PARLIAMENTARY PROCEDURE IN INDIA

PARLIAMENTARY PROCEDURE IN INDIA

A. R. MUKHERJEA, M.SC., LL.B., D. PHIL.

OXFORD UNIVERSITY PRESS
1967

Oxford University Press, Ely House, London W. 1

GLASGOW NEW YORK TORONTO MELBOURNE WELLINGTON
CAPE TOWN SALISBURY IBADAN NAIROBI LUSAKA ADDIS ABABA
BOMBAY CALCUTTA MADRAS KARACHI LAHORE DACCA
KUALA LUMPUR HONG KONG TOKYO
Faraday House, P-17 Mission Row Extension, Calcutta 13

A. R. **MUKHERJEA**

First published 1958
Second edition 1967

Printed in India by P. K. Ghosh at Eastend Printers, Calcutta,
and published by John Brown, Oxford University Press, Calcutta.

TO THE
PRESIDING OFFICERS
OF THE
INDIAN PARLIAMENT
AND OF THE
STATE LEGISLATURES OF INDIA
IN WHOSE HANDS REST
THE HIGH TRADITION
AND
THE DIGNITY
OF
THE CHAIR

FOREWORD

By

SIR BARNETT COCKS

CLERK OF THE HOUSE OF COMMONS

AT THE present stage of Parliamentary development throughout the Commonwealth, nine years is not a short period to elapse between editions of an authoritative textbook. Although retired since 1963 from his former position of Secretary to the West Bengal Legislative Assembly, Dr Mukherjea has not eased his grasp upon the pulse of Parliament, and the second and much-expanded edition of this book bears testimony not only to his enduring interest in the institution which he once so creditably served, but also to the way in which the legislatures of India and the United Kingdom have continued their procedural development. There are few pages which contain no addition or amplification, and a good deal of the matter is quite new. A chapter on the System of Committees, not present in the First Edition, brings into one compass a description of the functions of all the Committees which are regularly set up by Indian Legislatures, and sets forth the rules by which their business is conducted; matters such as the plight of legislatures where there is a substantial body of Members bent upon obstructing the ordinary conduct of business are canvassed in thoughtful detail; and a new section in Chapter XIII provides a lucid historical conspectus of the growth of the Indian financial system.

As in the previous edition, constant comparison is made between the procedural modes in the Parliaments of Westminster and India (indeed, the scope of Dr Mukherjea's knowledge extends even further, as is evidenced by his succinct description of the case of the 'Bankstown Observer', a matter of Parliamentary privilege, involving the imprisonment of two journalists, which startled Canberra in 1955). Such comparison only serves to emphasise the unity of democratic spirit which informs that two systems of procedure, despite some quite startling divergences in detail—most of which relate to the far-reaching, almost autocratic, powers which Indian legislatures have seen fit to confer upon the Chair. Dr Mukherjea's book, infused with scholarship and devotion, will continue in its new form to give comfort and information to all whose interest it is to see that spirit grow and prosper.

PREFACE TO THE SECOND EDITION

THIS book has been out of print for some time, and in bringing out the second edition I have thoroughly revised it and added fresh material which has come into being since the first edition was published.

It appears that all the State legislatures have adopted the rules and procedures of Parliament and thus a uniformity of practice and procedure has been established throughout India.

In spite of upheavals in neighbouring countries, parliamentary democracy in India has not only flourished but has also been founded on a stable basis. The legislatures are functioning as perfectly mature bodies, and although the procedure followed by the Indian legislatures is mainly based upon the procedure of the British Parliament, there have been occasions where changes have been made, for example, the calling attention notice, in order to suit Indian circumstances. In particular, the Law of Privileges is developing fast in this country and it can be safely said that parliamentary practice and procedure stand on a firm footing. It may be mentioned in this connexion that the House of Commons has changed its financial procedure. It will no longer be necessary to have financial proposals originating in the Committee of Supply. In this it appears that the House of Commons is following the procedure which exists in the Indian legislatures where there are no Committees of Supply.

In preparing the second edition I have got valuable help from Mr M. N. Kaul M.P., former Secretary of the Lok Sabha, the present Secretary Mr L. S. Shakdher, and Mr B. N. Banerjee, Secretary of the Rajya Sabha and belonging also to the Secretariat of the Lok Sabha.

I owe a deep debt of gratitude to Mr Keshab Chandra Basu, Speaker of the West Bengal Legislative Assembly, the last Speaker I served under, for the help and guidance I received from him. The Index has been prepared by Mr Rafiqual Haque, Assistant Secretary to the West Bengal

Assembly and I must express my thanks to him. I also desire to express my thanks to Mr Shamapada Banerjee, Deputy Secretary, West Bengal Council, Mr Debabrata Chakravarty, Editor of Debates, West Bengal Assembly. And also to Mr Hiren Mitra, Mr Krisna Kanta Chatterjee, both of Durgapur Projects Ltd. and the others who have helped me. I am also indebted to the Secretaries of other legislatures in India who have always been generous enough to supply me with materials for the book. Mr Charu C. Chowdhuri, Director of Research, Indian Law Institute, West Bengal Branch, deserves my gratitude for helping me in various ways to publish this edition.

Mrs Subrata Sen Gupta who was my stenographer and who made the transcript ready for the press deserves utmost thanks for the labour she had undertaken and so does my wife Dr (Mrs) Niharkana Mukherjea, M.A., D.Phil. (Cal.), who has gone through the proofs thoroughly.

I would be failing in my duty if I did not mention the names of Sir Barnett Cocks, K.C.B., O.B.E., Clerk of the House of Commons, who besides helping me in other ways has very kindly written a foreword to this book, Mr W.D.S. Lidderdale and Mr C.A.S.S. Gordon of the House of Commons who have helped me in various ways. I also express my thanks to Dr John Broomfield of the University of Michigan for the many valuable suggestions which he made. Since the text of the book went to press, a number of points have come to my notice which seem of sufficient importance to bring to the attention of readers. On page 48, in dealing with contests for the Speaker's seat in General Elections, I have noted two such contests by Independent candidates in Britain since 1945. I would add that in 1964 the Speaker's seat was contested by candidates from both opposition parties. On page 62 the number of the Standing Order under which the House of Commons can be adjourned in case of grave disorder is given as 24, but this has recently been changed to 26. On page 81, in dealing with questions, I have written that when 'a member is mentioned in a motion before the House and he appears in a bad light in such a motion and a question also is put to such a member, the member can be allowed to make a statement to clarify his position, although the acts or words complained of may have been done or spoken outside the House'. I should note that this is not the position in the House of Commons, where personal statements are unprompted by any questions. They must also relate strictly to a member's actions in his parliamentary capacity (see, for example, page 164 in Vol. XXVIII of *The Table*). On page 110 the last paragraph on Rules of Admissibility should open with the words 'The Speaker may...', and on page 175 the date in the last paragraph on Closure should be February 1961 instead of 1963.

Consequent to recent changes affected in the Constitution and the Representation of People Act, 1951, the number of members of parliament in the Lok Sabha after the 1967 Election has gone up to 521. Of the 521 seats in the new Lok Sabha, 520 will be filled by direct election and the one (allocated to NEFA) by nomination. In the State Assemblies also there have been similar changes affected in the total number of seats by the amendment of the Constitution and the R.P. Act.

It is hoped that this edition will be received by the public with the same favour with which the first edition was received.

Calcutta, February 1967   A. R. Mukherjea

TABLE OF ABBREVIATIONS

A.C.	Law Reports, Appeal cases
A.I.R.	*All India Reporter*
A.I.R. (S.C.)	All India Report (Supreme Court)
And. L.A.D.	Andhra Legislative Assembly Debates
Art (s).	Article(s) of the Constitution of India
Audit code	*Audit code* published under the authority of the Comptroller and Auditor General of India
B.L.A.P.	Bengal Legislative Assembly Proceedings
B.L.C.P.	Bengal Legislative Council Proceedings
Bih. L.A.D.	Bihar Legislative Assembly Debates
Bom. L.A.P.	Bombay Legislative Assembly Proceedings
C.A. Debates	Constituent Assembly Debates
C.J.	Journal of the House of Commons
Cent. L.A.D.	Central Legislative Assembly Debates
Chubb	*Control of Public Expenditure* by Basil Chubb
Ch. D.	Law Reports, Chancery Division
C.L.A.D.	Central Legislative Assembly Debates
Con. A.L.D.	Constituent Assembly Debates (Legislative)
C.S.D.	Council of States Debates
C.W.N.	*Calcutta Weekly Notes*
Decisions	Selections from the *Decisions of the Chair*
Durell	*Parliamentary Grants* by Col. A.J.V. Durell
E.L.R.	Election Law Reports
Gauntlet	*Memorandum on the work of the Public Accounts Committee in India* by Sir Frederic Gauntlet
Hatsell	*Precedents of Proceedings in the House of Commons* by Hatsell (3rd ed.)

H.C.	House of Commons; followed by numeral & date, *Parliamentary Paper* printed by Order of House with page sessional year
H.C.D.	Parliamentary Debates (official report), 5th Series, House of Commons, 1909-current)
H.C. *Paper*	House of Commons *Paper*
H.P.	House of the People
H.P.D.	House of the People Debates
Hyd. L.A.D.	Hyderabad Legislative Assembly Debates
I.P.D.	Indian Parliamentary Debates
J. & K. L.A.D.	Jammu & Kashmir Legislative Assembly Debates
K.B.	Law Reports, King's Bench
L.A.D.	Legislative Assembly Debates (Central)
L.A.P.	Legislative Assembly Proceedings
L.S.D.	Lok Sabha Debates
L.S. Rules	Lok Sabha Rules
May	Erskine May's *Parliamentary Practice* (16th ed.)
M.P.C.	Moore's Privy Council Reports
Or. L.A.D.	Orissa Legislative Assembly Debates
Parl. Deb.	Parliamentary Debates (authorized edition), First to Fourth Series, 1803-1908
Parl. Hist.	Parliamentary History of England from earliest period to 1803
Prov. Parl. Deb.	Provisional Parliamentary Debates
P.P.D	Provisional Parliamentary Debates
Q.B.	Law Reports, Queen's Bench
Q.B.D.	Law Reports, Queen's Bench Division
Raj. A.P.	Rajasthan Assembly Proceedings
Redlich	*Procedure of the House of Commons*, 3 Volumes, 1908, by Joseph Redlich
R.S.D.	Rajya Sabha Debates
S.C.R.	Supreme Court Reports
S.O.	Standing Orders of the House of Commons

S.T.N.S.	State Trials New Series
Table	*Journal of the Society of Clerks at the Table*
T.C.L.A.D.	Travancore Cochin Legislative Assembly Debates
U.P.L.A.P.	Uttar Pradesh Legislative Assembly Proceedings
U.S.	United States Supreme Court Reports
Vind. L.A.D.	Vindhya Pradesh Legislative Assembly Debates
W.B.L.A.P.	West Bengal Legislative Assembly Proceedings
W.B.L.C.P.	West Bengal Legislative Council Proceedings

REFERENCES TO ERSKINE May in this edition are to the Sixteenth Edition. The Seventeenth Edition was published while the Second Edition of this book was in preparation and therefore for the convenience of readers using the new edition of Erskine May, the alternative page numbers are given below:

Page in this text	Foot-note in this text	Page in 16th edition	Page in 17th edition	Page in this text	Foot-note in this text	Page in 16th edition	Page in 17th edition
10	1	175	175	100	1	298	296
24	2	186	186	101	1	397	393
32	1	260-1	259	103	4	406	401
33	2	260	259	104	2	401	397
37	1	262	261	105	1	401	397
45	2	253	251	106	1	415	411
55	3	818	842	109	1	403	398
64	2	640	665	109	2	404	399
76	1	489-90	487	111	5	407	403
80	3	356	350	116	1	298	296
84	1	360	354	125	9	369	363
84	2	360	354	128	2	369	363-4
84	7	361	355	131	1	413	409
84	8	360	354	136	1	305	303
84	9	359	352	149	1	406	402
88	2	361	355-6	151	1	446	443
89	4	356	350	151	4	446	443-4
89	5	355	349	152	1	447	444
91	1	363	357	152	2	445	442
96	1	363	357	155	6	364	359

Page in this text	Foot-note in this text	Page in 16th edition	Page in 17th edition	Page in this text	Foot-note in this text	Page in 16th edition	Page in 17th edition
160	3	455	452	239	5	556	551
167	3	124	124	239	7	555	550
168	2	459	456	240	1	555	550
168	3	459	456	242	1	564	560
172	1	53	53	242	2	578	572
180	1	443	440	248	2	820	844
181	1	435	431	252	1	818	842
182	1	436	433	256	3	280	279
187	8	105	105	257	2	522	518
191	3	268	267	261	1	306	304
222	4	646	673	291	1	733	760
222	5	612	637	292	1	746	773
223	1	574	568	296	1	738	765
223	2	576	570	297	1	749	775-6
224	1	536	533	299	4	720	748
225	1	575	568	300	1	720	748-9
226	1	665	693	300	2	711	739
226	2	568	563	302	2	737	763-4
227	1	500	497	322	1	739	766
232	1	644	669	357	2	42-3	42
233	2	636	661	359	1	173	173
234	1	628	653	378	2	63	63
234	3	627	652	382	1	79	79
234	4	627	652	389	1	109	109
235	3	631	656	402	1	89	89
237	1	568	563	403	1	82	82
238	1	572	566	403	2	83	83

CONTENTS

CHAPTER I
INTRODUCTORY

CHAPTER II
LEGISLATURES AND THEIR MEMBERS

CHAPTER III
SESSIONS OF LEGISLATURE

CHAPTER IV
ARRANGEMENT OF BUSINESS

CHAPTER V
QUESTIONS

CHAPTER VI
MOTIONS

CHAPTER VII
ADJOURNMENT MOTIONS

CHAPTER VIII
RESOLUTIONS

CHAPTER IX
MISCELLANEOUS MOTIONS

CHAPTER X
RULES OF DEBATE

CHAPTER XI

LEGISLATION

CHAPTER XII
SYSTEM OF COMMITTEES

CHAPTER XIII
FINANCIAL PROCEDURE

CHAPTER XIV
FINANCIAL COMMITTEES

CHAPTER XV

THE COMPTROLLER AND AUDITOR GENERAL OF INDIA

CHAPTER XVI

FINANCE DEPARTMENT

CHAPTER XVII

PARLIAMENTARY PRIVILEGE

CHAPTER I

INTRODUCTORY

THE Indian Constitution has adopted the system of parliamentary government as it obtains in England, and parliamentary procedure in India is essentially that which is followed in the British Parliament. The reason is not far to seek. It is beyond the scope of this work to discuss whether parliamentary government was known in India in ancient times. Parliamentary government as we know it now is of recent origin and is the outcome of the contact with the British system of government during British rule. Although full parliamentary control over the executive was not established until 1947, when the Government of India Act, 1935, was adapted by the Indian Constituent Assembly under powers conferred by the Indian Independence Act, 1947, yet the foundation had been laid by the creation of legislative bodies and the gradual introduction of responsible government by Acts passed by the British Parliament from time to time.

The power of legislation in the sense of making laws applicable generally to all persons and situations instead of making *ad hoc* orders was exercised from almost the very beginning of British rule, although legislatures as such, as distinct from executive authorities, did not come into existence until much later.

The power to legislate generally for a territory and its people appears to have been first conferred on the East India Company by the Charter of 1668, which authorized the Company 'to make laws, orders, ordinances and constitutions for the good government of the port and island (viz. Bombay) and of the inhabitants thereof.' The seed for the growth of future legislatures in India was, however, sown by the Royal Charter of 1726, which empowered the Governors and Councils of the Settlements to make bye-laws and ordinances etc. not contrary to the laws of England.

As has been observed by Keith:

'The Crown thus established in India itself a subordinate

power of legislation which was destined to supersede the authority in this regard vested in the Company itself.'[1] The Regulating Act of 1773 conferred on the Governor-General in express terms power 'to make laws for the good order and civil government of Fort William and subordinate factories'.

The Charter Act of 1833 for the first time made a differentiation between the executive authority and the legislative. Until then the laws were made by the Governor-General sitting with the Executive Council. By the Charter Act, the Executive Council was extended by the addition of one member who was not to be a member of the Executive Council, and the Governor-General, with this extended Council, was empowered to legislate for all British territories in the same way as the British Parliament, subject to certain restrictions. This may be said therefore to be the first Legislative Council although it was not so called in express terms. From this time on, laws made by the Governor-General in Council (Legislative) were called 'Acts' while the previous laws were designated 'Regulations'. The rules of procedure of this Council are said to have been drafted by Lord Macaulay.

The beginnings of legislative practice are to be found in the Charter Act of 1853, which further increased the number of the members of the Council for the purpose of making laws and who were now designated 'Legislative Councillors'. The sittings of the Council were made public and its proceedings were published. The Governor-General was given the power to withhold his assent from any bill. Standing orders were framed by the Legislative Council for regulating its own procedure.

The Council for the purpose of making laws (which will hereafter be referred to as the Legislative Council although it was not so called until 1909) began to act as a sort of parliament and wanted to exercise some control over the executive. This led to some dispute which came to a head when the Council desired to have some information about the grant made to the descendants of Tipoo Sultan. The Governor-General refused to give the information on the ground that neither the Council nor any of its members ought to ask for such information as they had no power to interfere in the

[1] Keith, *A Constitutional History of India*, 2nd ed., p. 18.

matter. A formal motion for the information was moved by Sir Barnes Peacock, Chief Justice of Bengal, who was a member and the Vice-President of the Council, and was carried by the casting vote of the Vice-President.[1] The result was that the powers of the Legislative Council were defined by the India Councils Act of 1861, and the Legislative Council was prohibited from transacting any business other than legislative business.

The Act of 1861 for the first time made provisions for the making of rules for the conduct of business of the Legislative Council. The rules were to be framed by the Governor-General in Council (Executive Council). The rules could be amended or altered by the Legislative Council only with the assent of the Governor-General. The first rules made under the Act may be said to be the origin of the rules of parliamentary procedure in India. Provision was made for the creation of provincial Legislative Councils, their powers and procedure.

It was in 1892 that two important rights were given to the Legislative Councils. The India Councils Act of 1892 empowered the Governor-General and the Governors or Lieutenant-Governors, as the case might be, to frame rules for the discussion of the Budget in the Legislative Councils and for the asking of questions by members. The right to ask supplementary questions was first conferred in 1909 and then also to the questioner only and not to other members. A further right was also given in 1909, the right to discuss any matter of general public interest.

The Montagu-Chelmsford Reforms gave an independent status to the legislatures. Until then the Governor-General or the Governor or the Lieutenant-Governor, as the case might be, had been the President of the Council and the laws were made by the Governor-General or the Governor or the Lieutenant-Governor, as the case might be, in Council (Legislative). Under the Government of India Act, 1919, the Governor-General or the Governor or the Lieutenant-Governor ceased to be associated with the legislatures. Provision was made for the appointment of Presiding Officers and for the voting of grants. Rules of procedure were divided into two classes, rules and standing orders. Rules for the central

[1] Proceedings of the Legislative Council of India, 1860, cc. 1343-99.

and provincial legislatures were framed by the Governor-General in Council with the approval of the Secretary of State and could not be amended or altered by the legislatures. Standing orders were framed by the Governors in Council for the provincial legislatures and could be amended or altered by the provincial legislatures with the consent of the Governors.

The Government of India Act, 1935, conferred on the provincial legislatures the power of full parliamentary control over the executive except for certain matters in regard to which the Governor was vested with special responsibility. But there was no responsible government at the centre although the legislature had power to refuse any grant of money for expenditure except those which were charged. The legislatures were empowered to frame rules for the conduct of their own business subject to certain restrictions. Rules relating to financial procedure and certain other matters for which the Governor-General or the Governor had special responsibility were made by them.

The history of the rules of procedure from 1861 to 1947, when India attained independence, is a history of tardy recognition, accompanied by some jealousy and want of trust, of the legislature as a part of the governmental machinery as distinct from the executive government. Because the government might not command a majority in the House, powers were reserved to the executive government to interfere with the business of the House, e.g., even in 1937, the Governor had the power to disallow questions, resolutions, adjournment motions, etc. Rules of procedure had been divided into two classes in 1921—rules and standing orders. The rules were framed by the Governor-General in Council but the standing orders made by the Governor (which were of minor importance) could be amended or altered by the Legislative Council with the consent of the Governor. Even under the Government of India Act, 1935, the Governor had the power to make rules regarding certain matters, e.g. financial business. The policy which dictated these precautions was expressed by the Joint Committee of the House of Lords and the House of Commons on Rules in a paragraph of their report,[1] as follows:

'The Committee think it desirable that a Governor's inter-

---

[1] *Report of the Joint Parliamentary Committee*, 1921.

vention in the proceedings of his Legislative Council should be confined to cases in which control by the executive (which for these purposes the Governor must represent) is essential, having regard to the fact that the Government will not command a majority in any Council, or to cases in which the President will not be in a position to give the requisite ruling. In all other cases they think that the last word should lie with the President of the Council. Following this principle, they have substituted the word "President" for "Governor" in rules 3, 7 and 11. But with regard to the last-mentioned rule, they think it necessary to retain for the Governor the power proposed by the Government of India to disallow a motion for adjournment even though it may have received the consent of the President, and of the Council if time permits of reference to the Governor before the adjournment takes place and if the Governor is of opinion that the proposed discussion cannot take place without detriment to the public interest. They have accordingly added a second paragraph to rule 22 to secure this power. The power to curtail public discussion in these newly constituted legislative bodies will obviously call for great discrimination in its use if it is not to prejudice their success, and to result, not in closing discussion, but in transferring it to less appropriate channels. But the Committee agreed with the Government of India that the power is one which the Government must have at its command, and they feel no doubt that the Governor-General and the provincial Governors will use their discretion in this matter wisely.'

The Constitution of India has effected a radical change in the conception of governmental machinery. The legislature is now the supreme authority to which the executive government, the Council of Ministers, has been expressly made responsible. The legislature by itself has of course no executive power but each and every action of the executive government can be scrutinised and questioned by the legislature and is subject to its ultimate control, and if it thinks necessary it can even remove the Council of Ministers. The legislature and the executive are not, however, as in pre-independence days, arrayed against each other—the one to obstruct or to evade the other. Each is a part of the same governmental machinery, and if the legislature is endowed with the right to control the executive, it has also the duty of seeing that the country's government goes on. The guiding principle should therefore be that the rules of procedure should be such as not only to ensure effective parliamentary control over the executive but also to ensure the smooth and expeditious running of the executive machinery.

The Indian Constitution has conferred upon the legislatures the power to regulate their own business. But the procedure in regard to certain matters, e.g. voting of demands for grants or the passing of bills, has been, to some extent, enunciated in the Constitution itself. Parliamentary procedure as it now obtains in India will be discussed in the following chapters.

CHAPTER II

LEGISLATURES AND THEIR MEMBERS

CONSTITUTION AND COMPOSITION OF LEGISLATURES

SOME of the legislatures in India are bicameral and some uni-cameral. The Head of the State, i.e. the President in the case of the Union and the Governor in the case of the State, is an integral constituent part of the legislature. In this respect the Indian Constitution has departed from the Constitution of the United States where the President is not a constituent part of the Congress but has followed the English Constitution where the Queen is a constituent part of the Parliament. Though the Constitution itself provides for a Second Chamber in some of the States and leaves the others to be unicameral, it makes it possible either to abolish the Second Chamber in the States having one, or to create a Second Chamber in any of the remaining States without the necessity of going through the process of Constitutional amendment. The only require-ment for effecting such a change is a resolution passed by a special majority of the Lower House of the State legislature itself, as provided in clause (1) of Article 169, followed by an appropriate Act of Parliament. Such a resolution under Article 169(1) of the Constitution was passed by the Bombay Legislative Assembly on 26 September 1953.[1]

The Union Parliament consists of two Houses—the Council of States (Rajya Sabha) and the House of the People (Lok Sabha).[2] The Council of States consists of not more than 238 representatives of the States and the Union territories and twelve members nominated by the President.[3] The above numbers are, however, the maximum fixed by the Constitu-tion, the total number of representatives of different States being in fact less than the maximum. The Fourth Schedule

---

[1] Bombay Legislative Assembly Proceedings, vol. 24, p. 1855, and vol. 25, p. 109.
[2] Art. 79. For adoption of the nomenclatures Lok Sabha and Rajya Sabha see Parl. Deb. part ii, 14 May 1954, cc. 7389-90 and C. S. D. 23 Aug. 1954, cc. 36-37.
[3] Art. 80.

of the Constitution shows the allocation of seats in the Council
to different States. Unlike the United States, Australia and
Switzerland where local states (cantons) are represented in
the Second House by an equal number of seats, local States
in India do not enjoy equal representation in the Council of
States. The framers of the Constitution accepted the scheme
suggested by the Union Constitution Committee regarding
the allocation of seats in the Council of States on the basis
of one seat for every million of the population of the States
up to five millions, plus one representative for every additional two millions, plus twelve members to be nominated by
the President.[1] The nominated members must be persons
having special knowledge or practical experience in such
matters as literature, science, art and social service.[2] The
qualifications for membership of the Council of States are
the same as those for the House of the People except that the
minimum age is thirty instead of twenty-five.

The House of the People consists of not more than five
hundred members from the States elected on adult franchise
and not more than twenty-five members from the Union
territories partially elected on adult franchise and partially
nominated. The President may, if he is of opinion that the
Anglo-Indian community is not adequately represented,
nominate not more than two members of that community to
the House of the People.[3] As in the case of the Council of
States, the above numbers are the maximum fixed by the
Constitution, the actual number being fixed by the Parliament by law, viz. the Representation of the People Act, 1950.

The members of the Upper Houses of State legislatures
known as Legislative Councils are partially elected and partially nominated. The total number of members of a Legislative Council of a State shall not be less than forty and
shall not exceed one-third of the members of the Legislative
Assembly of that State. One-third, as nearly as possible, of
the total number of members is elected by the Lower House,
the Legislative Assembly, one-third by specified local bodies,
one-twelfth, as nearly as possible, by graduates, one-twelfth

[1] C. A. Debates, vol. x, pp. 407-10, 17 Oct. 1949.
[2] Art. 80.
[3] Arts. 81, 331.

by teachers, and one-sixth, as nearly as possible, is nominated by the Governor.[1] This composition was provisionally fixed by the Constitution which made it liable to variation by Act of Parliament. By the Legislative Councils Act, 1957, and other Acts relating to the reorganization of States, the the composition as provisionally fixed by the Constitution has been varied. The members of the Lower Houses known as Legislative Assemblies are elected on adult franchise, and there is provision for the nomination of a few members from the Anglo-Indian community when they are not properly represented.[2] Unlike the Lok Sabha, the number of Anglo-Indian members for a State Assembly has not been limited by the Constitution, the matter being left to the discretion of the Governors of the States. The question of fixing a maximum for this purpose was, however, under consideration by the Central Government.[3] The members (other than those nominated) of the Upper House, both Union and States, are elected under the system of proportional representation by means of the single transferable vote. (For the method of proportional representation see Appendix IV).

The question of the due constitution of the House in India is not a matter of privilege, as it is in the British House of Commons. General Elections and bye-elections to the legislatures are conducted by the Election Commission, but are held when directed by the President or the Governor, as the case may be, that is to say, by the Government concerned,[4] in the case of general elections to the Lower Houses and biennial elections to the Upper Houses, and by the Election Commission in the cases of bye-elections. Article 324 provides for the creation of an independent body, referred to in the Constitution as the Election Commission, which is in charge of all matters connected with elections under the Constitution in order to ensure their freedom. Article 327 empowers the Parliament to make provision with respect to elections to

---

[1] Art. 171.

[2] Art. 333.

[3] A Constitution Amendment Bill (Bill no. 79 of 1959) was introduced, fixing a maximum for the State Assemblies, but the relevant clause was not passed by the required majority; see also Mr. Jyoti Basu's speech in W.B.L.A.P. 1957, vol. xvii, no. 1, p. 61.

[4] Art. 324; secs. 12, 14, 15, 16, 147, 149, 150 and 151 of the Representation of the People Act, 1951.

Houses of legislatures (including Parliament) and all other matters for securing the due constitution of such Houses.

In England, however, it is a privilege of the House of Commons to provide for its due constitution. The privilege, as May says,[1] 'is expressed in three ways: first, by the order of new writs to fill vacancies that arise in the Commons in the course of Parliament; secondly, by the trial of controverted elections; and thirdly, by determining the qualifications of its members in cases of doubt.' In the British Parliament, the House itself decides such matters. In the case of sitting members the House claims the right to decide any question of law or fact which arises as to their disqualifications. 'Any doubtful question, whether of law or fact, which arises concerning the seat of a member is habitually referred to a Select Committee and the House awaits its report before taking a decision.'[2] The expulsion of a member or the declaration of a vacancy is made by resolution of the House. 'When a vacancy occurs during the session by death, elevation to the Peerage, acceptance of office, etc., the House on motion orders the Speaker to issue his warrant to the Clerk of the Crown to make out a new writ for the election of a member. This is generally moved by the Chief Whip of the party to which the member whose seat is vacated belonged.'[3] During recess an elaborate procedure is laid down by an Act relating to the formalities to be observed by the Speaker in issuing writs, e.g. the receipt of a certificate from two members specifying the cause of the vacancy, etc. Under the Lunacy (Vacating of Seats) Act and the Bankruptcy Act, provisions have been laid down for the vacation of seats and the issue of new writs. It therefore appears that these matters are not decided on points of order but must be moved by motions. There appears to be also a procedure under which the court gives information to the Speaker of any conviction of a member. In the case of Horatio Bottomley, Mr. Justice Salter informed the Speaker about his conviction and Bottomley was called upon to attend the House on a day on which the then Leader of the House moved a resolution for his expulsion.[4] Only in the

[1] May, p. 175.
[2] Campion, 2nd ed., p. 70.
[3] Ibid. p. 67.
[4] H.C.D. 1922, vol. 157, c. 1288.

matter of disputed elections is the decision left to the court. The decision of the court is communicated to the House, and orders are made by the House to give effect to the decision.

In India due constitution of the House is not a matter of privilege as it is in England because specific provisions are outlined in the Constitution for this purpose. The House of Commons has power to determine all matters touching the election of its members. Contrary to the English practice, the decision of questions as to the disqualification of members is left to the President of India or the Governor of the State concerned who, however, is required to act according to the opinion of the Election Commission. The decision of the President or the Governor is final. The courts in India have no jurisdiction to question the validity of the decision of the President or the Governor on the opinion of the Election Commission.[1] However, there was a case in India in which the Supreme Court entered into the question of due constitution of the Assembly. A judgment[2] of the Supreme Court declared that the Himachal Pradesh Legislative Assembly had not been properly and validly constituted. The facts out of which the judgment arose are as follows.

Himachal Pradesh and Bilaspur were two contiguous States of the category Part C under the Constitution passed in 1950. In 1951 an Act known as the Part C States Act was passed by Parliament which provided for a Legislative Assembly and a consequent ministry in some of the Part C States. The powers, privileges and immunities of these Assemblies were defined by the same Act as to be those of the House of the People. Himachal Pradesh was one such State having a Legislative Assembly (of thirty-six members) whereas Bilaspur was not brought under the said Act. In the General Election of 1952 members were elected to the Himachal Pradesh Assembly. While this Assembly was functioning, a bill known as the Himachal Pradesh Abolition of Big Landed Estates and Land Reforms Bill was introduced in 1953, and while it was pending before the said Assembly an Act was passed by Parliament known as the Himachal Pradesh and Bilaspur (New State) Act (Act 32 of 1954) which came into

[1] Arts. 103, 192.
[2] A.I.R. 1959, S.C. 223.

effect from 1 July 1954. This Act provided for a House of forty-two members (five for Bilaspur territories) for the new State. In the meantime, on 7 May 1954, the Lieutenant-Governor of Himachal Pradesh summoned the second session (the first session being held in 1953, i.e. prior to 1 July 1954) of the Himachal Pradesh Assembly to commence on 16 July 1954. The Bill introduced in 1953 regarding abolition of zamindaris and introducing certain reforms was passed during the said session, and the Act was given effect from 26 January 1955. Certain landlords who believed that their rights had been curtailed by the Act filed applications before the Supreme Court of India. The validity of the Act passed by an Assembly which purported to be the legislative House of Himachal Pradesh after its merger with the State of Bilaspur, the latter having no representation in the House, was impugned for the purpose of assailing the Land Reforms Act. In *Vinod Kumar and others* v. *the State of Himachal Pradesh*, referred to above, the Supreme Court declared the Land Reforms Act *ultra vires* on the ground that the Legislative Assembly which passed the Act had not been properly and validly constituted.

A bill had to be introduced in the Lok Sabha on 3 December 1958, to validate the constitution and proceedings of the Legislative Assembly of the New State of Himachal Pradesh formed under the Himachal Pradesh and Bilaspur (New State) Act, 1954.[1] This was in due course enacted into law.[2]

QUALIFICATIONS

The qualifications and disqualifications for membership of a legislature are laid down in the Constitution[3] and also by the Representation of the People Act, 1951. In order to be eligible for election or nomination to a legislature, a person must be:

(i) a citizen of India,

(ii) registered as a voter

(a) in any parliamentary constituency in any State in India, in the case of the House of the People

---

[1] L.S.D. 3 Dec. 1958, c. 2939.
[2] The Himachal Pradesh Legislative Assembly (Constitution and Proceedings) Validation Act, 1958: Act 56 of 1958.
[3] Arts. 84, 102, 173, 191.

    (b) in any parliamentary constituency in the State from which election is sought, in the case of the Council of States

    (c) in any assembly constituency of the State, in the case of the legislature of that State,

  (iii) not less than

    (a) twenty-five years of age, in the case of the House of the People and the State Legislative Assemblies

    (b) thirty years of age, in the case of the Council of States and the State Legislative Councils.

In India there appears to be a departure from the general principle that any person who is qualified to be a voter may become a member of the House unless he incurs any disqualification under any statute in force. The departure lies in the fact that our Constitution[1] has accepted the adult franchise, that is to say, a voter must attain the age of twenty-one, while a candidate must be aged twenty-five or thirty, as the case may be, to become a member of a Lower House or an Upper House of a legislature.

DISQUALIFICATIONS

A person is disqualified for being or remaining a member of any House of a legislature:

  (i) if he holds any office of profit under the Government of India or the Government of any State other than an office declared by the Union Legislature or the State Legislature, as the case may be, not to disqualify its holders,[2]

  (ii) if he is of unsound mind and stands so declared by a competent court,

  (iii) if he is an undischarged insolvent,

  (iv) if he is not a citizen of India or has voluntarily acquired the citizenship of a foreign State or is under any acknowledgment of allegiance or adherence to a foreign State.

Further disqualifications are prescribed by section 7 of the Representation of the People Act, 1951 which is as follows:

'*Disqualification for membership of Parliament or of a State Legislature.* A person shall be disqualified for being chosen as, and for being, a member of either House of Parliament or

---

[1] Art. 326.
[2] Arts. 102, 191.

of the Legislative Assembly or Legislative Council of a State:

(a) if, whether before or after the commencement of the Constitution, he has been convicted, or has, in proceedings for questioning the validity or regularity of an election, been found to have been guilty, of any offence or corrupt practice which has been declared by section 139 or section 140 to be an offence or practice entailing disqualification for membership of Parliament and of the Legislature of every State, unless such period has elapsed as has been provided in that behalf in the said section 139 or section 140, as the case may be or the Election Commission has removed the disqualification;

(b) if, whether before or after the commencement of the Constitution, he has been convicted by a Court in India of any offence and sentenced to imprisonment for not less than two years, unless a period of five years, or such less period as the Election Commission may allow in any particular case, has elapsed since his release;

(c) if he has failed to lodge an account of his election expenses within the time and in the manner required by or under this Act, unless three years have elapsed from the date by which the account ought to have been lodged or the Election Commission has removed the disqualification;

(d) if there subsists a contract entered into in the course of his trade or business by him with the appropriate Government for the supply of goods to, or for the execution of any works undertaken by that Government;

(e) if he is a director, managing agent, manager or secretary of any company or corporation (other than a co-operative society) in the capital of which the appropriate Government has not less than twenty-five per cent share;

(f) if, having held any office under the Government of India or the Government of any State or under the Crown in India or under the Government of an Indian State, he has, whether before or after the commencement of the Constitution, been dismissed for corruption or disloyalty to the State, unless a period of five years has elapsed since his dismissal.'

Electoral offences entailing disqualifications are bribery or undue influence or personation in connection with any election (sections 171E and 171F of the Indian Penal Code) and offences defined under section 135 and clause (a) of sub-section 10 of section 136 of the Representation of the People Act, 1951. Practices entailing disqualification are corrupt practices as specified in section 123 of the above-mentioned Act. The disqualification for conviction for an electoral offence lasts for six years from the date on which the finding of the Election Tribunal takes effect, i.e. the date on which the order of the Tribunal is pronounced. The Election Commission can, however, remove any disqualification or reduce the period of such disqualification.

There are certain exceptions to these disqualifications which are laid down in section 8 of the Representation of the People Act, 1951, as follows:

'8. *Savings*. (1) Notwithstanding anything in section 7:

(a) a disqualification under clause (a) or clause (b) of that section shall not, in the case of a person who becomes so disqualified by virtue of a conviction or a conviction and a sentence and is at the date of the disqualification a member of Parliament or of the Legislature of a State, take effect until three months have elapsed from the date of such disqualification, or if within these three months an appeal or petition for revision is brought in respect of the conviction or the sentence, until that appeal or petition is disposed of;

(b) a disqualification under clause (c) of that section shall not take effect until the expiration of two months from the date on which the Election Commission has decided that the account of election expenses has not been lodged within the time and in the manner required by or under this Act;

(e) a person shall not be disqualified under clause (e) of that section by reason of his being a director unless the office of such director is declared by Parliament by law to so disqualify its holder;

(f) a disqualification under clause (e) of that section shall not, in the case of a director, take effect where the law making any such declaration as is referred to in clause (e) of this section in respect of the office of such director has come into force after the director has been chosen a member of Parliament or of the Legislature of a State, as the case may be, until the expiration of six months after the date on which such law comes into force or of such longer period as the Election Commission may in any particular case allow.'

OFFICE OF PROFIT

The disqualifying provision that a holder of an office of profit under the Government could not become or remain a member of a legislature was first enacted in England in the Act of Settlement of 1700-1, and subsequently re-enacted in a somewhat amended form in the Succession to the Crown Act, 1707. This was done obviously to prevent the Government of the day from exercising influence over members of Parliament by appointing them to sinecure posts created for the purpose. On the other hand, when parliamentary government came to be established, ministers had, of necessity, to be members of the House. The phrase 'office or place of profit' and the distinction of 'old' and 'new' offices introduced by the Act of 1707 gave rise to various difficulties, and a Select Committee of the House of Commons went into the question in 1941[1] and made certain recommendations which are worth consideration in India. The Committee summarizes the gradual development of the law in the following words:

'There can be traced the genesis and gradual development of the three chief principles which by the beginning of the eighteenth century had become, and have since been, and should still be, the main considerations affecting the law on this subject: these, in the order of historical sequence, are (1) incompatibility of certain non-ministerial offices with membership of the House of Commons (which must be taken to cover questions of a Member's relations with, and duties to, his constituents); (2) the need to limit the control or influence of the executive government over the House by means of an undue proportion of office-holders being members of the House; and (3) the essential condition of a certain number of ministers being members of the House for the purpose of ensuring control of the executive by Parliament. The Act of 1707 was the first effective attempt to establish these principles in an Act of Parliament.'

The Committee recommended the passing of a bill which subsequently emerged as the House of Commons Disqualification Act, 1957, the chief provisions of which are as follows.

Except as provided by the Act, a person shall not be dis-

[1] H.C. *Paper* 120 of 1941.

qualified for membership of the House of Commons by reason of his holding an office or place of profit under the Crown or any other office or place; and a person shall not be disqualified for appointment to or for holding any office or place by reason of his being a member of that House.

With the exception of holders of political or ministerial offices, all persons employed either whole or part-time in the Civil Service under the Crown are disqualified for membership. Holders of certain judicial offices, members of the regular armed forces, members of any police force, members of legislatures of any country or territory outside the Commonwealth, and holders of certain specified posts, including membership of certain committees, commissions, boards, etc., are also disqualified. The lists of disqualifying offices may be amended by Order in Council made in pursuance of a resolution of the House of Commons.

Of the holders of ministerial offices not more than twenty-seven of the Ministers named in part I of the Second Schedule and not more than seventy of the Ministers named in both parts I and II of the said Schedule are entitled to sit and vote in the House.

No Member of the House of Commons is required to accept any office or place by virtue of which he would be disqualified for membership.

A person shall not be disqualified by reason of his holding a pension from the Crown.

In India the 'office of profit' has also a long history which is best described by the Committee[1] on Offices of Profit, 1955.

The Committee after discussing the history of the office of profit came to the following conclusion:

'Broadly speaking there are five categories of offices from the point of view of emoluments, which may be deemed to be offices of profit, namely:

(i) Where a person is appointed to an office of profit and takes remuneration which may, when set against expenses or loss incurred by not being able to follow his ordinary avocation, be less.

(ii) Where a person is appointed to an office of profit even though he does not take remuneration.

[1] See *Report of the Committee on Offices of Profit*, 1955, paras 18-23.

2

(iii) Where a person is appointed to an office of profit although the payment of remuneration may have fallen into disuse.

(iv) Where a person is appointed to an office of profit which is not financed from Government funds.

(v) Where a person is appointed to an office which may not give any advantage by way of monetary gain but is an office which carries with it honour, influence or patronage.'[1]

As regards the word 'under' used in the term 'under the Government of India or of a State' the Committee have come to the conclusion that the word 'under' in Articles 102(1)(a) and 191(1)(a) of the Constitution has been used in a broad sense and must be construed to include even offices which may be remotely under the control of the Central or State Governments.[2]

Thus having examined the question as to what should be considered as 'offices of profit under the Government of India or of a State' the Committee on Offices of Profit submitted their report in November 1955, recommending that a bill embodying such of their recommendations as were acceptable to Government should be passed. The Committee also recommended that frequent scrutiny should be made by a Standing Parliamentary Committee in respect of offices of profit in the case of committees which had escaped their notice or which might come into existence in future.

Thereafter, the Parliament (Prevention of Disqualification) Bill, 1957, was introduced before the Lok Sabha and referred to a Joint Committee of both Houses of Parliament. The report of the Joint Committee was presented in September 1958. The Bill was subsequently enacted into law known as the Parliament (Prevention of Disqualification) Act, 1959, which superseded all previous enactments made since 1950.

The Act exempted the holders of the following offices from any disqualification for being chosen as or for being a member of Parliament:

(i) any office held by a Minister, Minister of State or Deputy Minister for the Union or for any State, whether ex-officio or by name,

---

[1] *Report of the Committee on Offices of Profit*, 1955, para 36.
[2] Ibid. para 37 conclusion.

(ii) offices of Whips in Parliament and Parliamentary Secretaries,

(iii) offices of members of forces in the National Cadet Corps, Territorial Army, Reserve or Auxiliary Air Forces,

(iv) offices of members of Home Guards formed in States,

(v) offices of Sheriffs of Bombay, Calcutta and Madras,

(vi) offices of chairmen or members of Universities or bodies connected therewith,

(vii) offices of members of Delegations or Missions sent abroad,

(viii) offices of chairmen or members of committees set up for advising the Government or for any enquiry etc. if no remuneration other than compensatory allowance is paid,

(ix) offices of chairmen, directors and members of statutory or non-statutory bodies other than those included in the Schedule, when no remuneration other than compensatory allowance is payable,

(x) offices of village Revenue Officers not discharging any police function and paid by share of their collections.

The Act has declared offices of chairmen and secretaries of certain statutory and non-statutory bodies (enlisted in the Schedule) as not exempt from disqualification. The Constitution has expressly excluded the office of a Minister, whether of the Union or of a State, from the category of disqualifying offices. In the Parliament (Prevention of Disqualification) Act, 1950 (repealed by the Act of 1959), the office of a Minister of State or a Deputy Minister was expressly declared as not disqualifying. In some of the State Acts such offices have been expressly declared as not disqualifying. Evidently this has been done to obviate any misconception. In the Acts of other States there is no mention of Ministers of States or Deputy Ministers, although such Ministers have been appointed from among the members of the legislature.[1] These offices are included in the office of a Minister for which the Constitution has made express provision. The language of the present Act of Parliament regarding Ministers, Ministers of States, or Deputy Ministers closely follows that of the similar

---

[1] Calcutta High Court Order no. 3360 of 1952 (16 Dec. 1952), *Jatish Chandra Ghosh* v. *Amulyadhan Mukherjee and Others*, Order no. 3363 of 1953 (9 Sept. 1953), *Jatish Ghosh* v. *Jibanratan Dhar and Others*.

provision in the House of Commons Disqualification Act, 1957, declaring all offices of profit held by a Minister etc. ex-officio as not disqualifying. There is no such provision in any of the State Acts. The basic distinction between the present English law as contained in the House of Commons Disqualification Act, 1957, and the provisions of the Constitution of India in regard to offices of profit is noticeable. According to English law no office entails disqualification unless it is included in the schedule of disqualifying offices appended to the Act, whereas according to the Constitution of India all offices of profit under any Government in India are disqualifying unless exempted by the legislature concerned.

The provisions of the State Acts are not uniform. Offices of Parliamentary Secretaries, members of National Cadet Corps, and some other forces, part-time officers or offices (including membership or chairmanship of a committee) remunerated by compensatory allowance or fees have more or less been exempted everywhere. Other exemptions have been made according to local needs. It may be mentioned in this connection that in the Central Act, the term 'compensatory allowance' means daily allowance up to an amount admissible to a Member of Parliament for attending a meeting of Parliament, and other allowances, namely conveyance allowance, house rent allowance, travelling allowance, which are necessarily spent for performing the duties for which they are paid. No such restriction in the amount of daily allowance has been made in any of the State Acts. This is because in the States the rates of daily allowance of members of committees seldom exceeds those paid to members of the legislature. However, disqualification applies to any holder of an office of profit where salary or allowance is payable in excess of compensatory allowance but is not drawn.

A question may also arise in regard to holders of pensions from the Government. In England holders of Civil Service pensions under the Superannuation Act were exempted from disqualification by a special Act, the Pensioners Civil Disabilities Relief Act, 1869. This Act has, however, been repealed by the House of Commons Disqualification Act, 1957, which has re-enacted the same provisions. There is no such Act in India. It may be noted that pension-holders were thought in

England to be disqualified not because of the provisions as to 'office or place of profit' in the Succession to the Crown Act, 1707, but because section 24 of that Act disqualified persons having any pension from the Crown at pleasure. It seems, therefore, that holders of pensions from the Government would not be disqualified from membership at the will of the Government. In fact, in the legislatures in India, there have been members who are in receipt of pensions from the Government.

FOREIGN STATE

A country within the British Commonwealth is not a foreign State for the purposes of the Constitution.[1] 'Any acknowledgment of allegiance or adherence to a foreign State'—an expression which has a much wider meaning than acquiring the citizenship of a foreign State—will not, it seems, disqualify a person under Article 102 and Article 191, if the State concerned is a State within the Commonwealth, e.g. Pakistan.

Under Article 191, a person is disqualified from being a member of a State legislature if he has voluntarily acquired the citizenship of a foreign State or is under any acknowledgment of allegiance or adherence to a foreign State. The last disqualification clause is very wide and will cover the case of a person who may be a citizen of India but nevertheless is under an acknowledgment of adherence to a foreign State. This clause was enacted to cover the case of fifth-columnists. The President's Order, namely the Constitution (Declaration as to Foreign States) Order, 1950, says that a State within the British Commonwealth of Nations will not be treated as a foreign State 'for the purpose of the Constitution'. It is not correct to say that no purpose has been mentioned. The purpose mentioned is quite clear, that is to say, wherever there is a reference to a foreign State in the Constitution, that provision will not apply to a State within the Commonwealth. Consequently, Article 191 will not apply to such a case. Pakistan is a State within the British Commonwealth (Declaration at the Prime Ministers' Conference,

---

[1] Constitution (Declaration as to Foreign States) Order, 1950, made under Art. 267 of the Constitution, C.O. 2, 23 Jan. 1950, *Gazette of India Extraordinary*, 24 Jan. 1950.

London, 27 April 1949), and any person, even if he is a citizen of India, will not be disqualified from being a member of a legislature, although he may owe allegiance to Pakistan.

DECISION AS TO DISQUALIFICATION

When a member becomes subject to any of the disqualifications his seat becomes vacant.[1] Whether a member has become subject to any disqualification is a matter of evidence. In the British Parliament the House itself decides such matters. Any doubtful question, whether of law or of fact, which arises concerning the seat of a member is habitually referred to a Select Committee and the House awaits its report before taking any action.[2] It appears that the case of Mr. Anthony Wedgwood Benn was referred to a Committee of Privileges which reported that he was disqualified for membership.[3] The case of the Reverend James George MacManaway, Member for Belfast, West, was also referred to a Select Committee. The Judicial Committee of the Privy Council was also consulted, and on the report of that Committee the House declared Mr. MacManaway disabled from sitting and voting in the House of Commons.[4] It may be pointed out, however, that the decision of an Election Petition Court, if any, cannot lawfully be overridden by the House of Commons. In the case of Mr. Wedgwood Benn the Election Court held that he had not been duly elected to the House of Commons. In India, however, the decision on a question whether a member has become subject to any disqualification has been left to the President in the case of the Indian Parliament and to the Governors in the case of the State legislatures.[5] The President and the Governors, however, cannot take any decisions themselves. The matter has to be referred to the Election Commission for its opinion, and the decision has to be given in accordance with its opinion.[6] The question may arise either as one of law or as one of fact. For example, if

[1] Arts. 101, 190.
[2] H.C.D. 1955-6, 545, c. 73.
[3] H.C.D. 1960-1, 638, cc. 641-2.
[4] H.C.D. 1950, 478, cc. 2243-76.
[5] Arts. 103, 192.
[6] Ibid.

a point is raised that a member has accepted an office of profit under the Government and it is open to dispute whether that office is an office of profit or not, the question is a question of law. Or, the question may arise whether a member is an undischarged insolvent, which is a question of fact. In either case, in the event of a dispute, the question must be referred to the Head of the State, and his decision will be final.

It may, however, be stated that the jurisdiction of the President or Governor under Articles 103(1) or 192(1) of the Constitution is restricted only to cases where a member *becomes* subject to a disqualification *after* his election to a House. This is evident from the words 'whether a member ...*has become* subject to any of the disqualifications...' used in those Articles. The President or Governor or the Election Commission have no jurisdiction to enquire into a member's disqualification which arose before his election.[1]

The Articles do not say where this question can arise and who is to refer the dispute. It will be noticed that under Articles 101(3) and 190(3) a seat becomes *ipso facto* vacant if the member incurs any of the disqualifications, and the date on which the vacancy occurs is the date of becoming disqualified and not the date on which any decision of the Head of the State may be given. No declaration of vacancy is necessary. A duty has, therefore, been cast upon a member to refrain from attending the House after incurring any of the disqualifications on penalty of a daily fine. The question may arise in the House on a point of order if a disqualified member takes his seat or by communication, for example, from a court that a member has been adjudged insolvent. The Presiding Officer may also see that the House is properly constituted, and he may take notice of any disqualification of a member either of his own knowledge or from any communication made to him. In such cases, unless the member admits the disqualification, the question will have to be referred to the Governor.

An anomalous position has arisen by reason of the phrasing of Articles 101 and 190 which provide that if a member 'becomes subject to any of the disqualifications', his seat shall become

---

[1] *Election Commission* v. *Saka Venkata Rao*, 2 E.L.R. (1952-3), 499.

vacant. It has been held by the Supreme Court that the expression 'becomes subject to' means becomes subject to any disqualification after a person has been elected a member, and does not cover the case of a person who was disqualified from standing for an election but has in fact been elected without challenge. Therefore, if a disqualified person has been elected a member, his seat does not become vacant under the above-mentioned Articles, and the provision regarding enquiry by the Election Commission under Article 103 or Article 192 would not apply.[1] The election of such a person can be challenged by an election petition under section 100 of the Representation of the People Act, 1951, on the ground that the nomination paper of the person was improperly accepted, and the Election Tribunal may declare the election void.

Whether the House can declare the election of a disqualified person void is a difficult question to answer. In the British House of Commons the question of the due constitution of the House is one of privilege of the House, and as stated by May: 'The House is bound to take notice of any legal disabilities affecting its Members and to issue writs in the rooms of Members adjudged to be incapable of sitting.'[2]

There are many instances in the British House of Commons where the elections of disqualified persons have been declared void. In India, however, the question does not seem to be one of privilege, and the House has no authority to issue any writ for bye-election. Whether the House can do so by reason of the fact that the privileges of the House of Commons attach to the House, and therefore the privilege of the House of Commons to declare a person disqualified for membership is attracted, is also a difficult question to answer.

The penal provisions of Articles 104 and 193 of course would apply, and a disqualified person would be liable to pay the fine if he sits or takes part in the proceedings of the House. But beyond that there seems to be no remedy. Of course, if such a person desists from attending the House for a period of sixty days for fear of incurring the penalty, his seat can be declared vacant by the House.

[1] A.I.R. 1953, S.C. 210.
[2] May, p. 186.

DOUBLE MEMBERSHIP

If a person becomes a member of both the Parliament (either House) and a State legislature (either House), then his seat in the Parliament becomes vacant unless he resigns his seat in the State legislature within fourteen days of the latest date on which his election is published in the Official Gazette.[1]

If a person is elected to any Houses of legislatures of more than one State, all the seats become vacant unless the person elects to resign all but one seat within ten days from the latest day of publication of his election to any of the seats.[2]

If a person is elected to both the Houses of Parliament he has, before taking his seat, to select the House he desires to be in within ten days of the latest date on which his election is notified in the Official Gazette. In the absence of any election, his seat in the Council of States becomes vacant.[3] If within ten days he takes his seat in any of the Houses, it seems that his seat in the other House would become vacant.

If a member of one of the Houses is elected to the other House, his seat in the House of which he is a member becomes vacant. [4]

If a person is elected to either House of Parliament from more than one constituency, he has to resign all but one seat within fourteen days of the latest date of publication of his election in the Official Gazette, and unless he does so all the seats become vacant.[5] The provisions as regards State legislatures are similar, and are governed by Acts of different State legislatures.

VACATION OF SEATS

A member may resign his seat by writing to the Presiding Officer of the House of which he is a member. When a member has been elected from more than one seat of a House and the offices of the Presiding Officers (including the Deputy Speaker

[1] Arts. 101, 190; Prohibition of Simultaneous Membership Rules, 1950.
[2] Ibid.
[3] Representation of the People Act, 1951, s. 68.
[4] Ibid. s. 69.
[5] Ibid. s. 70 and Rule 91 of the Conduct of Elections Rules, 1961.

or the Deputy Chairman as the case may be) are both vacant at the time, the resignation is to be addressed to the Election Commission.[1] Resignation takes effect as soon as the letter is received by the authority concerned. No acceptance of resignation is necessary.

A rule of the Lok Sabha and also of some State legislatures prescribes a form of letter intimating the resignation of a member to take effect from the date of resignation specified in the letter. If, however, no date from which the resignation should take effect is specified in the letter, the resignation takes effect from the date of the letter; if the letter of resignation does not bear any date the resignation takes effect from the date of the receipt of the letter in the Lok Sabha Secretariat. Such a rule may lead to several anomalies.

So far as the coming into operation of Statutes is concerned, the General Clauses Act lays down a presumption that, unless otherwise provided, an Act comes into operation on the expiry of the day previous to the day on which it comes into force. There is also such a presumption in regard to judicial acts. There is no such presumption, however, with regard to acts of parties which are deemed to take effect at the time when they are actually performed (see *Clarks* v. *Bradlaugh*, 8 Q.B.D. (63)). Resignation of a seat is the act of a private individual, and it takes effect at the time when it is performed (or is deemed to be performed). If a letter is dated as of a particular day, resignation takes effect not on the expiry of the previous day but at the time on that day at which the letter is written. If any time is indicated on the letter, resignation takes effect and the seat becomes vacant at that time. If no time is indicated, enquiry will have to be and can be made (as was held in the case cited above) as to the exact time when the letter was written. There are a number of cases where members indicated not only the dates but also the time in their letters. Notifications in such cases stated that the seats become vacant on the date either at forenoon or afternoon, as the case might be.

Another alternative might be considered. When a member hands in his letter of resignation personally to the Speaker, the resignation must take effect at the time when the letter is

[1] Rule 91 of the Conduct of Elections Rules, 1961.

handed over. There are instances (e.g. resignation of the Judicial Minister of West Bengal in 1958, and that of Mr. Mudgal in the House of the People in 1951) where members have handed over their resignation after attending the House. It cannot be said that the seat became vacant on the expiry of the previous day, as, in that event, the member would have become *functus officio*, and could not have taken part in the proceedings on the day on which he tendered his resignation.

The question can now be considered whether resignation takes effect on the date which the letter of resignation bears. Article 190 says that a member may resign his seat by writing under his hand to the Speaker (this term hereinafter includes the Chairman). The Article obviously implies that a member must resign into the hands of the Speaker. A declaration at large addressed to the Speaker and signed by the member will be of no effect. Such a declaration will not cause resignation even if it is posted on the Notice Board of the Legislatures. No period of notice is prescribed, and the Speaker cannot refuse to accept resignation, but the fact of resignation must be communicated to the Speaker. The mere signing of a letter of resignation addressed to the Speaker does not cause the seat to become vacant at the moment of signature. Something more is necessary, and that is that the letter of resignation must reach the hands of the Speaker. The material point of time is, therefore, not the date of the letter but the date on which the Speaker receives it.

No precedent of the House of Commons is available because there is no provision for the resignation of the member there. As an analogy, however, the case of a Company Director may be cited. A Director resigned his seat by a letter dated 17 June 1884, which was considered by the Board of Directors on 15 July 1884. It was held that the Director was to resign into the hands of the Company in General Meeting. The Company in General Meeting considered the letter on 31 December 1884. It was held that, although no period of notice was necessary, the Company could not have declined to accept the resignation. The resignation took effect on the day when the letter was considered by the Company in General Meeting, namely 31 December 1884, and not on the date on which the letter was written, 17 June 1884. The

Director remained liable up to 31 December 1884, although, after his resignation on 17 June, he did not take any part in the Company's affairs. The following passage[1] from the judgment will make the point clear:

'The real legal question is, what was the contract of service on the one hand and the Company on the other? Had he contracted to serve until he resigned into the hands of the Company and he accepted the office which he had undertaken? It is not contended on the part of the Company that they could have refused to accept it, but they say that the office must have been resigned into their hands to accept. They do not place themselves in the position of a sovereign, who can, if so pleased, decline to accept the resignation of a Minister or an Officer. They only say, "resignation must be made to us and not to our colleagues. Now on principle that seems to be so."'

This case is, therefore, an authority for the proposition that when resignation has to be made to a particular person resignation does not take effect until it is communicated to that person. Resignation of a member, therefore, takes effect at the time and date on which the Speaker receives the letter, whatever may be the date of the letter.

Any other conclusion would result in various anomalies. The following instances may be considered:

(i) a letter of resignation is received by the Speaker but it does not bear any date. On which date then is his resignation to take effect? The Speaker cannot engage in an investigation as to when the letter was written or posted or handed over for delivery. The material time in such a case is the time when the Speaker receives the letter.

(ii) a member writes a letter of resignation dated as on a particular day, keeps it in his pocket because he is not quite decided about resignation, but afterwards posts the letter when he comes to a firm decision. It may also be that he forgets to post the letter and posts it afterwards. If the time of posting is the material time, an investigation will have to be made not only as to when the letter was posted but also as to the state of the mind of the member—whether he was undecided on the day when he wrote the letter, or whether

---

[1] *Municipal Freehold Land Co.* v. *Pollington* (1890) 63, L.T. 238.

his decision was firm but he merely forgot to post it. The Constitution does not envisage any such investigation.

(iii) a member posts his letter of resignation, but before the letter reaches the Speaker he withdraws the letter by a telegram or the member may recall the letter from the post office on payment of the necessary fee so that the letter does not reach the Speaker at all. Can it be said that the resignation became operative and irrevocable on the date on which the letter was written or posted? It may also be that the letter becomes mislaid and is not delivered to the Speaker. In neither case can it be said that the resignation was effective on the date of posting. There is nothing to prevent a member giving a back date in his letter and posting it. In that way he can make his resignation retrospective in effect—something which he certainly cannot do.

(iv) a member sends his resignation by messenger. The messenger makes delay in delivering the letter or does not deliver the letter at all; or it may be that the letter was exacted from the member by coercion and sent to the Speaker. In any such case a detailed investigation would be necessary, and there will be ample scope for putting up various legal pleas either in support of or against resignation. The Speaker surely cannot constitute himself a court of law to determine whether there was fraud or coercion or some other legal defect on the part of the member, the messenger or any third party. It may also be that before a letter sent by a messenger is actually delivered to the Speaker, the member states that this letter of resignation stands withdrawn; it cannot be contemplated that in such a case the letter of resignation will be effective over the express intention of the member.

As for a member who has given notice of resignation from a future date, it is only a notice of intention to resign on a particular date. It cannot take effect as resignation on the day on which the letter is delivered to the Speaker.[1] The member may change his mind before the future date arrives, and withdraw his letter of resignation at any time before that date.

It is evident, therefore, that in all such cases an investigation as to the time when a seat becomes vacant will be neces-

---

[1] *M. Kunju Krishnan Nadar* v. *Speaker, Kerala Legislative Assembly*, Kerala Law Journal, 7 July 1964, p. 130.

sary. That cannot be in the contemplation of the Constitution. The Speaker is to give notice of any casual vacancy to the Election Commission. He cannot spend his time in investigation into the various pleas that may be raised in such circumstances.

It seems, therefore, that resignation of a member takes effect as soon as, and not until, a communication addressed to the Speaker in writing under the hand of the member resigning his seat is received by the Speaker.

It is a debatable question as to how far a court has jurisdiction to enquire whether a letter of resignation is a void document on the ground that it is forged or obtained by force or fraud, and to direct the Speaker to allow the member to continue to take his seat after declaring that the member has not lost his seat by the alleged resignation. Such a question arose in the case of *Thankama* v. *Speaker* (A.I.R. 1952, T.C. 166) in which the Travancore High Court held that the resignation under sub-clause (b) of clause (3) of Article 101 must be a voluntary act of the member, and that accordingly a civil court has the jurisdiction to do so. But if the resignation tendered by a sitting member be considered as a part of the 'business of the house' it may be argued that the court cannot *prima facie* have any jurisdiction in it under Article 122(2). The judgment of the Travancore High Court may be considered to be open to criticism from this point of view, for the Speaker or Chairman is an officer in whom powers are vested for this purpose, as contemplated in Article 122(2) of the Constitution.

The House may declare a member's seat vacant if he absents himself without leave of the House for more than sixty days. In computing the period of sixty days no account is taken of days during which the House is prorogued or adjourned for more than four consecutive days.[1]

The procedure for asking for leave of absence is laid down in the rules of the various legislatures. The usual procedure is to read the letter asking for leave of absence in the House, and, if no one objects, the leave is deemed to have been granted. If there is any objection, the matter is put to the vote of the House without any debate or discussion.

[1] Arts. 101, 190.

PARTY ORGANIZATION AND WHIPS

As is well known, the members of a legislature are usually divided into two distinct blocks, the Government and the Opposition. Each block may be composed of a single party or a combination of several parties or groups. Although the party system has an important bearing on the work of the legislature, the standing orders or the rules of procedure do not formally recognize the parties or party officials as such; on the other hand, the members of the Government and other members, whether supporting the Government or in the Opposition, are theoretically treated as on the same footing. The respective rights of the Government Party and the Opposition in the arrangement of the business of the House and allocation of time etc. have been discussed in their proper places.

LEADER OF THE HOUSE

In India the leader of the majority, i.e. the Government Party, usually the Prime Minister or the Chief Minister, as the case may be, is known as the Leader of the House of which he is a member. But any other member, usually a Minister, may be nominated by the Government Party to be the Leader of the House, and that is always done in the House where the Prime Minister or the Chief Minister is not a member. In the House where the Prime Minister or the Chief Minister is a member such a course is adopted only when he requires to be relieved of a part of his burden, namely the day-to-day management of the sittings of the House, but nevertheless nothing can deprive him of the ultimate responsibility. The Leader of the House is the chief spokesman of the Government in the House, and it is he who usually keeps the House informed about the Government's intentions.

The title of Leader of the House appears in almost all the rules of procedure of the legislatures in India, though the term has not been defined. The functions of the office are, of course, the same as in the British Parliament, i.e. suggesting and to a great degree fixing the course of all principal matters of business, viz. arranging business with the Chief Whip, settling procedure and distributing time with the

Opposition, and giving assistance to the Speaker or the Chairman in the maintenance of order and decorum, supervising and keeping in harmony the actions of other Ministers and members, taking the initiative in matters of ceremonial procedure and advising the House in every difficulty as it arises. The term does not appear to have been established in the British Parliament before the middle of the last century.

As May says:[1]

'The member of the Government who is primarily responsible to the Prime Minister for the arrangement of Government business in the House of Commons is known as the Leader of the House. He controls arrangement of business in that House while the programme and details are settled by the Government Chief Whip.

'When each week's programme of business has been arranged the Leader of the House states the business for the following week in answer to a question put to him at the end of Questions on Thursdays by the Leader of the Opposition, and, whenever necessary, makes further business statements from time to time. He may also move procedural motions relating to the business of the House.

'In the absence of the Prime Minister the Leader acts as spokesman of the House on ceremonial and other occasions; and at all times, being responsible to the House as a whole, he "advises the House in every difficulty as it arises."

'The leadership of the House is not a statutory office, nor is the Leader formally appointed by the Crown; for these reasons the post has usually been held together with another office. Until 1917 the Prime Minister, if a member of the House of Commons, also acted as leader of the House; if he was a member of the House of Lords the duties of the Leader of the House of Commons were performed either by the First Lord of the Treasury or by the Chancellor of the Exchequer. In 1917, Mr. Lloyd George appointed Mr. Bonar Law as Chancellor of the Exchequer and Leader of the House, but the practice of having a separate Leader of the House while the Prime Minister was in the House of Commons was not continued between 1922 and 1942. It has, however, been the regular practice since the latter date.'

[1] May, p. 260.

LEADER OF THE OPPOSITION

When the Opposition consists of a single party, the leader of that party is known as the Leader of the Opposition. When the Opposition consists of several parties, the parties may by agreement among themselves nominate a member to be the Leader of the Opposition. The expression 'Leader of the Opposition' has been defined in the Ministers of the Crown Act, 1937, as 'the Leader in that House of the Party in Opposition to His Majesty's Government having the greatest numerical strength in the House.' If any question arises as to which party in opposition has the greatest numerical strength, the Speaker has been given the power to decide the issue. The prevalence on the whole of the two-party system in the House of Commons has, as pointed out by May, usually obviated any uncertainty as to which party should be recognized as the official Opposition. The test of determining which party has a right to be called the official Opposition and its leader, the Leader of the Opposition, has been laid down by Mr. Speaker Fitzroy. It must be 'a party in Opposition to the Government from which an alternative Government could be formed.'[1] Or, as May has paraphrased it, 'It is the largest minority party which is prepared, in the event of the resignation of the Government, to assume office.'[2]

Therefore, where there are more parties than one in Opposition, the party which is numerically the largest of them all cannot necessarily be recognized as the official Opposition. The other test must also be satisfied, that is to say, it must be one from which an alternative Government may be formed. In 1935, when there were more than two parties in the House of Commons, the Conservatives having 387 members, the Labour Party 154, the National Liberals 33 and the Liberals 17, it appears that the Labour Party was recognized as the official Opposition and its Leader, Mr. Attlee, was the Leader of the Opposition. On the other hand, in 1940, a small party led by Mr. Maxton,[3] when there was no other party in opposition, was not recognized as the official Opposition. Three

[1] H.C.D. 1939-40, vol. 361, c. 28.
[2] May, p. 260.
[3] H.C.D. 1939-40, vol. 361, c. 21.

3

things are, therefore, necessary before a party can be recognized as, and given the privileges referred to above of, the official Opposition. It must be an organized Opposition in the House, it must have the largest numerical strength, and it must be prepared to assume office. Where there are numerous small parties or groups, it cannot always be said that these three tests are satisfied. In such circumstances the party which has the largest numerical strength among the Opposition Parties need not necessarily be recognized as the official Opposition and its leader given the status of Leader of the Opposition unless all the parties unite as a single Parliamentary Opposition Party.[1] Moreover this is quite reasonable in that the other Opposition Parties would be deprived of the right of selection of subjects for debates and other privileges of the Opposition Parties.

This view has been taken in the West Bengal Legislative Assembly.[2] It is understood that in the House of the People the following principles are followed in recognizing the official Opposition.[3]

(i) Unity of ideology and the programme of the members who form a party or group.

The function of a party is not merely to have a fluid partnership of individuals or members for the purpose of opposing Government. For a party to pull its weight in a legislature, it should have a distinct ideology and programme of its own whether on the political, economic or social side. In this view a group of independents can never be a homogeneous party capable of developing into a well-knit Opposition, as it would never stand the chance of forming the Government in an emergency. The Opposition should have all the potentialities of enlarging their numbers from election to election.

(ii) Number of members of party or group.

A parliamentary party should be able to command a minimum strength which will place it in a position to keep the House. In other words, the number of members to form a

---

[1] *Table*, vol. xxiii, pp. 153-4.

[2] W.B.L.A.P. vol. vii, no. 3(1953), c. 255; ibid. 25 June 1957, p. 947.

[3] In accordance with these principles the Speaker has recognized no one as a party in the House of the People. He has, however, recognized the Communist Block as a Group as they satisfy all the three conditions laid down above. The Leader of the Group has not been recognized as Leader of the Opposition.

party should not be less than the quorum fixed to constitute a sitting of the House.

(iii) Party organization.

A party should have a party organization not only inside the House, but outside the House, which is in touch with public opinion on all important issues before the country.

A group has to satisfy all the above conditions, except that the number of members to form a group has been fixed at thirty in the House of the People which consists of more than five hundred members.

In England the Leader of the Opposition receives a salary under the Ministers of the Crown Act, 1937. In West Bengal an amendment was made in 1957 in the Legislative Assembly (Members' Emoluments) Act, 1937, providing for the payment of a salary to the Leader of the Opposition. The Leader of the Opposition is a private member. He owes no allegiance to the Government.[1] No action of his can in any way implicate the Government. He is responsible only to his constituents and to the members from whom he derives his position. He is under a special obligation to defend the rights and privileges of private members, particularly the right of every member to express his opinion freely on all matters of public policy.

WHIPS

The parties inside the legislature have elaborate organizations of party members and officials. The officials who are closely connected with the business of the House are the Whips. Each party has its own Whips, one of whom acts as the Chief Whip. The Government Chief Whip is usually a member of the Government—a junior Minister or a Parliamentary Secretary. There seems to be some misconception in India about the status of the Chief Whip. The Chief Whip is only a party official and as such has no official status in the Government, although he may be a junior Minister or a Parliamentary Secretary. This misconception has led some State Governments to have the Government Chief Whip nominated by the Governor. The Governor as the head of the executive government has no party affiliation, and it

[1] H.C.D. 1937-8, vol. 330, c. 824.

would be improper for him to nominate the Chief Whip of a Party. The main function of the Whips when the office came into existence was to shepherd party members to support the Government or the Opposition, as the case may be, when voting was demanded. The word 'Whip' is said to have been borrowed from the expression 'whipping in' used in hunts.

In modern times, however, the functions of the Whips have become much more elaborate and onerous. They have been succinctly described by May as follows:

'The efficient and smooth running of the parliamentary machine depends largely upon the Whips. Certain duties are common to Whips of all parties, but by far the most important duties devolve upon the Government Chief Whip. He is concerned with mapping out the time of the session; for applying in detail the Government's programme of business; for estimating the time likely to be required for each item, and for arranging the business of the individual sitting. A statement is made in the House, usually on Thursday, of the business to be taken in the following week. In drawing up the programme he is limited to a certain extent by the standing orders, which allot a modicum of time to private Members; and by statute law or standing orders, which require, or may require, certain business to be completed by specific dates; as well as by certain conventions which make it obligatory upon him to consult the Whips of Opposition Parties and even to put down items of their selection. In carrying out his duties, he is directly responsible to the Prime Minister, as Leader of the House. It is also part of his duties to advise the Government on parliamentary business and procedure, and to maintain a close liaison with Ministers in regard to parliamentary business which affects their departments. He, together with the Chief Whips of other parties, constitutes what is known as the 'usual channels,' through which communications pass as to business arrangements and other matters which concern the convenience of Members as a whole.

'The duties which are common to Whips of all parties are the following: they keep their Members supplied with information about the business of the House, secure the attendance of Members, arrange for their Members who are unable to attend divisions to "pair" with Members of the opposite side of the House so that their votes may be neutralized and lost, and supply lists of Members to serve on standing and select committees. They also act as intermediaries between the leaders and rank and file of their parties in order to keep the former informed as to the trend of party opinion.'[1]

The notices which are sent out to party members by the Whip informing them about important debates and votes in which they should be present are also known as 'whips'. The importance of debates is indicated by lines (one, two or three) with which a whip is underscored, and it is assumed that a member receiving a whip will support the policy of the party. To ignore a whip without sufficient reason, e.g. illness, is considered to be a serious offence against party discipline. Whips are not issued for all debates—sometimes members are allowed a 'free vote'. To decline a whip is a method of resignation from a party, and withdrawal of a whip is a means of expelling a member from a party.

[1] May, p. 262.

CHAPTER III

SESSIONS OF LEGISLATURE

SUMMONING THE LEGISLATURE

THE right to summon the legislature is vested in the Executive Head of the State—the President of the Union, or the Governor of the State, as the case may be. He can summon the legislature at any time; but the Constitution[1] requires that not more than six months shall elapse between the day appointed for the first meeting of one session and the day of the last meeting of the previous session. The legislature is summoned by an order under the signature of the Executive Head of the State published in a notification in the Official Gazette; the time and place of meeting are specified in the notification. Individual summonses to the members are issued by the Secretary to the legislature.

A rule of the Lok Sabha provides that if a session is called at short notice, summonses may not be issued separately but an announcement will be published in the Official Gazette and in the Press and the members may be informed by telegram. In other legislatures where their rules carry no such provisions, when a session is summoned at very short notice, summonses are issued as usual to individual members, and an announcement is made in the Gazette and in the Press, and telegraphic intimation sent to members. Apart from the summonses to members, intimation is also given of a session to persons who, although not members of the legislature, are entitled under the Constitution[2] to take part in its deliberations, e.g. Ministers who are not members of the House concerned, the Attorney-General, the Advocates-General of the States.

The question whether, once a House has been summoned to meet on a particular date, the date can be changed by a subsequent notification, arose in the Council of States in

[1] Arts. 85, 174.
[2] Arts. 88, 177.

1953. On 28 May the Rajya Sabha was summoned to meet on 17 August 1953. By a subsequent notification purporting to supersede the previous notification dated 5 August 1953, the House was summoned to meet on 24 August 1953. A protest was made by the members of the Rajya Sabha that the House should be treated with more consideration. It was also argued that the President had no authority to alter the date once he had issued the summons. As regards the second point, the Government contended that the President had the right to alter the date on the ground that the authority which could summon a meeting had also the power to cancel the notice and summon a meeting on a later date. The Law Minister, however, added that he was expressing the opinion off-hand, as the matter had not been considered from the legal or constitutional point of view. In the end, the Chairman said that when lawyers differed on the question of legality he would not express any opinion, but it should be presumed that the President had obtained the best legal advice and his action should be presumed to be regular. He also added that he had no doubt that the House would have no occasion to be called on one date and then be asked to come on another. Such a change of date was also made in West Bengal in July 1956.

The general proposition that the authority which can convene a meeting has also the authority to postpone or alter the date of the meeting does not appear to be correct so far as the ordinary law of meetings is concerned. It was held in *Smith* v. *Paringa Mines* [1906] 2 Ch., p. 193, that when a meeting has been properly convened by the directors of a company for a certain date, they have no power to postpone the meeting to another date.

In the British Parliament the King has the authority to defer or accelerate by subsequent proclamation the date fixed for a meeting of Parliament. That authority is however derived from the Meetings of Parliament Act, 1797, and the Prorogation Act, 1867. Various other Acts authorize the King to summon Parliament on dates other than those previously fixed in a national emergency. If the general propositions mentioned above are correct, there would have been no necessity for authorizing the King to summon Parliament by special enactments.

The Indian Constitution says that the President shall from time to time summon each House of Parliament at such time and place as he thinks fit. But no power is given to him expressly to postpone a meeting or accelerate a meeting. In the absence of such power it is doubtful whether the President has the power to alter the date of a meeting once he has summoned it for a particular date.

Even if the President has the power, it is submitted that summoning a House should not be made a light affair which a frequent or hasty change of date may imply. Only in the case of a national emergency or in grave circumstances may the dates, once fixed, be altered.

The same considerations will apply in the case of the summoning of State legislatures also.

OATH OR AFFIRMATION

The first duty of a member elected or nominated to the legislature is to make and subscribe the oath or affirmation of allegiance; for, if any member sits or votes as a member without taking the oath or making the affirmation, he is liable to pay a penalty of Rs. 500 in respect of each day on which he sits or votes.[1]

The oath or affirmation[2] is in the following form:

'I...having been elected/nominated a member of...do swear in the name of God/solemnly affirm that I will bear true faith and allegiance to the Constitution of India as by law established, that I will uphold the sovereignty and integrity of India, and that I will faithfully discharge the duty upon which I am about to enter.'

The Executive Head of the State or any person authorized by him can administer the oath or affirmation. The Presiding Officer of the legislature, the Speaker or the Chairman, as the case may be, is generally authorized to adminster the oath or affirmation to members. The oath may be taken or the affirmation made either in the House or in the Chamber of the Presiding Officer.

When the Lower House meets for the first time after a

---

[1] Arts. 99, 104, 188, 193.
[2] Constitution, Schedule III.

General Election, the Presiding Officer of the former House, who continues to be so until immediately before the first meeting of the new House,[1] can administer the oath or affirmation to the newly elected member(s) by virtue of the power, if any, previously delegated to him. In the case of the Upper House, the Chairman continues in office unless his seat is vacated and he can administer the oath to any newly elected member.

The practice in the Lok Sabha, however, is that the first sitting after a general election is devoted to oath-taking by members. Since the Speaker of the former Lok Sabha relinquishes his office immediately before that sitting, the President appoints the seniormost member of the Lok Sabha as the Speaker *pro tem.*, and he is administered the oath by the President himself at the President's House several hours before the time fixed for the sitting of the Lok Sabha. The Speaker *pro tem.* and two other members of the Lok Sabha are also appointed by the President as the persons before whom members of the Lok Sabha can make and subscribe the oath or affirmation. Those two members are nominated by the Speaker *pro tem.* on the Panel of Chairmen of the Lok Sabha in order to enable them to preside over the Lok Sabha in his absence and to administer the oath to members. Immediately after oath-taking by members, the Lok Sabha elects its Speaker, whereupon the Speaker *pro tem.* relinquishes his office.

ELECTION OF THE PRESIDING OFFICER

After the members have taken their oaths, the first business that the House of a legislature enters into is the election of its Presiding Officers.[2] The Presiding Officer of the House of the People or of a State Legislative Assembly is called the Speaker, and that of the Council of States or of a Legislative Council is called the Chairman. Two Deputies, the Deputy Speaker and the Deputy Chairman, must also be elected.[3] In the case of the Upper House, the members of which retire

---

[1] Arts. 94, 179.
[2] Arts. 93, 178, 182.
[3] Art. 89.

by rotation, a Chairman or a Deputy Chairman has to be elected if the previous Chairman or the Deputy Chairman vacates his seat by rotation. As there is no one to preside over a meeting until the election of the Presiding Officer takes place, it is necessary to have somebody to preside over the meeting which is to elect the Presiding Officer. In the British House of Commons no one actually presides at the election of the Speaker, but the Clerk of the House practically acts in that capacity. In India, however, the Constitution provides that if the offices of the Presiding Officer and his Deputy are vacant, the Executive Head of the State may appoint any member of the House to act as the Presiding Officer.[1] Under a similar provision of the Government of India Act, the Executive Head of the State used to appoint a member of the House to preside at the election of the Presiding Officer. The same procedure has been followed under the Constitution also.

The election of the Speaker in the British House of Commons is a picturesque affair, and follows the tradition of a time when to be elected Speaker was rather risky. For it was upon the Speaker that the wrath of the King ordinarily fell if there was a conflict between the King and the House of Commons.

The King directs the Commons to elect one of their members as Speaker, and the King's directive is conveyed by the Lord Chancellor from the House of Lords. So, when Parliament assembles after a General Election, the Commons are summoned by the Gentleman Usher of the Black Rod (the messenger from the House of Lords, so called because he carries an ebony rod as the insignia of his office) to attend the House of Lords. A few members go there and hear from the Lord Chancellor the message of the King. Before that, each party tends to arrange whom it is going to support for election as Speaker, and two members, usually backbenchers, are selected who will respectively propose and second the proposal. If there is no contest and the parties have agreed on the person to be elected, it is usual for the Government party to make, and for the Opposition to second, the proposal. When the message of the King has been re-

[1] Arts. 95, 180, 184.

ceived, the House of Commons proceeds to elect its Speaker. The Clerk of the House calls upon the member or members as prearranged, not by words but by pointing his finger at him, to propose or second, as the case may be, the name or names of candidates. If there is a contest, he takes a division.

A curious question was raised by the Canadian House of Commons as to what would happen if there was a tie in the division for the election of the Speaker. It appears that no precedent was available, but the Clerk of the British House of Commons, Sir T. L. Webster, gave the following opinion:

'My personal opinion on the precise question asked by you is that in the event of an equality of votes on the first question (i.e. on the first name) proposed from the Chair, the question should be treated as void and the question should be proposed on the second name. I am quite clear that a Clerk of the House has not any power of voting. The question not having received a majority of votes in its favour has not been decided one way or the other, and the decision should be treated as void.'[1]

After the election is over, the Speaker-elect makes a show of unwillingness and he has to be conducted to the Chair by pretence of force by the two members who had proposed and seconded his name. Felicitations then follow and a suitable reply is made by the Speaker.

The election of the Speaker is subject to the approval of the King. But it is inconceivable nowadays that such approval would be refused. Approval is given as a matter of course.

In India the procedure for the election of the Presiding Officer is regulated by the rules of procedure of the House concerned. The procedure followed in some States is for a member to nominate a candidate from among the members of the House and for another member to second the nomination. The consent of the proposed candidate has to be obtained by the proposer. If there is only one nomination, the proposed candidate is at once declared elected. If there is more than one nomination, a ballot takes place. In case there are more than two nominations, the decision is made by the system of the second ballot. That is to say, if any of the candidates secures a number of votes more than the

[1] Beauchesne, *Parliamentary Rules and Forms*, 2nd ed., p. 9.

aggregate number of votes of all the other candidates, he is declared elected. If no one obtains such a number of votes at the first ballot, the candidate who obtains the smallest number of votes is excluded and a second ballot takes place, and the ballot is repeated until one of the candidates succeeds in obtaining more votes than the aggregate votes of all the remaining candidates. If two or more candidates obtain the same number of votes, lots are drawn as to which of them should be elected or excluded.

The procedure in the Lok Sabha and some other States is different. Election is made on a motion proposed by one member and seconded by another. If more than one motion is proposed, all the motions are moved and seconded. They are put to the vote in the order in which they have been moved. If any motion is carried, the member proposed by that motion is declared elected. The later motions, if any, are not put.

As soon as a member is declared to have been elected as the Presiding Officer the member appointed to preside at the election vacates the chair and the elected Presiding Officer takes it. Thereafter the election of the Deputy Presiding Officer takes place in the same manner as that of the Presiding Officer. No approval by the Executive Head of the State of the persons elected as Presiding Officers is necessary.

PRESIDING OFFICER OF THE COUNCIL OF STATES

The Vice-President of India is the *ex-officio* Chairman of the Council of States,[1] and therefore the election of a Chairman is not necessary; the Deputy Chairman is, however, elected in the same manner as the Speaker of the Lok Sabha.

TEMPORARY PRESIDING OFFICERS

The Presiding Officer, and in his absence his deputy, presides over the deliberations of the House. In case both of them are unable to preside, a panel of temporary presiding officers is nominated by the Presiding Officer. If neither the Presiding Officer, his deputy nor the temporary presiding

[1] Art. 89.

officers are available, such other member as may be determined by the House shall act as the Presiding Officer.[1]

In the British House of Commons, besides the Speaker, another officer known as the Chairman of Ways and Means is appointed by the House on a motion.[2] The Chairman of Ways and Means presides when the House goes into Committee. He also acts as Deputy Speaker and presides over the meetings of the House when the speaker is absent. There is also a Deputy Chairman, similarly appointed, who acts for the Chairman in his absence and also for the Speaker in the absence of both. The Speaker nominates a panel of ten members to act as temporary chairmen of committees when requested to do so by the Chairman of Ways and Means.

HISTORY OF THE OFFICE OF THE SPEAKER

Previous to the Montagu-Chelmsford Reforms, the Head of the State used to preside over the deliberations of the legislature. The Government of India Act, 1919, first provided for a separate Presiding Officer of the legislature. The Presiding Officer was called the President, and the first President of the Central Legislative Assembly was Sir Fredrick Whyte. Although the Government of India Act provided for the election of the President, it was also provided that the first President should be appointed by the Government. Sir Fredrick Whyte was a member of the House of Commons and he was selected for the post for his deep knowledge of parliamentary procedure.

When the term of Sir Fredrick Whyte expired in 1925, Mr. V. J. Patel was elected as President, beating his rival Mr. Rangachari by two votes. He had an eventful career as President and came into frequent conflict with the Government, but it was he who laid the foundation of the independence of the Speaker, the Speaker's severance from party politics and the independence of the legislature's own secretariat. His first conflict was with regard to the Public Security Bill. When the Bill was pending before the Assembly, the Meerut conspiracy case had been launched. Mr. Patel took

[1] Arts. 91, 95, 180, 184.
[2] May, p. 253.

the view that no proper discussion of the Bill could take place without reference being made to the Meerut Conspiracy Case, and the matter being *sub judice* all such references would have to be ruled out of order. In consequence there could be no proper discussion, and he refused to place the motion for the consideration of the Bill before the House. On the next day the Viceroy addressed the House and said that the interpretation given by the President was not in accordance with the intention of the rule, and the rule was amended taking away the powers of the President to refuse to place a motion before the House. The next encounter with the Government was when the Government made certain security arrangements within the precincts of the House without consulting the President. Mr. Patel closed the public galleries for a month. A compromise was arrived at whereby all security arrangements were to be under the control of the President, who exercised his authority through officers directly appointed by him (the Watch and Ward staff).

The foundation of a separate and independent secretariat for the legislature was also laid by President Patel. Although from the very inception the need for a separate Assembly Department had been felt and canvassed, it was not till 1928 that a separate Assembly Department was created to be under the control of the President in pursuance of a resolution passed by the Assembly on a motion moved by Pandit Motilal Nehru on 22 September 1928. The Indian Constitution adopted the same principle by Articles 98 and 187, which lay down that each House of legislature should have a separate secretariat.

President Patel also extracted an apology from the Government when it came to his notice that his rulings were commented upon by official members in the lobby.

President Patel resigned in 1930 and was succeeded by Mohammed Yakub. Then came Ibrahim Rahimutulla and Shanmukhan Chetti. After the resignation of Patel it seemed as if life had almost left the Assembly; its proceedings became completely spiritless. Sir Abdur Rahim held the office of President from 1935 to 1945, by which time the office of the President came to be known as that of the Speaker. Abdur

Rahim maintained the dignity of the chair, and once when Bhulabhai Desai and Aney criticized one of his rulings in a statement to the Press he took great exception. Ultimately, after a conference between the various leaders of the parties, it was agreed and stated in the Assembly that it should not be open to any member of the House to criticize directly or indirectly outside the House any ruling given, opinion expressed or statement made by the Speaker in the discharge of his duties.

The next Speaker was Mr. Mavlankar, who was elected in January 1946 after defeating his rival Sir Cawasjee Jehangir, a nominated member set up by the official circle. But it was the vote of some officials which turned the scale in his favour. In his time certain conventions were established as regards the independence of the secretariat. One was that the officials were to be selected not by the Selection Board of the Government but by the Speaker, and the other was when he insisted that the Economy Committee set up by the Government should make its report, so far as the Parliament Secretariat was concerned, to the Speaker, and it would be for the Speaker to implement the recommendations of the Committee. It also appears that he had a hand in the incorporation in the Constitution of the provision of the President's address at the opening of a session in imitation of the King's speech, and the financial procedure of having Appropriation Bills. The privileges of Parliament also were equated with those of the House of Commons at his suggestion, and Articles 105 and 194 were accordingly incorporated in the Constitution.

PRESIDING OFFICER AND POLITICAL PARTY

What the position of the Presiding Officer should be, when once elected, *vis-à-vis* the political party to which he belongs, has received considerable attention not only in India but also in England. The question may be considered in three aspects: (i) whether the Presiding Officer after being elected should remain a member of the political party; (ii) whether he should be opposed when seeking re-election in a General Election or when seeking re-election as Speaker; (iii) how the grievances of the constituency from which he is elected can be brought before the House.

As regards (i), it has been the strict convention in the British Parliament that the Speaker of the House of Commons severs all connections with the party to which he belonged before his election, and does not participate in any activities of the party. In India, however, the Presiding Officers remain members of the party, but do not usually attend or participate in any party meetings except on ceremonial or social occasions.

As regards (ii), whether the Speaker's seat should be contested in a General Election if the Speaker desires to continue his services, the question was raised in the British Parliament in 1939, and a Select Committee of the House of Commons went into the question thoroughly. A number of schemes providing for a safe seat for the Speaker, including the setting up of an imaginary constituency where a contest would not take place and an agreement among the various parties not to contest the Speaker's seat, were examined by the Committee but all were rejected. It may be pointed out that in practice the Speaker's seat is seldom contested. As a matter of fact, from 1714 to 1945 only five contests have taken place, in 1806, 1885, 1895, 1935 and 1945. Since 1945 there have been three more instances of a contest, namely in 1950, 1955 and 1964, but the seat was contested by an Independent candidate except in 1964. But there is no convention that the Speaker's seat should not be contested at all. On the other hand, it has been recognized that the ex-Speaker cannot stand as a party candidate. A tradition has therefore grown up that if the Speaker signifies his desire to accept the Speakership for the next term, his seat is not contested unless there are very special reasons for doing so. On the reassembling of Parliament the ex-Speaker is again elected Speaker. On retirement from the Speakership the Speaker quits politics— usually with a peerage.

The Select Committee, which consisted of such eminent persons as Mr. Lloyd George, Mr. Churchill and Mr. Lansbury, reported that the existing practice should continue and no safe seat should be provided for the Speaker either by legislation or by agreement.

The recommendation of the Select Committee may best be given in their own words:

'Your Committee attach the greatest importance to the preservation of the right of the electors to choose their own candidate, and they are not prepared to recommend any proposal which would secure the immunity of the Speaker from opposition in his constituency by a statutory limitation of this right.

'Your Committee have carefully considered the possibility that opposition to the Speaker might be avoided by an agreement between all parties. But, even if the principal parties were to accept such an agreement and, in defence of it, were prepared to withdraw all support from a local organization which was insisting on its undoubted freedom of choice, it is not certain that such contests would be abandoned or even that their frequency would be abated.

'If the Speaker is to be faced with opposition at general elections the crux of the matter is the extent to which he and his supporters can properly go in the defence of his candidature. Your Committee have already set out above the course which has previously commended itself to Speakers who have been placed in this dilemma. And, in their opinion, the adoption of this line of conduct displays the great political wisdom which the House now confidently expects from those who are called upon to preside over its deliberations. While your Committee cannot but regret—and they are in no doubt that this regret is fully shared by members of all parties—that the weight of any additional anxiety should be added to the heavy burden already laid upon the Speaker, they are convinced that it is by the ability to meet such opposition with the same consistent impartiality, which marks his conduct in the Chair, that the highest traditions of the Speakership are best served. It would be better that a Speaker should suffer defeat through strict adherence to his principles than that he should deviate in the slightest degree towards political controversy. Your Committee can envisage no half-way house, and a return to partisan Speakership would be inevitable.

'If the modern Speaker is to be required both to face contests in his constituency, even though perhaps not with the

4

same frequency and regularity as other members, and at the same time to maintain the traditions of his office in such a way that he can continue to discharge to the full satisfaction of the House and of himself the onerous duties that today rest upon him, what course of action is open to him? He clearly cannot stand as a party candidate;[1] but he can stand as the Speaker seeking re-election—a course which has been followed not only by the present Speaker in 1935, but by those Speakers in New Zealand who have most closely adhered to the British tradition. As a non-party and independent candidate with no political proposals to put before the electors, he can but offer them the high ideals of his office, the historical background from which these have developed, and the need for their preservation if freedom of speech and a proper regard for minority opinions are to remain outstanding characteristics of the House of Commons. Thus confining himself to the pure statement of a case without in any way being drawn into argument with his opponents or attempting to controvert any statements that they may make, he is placed in the embarrassing position of being a party to a fight in which he can take no part. The difficulties of such a position may be felt even more keenly by his supporters than they are by the Speaker himself.

'Your Committee cannot but agree that such a state of affairs is far from desirable. On the other hand, they are emphatically of opinion that any departure from these traditions that would again bring the Speaker back into the mill of party controversy, and so strip him of that great authority he can now wield in the defence of democracy, would be a retrograde step which would inevitably tend to cast doubt upon the impartiality of the occupant of the Chair and thus impair that confidence which is essential to its unique influence and prestige.'[2]

As for the question whether the Speaker should be opposed when seeking re-election, it appears that the convention

[1] It appears, however, that Mr. Speaker Morrison stood as a Conservative candidate in the General Election, 1955, and was opposed by an Independent Labour candidate. See *Dod's Parliament Companion*, 1955. In India Speakers generally stand as party candidates. In Madras the Speaker stood and was elected as an Independent candidate in the General Election 1952, and was also elected Speaker subsequently.

[2] H.C. *Paper* 98 of 1939.

that a Speaker is usually re-elected as long as he is willing to serve, irrespective of changes in the political complexion of the House, has been established in England for more than a century. But even then the Select Committee says that there can be no absolute bar to a contest on the re-election of a willing former Speaker:

'Though it is now over a hundred years since the re-election to the Chair of a willing Speaker has been challenged, there is no question that the members of each new Parliament have been, and still are, free to take that course. The retention of that full freedom is a vital safeguard in the defence of the high traditions of the Speakership, and it might be so exercised against some occupant of the Chair who, entirely innocent of any offence, might yet prove himself unequal to the weight of the immense and growing burden of his office.'

As regards (iii), this question was also considered by the Select Committee; in fact the inability of the Speaker to bring forward the grievances of his constituency before the House was advanced as an argument for changing the system of election by either creating an imaginary constituency for the Speaker or making his constituency a two-member one. The Select Committee met the arguments as follows:

'It has been argued by those who advocate some change in the existing system that the Speaker's non-political position after election further disenfranchises his constituents, in that he cannot express their views in the debate or by his vote in divisions, nor can he by political means seek to redress their grievances. Your Committee do not find themselves impressed by these arguments. In the British political system, whatever may be its merits or demerits, there is a strong party control over the actions of members in the House and the sterilisation of a single vote on whichever side it might have been delivered will have so small an influence on matters which are the subject of party decisions as to be entirely negligible. On the other hand, on non-controversial matters and particular grievances your Committee feel assured that there are many members in any House who would most willingly place their services at the disposal of the Speaker and his constituents.

'In matters of individual interest or grievance the Speaker's constituents are in fact in a peculiarly favoured position. Though the Speaker himself can put down no questions, any matter affecting them which he feels justified in raising privately with a Department of State will, in the nature of human reactions, coming from such a source, receive the most careful consideration. Again, if the circumstances of a particular case require that a question should receive public expression, it would be, and in fact, is willingly sponsored by other members.'

OUTSIDE INTERESTS OF PRESIDING OFFICERS

The question whether Presiding Officers or Deputy Presiding Officers can have outside interests, for example, whether they can hold directorships of companies or follow any pro- fession such as the profession of law, has been occasionally asked, but no authoritative decision seems to have been laid down.

In England the question has been raised in the case of Ministers and once at least in the case of a Deputy Speaker. In the case of Ministers a rule was laid down by Sir Henry Campbell-Bannerman in 1906 in the following terms:

'The condition which was laid down on the formation of the Government was that all directorships held by Ministers must be resigned except in the case of honorary directorships, directorships in connection with philanthropic undertakings, and directorships in private companies.'[1]

In 1937 the then Prime Minister, Mr. Baldwin, declared that this rule had been followed by successive Prime Ministers and would be followed by him. The rule was further eluci- dated in 1939 in respect of private companies which had been excepted in the Campbell-Bannerman rule:

'At the time when this rule was announced the term "private company" had no statutory significance and was used probably to cover companies dealing wholly or mainly with family interests. Since then the term has received a statutory definition which covers a very wide field and examples of existing private companies submitted by the hon. and learned Gentleman show that such companies may

[1] H.C.D. 1906, vol. 154, c. 234.

control very large amounts of capital while their shares may be in turn controlled by public companies engaged in the widest possible range of activities. In these circumstances it is clear that if the term "private companies" in Sir Henry Campbell-Bannerman's ruling were to be interpreted in the statutory sense it would travel far beyond the intentions of the original framers of the rule.'[1]

The Prime Minister proposed to interpret the term in future as applying only to concerns dealing wholly or mainly with family affairs or interests and not principally engaged in trading.

As regards following independent professions, the question was raised with respect to solicitors in private practice. Mr. Baldwin said in 1937 that it would be unreasonable to require that a solicitor, on becoming a member of the Government, should dissolve his partnership or should be obliged to allow his annual practising certificate to lapse; on the other hand he should, in accordance with the principle laid down in Sir Henry Campbell-Bannerman's rule, cease to carry on the daily routine work of the firm or to take any active part in his ordinary business although he should not be precluded from continuing to advise in matters of family trusts, guardianships and other similar cases; a certain amount of discretion was to be allowed since it was impossible to cover all conceivable cases in any rule.

This principle was accepted by the House, and it was applied to Ministers both inside and outside the Cabinet.

As regards the Speaker, a question was put to Sir Gilbert Campion, as he then was, by a Select Committee which was appointed to consider the case of private practice by the Chairman of Ways and Means who is also the Deputy Speaker, whether Sir Henry Campbell-Bannerman's rule applied to the case of the officers of the House. Sir Gilbert Campion replied that it had never been explicitly applied, but he said that the Speaker did not have any outside interest. The Speaker of the House of Commons after election to the office resigns all public directorships; as regards private directorships it depends on the nature of the company, but the Speaker does not take any part in the activities of a

[1] H.C.D. 1938-9, vol. 350, cc. 1937-8.

company likely to be connected with Parliament or Parliamentary business in any way. There does not appear to be any precedent in India. In West Bengal, however, it appears that a former President of the Bengal Legislative Council continued to hold directorships in companies while in office. It appears that a convention has now been established in West Bengal that a member on being elected Speaker should resign any directorship of a company.[1]

So far as the Deputy Speaker is concerned, a Select Committee of the House of Commons considered the matter, and it transpired in evidence that a distinction was made between the Speaker and the Deputy Speaker, and that several Chairmen of Ways and Means continued to have outside interests such as holding active directorships of companies or practising the profession of a barrister or solicitor.[2]

As a result of the report of the Committee, a rule was laid down by the House of Commons that the Chairman and the Deputy Chairman, if they happen to be lawyers, should refrain from acting in a professional capacity on behalf of or against members of the House.[3]

In West Bengal successive Deputy Speakers and Deputy Presidents have practised the legal profession.

POWERS OF DEPUTY SPEAKER

Article 95, clause (1) and Article 180, clause (1) of the Constitution provide that when the office of the Speaker is vacant, the duties of the office shall be performed by the Deputy Speaker. Clause (2) of these Articles lays down that when the Speaker is absent from any meeting, the Deputy Speaker shall act as Speaker. Clause (2) refers to the circumstances when the office of Speaker is not vacant, but the Speaker, for some reason or other such as illness, is unable to attend the meeting, and obviously authorizes the Deputy Speaker only to preside at the meeting and exercise such functions of the Speaker as are exercisable in a meeting, e.g. keeping order, deciding points of order and so on.

[1] W.B.L.A.P. 20 Mar. 1959.
[2] H.C. *Paper* 104 of 1947-8.
[3] H.C.D. 1947-8, vol. 452, c. 663.

But besides presiding at meetings the Speaker has other duties to perform in regard to the work of the House. Some such duties are enjoined by the rules of procedure and some by the Constitution itself. One of the duties cast upon the Speaker by the Constitution[1] is to certify Money Bills when they are sent to the Upper House or to the Head of the State for assent. Articles 110 and 199[2] specifically mention the Speaker, and under Articles 95, clause (1) and 180, clause (1), the Deputy Speaker can perform this duty only when the office of the Speaker is vacant. He cannot, it seems, certify Money Bills when the office of Speaker is not vacant but for some reason (e.g. absence from the country) the Speaker is not available. In the British House of Commons, Money Bills are required to be endorsed by the Speaker in accordance with the provisions of the Parliament Act, 1911. The Deputy Speaker has, however, endorsed Money Bills during the absence of the Speaker.[3] This is in accordance with the Deputy Speakers Act, 1855.[4]

The rules of procedure of the House require that all bills should be authenticated by the Speaker when they are transmitted to the Upper House or sent to the Head of the State for assent. The rules also require the Speaker to decide on the admissibility of adjournment motions, questions etc., before they come before the House. The question is whether, when the Speaker is not available, the Deputy Speaker can exercise these functions of the Speaker. Unless the rules specifically authorize the Deputy Speaker, it seems that the Deputy Speaker would have no authority to do so. Rules of many Houses provide that the Speaker may give such directions as may be necessary for giving effect to the rules; under such a rule, the Speaker may authorize the Deputy Speaker to exercise his functions or he may delegate the authority to the Deputy Speaker. If this view is correct, there may not be any difficulty about these matters.

So far, however, as Money Bills are concerned, the Constitution will stand in the way, for the Constitution enjoins the Speaker to certify Money Bills, and the Constitution itself

[1] Arts. 110, 199.
[2] Ibid.
[3] May, p. 818, footnote.
[4] 18 and 19 Vic., c. 84.

provides for the exercise of the functions of the Speaker in the absence of the Speaker. There seems to be a lacuna here which should be removed.

RESIGNATION AND REMOVAL OF PRESIDING OFFICERS

The Presiding Officer may resign his office by a letter addressed to the Deputy Presiding Officer; similarly the Deputy Presiding Officer may resign his office by a letter addressed to the Presiding Officer.[1] If either of the offices is vacant, it seems that the occupant of the other office cannot resign until the vacant office is filled. It appears, however, that in the Lok Sabha, when Mr. Speaker Mavalankar died, Mr. Ananthasayanam Ayyangar resigned his office of Deputy Speaker on 7 March 1956 by a letter addressed to the office of the Speaker, although there was no incumbent of the office at the time. Thereafter the Secretary of the Lok Sabha informed the President of India that the office of both the Speaker and the Deputy Speaker were vacant, and the President appointed another member to perform the duties of the Speaker until a Speaker had been elected. Mr. Ananthasayanam Ayyangar was then duly elected as Speaker of the Lok Sabha on 8 March 1956.[2] If both the Presiding Officer and Deputy Presiding Officer desire to resign at the same time it appears they cannot do so. The solution may be found in each of them resigning their offices in a letter addressed to the other; for it may be argued that resignation does not take effect until the letter reaches the addressee, and each continues to hold office up to that time. How far this view is correct may be open to question.

As regards the removal of Presiding Officers see Chapter IX.

SITTING ARRANGEMENT

The sitting arrangement for members is left, by the rules of procedure, to the discretion of the Presiding Officer. In accordance with the universal practice in parliaments, members

[1] Arts. 90, 94, 179, 183.
[2] *Journal of Parliamentary Information*, vol. ii, no. 1, p. 44; L.S.D. 1956, part ii, vol. ii, cc. 1953-4.

belonging to the Government Party take their seats on the right of the Presiding Officer, and those in the Opposition to his left. If there is more than one party in the Opposition, the Presiding Officer allots, on the application of parties, a block of seats for each party. Each party then may allot the seats to its members as it chooses. The Presiding Officer may also reserve seats for particular members once seats have been allocated to them. A group of members in order to be considered a party is usually required to consist of at least one-tenth of the total number of members of the House. A smaller number of members may also be recognized as a group for the allotment of a compact block of seats.

The Chamber in most Indian legislatures is, unlike the British House of Commons which is oblong and which has accommodation only for about two-thirds of the members, circular or semi-circular in shape, and has ample accommodation for all the members of the House; desks are also provided for the members. The House of Commons was destroyed by bombs during the Second World War, and when it was going to be rebuilt a question was raised whether the shape should be changed and a large chamber built to provide accommodation for a larger number of members.[1] The conservative spirit of the British people prevailed, and the chamber was rebuilt almost as it was before it was destroyed. The speech of Sir Winston Churchill in that connection is well worth quoting. The Prime Minister said:[2]

'The semi-circular Assembly which appeals to the political theorists, enables every individual and every group to move round the centre adopting various shades of pink according as the weather changes. I am a convinced supporter of the Party system in preference to the group system. I have seen many earnest and ardent Parliaments destroyed by the group system. The party system is much favoured by the oblong form of Chamber. It is easy for an individual to move through these insensible gradations from Left to Right, but the act of crossing the floor is one which requires serious consideration. I am well informed on this matter, for I have accomplished that difficult process, not only once but twice. Logic is a

[1] *Report of the Select Committee*—H.C. *Paper* 109 of 1943-4.
[2] H.C.D. 1943, vol. 393, c. 403.

poor guide compared with custom. Logic which has created in so many countries semi-circular Assemblies which have buildings which give to every member, not only a seat to sit in, but often a desk to write at, with a lid to bang, has proved fatal to Parliamentary Government as we know it here in its home and in the land of its birth. . . . If the House is big enough to contain all its members, nine-tenths of its debates will be conducted in the depressing atmosphere of an almost empty or half empty Chamber. The essence of good House of Commons speaking is the conversational style, the facility for quick, informal interruptions and inter-changes. Harangues from a rostrum would be a bad substitute for the conversational style in which so much of our business is done. But the conversational style requires a fairly small space, and there should be on great occasions a sense of crowd and urgency.'

OPENING OF LEGISLATURE

The first session of the legislature in each year is opened by the Executive Head of the State by a speech informing the legislature of the causes of its summons.[1] In the legislatures which have two Houses, the Executive Head of the State addresses the two Houses assembled together. If the legislature meets for the first time after a General Election, the Executive Head addresses the legislature on the first sitting day after the election of the Presiding Officer;[2] otherwise he addresses it on the first sitting day before any business is entered upon.

This provision for the opening of the legislature by the Executive Head of the State has been taken from the practice obtaining in England, where the King opens Parliament annually with a speech. In the Dominions of the British Commonwealth also, there is the practice of the Governor-General addressing the legislature.

The King's speech enunciates the policy of the Government, and discussion on the King's speech is initiated by a motion for giving an address to the King. Formerly, the address to the King's speech used to be in the form of an answer,

[1] Arts. 87, 176.
[2] *Saradhkar* v. *Legislative Assembly*, A.I.R. 1952, Orissa, 234.

paragraph by paragraph, to the speech, and a committee was formed to draft the address. Since 1890-91, no such detailed address has been given. But the answer is recorded in the form of a single resolution expressing the thanks of the House for the most gracious speech delivered by His Majesty, and amendments are moved by way of addition thereto. In some of the Dominions the older form is in use. The procedure is as follows. The House assembles to hear the King's speech or the Governor's speech or Governor-General's speech, as the case may be. As the speech is delivered to the two Houses assembled together, the Presiding Officer of each House then reports the speech to the House, and upon such report, discussion on the speech follows by means of a motion for address and amendment. But before that is done, some formal business is transacted in the House in order to assert the right of the House to deliberate without reference to the immediate cause of summons. This formality has its origin in history in the struggle between the King and Parliament. It is unnecessary to introduce such formality in our country where the Constitution is written and fixed, particularly in view of the fact that the legislature has no right to meet unless summoned by the Executive Head of the State.

As in England, the speech of the Executive Head of the State in India usually deals with the legislative programme, the financial recommendations and administrative policy of the Government. Each House of the legislature has the right to discuss the speech of the Executive Head,[1] and usually the debate on the speech is given precedence over other business. Formerly the Constitution specifically provided for such precedence, but that provision has now been amended and it is not obligatory now to give precedence to the debate on the speech.

WALK-OUT IN PROTEST AGAINST THE SPEECH OF THE EXECUTIVE HEAD

On 18 February 1963, when the President of India was addressing the two Houses of Parliament, five members staged a walk-out in protest against the President's speech

[1] Arts. 87, 176.

being read in English. A committee was appointed to consider their conduct, and the committee reported that any interruption or walk-out during the President's speech would be considered grossly disorderly conduct, and for such disorderly conduct a member could be suspended for a period extending to one year. Three offending members in this case were reprimanded by the House and the conduct of the other two disapproved.[1]

In the Kenya Legislative Assembly a walk-out on the occasion of the Governor's speech was held to be grossly disorderly conduct.[2] In England, however, when Charles I came to arrest certain members, the members protested crying, 'Privilege, privilege'.

This point of view is, however, open to the objection that the discourtesy shown to the President was outside the House, because a joint sitting of the two Houses is not considered a sitting of the two Houses but is merely an assemblage of the members of the two Houses. Whether a member can be punished for his misbehaviour outside the House is open to question.

DEBATE ON THE SPEECH OF THE EXECUTIVE HEAD

The speech as such cannot be the subject matter of discussion. The debate is therefore initiated, as in England, by a motion of thanks proposed by a member and usually seconded by another. As all communication between the legislature and the Head of the State has to be by an address, the motion generally takes the form of a proposal for presenting an address in reply to the Executive Head expressing the thanks of the members for the speech delivered by him. The motion is moved on the day the speech is delivered, but is usually postponed for discussion to a subsequent day.

To this motion amendments may be moved by way of adding words at the end of the address in reply. The words sought to be added usually take the form of an expression of regret for any matter omitted from the speech or for the policy contained therein. Amendments may also be moved in any other form that may be deemed appropriate by the Speaker.

[1] *Report of the Committee on the Conduct of Members* presented on 12 March 1963.
[2] See *Table*, 1961.

SCOPE OF DEBATE

Not only can the administrative policy contained in the speech of the Executive Head be criticized, but any other matter may be raised by amendments moved to the motion of thanks. Although the Constitution provides that the debate is to be on points raised by the speech, in practice debate is allowed on matters which are not referred to in the speech.[1] The whole administration of the Government, whether referred to in the speech or not, may therefore form the subject matter of the debate. The debate generally falls into two parts, the first part consisting of a general discussion on the speech covering the whole field of Government policy, and the second a discussion on specific matters raised by the amendments.

The motion of thanks is taken to be a motion of confidence. In the British House of Commons a specific question of Government policy is usually raised by an amendment to the motion, e.g. the question of nationalization of iron and steel in 1950.[2] An amendment in specific terms that the House has no confidence in the Ministers may also be proposed to the motion of thanks. If an amendment is carried, and the address in reply as amended is agreed to, it is generally taken to be a motion of no-confidence and the Ministry resigns. In 1924 the Baldwin Ministry resigned after an amendment to the address in reply that the House had no confidence in His Majesty's Advisers was passed by the House of Commons.[3]

A division can be claimed on the amendment to the motion of thanks as also on the main motion if amended.[4]

PRESENTATION OF ADDRESS AND REPLY

After the motion of thanks has been agreed to, with or without amendments, the address in reply is sent to the Executive

[1] H.P.D. 1952, vol. i, p. 88.
[2] H.C.D. 1950, vol. 472, c. 474.
[3] H.C.D. 1924, vol. 169, c. 680. In 1964, in Ceylon, the Ministry of Mrs. Bandaranaike resigned when an amendment was carried to the motion of address in reply.
[4] Ibid.

Head of the State who usually makes a formal acknowledgment which is communicated to the House by the Presiding Officer. In the United Kingdom the communication is made by a member of the Royal Household.

ADJOURNMENT OF THE HOUSE

In England the sittings of the House of Commons are ordinarily adjourned whether for the day or for a period by means of a motion of adjournment, but a sitting can be adjourned without question being put (a) on a count showing that there is no quorum or (b) in case of grave disorder under S.O. No. 24. In India, however, no such motion is necessary. The Presiding Officer has the power to adjourn the daily sittings at any time and for any purpose. The times of commencement and termination of a sitting are usually prescribed by the rules of procedure, but by the rules of some legislatures the Presiding Officer is given the authority to relax the rules. The days on which the legislature is to sit are generally arranged by the Government, or, where so allowed by the rules, by the Presiding Officer in consultation with the Leader of the House having regard to the volume of business to be transacted in a session. In fixing the days, notice is taken of any holiday intervening or of days on which the House would not be willing to sit. If any prearranged sitting on any day has to be adjourned, the adjournment is decided upon by the House—not by a formal motion but by the Presiding Officer taking the sense of the House.

ADJOURNMENT SINE DIE

In India legislatures are often adjourned *sine die*, that is, without naming a day for reassembly. There is nothing unconstitutional or illegal in this. In the rules framed under the India Council Act, 1861, it was provided that the Council should meet every Wednesday and the President used to adjourn the Council on Wednesday. Even then, on 20 April 1862, the President adjourned the House *sine die*, although there was no specific rule for the purpose. Sometimes the legislature is adjourned *sine die* and thereafter recalled, or after adjournment *sine die* the legislature is prorogued by notification.

The Lok Sabha in its *Rules of Practice and Procedure* (3rd edition) for the first time framed a rule allowing the House to be adjourned *sine die*. Many State legislatures have adopted the Lok Sabha rules.

Whether a House can be adjourned *sine die* or prorogued when there is business pending before the House is a political question. There are instances when such adjournments have been made.[1]

PROROGATION

The termination of a session of the legislature is called prorogation, and the Executive Head of the State has the right to prorogue the legislature.

In England the Parliament is prorogued either by a commission when the Parliament is sitting or by a proclamation during the period when it stands adjourned. The British Parliament is always prorogued until a specified date. In India the order of prorogation is ordinarily sent at the end of a session to the Presiding Officer who announces that the legislature stands prorogued by command of the Executive Head. But there are precedents when legislatures have been prorogued by notifications published in the Official Gazette after the legislature had been adjourned.[2] No date is specified in the order of prorogation on which the legislature is to reassemble.

EFFECT OF PROROGATION ON PENDING BUSINESS

The effect of prorogation is not, as in England, 'to pass a sponge over the Parliamentary slate'. The Constitution[3] provides that bills pending in the legislature at the time of prorogation shall not lapse. The rules of procedure of the

[1] See B.L.A.P. vol. lxiii, no. 2, p. 188, 30 Sept. 1942; *In re Veerabhadrayya*; A.I.R. 1950, Mad. 256.

[2] In November 1942, April 1943, March 1945 and May 1953, such a course was adopted in West Bengal.

[3] Arts. 107, 196.

different legislatures prescribe whether other matters such as questions, resolutions, etc., should or should not lapse. For instance, the rules of the Indian Parliament prescribe that all pending notices, except those for motion for leave to introduce certain bills, shall lapse. A motion, resolution or an amendment which has been moved and is pending in the House does not lapse. If any bill has been partly dealt with in any session, the bill can, under the precedent followed in the West Bengal Legislature, be taken up in the next session from the stage at which it was left in the previous session.[1]

EFFECT OF PROROGATION ON COMMITTEES OF
THE HOUSE

In the British House of Commons, all committees cease to exist upon prorogation, and any reference to any select committee appointed in one session cannot be taken up by it after prorogation of the session. The procedure is for the House to appoint a new committee and make a fresh reference.[2]

The underlying principle seems to be that any reference to a committee which itself becomes *functus officio* becomes infructuous and cannot be continued without a fresh order of the House.

In India select committees do not cease to exist after prorogation, and therefore a select committee appointed in one session can and does continue its work even after prorogation, and may make its report in a subsequent session.

There are, however, certain committees which cease to function by efflux of time, e.g. the Committee of Privileges which is elected annually. The question, therefore, is whether the work of a Committee of Privileges which has not finished its work during its lifetime can be taken up by its successor. The principle seems to be this, that when a committee ceases to function for whatever reason—whether it is by prorogation or efflux of time—all references fall through. If the committee has not reported within its lifetime, the reference

[1] B.L.C.P. 10 Mar. 1934; W.B.L.A.P. 30 Sept. 1954.
[2] May, p. 640, and the references cited there.

becomes infructuous and the successor committee has no jurisdiction to take up the matter left unfinished without a further reference from the House or from the Speaker as the case may be.[1]

DISSOLUTION

The House of the People and the Legislative Assemblies of the States stand dissolved by efflux of time after the expiry of five years from the first meeting of the House concerned after a General Election.[2] The period, however, can be extended during a declared emergency by Parliament by law for a period not exceeding one year at a time.[3]

The Executive Head of the State can dissolve the Lower House at any time.[4] The question as to the circumstances in which the Executive Head would be entitled to dissolve the House is a matter not of procedure but of constitutional convention.

The Council of States and the Legislative Council of the States are not liable to be dissolved at any time. But one-third of the members of such Councils retire by rotation every second year and a fresh election is made in their place.[5]

EFFECT OF DISSOLUTION ON BUSINESS PENDING IN COUNCILS

If the House of the People is dissolved, any bill pending in the Council of States, but not passed by the House of the People, does not lapse.[6] Similarly, bills pending in the State Legislative Councils but not passed by the State Assemblies do not lapse.[7] Any bill which has been passed by the House of the People but is pending in the Council of States lapses on the dissolution of the House of the People,[8] but if in respect

[1] See also *Searchlight Case* (2nd reference to Supreme Court), 1961 (1) S.C.R., p. 96.
[2] Arts. 83, 172.
[3] Ibid.
[4] Arts. 85, 174.
[5] Arts. 83(1), 172(2).
[6] Art. 107.
[7] Art. 196.
[8] Art. 107.

5

of any such bill the President has summoned a joint session of the House of the People and the Council of States and if the House of the People is subsequently dissolved, the bill will not lapse and a joint sitting of the two Houses may be held in spite of the dissolution of the House of the People.[1]

In the States, however, all bills passed by the Assembly and pending in the Council lapse on the dissolution of the Assembly.[2]

SUSPENSION OF LEGISLATURE

If the President is satisfied that a situation has arisen in which the Government of a State cannot be carried on in accordance with the Constitution, he may by proclamation suspend the legislature of the State and direct that the powers of the legislature shall be exercised by or under the authority of Parliament.[3] Such a proclamation remains in force for two months, and, if approved by Parliament, for six months from the date of approval. The period of six months can be extended by six months at a time by successive approvals of the proclamation. But no such proclamation can remain in force for more than three years.[4] A question may arise as to the position of the Presiding Officers in the case of a suspension of the legislature. There can be no doubt that a proclamation under Article 356 does not operate as an order of dissolution of the legislature. The Article does not authorize the President to dissolve the legislature. What it does is to authorize him to assume to himself certain powers, to direct that the powers of the legislature shall be exercisable by or under the authority of Parliament, and to suspend the Constitution in so far as is necessary to attain the above-mentioned objects. The effect, therefore, is that the legislature remains in existence although it cannot function, i.e. exercise any of its powers. In fact the exercise of the powers of the State legislature by Parliament presupposes the existence of a State legislature, and it may have been noticed that Article 168, which provides that every State must have a legislature,

[1] Art. 108.
[2] Art. 196.
[3] Art. 356.
[4] Ibid.

was not suspended in the case of East Punjab and other States. Indeed it could not have been suspended.

What then would be the position of the Presiding Officer when the legislature is suspended? If the legislature does not cease to exist, the Presiding Officer does not, it may be assumed, vacate his office. A Presiding Officer can be removed only in one of the three ways enumerated in the Constitution (Articles 179, 183), viz. by (i) ceasing to be a member of the legislature, (ii) resignation, and (iii) removal by a vote of no-confidence. There is no other way in which a Presiding Officer can be removed from his office. Once a Presiding Officer has been elected, any suspension of the Articles relating to the Presiding Officer cannot in any way have the effect of removing him from his office. Indeed it seems that if the Article relating to Presiding Officers is suspended, none of the above-mentioned ways of removing a Presiding Officer would be available. It may be noted that the Speaker continues in his office even after a dissolution until the first meeting of the Assembly after the dissolution (Article 179). As there is no power to remove a Presiding Officer from his office, except as provided by the Constitution, the Presiding Officer does not vacate office during the period of suspension of the legislature.

It may be noted that if the Article as to prorogation and dissolution is also suspended, the Assembly cannot be dissolved until and unless the proclamation is revoked. In Bengal, when section 93 of the Government of India Act was applied in 1945, the proclamation under section 93 was revoked before dissolution of the Assembly and fresh elections were ordered.

Article 356 of the Constitution in all material particulars is in almost the same language as section 93 of the Government of India Act, 1935, and a question regarding the Speaker arose in Bengal in 1945 when that section was brought into operation. The Government declined to pay the salary of Mr. Speaker Nausherali on the ground not that Mr. Nausherali had ceased to be the Speaker but on the ground that the section under which the Speaker was entitled to draw his salary had (as in the Punjab) been suspended. Mr. Nausherali continued to exercise his administrative functions as Speaker, and indeed it was in effect recognized by the Government that he should continue to be the Speaker, for he was allowed to draw his compensatory allowance although the payment of his salary was objected to. After the revocation of the order of suspension, Mr. Speaker Nausherali was paid all his arrears of salary. That could be done only on the basis that he had not ceased to be the Speaker in the meantime.

It appears, therefore, that the suspension of the Articles as aforesaid cannot have the effect of removing the Presiding Officer from his office and would not affect his right to receive his salary.

A question may arise whether the House can assemble under the direction of the Presiding Officer if a proclamation of suspension is made during a period of adjournment of the House without proroguing the House. It is unlikely in fact, for a House is sure to be prorogued before any such proclamation is issued. But even if the House is not prorogued and the House assembles, it cannot function as a legislature, for all its powers are to be exercised under the proclamation of Parliament.

CHAPTER IV

ARRANGEMENT OF BUSINESS

NATURE OF BUSINESS

THE main business before the legislature consists of legislation, i.e. the passing of laws, and the sanctioning of expenditure out of the public revenues, i.e. passing the annual Budget. There are, however, many other matters which come up before the legislature for consideration. One of the more important of these are the questions put by members to Ministers regarding matters under their administrative control. Resolutions and other motions, e.g. adjournment motions or motions of no-confidence, are other kinds of business that frequently come up before the legislature. Then there are various matters about which information has to be given to the legislature. If ordinances have been passed, they have to be laid before the legislature. The report of the Comptroller and Auditor General and that of the Public Service Commission are required by the Constitution to be laid before the legislature. Rules made under various statutes and reports and/or accounts of statutory bodies may also be required by those statutes to be laid before the legislature. Petitions from the public are also presented to the House not infrequently. The business before the legislature may, therefore, be classified as follows:

1. Legislation, i.e. the passing of bills.
2. Financial business, i.e. the passing of the annual Budget, vote on account, supplementary budget, excess grants and exceptional grants, if any, and the Finance and the Appropriation Bills.
3. Questions.
4. Resolutions.
5. Motions:
    (a) Motion of thanks in address in reply,
    (b) Adjournment motions,
    (c) Motion of no-confidence,

(d) Other motions.
6. Information to be laid before the legislature:
   (a) Ordinances,
   (b) Statutory Rules,
   (c) Report of the Comptroller and Auditor General,
   (d) Report of the Public Service Commission,
   (e) Reports and Accounts of statutory bodies,
   (f) Reports of Committees of the House,
   (g) Communication of messages from one House to another.
7. Presentation of public petitions.
8. Miscellaneous:
   (a) Oath or affirmation,
   (b) Obituary references,
   (c) Communications regarding arrest, detention or release of members,
   (d) Leave of absence of members,
   (e) Communications regarding resignation of members, nomination to panel of Chairmen or temporary Presiding Officers, Committees, etc.
   (f) Rulings or announcements of Presiding Officer,
   (g) Personal statements by ex-Ministers,
   (h) Miscellaneous statements by Ministers.

CLASSIFICATION OF BUSINESS

The business of the legislature is usually classified into two categories, (a) official and (b) non-official. Official business is business which is initiated on behalf of the Government by Ministers. All business which is initiated by members (even though belonging to the Government party) other than Ministers is non-official business. It is necessary to bear this classification in mind, as non-official business, except questions and certain other matters, cannot be taken on any day not allotted for such business.

It will be seen that some of the business of the legislature mentioned above may be either official or non-official, some exclusively official and some exclusively non-official. For example, legislation may be initiated by the Government or by non-official members; financial business is exclusively official business; questions are by their nature non-official business; resolutions may be either official or non-official. Similarly, other motions may be official or non-official. There are some matters which although initiated by non-official members (e.g. questions, adjournment motions) are not treated as non-official business but may be and are taken up on days allotted to official business (see below).

ARRANGEMENT OF SESSIONAL BUSINESS

As the Government is responsible for carrying on the administration, it must have its financial estimates and its legislative proposals in the form of bills passed by the legislature. Consequently, it must have the power to control the time of the House, that is to say, to decide, having regard to the volume of business, how long a session of the House will last, on what days the House will sit, what business will come up before the House and what business should get priority. The programme of sessional business is therefore settled by the Government. In India, however, it is the Business Advisory Committee which settles the time for different kinds of Government bills and other Government business which may be referred to the Committee by the Speaker in consultation with the Leader of the House. There is another committee, the Committee on Private Members' Bills and Resolutions which settles the programme of non-official business. Even when the Presiding Officer fixes the days of sitting, he is required by the rules to do so in consultation with the Leader of the House, and in practice it is the Government which fixes the days.

NON-OFFICIAL DAYS

The last two and a half hours of every sitting on a Friday are reserved for non-official business;[1] the Speaker may allot the requisite hours on any other day. Any day other than a Friday may also be allotted for such business in consultation with the Leader of the House.

[1] For the practice in the House of Commons, see *Report of the Select Committee on Procedure*, H.C. 189, Third Report, p. 16.

BALLOT OF NON-OFFICIAL BUSINESS

If a large number of notices relating to non-official business, which ordinarily consists of bills and resolutions, is received, it may not be possible to finish all of them within the time allotted for such business. It becomes, therefore, necessary to determine the order in which non-official business is to be taken up. Usually certain dates are allotted for non-official bills and certain others for resolutions etc. The order of priority is determined separately for each class of business by taking a ballot. The rules of procedure of certain legislatures, e.g. West Bengal, provide that a resolution may be taken out of its turn as obtained in a ballot by a requisition made by a specified number of members.

NON-OFFICIAL BUSINESS WHICH CAN BE TAKEN UP ON GOVERNMENT DAYS

As has already been stated, certain kinds of business, although initiated by non-official members, are not treated as non-official and may be taken up on days which are not non-official days.

(a) Questions: a fixed period, usually one hour, is set apart at the beginning of each day's sitting for the answering of questions.

(b) Motion of thanks to the Head of the State: the Constitution requires that time must be provided for a debate on the opening speech of the Head of the State.[1] The motion of thanks initiating such debate is proposed by a non-official member but some days are allotted for the discussion of the motion.

(c) Adjournment motions: if leave is granted for moving an adjournment motion for the purpose of discussing a definite matter of urgent public importance, the motion is taken up on the day on which it is moved which is always an official day; such adjournment motions are invariably moved by members of the Opposition.

(d) No-confidence motion: if any motion of no-confidence in the Ministry is tabled, the Speaker allots a day or days or part of a day for discussing the motion.

[1] Arts. 87, 176.

(e) If any motion of disapproval of an ordinance or amendment of any statutory rule laid before the House be tabled, or if any motion is made for the consideration of any report of the Auditor and Comptroller General or the Public Service Commission, time may be allotted for the purpose.

ARRANGEMENT OF DAILY BUSINESS

The hours of commencement of a daily sitting and the termination thereof are fixed by the rules of procedure of the respective Houses. The first hour of every sitting is, as already stated, set apart for the asking of questions and the giving of answers. If, however, the questions are finished before the expiry of one hour, other business may be entered into at the time. In the Lok Sabha and in some of the States, the Presiding Officer is required to allot half-an-hour for the discussion of matters of sufficient public importance raised by questions if a member gives notice of raising such a matter. In the Lok Sabha and in the States the Presiding Officers allot the time when notices requesting such discussion are received and admitted. In the Rajya Sabha two days in a week are fixed for such discussion, but the days can be varied by the Chairman. This is taken from the practice obtaining in the British House of Commons where at the interruption (which is fixed by the standing order at 10 o'clock p.m.) or conclusion of business, an adjournment motion is moved, and for half an hour thereafter members can discuss any matter of which notice has been given. Such matters are not, however, limited in the House of Commons to matters raised by questions. In India two matters can be set down for discussion on any particular day, and if more than two notices are received lots are drawn for two. If any matter is not disposed of on the day allotted it can be raised on a subsequent day only if it is drawn on the ballot for that day. No formal motion is moved but the Minister concerned is bound to reply.

As regards other business, the Government arranges the business in any way it likes for the days allotted to official business. In some legislatures there is a practice that on days allotted to the voting on demands for Budget grants no other business can be taken up earlier than one hour before the time fixed for the daily adjournment except with the consent of the Speaker.[1] This prohibition, however, does not apply to the moving of adjournment motions if otherwise in order. Leave for such adjournment motions has to be asked for just after the questions are over.

In the Lok Sabha the Speaker has prescribed that the daily business should be taken in the following order unless the Speaker otherwise directs: (1) Oath or affirmation; (2) Questions (including short notice questions); (3) Obituary references; (4) Papers to be laid on the Table; (5) Communication of messages from the President; (6) Communication of messages from the Council of States; (7) Intimation regarding President's assent to bills; (8) Communications from Magistrates or other authorities regarding arrest or detention or release of members of the House; (9) Presentation of reports of Committees; (10) Laying of evidence before Select/Joint Committees in respect of bills; (11) Presentation of petitions; (12) Questions involving a breach of privilege; (13) Leave to move motions for adjournment of the business of the House; (14) Calling attention notices; (15) Announcement by the Speaker regarding leave of absence of members from the sittings of the House; (16) Announcements by the Speaker regarding various matters, e.g. resignations of members of the House, nominations to panel of Chairmen, Committees, etc.; (17) Rulings or announcements by the Speaker; (18) Miscellaneous statements by Ministers; (19) Personal statement by ex-Minister in explanation of his resignation; (20) Motion for election to Committees; (21) Motion for extension of time for presentation of report of Select/Joint Committees on a bill; (22) Bill to be withdrawn; (23) Bill to be introduced; (24) Laying of explanatory statement giving reasons for immediate legislation by ordinances; (25) Motion for adoption of Report of Business Advisory Committee; (26) Motion for leave to move a resolution for removal of Speaker/Deputy Speaker; (27) Motion for leave to make a motion of no-confidence in the Council of Ministers; (28) Consideration of report of Committee of Privileges; (29) Other business, e.g. legislation, resolution, financial business, etc.

[1] W.B.L.A. Procedure Rules, Rule 209.

BUSINESS ADVISORY COMMITTEE

Rules of legislatures provide for the setting up of a Business Advisory Committee and for the passing of an Allocation of Time Order by the House. The Business Advisory Committee consisting of members from all parties is nominated by the Speaker and is presided over by him. Government bills and other Government business may be referred to this committee by the Speaker in consultation with the Leader of the House. The committee fixes a time-table for the different stages of a bill or other business, and makes recommendations to that effect. A motion to approve of the recommendation of the committee is made in the House, and if the motion is accepted, the allocation of time made by the committee becomes an order of the House, and on the expiry of the time limit for each stage all motions pending at the time are guillotined. A debate on the motion for allocation of time can last half-an-hour, and amendments to refer the matter back to the committee may be moved. An allocation of time can, however, be varied by a motion made with the consent of the Speaker and accepted by the House.[1] The Speaker can also without any motion increase the time by one hour after taking the sense of the House.

The procedure followed in the House of Commons will appear from the following extracts from May:

'The detailed task of drawing up a time-table for the proceedings on a bill in Committee of the whole House and on report, in respect of which an Allocation of Time order has been made, is delegated by Standing Order No. 41 to a Business Committee unless alternative arrangements are made in the original order. For the Committee stage of a bill committed to a standing committee this detailed task is referred, without question put, to a business sub-committee of that standing committee.

'The Business Committee consists of the members of the Chairmen's Panel and not more than five other members nominated by the Speaker; its quorum is seven. It is the duty of the Business Committee to allot to each portion of the bill as many days or portions of days as may seem appro-

[1] L.S.D. 1954, vol. v, pp. 6565; ibid. vol. vii, p. 1653, 1722.

priate, within the limits laid down by the Allocation of Time order. Any recommendations which it makes must be reported to the House, and a time limit within which the report must be made has sometimes been prescribed in the Allocation of Time order. On consideration of any such report the question "That this House doth agree with the Committee in the said report" is put forthwith and decided without amendment or debate. If agreed to, such recommendations have effect as if they were part of the Allocation of Time order.

'The Allocation of Time order may however have provided for any amendment of the Business Committee's Resolution that might prove necessary after the House had agreed to it. Such provision might lay down that any motion moved by a member of the Government to vary or supplement the Business Committee's Resolution must be concluded within a fixed time.

'Standing Order No. 41 also provides that the Business Committee may be used to perform a similar function when there is a voluntary agreement, notified orally to the House by a Minister of the Crown, to limit the proceedings on a bill; and although this has not yet been done under the present Standing Order, there is a precedent for such procedure, which is quoted immediately below.

'Instead of the compulsory provisions of an Allocation of Time order, an agreement between parties in the House for the purpose of securing the completion of business within a limited time has occasionally been made. An outstanding instance of such an agreement was that in the case of a complicated and contentious bill but one which did not reproduce the ordinary lines of party cleavage—the Government of India Bill, 1935.'[1]

LIST OF BUSINESS

A list of business for each day is prepared and circulated to members, and no business not included in such list can be taken up without the leave of the Presiding Officer. In giving leave the Presiding Officer has of course regard to the urgency of the matter and the convenience of the members in parti-

[1] May, p. 489-90.

cipating in the discussion.[1] The order in which the daily business appears in the list is followed, but it may be varied with the general consent of the House.[2]

BUSINESS NOT DISPOSED OF

Any business which is appointed for any particular day but not disposed of on that day is generally carried over to the next day appointed for the business of the class to which it belongs. In the case of non-official business, however, rules of legislatures provide that such business (unless discussion has actually begun) should receive priority by ballot also for the next day.

[1] L.A.D. 1922, vol. iii, p. 688.
[2] L.A.D. 1932, vol. ii, p. 938.

CHAPTER V

QUESTIONS

The right of putting questions to Ministers for the purpose of eliciting information regarding matters under their administrative control is one of the later developments in parliamentary practice. Indeed, in India, the right of putting questions was given to the members of the legislatures for the first time in 1892 by the Indian Councils Act of that year. Even then, the right was given not so much as an accession to any demand but out of necessity, as the Government felt the want of a medium through which Government policy might be made public. The Government of India was pressing for conferring the right of asking questions on the legislatures.[1] In recent times questions have been used for the purpose of focussing public attention on specific grievances or of eliciting information regarding the Government's intentions. It is also extensively used by members to bring the grievances of their constituencies to the attention of the Government. The right to ask questions was first granted in 1892. Lord Curzon said during the debate on the Indian Councils Bill:[2]

'The second change introduced by the Bill is the concession of the right of interpellation or of asking questions...It is proposed to give to members of both classes of Councils, the Supreme and the Provincial Councils, this right of asking questions on matters of public interest. But both this privilege and the one to which I have previously alluded will be subject, under the terms of the Act, to such conditions and restrictions as may be prescribed in rules made by the Governor-General or the Provincial Governors... The merits of this proposal are self-evident. It is desirable in the first place in the interest of the Government, which is at the present moment without the means of making known its policy, or of answering criti-

---

[1] *Dispatch of Lord Dufferin*, Nov. 1888, and also *Dispatch of Lord Landsdowne*, Aug. 1889.
[2] Parl. Deb. 28 Mar. 1892, cc. 60-61.

cism or animadversions, or of silencing calumny,...and it is also desirable in the interests of the public, who, in the absence of correct official information, are apt to be misled, and to entertain erroneous ideas, apprehensions and to entertain unjust ideas.'

The right to ask supplementaries was given in 1909. As Lord Morley explained in his dispatch to the Government of India:[1]

'In respect of rules on the asking of questions, I have come to the conclusion that, subject to such restrictions as may be found requisite in practice and to the existing general powers of the President, the asking of supplementary questions should be allowed. Without these, a system of formal question met by formal replies must inevitably tend to become unreal and ineffective, and in an assembly in which under proper safeguards, free discussion and debate is permitted and encouraged, there can be no sufficient reason for prohibiting that method of eliciting information and expressing indirectly the opinions and wishes of the questioners.'

The right to ask supplementaries was, however, restricted to the questioner. The right was given to all members by the Government of India Act, 1919.

INTERPELLATION

Lord Curzon, when introducing the Indian Councils Act in 1892, and Lord Lansdowne, in his speech before the Indian Legislative Council, used the expression 'right of interpellation' when speaking of the new right which was conferred on the Councils.[2] The right that was given was not, however, strictly the right of interpellation which has a technical meaning in parliamentary procedure. What was conferred was the right to put questions for eliciting information as it obtained in the British House of Commons.

An interpellation (as known in France) is 'a request made through the President of either House to a Minister by a

[1] *Dispatch*, 27 Nov. 1908.
[2] Parl. Deb. 28 Mar. 1892, c. 60; Proceedings of the Legislative Council of India, 1893, p. 47.

private member for an oral explanation of some matter for which the Minister is responsible. The President invariably informs the House of this request, and in some parliaments the House concerned may disallow its further proceeding. The delivery of the explanation initiates a debate, which is usually (but not always) brought to a conclusion by the taking of a vote. In those countries where a vote is taken, a reverse in the Upper House is not as damaging to the Government as a defeat in the Lower. Limits are frequently set to the length of speeches. The procedure of interpellation does not exist in *British* or *Irish* procedure.'[1]

STARRED AND UNSTARRED QUESTIONS

Questions are classified in two categories, (a) questions to which oral answers are required, that is to say, questions which must be answered by the Minister on the floor of the House; and (b) questions to which oral answers are not required.[2]

If a member wants an oral answer to his question he has to put a star mark on the question; such questions have therefore come to be called 'starred' questions. The other kind of question is consequently known as 'unstarred'. In Indian legislatures the Presiding Officer is authorized by the rules to treat a question as unstarred if he thinks a written answer would be more suitable, provided that if a member can satisfy him that an oral answer is necessary, the question may be treated as a starred one.

PERSONS TO WHOM A QUESTION CAN BE PUT

Although it is mainly Ministers to whom questions are put, a question can also be put to another member; but a question to a member must relate to a particular matter, e.g. a bill, connected with the business of the legislature for which the member is responsible[3] and not to any matter, e.g. acts done

[1] Campion and Lidderdale, *European Parliamentary Procedure*, p. 33.
[2] L.A.D. 1921, vol. ii, p. 98 (b).
[3] May, p. 356; see also Sir Herbert Williams, *A Question in Parliament*, p. 14; Parl. Deb. 4th series, vol. cxxxvi, c. 1013; ibid. 5th series, vol. 381, c. 215; ibid. 3rd series, vol. ccix, c. 141; ibid. 3rd series, vol. cxcii, c. 717.

or words spoken by a member outside the House,[1] or to any
matter for which another member is responsible.[2]

When, however, a member is mentioned in a motion
before the House and he appears in a bad light in such a
motion and a question also is put to such member, the member
can be allowed to make a statement to clarify his position,
although the acts or words complained of may have been
done or spoken outside the House.

The following ruling of the Speaker of the West Bengal
Legislative Assembly will clearly indicate the position.[3]

'I allowed Sj. Majumdar only to make a statement because
he was the subject of an adjournment motion tabled by
Sj. Jyoti Basu in which he seemed to appear in a bad light
as his name had been unfortunately mentioned in connection
with some business of the House namely Sj. Jyoti Basu's
adjournment motion. In such a case Sj. Majumdar was
perfectly entitled to clear up the position by making a statement and I gave him permission accordingly.

'In a similar case in the House of Commons when Mr. Attlee,
the Leader of the Opposition in the House of Commons, became subject of a criticism in a motion, he had been allowed
to make a personal statement with a view to clearing himself of the charge (see House of Commons Debates dated 13
December 1937).

'In another case in the House of Commons, Mr. Speaker
ruled that it was in Order for an unofficial hon. Member
to ask another unofficial hon. Member a Question on some
subject with which the latter Member was connected, that
is to say, with a motion or a Bill. I quote the words of
Mr. Speaker:

"There is a definite Rule that it is not in Order for an hon.
Member to ask another hon. Member a Question, but there
are exceptions to that Rule. It has taken place in the past.
It is not in Order for an unofficial hon. Member to ask another
unofficial hon. Member a Question on general knowledge or

---

[1] Parl. Deb. 5th series, vol. lxii, c. 1270; ibid. vol. xii, c. 1181; H.C.D. 3rd
series, vol. cclxviii, c. 556; ibid. vol. cccxviii, c. 1382; ibid. vol. clxxiv, c. 1914;
ibid. vol. ccxxviii, c. 1758; ibid. vol. ccliii, c. 974.
[2] Parl. Deb. 5th series, vol. 141, c. 194.
[3] W.B.L.A.P. 22 Nov. 1960; Parl. Deb. 1887, vol. cccxiii, c. 1249; ibid. 5th
series, vol. 330, c. 821; H.P.D. 1953, 11 Mar. 1953, part ii, c. 1772.

on the merits of a particular case, but on some Question with which an hon. Member is connected, that is to say, with a Motion or Bill, it has been ruled in the past that an un-official hon. Member is entitled to ask a Question on that subject". (See House of Commons Debates dated 1 July 1942.)

'In similar circumstances in Indian Parliament statements by Members whose conduct inside or outside the House has been referred to on the floor of the House has been permitted and it has been decided that any hon. Member to whom a reference is made on the floor of the House with respect to his conduct whether inside or outside the House must have an opportunity to explain (see H. P. Debate, 11 March 1953). The same practice has been followed here in this House in a number of cases of which hon. Members are aware. Whether Rule 31 (2)[1] applied in terms or not, what I did was to permit Sj. Satyendra Narayan Majumdar to make a personal statement to clear up his position in respect of the unfavourable light in which he was made to appear in Sj. Basu's adjournment motion.'

A question to a Minister must also relate to public affairs with which he is officially connected or to a matter of administration for which he is responsible.

ADMISSIBILITY OF QUESTIONS

The Presiding Officer has the authority to decide whether a question is admissible or not, and may disallow a question if in his opinion it is not admissible. If a question is admitted or disallowed by the Presiding Officer, his decision cannot be challenged.[2] There are certain rules of practice, often embodied in the rules of procedure of legislatures, by which the admissibility of a question is judged. A question must relate to a matter which is primarily the concern of the Union Government or the relevant State and also with which the Minister to whom the question is put is officially concerned. In the case of certain matters which are within the cognizance

[1] New Rule 42 of the W.B.L.A.P. Rules (Question to private members).
[2] L.A.D. 1929, vol. iv, p. 128; H.P.D. part i, 3 June 1952, c. 447-48; Bih. L.A.D. vol. 2, 23 Dec. 1937, p. 896; Ben. L.A.D. vol. lxxii (no. 1), 11 Feb. 1947, p. 99.

of the Union Government, e.g. Railways, questions are asked in the State legislatures if they relate to matters of local interest, e.g. level crossings, accommodation in stations, etc., within the State concerned.[1] If a question is asked of a Minister regarding a matter within the administrative responsibility of another Minister, the question is ordinarily transferred to the Minister concerned by the secretariat of the legislature, or as in the case of the Indian Parliament by the Ministry to which the question is put.

A question must be asked with the object of eliciting information;[2] it must not supply any information or be put in such a way as to suggest the answer. If any facts are stated in the question, the member must take the responsibility for the accuracy of the facts stated.[3] A question therefore cannot be put on the basis of newspaper reports.[4] A question cannot also ask for the solution of a hypothetical proposition,[5] or the expression of opinion,[6] or interpretation of law.[7] If the information sought is available in accessible documents or books or in ordinary works of reference, and does not come within the official knowledge or duties of the Minister, no question can be asked for such information.[8] A question must not relate to a matter which is pending in, or reflect on the decision of, a court of law.[9] A question was asked in the House of Commons about Podola[10] who was accused of murder pending his trial before the court. When the time came for answering the question the Home Secretary was able to announce that a charge of murder had been made and that he did not wish to say anything which in any way might influence the course of justice. In fact the Home Secretary was implying that the case was now *sub judice*, and that he supposed the usual rules would operate under which

[1] Railway Department *Circular* no. 447-E/21, 28 Nov. 1923.
[2] Parl. Deb. 1893-4, vol. ix, c. 1620.
[3] Parl. Deb. 1882, vol. 270, c. 1132.
[4] Parl. Deb. 1907, vol. 172, c. 225; Bih. L.A.P. 29 May 1952, p. 10; Beng. L.A.D. vol. lxxii (no. 3), 23 Apr. 1947, p. 167; ibid. vol. li (no. 2), 9 Aug. 1937, p. 8.
[5] Parl. Deb. 1898, vol. 63, c. 705; ibid. 1907, vol. 172, c. 600; Hyd. L.A.D. vol. ii, 2 July 1952, p. 1096; Bih. L.A.D. 21 Nov. 1952, p. 12.
[6] H.C.D. 1915, vol. 73, c. 14.
[7] Parl. Deb. 1901, vol. 89, c. 1056; ibid. 1905 vol. 143, c. 36.
[8] H.C.D. 1914, vol. 66, cc. 162, 939.
[9] Parl. Deb. 1901, vol. 96, c. 1365; ibid. 1907, vol. 177, c. 1614; Bom. L.A.D. vol. iv, 2 Sept. 1938, p. 804; Bih. L.A.D. 15 Mar. 1939, p. 1345.
[10] H.C.D. 1958-59, vol. 609, cc. 873-882.

members do not ask questions about such cases. The Speaker, while admitting that the line between what is *sub judice* and what is not is sometimes difficult to draw, brought the supplementary questions to a conclusion and the matter was regarded as closed in the interests of justice. It appears that instruction was given not to accept questions dealing with any aspect of the matter, including such details as Podola's deportation from Canada, his arrival in England and so on. A question was even removed which was already on the paper, having been put down before the above-mentioned question. A question must not relate to the character of any person except in his official and public capacity;[1] a question which implies a charge of a personal character will be disallowed.[2] A question must not be of excessive length.[3] Rule 41 of the Lok Sabha Rules lays down that a question must not ordinarily exceed one hundred and fifty words; a question must be couched in proper language;[4] it must not contain any arguments, imputations, ironical expressions or abusive epithets,[5] and it must not bring in the name of any person not strictly necessary to make the question intelligible.[6] A question should not be asked about trivial matters.[7] A question should not repeat in substance a question which has already been answered or to which an answer has been refused.[8] A question cannot ask for information about matters which are in their nature secret, e.g. a decision of the Cabinet,[9] and should not raise any matter of policy too large to be answered in a question. A question would be inadmissible if it refers to:

(a) matters relating to proceedings in a Committee which have not been placed before the House,

(b) character or conduct of any person whose conduct can only be challenged in a substantive motion,

(c) matters of past history,

(d) discourteous reference to a friendly foreign country,

---

[1] May, p. 360.
[2] Ibid.
[3] Parl. Deb. 1887, vol. 318, c. 42.
[4] L.A.D. vol. ii, 5 Sept. 1921, p. 98 (a).
[5] Parl. Deb. 1860, vol. 160, c. 1827.
[6] Parl. Deb. 1880, vol. 253, c. 1631; H.C.D. 1912-13, vol. 46, c. 1005.
[7] May, p. 361.
[8] Ibid. p. 360.
[9] Ibid. p. 359.

(e) matters pending before a Parliamentary Committee,

(f) matters pending before Statutory Tribunals or authorities performing any judicial or quasi-judicial function or any Commission or Court of Enquiry.

In the Indian legislatures[1] the right to ask a question is governed by the following conditions:

(a) it shall not bring in any name or statement not strictly necessary to make the question intelligible;

(b) if it contains a statement the member shall make himself responsible for the accuracy of the statement;

(c) it shall not contain arguments, inferences, ironical expressions, imputations, epithets or defamatory statements;

(d) it shall not ask for an expression of opinion or the solution of an abstract legal question or of a hypothetical proposition;

(e) it shall not ask as to the character or conduct of any person except in his official or public capacity;

(f) it shall not ordinarily exceed one hundred and fifty words;

(g) it shall not relate to a matter which is not primarily the responsibility of the Government concerned;

(h) it shall not ask about proceedings in a committee which have not been placed before the House by a report from the committee;

(i) it shall not reflect on the character or conduct of any person whose conduct can only be challenged on a substantive motion;

(j) it shall not make or imply a charge of a personal character;

(k) it shall not raise questions of policy too large to be dealt with within the limits of an answer to a question;

(l) it shall not repeat in substance questions already answered or to which an answer has been refused;

(m) it shall not ask for information on trivial matters;

(n) it shall not ordinarily ask for information on matters of past history;

(o) it shall not ask for information set forth in accessible documents or in ordinary works of reference;

[1] See, for example, Lok Sabha Rule 41.

(p) it shall not raise matters under the control of bodies or persons not primarily responsible to the Government concerned;

(q) it shall not ask for information on a matter which is under adjudication by a court of law *having jurisdiction in any part of India;*

(r) it shall not relate to a matter with which a Minister is not officially connected;

(s) it shall not refer discourteously to a friendly foreign country;

(t) it shall not ask for information regarding Cabinet discussions, or advice given to the Head of the State in relation to any matter in respect of which there is a constitutional statutory or conventional obligation not to disclose information;

(u) it shall not ordinarily ask for information on matters which are under consideration before a *parliamentary* committee; and

(v) it shall not ordinarily ask about matters pending before any statutory tribunal or statutory authority performing any judicial or quasi-judicial functions or any commission or court of enquiry appointed to enquire into or investigate any matter, but may refer to matters concerned with procedure or subject or stage of enquiry, if it is not likely to prejudice the consideration of the matter by the tribunal or com- mission or court of enquiry.

QUESTIONS REGARDING AUTONOMOUS BODIES

One of the rules against admitting a question is that it must not raise any matter not under the control or direction of Ministers but which has been delegated to other autonomous bodies.[1] Under this rule, questions relating to statutory corporations, such as Universities, Municipal Corporations, Boards of Education, etc. are often disallowed. But in these days when statutory bodies are created for the purpose of

[1] H.C.D. 1929-30, vol. 233, c. 246; I.P.D. 8 Apr. 1950, p. 1386; H.P.D. part i, 10 June 1952, c. 746; H.C.D. 1947-48, vol. 448, c. 391; ibid. vol. 449, c. 1630-34; ibid. 445, cc. 565-72; ibid. 1950-51, vol. 481, cc. 781-83.

carrying on the activities of a welfare State, some modification of the rule has been found to be necessary. Questions relating to details of day-to-day administration are not allowed, but questions relating to matters of policy or matters over which the Ministry retains some amount of control are admitted. Sir John Anderson put the matter succinctly when he said:

'The extent of ministerial control should be defined as clearly as possible in the instrument constituting the authority. In regard to matters falling within the Minister's power of control, he would be liable to be questioned in Parliament in the usual way. On the other hand, in regard to all matters declared to be within the discretion of the authority, the Minister would be entitled and, indeed, bound to disclaim responsibility'.[1]

The matter was considered by a Select Committee of the British House of Commons in relation to questions about nationalized industries. The Committee in their Report said:

'The basic feature of the Parliamentary Question is that it is answered by the Minister ultimately responsible for the decisions about which he is questioned. Under their existing constitution, the Nationalized Industries are not subject to any direct control by Ministers in individual matters of detail. Your Committee therefore feel that without altering the terms of the statutes under which the public corporations are constituted, which they are not empowered to recommend, questions on matters of detail in the Nationalized Industries are inappropriate...

'But in the case of questions which are not obviously matters of repetition or matters of detailed administration the questions should be allowed to appear on the Order Paper and the Minister would have to answer or refuse to answer on the floor of the House.'[2]

Questions relating to matters over which the Government exercise some amount of control, e.g. questions of policy, appointments, which are subject to the approval of the Government, schemes on expenditure subject to such approval etc. would therefore be admissible:

[1] Sir John Anderson, *The Machinery of Government*, Romanes Lecture, Oxford, 1946.
[2] H.C. *Paper* 332 of 1951-52, p. ix.

'But within the Speaker's discretion questions relating to matters of day-to-day administration may exceptionally be allowed, provided that in his opinion the matters are of sufficient public importance to justify this concession.'[1]

'In order to meet some of the difficulties which a strict application of this rule might cause, the Speaker has undertaken to allow certain questions on what might otherwise be called day-to-day administration provided they raised matters of urgent public importance.'[2]

In the House of Commons questions about the nationalized industries are allowed if they concern matters for which the Minister has statutory responsibility. The Minister's responsibility is broadly limited to his power to give the board of the industry concerned a general direction in the national interest and the power to ask for certain information. The admission of questions about nationalized industries depends firstly on the statutory responsibility of the Ministers concerned, and secondly on the application of the general rules of questions. Questions on nationalized industries can be divided into three classes, depending on the statutory responsibility in the hands of the Minister: (a) where the statute nationalizing the industry gives the Minister concerned specific duties, e.g. in nominating members of boards or approving borrowing powers, any question on the exercise of these duties can be asked, (b) where the statute gives the Minister concerned power to give general directions in the national interest, questions can be asked on any matter that can be the subject of such general direction, but such subject must be general and must be in the national interest; (c) where the statute empowers the Minister to require information from the nationalized industry, the Minister would in general refuse to answer a question on matters of day-to-day administration, so that all matters except those on which a general direction by the Minister would be applicable would be outside the field on which questions could be asked. Questions falling into the latter category, i.e. day-to-day administration, are taken up by writing to the Minister concerned. As a result of the recent decision of the House of Commons in

[1] H.C.D. 1947-48, vol. 451, c. 1635-37.
[2] May, p. 361.

Strauss's Case,[1] such letters may make the writers liable to proceedings for libel. Another repercussion in England has been a slight increase in the number of questions, because matters containing allegations previously raised in correspondence between members and Ministers are now tabled as questions which are still absolutely privileged because they constitute a 'Proceeding in Parliament'.

The Presiding Officer has further authority to disallow any question which in his opinion shows an abuse of the right to put a question.[2] If a question is disallowed by the Presiding Officer his action cannot be a subject of debate in the House.[3]

In the British Parliament no written or public notice of questions relating to any matter within the jurisdiction of the Speaker is permissible on the ground that he is not a Minister, nor is his department a Government Department. Such questions can be put to the Speaker by private notice only.[4] The same practice is followed in India. No question relating to any matter within the jurisdiction of the Presiding Officer, e.g. questions relating to the legislature secretariat, can be put. Any information with regard to such matters may be obtained from the Presiding Officer privately.

The Presiding Officer has the authority to have a question edited in his office if it has not been properly framed or is not couched in proper language.[5] If a question has to be substantially altered in order to make it admissible under the rules, ordinarily the member putting the question is consulted as to whether he is agreeable to putting the question in the altered form.

QUESTIONS RELATING TO THE PRESIDENT'S OR GOVERNOR'S HOUSEHOLD

The services of members of the personal and household staff of the President or of a Governor are more or less of the nature of domestic service and the personnel do not stand

---

[1] H.C.D. 1957, vol. 568, cc. 819-22.
[2] *House of Commons Manual of Procedure* (1951), p. 52.
[3] Parl. Deb. 1903, vol. 127, c. 711.
[4] May, p. 356.
[5] Ibid. p. 355.

on the same footing as other Government servants. Other
staff, i.e. the secretarial staff, are, however, fully-fledged
Government servants, i.e. their duties and pay are regulated
and conditions of service determined by the Government.
Whatever may be the nature of their service, the expenditure
is met from the Consolidated Fund of the State and is charged
upon the Fund.

The legislature is not debarred from discussing estimates
on charged expenditure, nor are such estimates excepted
from the scrutiny of the Estimates Committee. Members
may require information for these purposes also.

It therefore follows that there is no bar to the asking of a
question relating to the staff of the President or the Governor,
but this is subject to limitations. In the House of Commons
questions were allowed on the expense of the Royal Wedding.[1]

In the House of Commons no question can be put which
brings the name of the Sovereign or the influence of the
Crown directly before Parliament, or which casts reflections
upon the Sovereign or the Royal Family. In the rules of
procedure of legislatures in India there is no rule relating to
questions of a similar kind, but there are rules to the effect
that questions shall not raise matters under the control of
persons not primarily responsible to the Government concerned. This being the case only broad questions of which a
Minister is supposed to have cognizance are permissible.

QUESTIONS BY IMPRISONED MEMBER

There is nothing to prevent a member under legal detention
from sending in notices of questions nor their being admitted.
When such questions appear on the Order Paper, the rule
or practice obtaining in the respective legislature relating to
questions of absent members applies. Under the Lok Sabha
Rules, a member authorised by an absent member is permitted
to ask the question standing in the name of the absent member.
In almost all legislatures similar provisions have been made
and before such rules were framed, by the practice obtaining
in India, such questions were allowed to be put by any other

[1] H.C.D. 1960, vol. 622, c. 4; ibid. 1960-61, vol. 640, c. 120 (written answers
to questions, 16 May 1961).

member of the party to which the absent member belonged or by any other member.

The question, however, remains whether a member who has been convicted of an offence should be allowed to participate in the proceedings of the House. If a member is convicted and is sentenced to a term of imprisonment for not less than two years, he becomes disqualified to sit as a member of the House. If a member is convicted for a lesser term, he is not *ipso facto* disqualified, but the House can expel him if the offence of which he is convicted makes him unfit to sit as a member, e.g. an offence involving moral turpitude.

If the House expels him and his seat is declared vacant, there will be no occasion for him to put questions, and any question already sent in by him will not be placed on the paper.[1] If the House which is necessarily apprised of the imprisonment of the member does not take any action, he continues to be a member. In such circumstances it would not be illogical to allow him to put questions which will be treated as questions of absent members. In the House of Commons notices of questions from members under legal detention can be accepted for written answer.[2] The same principle has been applied in the Lok Sabha. The case of a member kept in preventive detention stands on a different footing as no charge is framed in such a case. Members under preventive detention have been allowed to put questions or send notices of resolutions or amendments both in the Central and State legislatures.

It has been held that the withholding by the executive authority of any correspondence from a member detained in prison to the Presiding Officer of a legislature is not warranted,[3] and the executive authority has no power to withhold any correspondence of a prisoner with the Presiding Officer. Such correspondence may relate to the business of the House. It would, however, be for the Presiding Officer or the House to decide whether a member imprisoned for committing an offence involving moral turpitude should be allowed to participate in the proceedings of the House. When correspondence

[1] May, p. 363.
[2] *Ginnel's Case*, 183; H.C.D. 539.
[3] *In re Anand Nambiar*; A.I.R. 1952 Mad. 117.

from an imprisoned member to another member was withheld by the prison authorities it was held that there was no breach of privilege committed[1].

QUESTION BY SUSPENDED MEMBER

Notices of questions standing in the name of a member who is suspended from the services of the House are removed from the notice paper so long as the suspension lasts.

QUESTION BY MEMBER GRANTED LEAVE OF ABSENCE

Notices of questions of a member who has been granted leave of absence under Article 101(4) or 193(4) of the Constitution of India are accepted as questions for written answers.

NOTICE OF QUESTIONS

The period of notice necessary for the answering of a question varies according to the rules of procedure of particular legislatures. For example, in the Indian Parliament ten clear days' notice is necessary. In West Bengal it is twelve days. In the Indian Parliament, however, five days must elapse after a question is sent to the Minister concerned before the question can be put down for answer for any particular day.

NUMBER OF QUESTIONS ALLOWED TO MEMBERS

Rules of all legislatures prescribe a maximum number of questions that can be put by a member on any one day. In the Indian Parliament the number of starred questions that a member can put on any one day is three. If any member gives notice of more than three starred questions for any particular day, those in excess of three are treated as unstarred questions. There is no limit to the number of unstarred questions that a member can put in the Indian Parliament. In almost all legislatures the Lok Sabha practice is followed.

---

[1] *Fourth and Fifth Report of the Committee of Privileges* (Second Lok Sabha)— *Kansari Halder's Case.*

LIST OF QUESTIONS

As has already been said,[1] the first hour of every sitting of
the legislature is usually reserved for the answering of
questions. Under the Lok Sabha rules the 'first hour' is set
apart for the asking of questions. It has been ruled that when
part of the first hour has been spent on the administration of
the oath, the time for the asking of questions cannot be extended beyond the first hour from the commencement of
the sitting.[2] It appears, therefore, that no part of the first
hour may be utilized for any other kind of business. But in
the Lok Sabha an allocation of time order dispensed with
the question hour on a particular day. The Speaker also
ruled that the question due for answer on that day could not
be transferred to any other day.[3] The answers are printed
in the same way as answers to questions for written answers,
and no supplementaries can be asked.[4] In the Indian Parliament answers are not printed or available to members before
they are answered on the floor of the House. But if an answer
contains any lengthy statement or information of a statistical
nature, the statement is laid on the table of the House, and
copies of such statements are made available to members
half an hour in advance of the commencement of the question
hour. In the Indian Parliament questions are listed in three
rounds, so that one member cannot have more than one
question in each round. In almost all legislatures the practice
of the Indian Parliament has been adopted.

SHORT NOTICE QUESTIONS

Questions at shorter notice can be put with the consent of
the Minister concerned. The other provisions as to the admissibility and so on of questions apply to short notice questions
also. When a Minister agrees to answer a short notice question
he indicates the day on which he would be prepared to answer.
If a Minister is not agreeable to answering a question at
short notice, and if the Speaker is of the opinion that the

[1] See p. 73.
[2] L.A.D. vol. iv–vi, 8 Aug. 1938, p. 39-40; I.P.D. 1 Aug. 1950, c. 17.
[3] L.S.D. 1955, vol. vii, c. 12768, part ii.
[4] L.A.D. 1921, vol. i, p. 57.

question is of sufficient importance to be orally answered in the House, the question may be put down for oral answer as the first question on the day when it would be due for answer after the usual period of notice.

MANNER OF PUTTING AND ANSWERING QUESTIONS

The usual practice is to call upon the member who has given notice of a question to put his question. The member is not, however, required to read out the question.[1] He rises in his seat and only mentions the number of the question.

QUESTIONS OF ABSENT MEMBERS

The rules of various legislatures make different provisions as to what should happen when a member whose question appears in the list of questions is absent or does not put the question. The rules of the Indian Parliament provide that the Speaker may, at the request of any other member, direct the answer to be given; the rules also contemplate a second round of calling upon the members who were absent during the first round to put their questions.[2] If on the second round a member is still absent, any other member if authorized by the member who gave the notice of the question may be permitted by the Speaker to put the question.

In some legislatures the reply to a question which has not been put, or which has been withdrawn, or the answer to which the member concerned does not want to be read out, may nevertheless be given by the Minister with the permission of the Speaker on the ground of public interest.

QUESTIONS REMAINING UNANSWERED AFTER QUESTION HOUR

Questions which cannot be answered on a particular day for want of time are treated as unstarred questions, and the answers are laid on the table on that day and no oral reply can be demanded, neither can any supplementary question be asked.

[1] L.A.D. 1921, vol. i, p. 303.
[2] L.A.D. 1941, vol. iv, p. 69.

SUPPLEMENTARY QUESTIONS

When a reply to a question has been given any member may put a supplementary question for the purpose of further elucidating any matter of fact. Supplementary questions arise out of the answers given, and all the rules which apply to questions apply also to supplementaries. There is no limit to the number of supplementary questions that can be put, but the Speaker has a discretion to disallow further supplementary questions when in his opinion a sufficient number of supplementaries has been put. The report[1] of the Select Committee on Procedure of the House of Commons has recommended that the House should generally 'be prompt to support Mr. Speaker when he intervenes to curtail the number and length of supplementaries from either side of the House, or when a member endeavours to use question time for the purpose of giving information rather than seeking it', and has also urged Ministers and back-benchers to be concise in their questions and answers. The following extract from May will show the scope of supplementaries:

'An answer should be confined to the points contained in the question, with such explanation only as renders the answer intelligible, though a certain latitude is permitted to Ministers of the Crown; and supplementary questions, without debate or comment, may, within due limits, be addressed to them, which are necessary for the elucidation of the answers that they have given. The Speaker has called the attention of the House to the inconvenience that arises from an excessive demand for further replies, and, to hinder the practice, he has frequently felt it necessary to call upon the Member, in whose name the next question stands upon the notice paper, to put his question, and has for the same reason asked Members not to ask supplementary questions and has suggested that lengthy answers should be circulated with the Official Report instead of being given orally. A supplementary question may refer only to the answer out of which it immediately arises, must not be read, must not refer to an earlier answer or be addressed to another Minister

[1] H.C. *Paper* 92 of 1959.

and is governed by the general rules of order affecting all questions.'[1]

Although it has been observed time and again that the purpose of putting supplementaries is not to cross-examine the Minister concerned, it becomes in effect a cross-examination, and it is in the use of supplementaries and their answers that presence of mind, ready wit and parliamentary acumen come into full play.

WITHDRAWAL OF QUESTIONS

A member can withdraw a question at any time before it has been answered. A member, if the rules allow, may also ask for a postponement of his question to another day.

EFFECT OF PROROGATION

When a House of the legislature is prorogued, notices of all questions lapse.

REPLY TO QUESTIONS

A Minister is not bound to answer a question, and the Presiding Officer has no power to compel a Minister to answer a question or to answer it in any particular way. In the British House of Commons a Minister is not bound to answer a question if it is not in the public interest to do so. The same practice is followed in India, and Ministers answer questions unless they think that the public interest would suffer by answering the question.[2] An answer is never refused except on security grounds, or because the Minister does not possess the information and can convince the House that it is not reasonable for him to have it. If answers to questions are refused unreasonably it might lead to a feeling that the Government has something to conceal, and the Government would suffer politically as a result.

[1] May, p. 363.
[2] T.C.L.A.D. 21 Mar. 1951, p. 846; L.A.D. 21 Mar. 1935, p. 2427.

DISCUSSION

No discussion is allowed in respect of any question or answer during question time. In the Indian legislatures provision is made by rules for the discussion of any matter of public importance raised by a question during a fixed period. (For half-an-hour's discussion see p. 73).

IMPORTANCE OF QUESTIONS

The importance which questions have assumed will be evident from the fact that during the first term of the Lok Sabha, 1952-57, no less than 87,972 questions were put, out of which the maximum figure for one year was 22,651; and during the second term from 1957 up to the budget session of 1961 no less than 124,379 questions were tabled, out of which the maximum figure for one year was 32,686. The following passage from a publication of the Lok Sabha Secretariat[1] will show the utility of questions in parliamentary activities:

'To the members the Question Hour provides an unfailing opportunity to participate in the discussion of public affairs. Once a member's name is on the list of questions for a day he has every chance of being called without the necessity of either having to catch the Speaker's eye or solicit the patronage of the party whip. If a question is on a topic of national or international import even the back-bencher has the luck to hit the headlines in the following morning's papers. On account of this close liaison between the Question Hour and the Press, question time is utilised to the full both by the Opposition and other members.

'To the Press the Question Hour furnishes never-failing material for its columns and not a few topics discussed in the Press owe their inspiration to parliamentary questions and their answers.

'Far from being a source of annoyance the Ministers see in the Question Hour their daily opportunity to explain policy or acts of their administration; and many a statement of importance has been made by Ministers on national or international matters in answer to questions. It is through

---

[1] *Question Hour in Parliament* (March, 1957).

7

the Question Hour that the Government is able quickly to feel the pulse of the nation and adapt its policies and actions accordingly. Questions bring to the notice of the Ministers many an abuse which otherwise would have gone unnoticed. Sometimes questions may lead to the appointment of a commission, a court of inquiry or even legislation when matters raised have been grave enough to agitate the public mind.'

CHAPTER VI

MOTIONS

ANY matter on which a decision or an opinion of the House is sought must be brought before the House by means of a motion. A motion must be before the House also when the House desires to discuss any matter on which no decision or opinion is sought. For instance, when the Report of the Public Service Commission is laid before the House, a motion that the Report be discussed or taken into consideration must be moved by some member if it is desired that the Report should be discussed in the House. When it is desired to have a discussion on a matter of general policy, e.g. food policy or the international situation, the rules are not clear as to what form the motion should take. The usual practice is to move a motion that the food policy or the international situation be taken into consideration.[1]

There are certain matters, however, which can be brought before, or discussed by, the House without a motion being moved. Questions are one of such matters. Questions are asked and answered in the House, and supplementary questions may be asked by any member. (For Questions, see p. 78).

A general discussion on the Annual Estimates or the Budget takes place without any motion. In almost all legislatures, the rules of procedure allow debates on matters of public importance raised by a question during half-an-hour at the end of the sitting of the House on certain days without any specific motion being moved. (For half-an-hour debate, see p. 73).

KINDS OF MOTIONS

Motions may be of various kinds. Ordinarily the following kinds of motions are moved in a legislature:

(i) Motions for adjournment of the House for the purpose

---

[1] See *Parliamentary Forms and Formulae* published by the Lok Sabha Secretariat.

of discussing any matter of urgent public importance (shortly known as Adjournment Motions);

(ii) Resolutions;

(iii) Motions in respect of bills;

(iv) Motions in respect of demands for grants;

(v) Miscellaneous motions of which the following are types:

(a) motion for address in reply to the speech of the Head of the State in opening the legislature;

(b) motion for address to the Head of the State for any other purpose;

(c) motion of censure or no confidence in the Ministry;

(d) motion for removal of the Presiding Officer of the legislature;

(e) motion for the purpose of discussing any matter (other than an adjournment motion);

(f) any other special motion, e.g. for the purpose of sending a congratulatory message;

(g) privilege motions.

There are certain general rules applicable to all motions which will be discussed in this chapter, leaving the discussions of the special features of particular kinds of motions to the relevant chapters on them.

An amendment proposed to a motion is also a motion, and must conform to the rules governing motions of the particular class to which the main motion belongs.

Motions may again be divided into three classes, (a) Substantive motions; (b) Subsidiary motions; and (c) Dilatory motions. Substantive motions are independent motions moved for ascertaining the views of the House. 'A substantive motion is a self-contained proposal submitted for the approval of the House and drafted in such a way as to be capable of expressing a decision of the House.'[1] Subsidiary motions are again divided into '(i) ancillary motions dependent on an order of the day, such as the motion that the bill be now read a second time...; (ii) motions moved for the purpose of superseding questions, such as a motion for the adjournment of a debate...; and (iii) a motion dependent on another motion, such as an amendment'.[2] Dilatory motions are

[1] May, p. 298.
[2] Ibid. p. 397.

motions made for the purpose of obstructing or delaying the disposal of any other motion before the House. The Speaker of the Lok Sabha is authorized by the rules to put a motion which he considers dilatory to vote forthwith, or to decline to put such a motion to vote. Certain motions may be considered to be dilatory and an abuse of the rules of the House. These are, (i) motions for the adjournment of a debate, (ii) motions for the recirculation of a bill, and (iii) motions for the recommittal of a bill. An amendment that a bill be circulated to a motion that the Lok Sabha do concur in joining a Select Committee,[1] a motion for circulation on a motion for the consideration of a bill reported by a Joint Committee,[2] a motion that the further consideration of a motion that amendment made to a bill by the Rajya Sabha be postponed,[3] a motion to adjourn the debate on a bill[4] were all treated as dilatory motions.

In India motions are divided into three general classes, (a) Substantive motions; (b) Substitute motions; and (c) Subsidiary motions which are further sub-divided into three sub-classes, (i) ancillary motions, (ii) superseding motions, and (iii) amendments.

A substitute motion is a motion in substitution of the original motion for taking into consideration a policy or situation or statement or any other matter. Such motions, though drafted in such a way as to be capable of expressing an opinion by themselves, are not strictly speaking substantive motions inasmuch as they depend upon the original motion. The other kinds of motions have been discussed above.

NOTICE OF MOTION

Rules of procedure provide for the period of notice for any particular kind of motion. Notice is required not only in respect of substantive motions but also of amendments. The rules, however, also provide that the Presiding Officer may exempt any motion from the operation of such rules, and may accept any motion at a shorter notice than prescribed.

[1] L.S.D. 1954, vol. v, c. 6985.
[2] L.S.D. 1955, vol. iv, c. 6548.
[3] Ibid. vol. v, c. 8400.
[4] L.S.D. 1956, vol. i, cc. 414-17.

He may also accept motions for amendments on the floor of the House.

When any report or other paper is laid before the House on which a debate can arise or is desired, any member may forthwith give notice of his intention to move, or move that it be discussed. Indeed, if a debate is desired, notice must be given by the member rising at once and giving notice of moving a motion; if such notice is given, and the report or the paper concerns the Government, a day may be allocated for a debate. If the rules prescribe a written notice, such notice should be given afterwards. A written notice given subsequently is sufficient. Such motions are known as no-day-yet-named motions, and the Speaker is authorized in consultation with the Leader of the House to allot time for the discussion of such motions. All notices of motions must be given in writing. Notices must be addressed to the Secretary of the House concerned.

MOVING OF MOTIONS

A motion may be moved by any member or by the Presiding Officer himself. It is not usually necessary that a motion should be seconded. In the case of a motion for an address in reply to the speech of the Head of the State, rules of procedure require the motion to be seconded.

A member may speak on a motion proposed by him and then move the motion; but it is usual to move a motion formally first and then speak on it.

A motion after being moved becomes what is known as a Question (not to be confused with the question which is asked for eliciting information) and a debate ensues on the Question. Other members may speak on the Question before the House, subject to the rules of debate (for which, see p. 149).

DISCREPANCY BETWEEN TERMS OF MOTION IN NOTICE AND MOTION AS MOVED

The terms of the motion which is moved should be the same as those of the motion as given in the notice. A modification of the terms can, however, be made if the motion as modified does not extend the scope of the original motion.[1] The terms may also be varied, with the consent of the House, for the purpose of greater clarification of the motion. The secretariat of the legislature has the power under the authority of the Presiding Officer to edit the terms of a motion in order to bring it into conformity with the rules, to avoid irregularities or to leave out expressions or words which are unparliamentary or unbecoming of a legislature.[2] The rules of all legislatures authorize the Speaker to amend a notice if in his opinion it contains words, phrases or expressions which are argument-ative, unparliamentary, ironical, irrelevant, verbose or other-wise inappropriate. If a member desires to alter substantially the terms of a motion of which he has given notice, except as mentioned above, he must give a fresh notice of his motion.[3] When a motion has been moved without notice, the Presiding Officer may, when proposing the question, rectify any ir-regularity in the motion.[4]

ADMISSIBILITY OF MOTIONS

Motions must conform to certain rules of admissibility. There are some rules which are of general application; there are others which govern particular classes of motions. The Pre-siding Officer has the authority to decide the admissibility of a motion and to disallow or decline to put any motion which in his opinion transgresses any rule of admissibility. The general rules will be discussed in this chapter.

RULE AGAINST REPETITION

A motion, including an amendment, which is substantially the same as one on which the House has already given a verdict during the same session, is inadmissible. If, however, no verdict has been given, e.g. if a motion has been with-drawn, a similar motion may be brought forward.[5] When a

[1] Parl. Deb. 1907, vol. 171, c. 681.
[2] H.C.D. 1919, vol. 113, c. 604.
[3] Parl. Deb. 1872, vol. 212, c. 219; ibid. 1895, vol. 33, c. 961.
[4] May, p. 406.
[5] Parl. Deb. 1845, vol. 80, cc. 432, 798; L.S.D. 1955, vol. ii, c. 3392.

motion is superseded by the acceptance of an amendment in substitution for the substantive motion, a motion similar to the substantive one would be inadmissible in the same session, although strictly speaking no verdict has been given on it as it was not put to the House.[1] This rule of inadmissibility would apply not only as between two motions, but also as between a motion and a bill and as between two bills.

Whether a motion subsequently tabled is substantially the same as the one on which the House has already given a decision is often a difficult question to decide, particularly when the question arises in relation to a motion and a bill or to two bills. Even with two motions, considerable ingenuity is sometimes exercised by members for the purpose of avoiding this rule.

It is seldom likely that substantially the same question would be raised by a motion and a bill. As pointed out by May: 'A motion can do no more than affirm the desirability of legislation in general terms, whereas a bill is apt to contain qualifying provisions and conditions, generally sufficient to differentiate its subject-matter from that of a motion.'[2]

The following are some illustrations of the applicability of this rule.

A resolution which was subtantially in the same terms as an amendment to the address in reply to the King's speech was held to be inadmissible.[3] An amendment to the address in reply to the Governor's speech regretting that there was 'no mention of any effective measures to be taken by the Government in order to reorganize the boundaries of the State on the basis of language and contiguity; and to counter the move to amalgamate West Bengal and Bihar', was ruled not to be substantially the same as a substantive motion to the effect that 'this Assembly approves the proposal for the union of the States of West Bengal and Bihar.'[4]

A resolution impugning the general operation of an Act enumerating several particulars in which it had failed was negatived by the House. A motion subsequently tabled for leave to introduce a bill for the amendment of that Act in

[1] Parl. Deb. 1873, vol. 214, c. 287.
[2] May, p. 401.
[3] H.C.D. 1912, vol. 35, c. 1043.
[4] W.B.L.A.P. 23 Feb. 1956, vol. xiv, no. 1.

respect of one of the matters enumerated was held not to be affected by the rule.[1]

A resolution suggesting certain amendments to the West Bengal Bargadars Act, 1951, was disallowed on the ground that amendments to similar effect had been negatived when a bill for amending that Act was before the House during the same session.[2]

Where an amendment to a clause in a bill is rejected, another amendment to the same effect is not admissible.[3]

A resolution raising a matter which is substantially identical with a matter raised by a bill on which the House has given a decision is not admissible.[4]

A resolution regarding imbalance in price structure was not allowed to be moved because substantially the same question had been debated at length during the discussion on the demands for grants, and certain cut motions had been negatived.[5]

An adjournment motion on the Goan Freedom Movement was disallowed as the subject had been sufficiently discussed on a previous occasion.[6]

Although the above-mentioned rule is a rule of general application, it does not apply to the case of an open rescission of a previous decision of the House, because a motion that a decision be rescinded cannot be said to be the same as, for example, that a bill be passed.

May has expressed the same proposition in the following terms:

'But the practical inconvenience of a rigid rule of consistency, especially where the House as a whole wishes to change its opinion, has proved too great for a body confronted with the ever-changing problems of Government; and the rule prohibiting reconsideration of a decided question has come to be interpreted strictly according to the letter so as not to prevent open rescission when it is decided that it is desirable.

'Technically, indeed, the rescinding of a vote is the matter

---

[1] May, p. 401.
[2] Private ruling of Mr. Speaker S. K. Mukherjee; see also L.S.D. 25 Mar. 1955, vol. 2, cc. 3389-401.
[3] See L.S.D. 1954, vol. viii, c. 1230.
[4] L.S.D. 1955, vol. ii, c. 3392.
[5] Ibid. vol. ii, cc. 3395-400.
[6] Ibid. vol. vi, c. 10142.

of a new question; the form being to read the resolution of the House and to move that it be rescinded; and thus the same question which had been resolved in the affirmative is not again offered, although its effect is annulled.'[1]

Redlich states the same proposition in the following terms:

'It is necessary, finally, to refer to one principle which is of vital importance to the course of business and to the whole procedure of the House. A motion or bill on which the House has given a decision may not be brought before the House again in the same session. The rule is of great importance from a constitutional standpoint. It protects the judgment of the House on any point from being attacked in the same session as that in which it is given, and thus provides for some amount of stability in legislation. To a certain extent it is analogous to the rule of law which prevents *res judicatae* from being tried over again.'[2]

He goes on, however, to state: 'The rule has important practical results in the not impossible event of its being absolutely necessary to reconsider some decision at which the House has arrived. If the decision is positive in form the rule causes no difficulty: the direct negative (a motion to rescind) is technically a new matter.'

In the House of Commons decisions have been rescinded but the power is used sparingly.[3] In West Bengal two decisions that a bill be passed and that a bill be taken into consideration were rescinded.[4]

In moving for a rescission of a motion Lord Asquith, the then Prime Minister, said:

'Any other rule or law would really reduce the House to a condition of almost ludicrous impotence. To say that this House is not able, if it is so minded, under any circumstances whatever, to rescind a resolution which upon reconsideration it thinks ought not to have been passed, *is to deny to the House the first quality of a really deliberative Assembly.*'

Asquith goes on to cite two previous precedents in which the House of Commons had rescinded its previous decisions

---

[1] May, p. 415.
[2] Redlich, vol. iii, p. 36.
[3] C.J. 1834, 59; ibid. 1864-5, 463; ibid. 1867-8, 145; H.C.D. 1912, vol. 43, c. 1993; ibid. 1912, vol. 44, cc. 36, 121; ibid. 1918, vol. 105, c. 1956.
[4] W.B.L.A.P. 28 Feb. 1956, vol. xiv, no. 2.

taken during the current session, one in 1834 and the other in 1864. Asquith also points out that there is no distinction of any sort or kind between cases of resolutions, strictly so-called, and motions passed during the course of and in relation to the operation of a bill. This happened in 1912, and the motion that was moved by Asquith was, 'That the decision of this House on the amendment moved on...by... by which it was proposed to insert certain words in the Government of Ireland Money Resolutions as reported to the House be rescinded.'

The circumstances which led to the moving of the motion by Asquith are mentioned in his speech, and certain extracts from it are worth quoting:

'It is within the knowledge of the House that on Monday last an amendment moved by the Hon'ble Barnet, the Member for the City of London on the report stage of a resolution passed in Committee on the Government of Ireland Bill, was carried by a majority of 21. Of that amendment, no notice had been given. It was, I think, very briefly debated and it was not supported in debate by any gentleman sitting on the front Opposition Bench opposite, and although it was carried by the House, I think there is some doubt even now whether Hon'ble gentlemen either upon the one side or upon the other thoroughly appreciated its importance.

'Next, a matter to which I attach no less importance, the consideration which we have always put forward and which I strongly hold myself that in order that a Bill passing through this House should become law under the operation of the Parliament Act, it should receive upon all substantial and vital points the assent of a majority of this House. It follows that one ought, critical as the circumstances are, to consider—I think it is the duty of the House to consider—whether or not the ordinary presumption which I agree under normal conditions apply, that a decision of the House is the *considered judgment* of the House is applicable to this particular case and I am going to submit to the House stray reasons for thinking it is not.'

The same practice also prevails in the House of Commons in Canada.[1]

[1] See Beauchesne's *Parliamentary Rules and Forms*, 2nd ed., para 317.

A motion for rescission of a resolution or other vote of the House is also allowed in the other legislatures, e.g. New-Zealand (Standing Order 114), New South Wales (Standing Order 115). This is also the practice in all the Commonwealth Parliaments.

The motions in West Bengal referred to above were rescinded under the following circumstances. There was a *hartal* in Calcutta on the day when two motions in connection with two bills were accepted by the House in the absence of the entire Opposition members. The motions for rescission were not opposed by the Leader of the House on behalf of the Government on the ground that the Opposition should have such an opportunity to express its opinion. That the Opposition should have such an opportunity was also formulated by President Patel as long ago as 1926. On 8 March 1926, when the Opposition had walked out, President Patel adjourned the House with the remark that it would not be fair to the Chair to transact any business of a controversial nature in the absence of the Opposition.

A rather anomalous procedure was adopted in the House of the People with regard to the Constitution Seventh Amendment Bill, 1955. A bill, the Constitution Fifth Amendment Bill, 1955, was not passed by the requisite majority and was therefore deemed to have been rejected on 30 November 1955. A few days later another bill, the Constitution Eighth Amendment Bill, containing similar provisions was introduced. On objection being taken, Rule 388 of the Lok Sabha Rules of Procedure was suspended by a motion on 9 December 1955, and the later bill was passed. The result has become extremely anomalous. Both the verdicts of the House in regard to a bill of the same nature stand. It is precisely to guard against such a result that the rule against repetition has been invoked. It is not remedied by suspending the rule. The proper course would have been to discharge or rescind the previous verdict and then allow the later bill to proceed.

RULE AGAINST ANTICIPATION

A motion is out of order if it anticipates a matter about which notice has been given for consideration by the House, either in the form of another motion or bill. This rule is subject to two restrictions:

(i) The anticipatory motion must be less effective than the motion to be anticipated, e.g., when a notice of introduction of a bill has been given, any other motion relating to the subject matter of the bill would be out of order; or when a notice of a substantive motion is before the House, an amendment to another motion or to an address in reply to the speech of the Head of the State on the same subject matter would be out of order.[1]

As May has pointed out, 'A bill or other order of the day is more effective than a motion; a substantive motion more effective than a motion for the adjournment of the House or an amendment, and a motion for the adjournment is more effective than a supplementary question.'[2]

(ii) In order to prevent the abuse of the rule by means of tabling what are known as 'blocking motions', the Presiding Officer in deciding whether a motion is out of order under this rule must have regard to the probability of the matter anticipated being brought before the House within a reasonable time.[3] For example, if a motion for leave to introduce a bill has been given by a non-official member, an amendment to, say, an address in reply to the speech of the Head of the State raising the same subject-matter will not be inadmissible, if no non-official day for bills has been allotted up to the time when the amendment comes up.

Adjournment motions were disallowed because their subject matters might be raised during a debate on the motion of thanks[4] covered by amendments tabled to the motion of thanks[5], or on a debate which was to follow[6], or on a half-an-hour discussion.[7] A cut motion was disallowed as a date was fixed for the discussion of the matter by a resolution which raised the same matter.[8]

[1] See rulings cited in May, p. 403.
[2] May, p. 404.
[3] H.C.D. 1941-2, vol. 383, c. 533.
[4] Prov. Parl. Deb. 1951, 7 Aug. 1951, vol. xiv, cc. 29-31.
[5] H.P.D. 1953, vol. i, c. 32.
[6] H.P.D. 1952, vol. i, c. 65.
[7] Ibid. vol. vi, c. 1897.
[8] Ibid. vol. ii, c. 2526.

RULES OF ADMISSIBILITY

In order that a motion may be admissible it shall satisfy the following conditions:

(i) it shall raise substantially one definite issue;

(ii) it shall not contain arguments, inferences, ironical expressions, imputations or defamatory statements;

(iii) it shall not refer to the conduct or character of persons except in their public capacity;

(iv) it shall not revive discussion of a matter which has been discussed in the same session;

(v) it shall not anticipate discussion of a matter which is likely to be discussed in the same session;

(vi) it shall not relate to any matter which is under adjudication by a court of law having jurisdiction in any part of India.

No motion which seeks to raise discussion on a matter pending before any statutory tribunal or statutory authority performing any judicial or quasi-judicial functions or any commission or court of enquiry appointed to enquire into, or investigate, any matter shall ordinarily be permitted to be moved.

No Speaker may, in his discretion, allow any matter being raised in the House which is concerned with the procedure or subject or stage of enquiry if the Speaker is satisfied that it is not likely to prejudice the consideration of such matter by the statutory tribunal, statutory authority, commission or court of enquiry.

IDENTICAL MOTIONS BY SEVERAL MEMBERS

If several members give notice of motions in substantially identical terms, the Presiding Officer may ask one of them to move his motion. If one motion is moved, all other motions are deemed to be withdrawn.[1]

MOVING OF MOTION BY MEMBER OTHER THAN MEMBER GIVING NOTICE

It is possible that a motion of which notice has been given

[1] B.L.A.P. 1944, vol. lxvii, no. 5, p. 277; Bom. L.A.D. 23 Feb. 1949, p. 212.

by one member may not be moved by the member giving
notice, either because he is unwilling to move the motion or
because he is absent. If a member is unwilling, no other
member can move the motion.[1] A member may also authorize
any other member to move the motion standing in his name
on his behalf and the member so authorized, may, with the
permission of the Speaker, move the resolution.

There is an exception in the case of members of the Government. Any member acting for the Government may move a
motion standing in the name of any other member of the
Government; that is to say, any Minister can move a motion
standing in the name of any other Minister. A Minister may
move a motion even though he is not a member of the House.

WITHDRAWAL OF MOTION

Once a motion has been moved the motion can be withdrawn
only by leave of the House, and that also before the motion has
been put to vote.[2] A motion may be withdrawn only by the
member who has moved it.[3] A motion which has not been
moved but of which notice only has been given does not
become the property of the House, and no leave for withdrawal or not moving it is necessary. The Speaker of the
Lok Sabha allowed certain motions to be withdrawn without
expressly putting the request for leave to the House.[4]

A motion can be withdrawn only by the unanimous consent
of the House. If there is a single dissentient voice, when the
Speaker asks whether the member has leave to withdraw his
motion, the motion cannot be withdrawn. This is so even though
the dissentient member subsequently withdraws his dissent.[5]

No debate however is allowed on a request for leave to
withdraw.[6]

[1] B.L.A.P. 1944, vol. lxvii, no. 1, p. 462.
[2] Cf. Sec. 129, *H. C. Manual*, 7th ed., and Lok Sabha and other legislatures'
procedure rules.
[3] Rules of the Lok Sabha and Rajya Sabha and also of other legislatures.
[4] L.S.D. 1954, vol. v, c. 6853; ibid. 1954, vol. viii, c. 793; ibid. 1954, vol. ix,
c. 1934.
[5] May, p. 407. Although there are certain rulings of Speaker Azizul Haque of
Bengal that unanimous consent is not necessary, such rulings have not been
followed subsequently. (See for instance, W.B.L.A.P. 1950, vol. i, no. 2, p. 59,
Speaker Jalan's ruling).
[6] H.C.D. 1915, vol. 76, c. 1219.

If an amendment has been proposed to a motion, the practice in the House of Commons is that the motion cannot be withdrawn unless the amendment is first disposed of.[1]

The same practice is followed in India.

AMENDMENTS

When a motion has been moved, any member can propose an amendment to the motion, though it should be remembered that an amendment is also a motion, although subsidiary to the main motion to which it is proposed.

Notice is required of all amendments, and the period prescribed varies in different legislatures and in regard to different kinds of motions such as bills, resolutions etc. The Presiding Officer is invariably empowered by such rules to allow any amendment to be moved at short notice and even on the floor of the House when the main motion is before it.

The purpose of an amendment is to modify the main motion in the manner desired by the proposer, or to substitute an alternative to it.

Whatever may be the purpose, an amendment, in order to be admissible, must be relevant to and within the scope of the main motion.[2] And it must be so framed as to make the main motion intelligible and consistent with itself. An amendment to leave out all the words of a motion after 'that' which is allowed in the British House of Commons with the object of superseding the main motion is not in vogue in India. On the other hand, an amendment which has the effect of a negative vote, that is to say, an amendment which if accepted would totally nullify the main motion, is inadmissible according to the rules and practice obtaining in Indian legislatures. This rule, however, is not strictly followed. It appears that in the Lok Sabha two contradictory motions, one approving a statement of policy and the other disapproving it, may be moved in substitution for a motion that the policy be taken into consideration.[3] An amendment to the effect

[1] Parl. Deb. 1876, vol. 227, c. 787.
[2] L.S.D. 1957, vol. ix, c. 4035; ibid. 1953, vol. vi, c. 1190; ibid. 1953, vol. x, c. 1943; ibid. 1954, vol. viii, c. 708; ibid. 1956, vol. i, c. 100; ibid. 1956, vol. ii, c. 2933; ibid. 1956, vol. iii, c. 4006; ibid. 1956, vol. vii, c. 2389; ibid. 1957, vol. vi, c. 10288.
[3] See Directions by the Speaker.

that the House expresses its full confidence in the Speaker was allowed to be moved to the main motion that the House has no confidence in the Speaker.[1] An amendment to a motion, that this House disapproves of the manner in which Mr. Speaker discharges his function as a Presiding Officer, to the effect that this House expresses its full confidence in the Speaker was allowed to be moved in the House of Assembly, South Africa.[2] An amendment which is inconsistent with the words in the motion (including an amendment already agreed to), or which is substantially the same as an amendment that has been negatived by the House, is out of order. When amendment to a later part of a motion has been accepted or rejected by the House an amendment to an earlier part is inadmissible.

SELECTION OF AMENDMENT

The rules of the Lok Sabha and some other legislatures authorize the Speaker to select amendments to be proposed to any motion, and if he thinks fit to call upon any member who has given notice of an amendment to give such explanation of the object of the amendment as may enable the Speaker to form a judgment upon it.

AMENDMENT TO AN AMENDMENT

Amendments can be proposed to any amendment proposed to the main motion. The rules as to relevancy, notices, etc., apply in the case of such amendments in the same way as they apply to amendments to the main motion.

MOVING OF AMENDMENTS

A member who has given notice of an amendment must rise in his seat and move his amendment immediately the motion is moved. Similarly, an amendment to an amendment must be moved immediately after the latter amendment is moved. A member who is absent when his amendment is called may

---

[1] W.B.L.A.P. 20 Mar. 1959.
[2] *Table* (1954), p. 89.

8

move his motion subsequently.[1] But this is not an invariable rule.[2] Usually the Presiding Officer calls upon the members to move their amendments in the order in which the amendments are arranged in the Order Paper—the amendments to earlier parts of the motion coming earlier. If a member who has given notice of an amendment does not move it, the Presiding Officer usually allows any other member to move a similar amendment at short notice.[3] A member cannot authorize another member to move an amendment on his behalf. Amendments standing in the name of absent members are deemed not to have been moved.[4] An amendment like a motion can be withdrawn by unanimous leave of the House.

DEBATE ON A MOTION

When a member moves a motion he can speak upon it. Other members may also speak on it. The mover of a motion has a right of reply. Amendments are also kinds of motions. When an amendment has been moved the debate on the main motion is interrupted, and the debate proceeds upon the amendment. The mover of an amendment has no right of reply. In certain legislatures it is the practice to have all the amendments proposed formally moved first and throw the whole question, the main motion and the amendments, open to debate. This practice reduces the whole debate to a random discussion without clinching the issue pending before the House at the moment. Different members speak on different aspects, and the debate often assumes an unreal character. Whether such a practice saves the time of the House, on which ground this practice is supported, is doubtful. The better practice would be to confine the debate to a specific issue raised by an amendment or a motion, and to call to order any member who strays from the point.

[1] L.S.D. 1955, vol. vi, c. 11193; ibid. 1957, vol. vii, c. 12889.
[2] H.P.D. 1952, vol. vi, c. 2290; ibid. 1955, vol. vi, c. 11214.
[3] B.L.A.P. vol. liv, no. 7, p. 134.
[4] H.P.D. 1952, vol. vi, c. 1595; ibid. 1952, vol. iii, c. 4797; ibid. 1955, vol. vi, c. 11191; ibid. 1956, vol. x, c. 1968; ibid. 1957, vol. vi, c. 12142; ibid. 1957, vol. vii, c. 12382.

PUTTING OF MOTIONS AND AMENDMENTS

After the debate on a motion is over the Presiding Officer puts the motion before the House in this form: 'The Question before the House is that... (repeating the words of the motion)....'

A motion may be split up into parts if such splitting up facilitates voting, e.g., when there are several motions for circulation of a bill for eliciting opinion, and different motions specify different dates by which the opinions must be obtained, one of these motions can be split up into two, the first being only 'that the bill be circulated for eliciting opinion thereon.' If this part of the motion is negatived, no question arises about the date by which opinion is to be obtained. And all the other motions fall through. If the first part of the motion is carried, only the second part dealing with the date is put to the House beginning with the latest date.[1]

Where there is any amendment to a motion the amendment is put first. If there are several amendments to one motion, they are ordinarily arranged and put in such a way that the amendments to earlier parts of the question come earlier in order than those to later parts.

If there is an amendment to an amendment, the former is put before the latter.

If there is an amendment for the substitution of the entire motion, it is put before any amendment for the modification of the motion, either by adding words or substituting some of the words only.[2]

Amendments which are not pressed by members proposing them are not put.[3]

Precedence is given under the rules to an amendment proposed by the member in charge of a bill.

If more than one amendment in similar terms is moved, it is in the discretion of the Chair to select the amendment to be put to vote.

(For voting and division see chapter on Rules of Debate).

[1] B.L.A.P. 1940, vol. lviii, p. 296.
[2] C.L.A.D. 19 Sept. 1939, p. 734.
[3] H.P.D. 1952, vol. iii, 3840; ibid. 1952, vol. vi, cc. 1899, 2842, 2858, 2905; ibid. 1955, vol. vi, c. 11222; ibid. 1955, vol vii, cc. 13341, 14444; ibid. 1955, vol. viii, cc. 15300, 15329.

CHAPTER VII

ADJOURNMENT MOTIONS

As has already been stated, the British House of Commons cannot, with certain limited exceptions, be adjourned without a motion being made for the purpose. A motion that 'the House do now adjourn' is, therefore, made for the daily adjournment of the House as also when the House goes into recess for a few days. Curiously enough, when a motion is made for adjournment, the House never discusses the question whether the House should or should not adjourn, but it is made the occasion for the discussion of various matters raised by members. The reason why a motion for adjournment is made the peg on which to hang a debate on miscellaneous matters is obscure; but it seems it had its origin during the last War when the opportunity was conceded to private members as some compensation for all the time spent on motions and bills, and it has been retained ever since. But the underlying idea seems to be that before the House adjourns, members should be given an opportunity to air the grievances of their constituents. From this use of the adjournment motion, it appears that, by some sort of reverse process, a motion for adjournment came to be made out not only for the adjournment of the House, but also when it was desired to discuss any matter which was not in the Order Paper.

As May points out, 'The substantive motion for the adjournment is in fact a technical form devised for the purpose of enabling the House to discuss matters without recording a decision in terms.'[1]

A motion that 'the House do now adjourn' may also be made for the purpose of putting a stop to any debate which is going on in the House. The same purpose can be achieved by a motion, 'That the debate be now adjourned'.

A motion for the adjournment of the House may therefore be made in the House of Commons in the following circumstances:

[1] May, p. 298.

(i) When a motion is under discussion, a member may move a motion that the House do now adjourn. Such a motion is known as a dilatory motion and is intended to evade or supersede the motion that is before the House without a decision. If such a motion is carried, the motion is superseded and the House is immediately adjourned.

(ii) (a) Every day a motion is moved by a Government member, at the interruption or conclusion of business, proposing that the House do now adjourn. But on such a motion being moved the House, as stated above, proceeds to discuss various matters on which notice has been previously given by members. What motion should be discussed on what day is settled by ballot or by the Speaker every fortnight. After the expiry of half an hour from the time when the motion for adjournment is moved, the House is automatically adjourned without further question being put.

(b) Similarly, when the House goes into recess, a motion for adjournment is moved after the question hour, and on that occasion also topics selected by the Opposition or private members (selected by the Speaker if there are a number of motions) are discussed for the whole day.

(iii) If the Government intends to have a discussion on any matter of general interest, a member of the Government moves a motion for adjournment, and on that motion a discussion on the topic selected by the Government ensues. Such motions are also moved by the Government at the instance of the Opposition when it is not desired to challenge the authority of the Government but only to ventilate a subject without recording a decision of the House.

(iv) An adjournment motion may be made under certain restrictions by a private member to raise a discussion on any matter of urgent public importance.

NATURE OF ADJOURNMENT MOTION

It is only the adjournment motion of class (iv) that has been adopted in the Indian legislatures. Standing Order No. 9[1] of

---

[1] S.O. 9(1). No motion for the adjournment of the House shall be made until all the questions asked at the commencement of business on Monday, Tuesday, Wednesday, or Thursday have been disposed of, and no such motion shall be made unless by a Minister of the Crown before the orders of the day or notices

the House of Commons under which such a motion can be made is, as May says, 'designed to give the discussion of some recently occurring matter of emergency precedence over the programme of business arranged by the Government'. The adjournment motion is used in India also for the same purpose of discussing a definite matter of urgent public importance. And as the motion has the effect of upsetting the prearranged programme of the House, it is subject to the same restrictions.

In pre-Independence days, however, the restrictions were not strictly enforced, and the adjournment motion was almost a normal device for raising a discussion on any important matter. Since Independence a change has taken place, and the Presiding Officers are now reluctant to admit adjournment motions unless they strictly conform to the rules which obtain in the House of Commons. In fact, in England, the use of an adjournment motion of this nature is nowadays rare, and during the period from 1921 to 1939, the annual average of such adjournment motions in the House of Commons was only 1.25.[1] The Speaker always interprets the rule strictly, requiring that the matter be unquestionably urgent and of public importance. Not more than two or three times in any session has the Speaker allowed a matter to be raised in this way and in recent years the matter of time allowed has been as follows:

of motion have been entered upon, unless a Member rising in his place shall propose to move the adjournment for the purpose of discussing a definite matter of urgent public importance, and shall either obtain the leave of the House, or, if such leave be refused, the assent of not less than forty Members who shall thereupon rise in their places to support the motion, or, unless, if fewer than forty members and not less than ten shall thereupon rise in their places, the House shall, on a division, upon question put forthwith, determine that such motion shall be made. If leave is given or the motion is so supported, or the House so determines that it shall be made the motion shall stand over until seven of the clock on the same day.

(2) Any proceeding which has been postponed under this order shall be exempted from the provisions of Standing Order No. 1 (Sittings of the House) for a period of time equal to the duration of the proceedings upon a motion under this order, and may be resumed and proceeded with at or after ten of the clock.

[1] It appears, however, that the progressive decline in the moving of adjournment motions in the House of Commons was considered by a Select Committee (Committee on Procedure) which in its Third Report recommended that the rule regarding adjournment motions and their subject-matters should be more liberally construed (*Third Report of the Select Committee on Procedure*, H.C. 189, 1946, p. 18).

In 1955-56 — nil
In 1956-57 — nil
In 1957-58 — once
In 1958-59 — once
In 1959-60 — once
In 1960-61 — nil
In 1962-63 — twice
In 1963-64 — thrice
In 1964-65 — thrice

The changed attitude in India found expression in a ruling of Mr. Speaker Mavalankar in the Indian Parliament in the course of which he said:

'Successive Presidents of the Central Legislative Assembly including myself had considerably relaxed the rule of admission as it prevailed in the House of Commons, for the obvious reason that the private members, who were in opposition, had few opportunities of discussing matters of public importance. They were in perpetual political opposition to the Government of India, and the general political set-up of those days always induced the Presidents to relax the rule to give more scope for discussion and expression of the popular views. They had, in this matter, the general support of the Legislature. The Government then was not responsible to the Legislature, nor were they amenable to its control. There was, therefore, good ground for the presiding officers to relax the strict House of Commons practice and allow opportunities of discussion of all important questions on adjournment motions. Since 15 August 1947 the entire constitutional and political set-up has changed. The Ministry is fully responsible to this House and members have now ample opportunities of discussing various matters. They can discuss matters on Demands for Grants, again during discussions on the Appropriation Bill and the Finance Bill. The Government being responsive, time can be had by a pressing request made to Government. I may cite as an illustration the desire of the Government to allot time for discussion on the question of security to East Bengal refugees. They can put short notice questions and get information. They have now got a new rule for half-an-hour discussion. They can give notice of a motion of raising discussion on a matter of general public interest under Rule 126.

'It appears we have not yet got out of the old moorings, and continue to labour under a wrong impression that an adjournment motion continues to be a normal device for raising discussion on any important matter, as in the past. I have already stated how the conditions have entirely changed and therefore in the new set-up, with the various opportunities and the responsive and responsible character of the Government we cannot look upon an adjournment motion as a normal device for raising discussion on any important matter.'[1]

It may be mentioned that there is also scope for discussion in the debate on the address in reply to the speech of the Executive Head of the State.

It appears that in the Lok Sabha the consent of the Speaker was given to an adjournment motion on only twelve occasions up till now since 15 August 1947.

An adjournment motion may be treated as a censure motion and, if carried, may result in the fall of the Ministry.[2]

ADMISSIBILITY OF ADJOURNMENT MOTIONS

The admissibility of adjournment motions is governed by the following rules:

(1) *An adjournment motion must relate to a definite matter of urgent public importance*. What is a definite matter of urgent public importance would depend upon the facts of a particular motion. But the underlying principle of the rule was expressed by Mr. Speaker Peel of the British Parliament as follows:

'What I think was contemplated was an occurrence of some sudden emergency, either in home or foreign affairs. But I do not think it was contemplated—if the House will allow me to state my view—that a question of very wide scope which would demand legislation to deal with it in any effective manner should be the subject of discussion on a Motion for the Adjournment of the House, because if that was so we

---

[1] I.P.D., vol. iii, part ii, 21 Mar. 1950, p. 1894; see also H.P.D. 24 Aug. 1953, c. 1362.
[2] Ibid.; H.P.D. 1952, vol. vi, c. 1977.

might have repeated Motions made by the Opposition of the day, not so much in the direction of censuring the Government for action which had been taken or not taken for bringing to notice some grievance demanding instant remedy, as in the direction of wishing to introduce legislation on some particular subject.'[1]

We shall now analyse the several elements of the rule.

(a) *The matter must be definite.* It must relate to a specific issue and not raise wide and general issues.[2] A motion to discuss repressive measures taken against the student community was disallowed.[3] Similarly, a motion to discuss the food situation or famine condition in the country would be inadmissible. On the other hand, motions on individual cases, although definite, e.g. an order under section 144 served against a person,[4] or a strike in a particular concern,[5] would not be admissible unless some question of principle was involved.[6] The motion must not be couched in vague or general terms. A motion to discuss 'the giving of wrong information to the House by the Food Member', when it was not specifically stated what the information was,[7] or 'a situation arising out of some facts' is inadmissible.[8]

(b) *The motion must not be based on facts which are disputed, or made before correct facts are available.* Authentic official information must be available, and opportunity is usually granted for such information to be supplied. When facts are disputed, the Presiding Officer accepts the version of the Government as correct.[9]

(c) *The matter must be urgent.* It must be some grievance demanding, in the words of Mr. Speaker Peel, 'instant remedy'.[10] The matter must be of recent occurrence; the fact that a grievance is a continuing one is not sufficient;[11] if the incident

[1] Parl. Deb. 1894, vol. 23, c. 367. See also L.S.D. 22 Feb. 1955.
[2] H.P.D. 1952, vol. ii, c. 2432; ibid. 1952, vol. iv, c. 5155; ibid. 1952, vol. v, c. 4; ibid. 1952, vol. vi, c. 1570; ibid. 1954, vol. vi, c. 1051.
[3] B.L.A.P. 1942, vol. lxii, no. 1, p. 28.
[4] B.L.A.P. 1937, vol. li, no. 1, p. 198.
[5] B.L.A.P. 1939, vol. liv, no. 10, p. 58.
[6] L.A.D. (Central) 6 Oct. 1937, pp. 3118-19.
[7] L.A.D. (Central) 6 Apr. 1945, p. 2568.
[8] B.L.A.P. 1941, vol. lix, no. 1, p. 207.
[9] L.A.D. (Central) 19 Nov. 1940, p. 785; B.L.A.P. 1941, vol. lix, no. 6, p. 118; ibid. 1938, vol. liii, no. 3, p. 285; W.B.L.A.P. 1949, vol. iv, pp. 26, 43.
[10] See also H.P.D. 1950, vol. iii, c. 1893.
[11] H.C.D. 1933-34, vol. 283, c. 699; ibid. 1946-47, vol. 438, c. 387.

is of recent occurence, it is not necessary that the grievance should be a continuing one.[1] An occurrence is not recent merely because the facts have recently come to light.[2] A matter is not urgent if it is a continuing one.[3]

(d) *The matter must be raised at the earliest opportunity.*[4] This rule is a corollary to the preceding rule. If a matter is not of recent occurrence, it cannot be raised on an adjournment motion because there was no previous opportunity to raise it, e.g. because the legislature was not in session. An adjournment motion can, however, be postponed without prejudice to the question of urgency either for ascertainment of facts[5] or for convenience.[6] An adjournment motion was postponed for the next day because the day on which the notice was given was the last day allotted for the voting of demands.[7]

(e) *The matter must be of public importance.* Individual cases or questions cannot be raised on an adjournment motion, e.g. promulgation of an order under section 144 in a particular case,[8] an order passed on an individual,[9] or a strike in a particular factory.[10] The following cases were deemed to be not of public importance, the Delhi Tongawala strike,[11] the prohibition of cane crushing in U.P.,[12] the Delhi riot,[13] the situation arising in Andhra in the course of a General Election,[14] and a hunger strike.[15]

(2) (a) *The matter must not involve merely the ordinary administration of law,* such as banning of processions by the Commissioner

---

[1] B.L.A.P. 1937, vol. li, no. 2, p. 250.

[2] H.C.D. 1920, vol. 131, c. 1204.

[3] L.S.D. 1955, vol. iii, c. 4560; ibid. 1957, vol. iv, c. 6172; ibid. 1953, vol. i, c. 443.

[4] H.P.D. 1952, vol. i, c. 329.

[5] Ben. L.A.P. 1938, vol. liii, no. 3, p. 285.

[6] Ben. L.A.P. 1943, vol. lxvi, no. 1, p. 39; ibid. 1944, vol. lxvii, no. 1, p. 295; ibid. 1944, vol. lxvii, no. 5, p. 302; H.C.D. 1930-31, vol. 256, cc. 825, 1032; ibid. 1921, vol. 138, c. 1132; L.A.D. 23 Sept. 1929, p. 1239; ibid. 8 Mar. 1930, p. 1413; ibid. 6 Nov. 1944, pp. 264-65 and 285.

[7] *Selection from the Decisions from the Chair,* 1921-50, p. 14, Ruling no. 20 (Central Legislature).

[8] B.L.A.P. 1937, vol. li, no. 1, p. 198.

[9] Ibid.

[10] B.L.A.P. 1939, vol. liv, no. 10, p. 58; ibid. 1947, vol. lxxii, no. 3, p. 207.

[11] P.P.D. 1950, vol. v, c. 393.

[12] Ibid. vol. vi, c. 18.

[13] H.P.D. 1952, vol. i, c. 619.

[14] L.S.D. 1955, vol. i, c. 31.

[15] H.P.D. 1952, vol. i, c. 700.

of Police,[1] arrest of a candidate for election to the Assembly,[2] promulgation of an order under section 144 of the Criminal Procedure Code,[3] order of forfeiture under the Press Act,[4] arrest and detention of a Member of Parliament,[5] firing by police, lathi charge etc.,[6] a *satyagraha* in the Punjab.[7] In West Bengal consent was given to an adjournment motion on police firing at a violent mob in Calcutta during the food riot on 21 September 1959.

The scope of the rule was explained by the President of the Central Assembly when an adjournment motion was allowed on the arrest of the late Sarat Chandra Bose under the Defence of India Rules. The President said:

'I do not think this is a case which can be said to be covered by the doctrine relating to ordinary administration of law. A question like this is analogous to cases which have been dealt with by this House on an adjournment motion relating to persons arrested under Regulation III of 1818. The phrase ordinary administration of law, I might explain to the House, refers to cases where a person is arrested or detained under an ordinary process of law, for instance, by a magistrate or any other similar authority. Here what is complained of is an act of the Government of India itself.'[8]

An order served on the late Mrs. Sarojini Naidu directing her 'not to participate in public meetings and processions nor communicate with press anywhere in India' was allowed to be raised on an adjournment motion as being much too wide and general.[9]

(b) *In the same way any matter of day-to-day administration of a department*, (e.g. alleged wrongful dismissal of an employee)[10] cannot be the subject matter of an adjournment motion.

---

[1] L.A.D. (Central) 30 Mar. 1937, p. 2384.
[2] L.A.D. (Central) 22 Feb. 1941, p. 539.
[3] L.A.D. (Central) 23 Mar. 1944, p. 1463; H.P.D. 30 May 1952, c. 861.
[4] L.A.D. (Central) 7 Sept. 1933, p. 1119.
[5] P.P.D. 1950, vol. ii, p. 971; H.P.D. 1953, vol. ii, c. 1577; ibid. c. 1873; ibid. c. 1979.
[6] H.P.D. 1952, vol. i, c. 329; ibid. 1952, vol. iii, c. 3915; ibid. 1952, vol. vi, c. 1569; ibid. c. 2552; ibid. 1953, vol. i, c. 803; ibid. 1953, vol. ii, c. 1584; ibid. 1953, vol. iii, c. 4625; ibid. 1953, vol. v, c. 6477; ibid. 1953, vol. viii, c. 3801; ibid. 1953, vol. ix, c. 301.
[7] L.S.D. 1957, vol. ii, c. 3203.
[8] L.A.D. (Central) 12 Feb. 1942, p. 100. But see I.P.D. 28 Feb. 1950, p. 971.
[9] L.A.D. (Central) 7 Feb. 1944, p. 51.
[10] W.B.L.A.P. 1947, vol. i, p. 22.

(3) *The matter must not be sub judice.* The matter must not involve anything which is under adjudication by a court of law. A statement by the Government that a matter is *sub judice* will ordinarily be accepted by the Presiding Officer.[1] When a matter has been allowed to be raised by an adjournment motion, but becomes *sub judice* by the time allotted for the discussion of the motion, it cannot be discussed.[2] When the arrest of a person is sought to be raised, but it appears that proceedings against other persons arrested along with him are pending in a court of law, the arrest cannot be discussed.[3] As to when a matter is *sub judice*, see chapter on Rules of Debate.

(4) *The matter must not anticipate any matter which has already been fixed for discussion or for which notice of motion has been given*,[4] e.g. notice of a resolution drawn by ballot[5] and notice of a special motion;[6] a question on the Order Paper[7]—this is open to doubt because a question may or may not be answered by the Government; further, no discussion is allowed on a question except in the Union Parliament and some legislatures where the half-an-hour rule prevails.

(5) *The matter must not anticipate any matter for which an ordinary parliamentary opportunity will occur shortly.* This rule is often applied during the first session of the year or during the Budget session, when any matter relating to the administration may be raised by way of amendment to the address in reply to the speech of the President or the Governor,[8] or by way of motion for reduction of the demands for grants, or in the course of the debate on the Budget or the Appropria-

[1] L.A.D. (Central) 8 Mar. 1937, p. 1571.
[2] L.A.D. (Central) 23 Mar. 1939, p. 2632; ibid. 24 Feb. 1938, p. 1104; ibid. 25 Feb. 1938, p. 1220.
[3] L.A.D. (Central) 8 Mar. 1937, p. 1571; see also L.A.D. 13 Feb. 1946, p. 958.
[4] H.P.D. 1952, vol. i, c. 65; ibid. 1953, vol. i, c. 611; ibid. 1954, vol. vi, c. 14.
[5] L.A.D. (Central) 14 Feb. 1942, p. 170.
[6] B.L.A.P. 1938, vol. lii, no. 1, p. 77; W.B.L.A.P. 1948, vol. iii, no. 1, p. 13.
[7] H.C.D. 1923, vol. 161, c. 2526.
[8] H.C.D. 1944-45, vol 406, c. 360-61; ruling of Mr. Speaker on a motion o adjournment by Dr. Haden Guest on the subject of firing by the Greek police on a demonstration; L.A.D. 15 Feb. 1943, p. 212; ibid. 14 Feb. 1942, p. 172; ibid. 12 Feb. 1942, p. 105; ibid. 27 July 1943, p. 85; H.P.D. 13 Feb. 1953, c. 32; ibid. 20 Feb. 1953, c. 611.

tion Bill. Every case of course depends upon its merits. As
Mr. Speaker Jalan put it:

'When there would occur an opportunity to discuss the
subject matter of an adjournment motion shortly or in time,
such an adjournment motion would be disallowed. I would,
however, add that the rule is not an absolute one and a case
when it arises will have to be judged on the question of urgency
on its own merits. If a matter is of such grave importance or
sudden emergency that the discussion cannot be delayed at
all, the Speaker may permit the discussion of an adjournment
motion on such a matter.'[1]

(6) *The matter must not relate to anything which can otherwise
be raised in accordance with the rules of procedure*, e.g. the promulgation of an ordinance which can be discussed by means of
a resolution for disapproval cannot be raised on an adjournment motion.[2]

(7) *The matter must relate to the administrative responsibility of
the Government concerned.* A matter within the responsibility of
a State would not be allowed to be raised in the Central
legislature.[3] Similarly, matters for the Central Government
cannot be raised in the State legislature, e.g. questions of
foreign policy.[4] No matter can be raised for which another
authority, such as a local body[5] or a statutory body[6] or a
judicial authority,[7] is responsible.

(8) *The matter must not relate to anything which has already been
discussed in the same session.*[8] The failure of getting the leave
of the House to move an adjournment motion prevents its
subject matter being raised again during the same session.[9]

(9) *The motion must not raise matters entailing legislation.*[10]

(10) *The motion must not relate to any matter which should be
raised by a substantive motion*, e.g. the conduct of the Presiding

---

[1] W.B.L.A.P. 1951, vol. iii, no. 1, p. 16.
[2] B.L.A.P. 1939, vol. liv, no. 1, p. 41.
[3] L.A.D. (Central) 12 Feb. 1941, p. 106; ibid. 23 Feb. 1942, p. 404; ibid.
27 July 1943, p. 85; ibid. 18 Nov. 1943, p. 495; ibid. 20 Mar. 1944, p. 1270;
ibid. 11 Apr. 1945, p. 2759; H.P.D. 1954, vol. i, c. 138.
[4] W.B.L.A.P. 1952, vol. vi, no. 3, c. 1720.
[5] H.C.D. 1922, vol. 159, c. 1187.
[6] H.C.D. 1912, vol. 41, c. 816.
[7] H.C.D. 1923, vol. 164, c. 1288.
[8] L.A.P. 11 Feb. 1935, p. 628; H.P.D. 1954, vol. 1, c. 31.
[9] See rulings cited in May, p. 369.
[10] L.A.D. (Central) 23 Mar. 1936, p. 3057; ibid. 11 Apr. 1938, p. 2930.

Officer,[1] nomination of Anglo-Indian members by the Governor,[2] or discussion of which is prohibited by rules, e.g. the conduct of the Governor, apart from the Government.[3]

The above are the general principles guiding the admissibility of adjournment motions. It is not possible to give an exhaustive list of the grounds on which adjournment motions may be disallowed. The following are some of the grounds on which adjournment motions may be disallowed in the Indian legislatures:[4]

(1) It does not relate to a definite matter.

(2) It does not relate to a matter urgent enough to warrant interruption of the business of the day.

(3) It does not relate to a matter of sufficient public importance.

(4) It does not relate to a matter of recent occurrence, which has arisen suddenly, but to a continuing matter.

(5) It is not a matter for an adjournment motion. Other opportunities can be availed of to raise the matter.

(6) It raises more than one issue.

(7) Notice was not given in time.

(8) It relates to a matter which is likely to be debated in the near future, discussion on which has already been fixed.

(9) The matter should have been raised at the first opportunity.

(10) It relates to a matter which is *sub judice*.

(11) An adjournment motion cannot be moved merely to obtain information.

(12) In the case of the Central legislature, it relates to a matter of law and order which is a State subject; or any other State subject.

(13) No responsibility of the Government concerned is involved.

(14) It raises a question of privilege.

(15) It seeks to revive discussion on a matter which has already been discussed during the current session.

(16) It raises a question which under the Constitution or rules can only be raised on a distinct substantive motion.

[1] L.A.D. (Central) 11 Feb. 1935, p. 625; ibid. 8 Oct. 1936, p. 2664.
[2] H.P.D. 1954, vol. ii, c. 1385.
[3] L.A.D. (Central) 17 Mar. 1925, p. 2498.
[4] Lok Sabha Bulletin, part ii, 31 Aug. 1959.

(17) It involves wide questions of policy.

(18) It involves the conduct of a foreign government.

(19) It involves the interpretation of provisions of the Constitution.

(20) It raises matters entailing legislation.

(21) It relates to fasts undertaken by individuals or a body of people.

(22) It relates to service grievances.

(23) It refers to arrests made under the normal process of law.

(24) It involves the redress of grievances complained of available under the existing law.

(25) It relates to day-to-day administrative matters.

(26) The matter can be raised during discussion on the Demands for Grants of the Ministry, Finance Bill, the President's or Governor's address.

(27) It relates to a frivolous or trivial matter.

(28) It relates to an individual case.

(29) It relates to the affairs of an autonomous corporation or body.

(30) It relates to matters where a Minister exercises discretionary powers conferred upon him by a statute.

(31) It relates to matters where Ministers carry out treaty obligations under international law.

(32) It relates to industrial disputes such as lockouts and strikes of a normal character.

(33) It relates to an apprehended lockout or the threat of a strike.

(34) It relates to the Speaker's decision.

(35) It relates to action taken by authorities in due administration of law.

(36) It relates to policy continued from day to day.

(37) It involves demonstrations to get an Act modified.

(38) It relates to an unsatisfactory reply given to a question, or refusal by Government to answer a question.

(39) It relates to orders promulgated under section 144 of the Code of Criminal Procedure, 1898.

(40) The matter sought to be raised is covered by amendments to a motion of thanks on the President's or Governor's address.

An adjournment motion can be brought before the House only with the consent of the Presiding Officer. In giving or refusing his consent, the Presiding Officer will see whether the motion infringes any of the above-mentioned rules. If it does not and is in form, the Presiding Officer will give his consent. It has sometimes been argued that the consent of the Presiding Officer and his decision as to admissibility are two different things, and even if an adjournment motion is otherwise in order, the consent of the Presiding Officer may be withheld; or, after giving his consent, the Presiding Officer may yet declare that the motion is inadmissible.[1] It may be pointed out that this is not the correct approach; if the motion is admissible under the rules, the Presiding Officer should give his consent, leaving the matter for the final decision of the House. In withholding his consent the Presiding Officer cannot take into consideration any other factor than the admissibility of the motion. May says:

'It is a question for the decision of the Speaker whether a matter, to discuss which it is proposed to move the adjournment of the House under S.O. No. 9, complies with the provisions of that standing order. In accepting or rejecting such a motion the Speaker is, as in the case of a motion alleging breach of privilege... doing no more than deciding whether there is in his view a *prima facie* case of urgency, leaving the final decision to the House.'[2]

Before giving his consent finally, the Presiding Officer may, of course, ascertain from the Government on the floor of the House its viewpoint as to the accuracy or otherwise of the statements made in the adjournment motion, and he may give his decision accordingly. When consent is refused by the Presiding Officer, nothing can be mentioned about the adjournment motion in the House. The Speaker of the Lok Sabha has refused to read out the motions.[3] In some legislatures the Speaker reads out the subject matter of the adjournment motion and states that he has refused consent.

If the Presiding Officer gives his consent, leave to move the motion must be moved before the day's business commences

[1] Ben. L.A.P. 1937, vol. li, no. 2, p. 214; ibid. 1941, vol. lix, no. 6, p. 127.
[2] May, p. 369.
[3] H.P.D. 1952, vol. ii, c. 1993; ibid. vol. ii, c. 2820; L.S.D. 1954, vol. vi, c. 741.

and just after the questions are over. If there is no objection, leave is deemed to be granted; if there is any objection, the application for leave must be supported by a specified number of members rising in their seats. If the requisite number of members supports the motion, leave is deemed to be granted; otherwise the leave is deemed to be refused. When leave is granted, the motion is taken up at a specified hour or at an hour fixed by the Presiding Officer.

The debate on an adjournment motion, under the rules of all the legislatures, can last only for a specified time. If no vote is taken within the time, the adjournment motion is said to be talked out without a verdict.

The following procedure has been laid down by the Speaker of the Lok Sabha for the disposal of adjournment motions:[1]

(i) Where the Speaker is satisfied *prima facie* that the matter proposed to be discussed is in order under the rules, he will give his consent to the moving of the motion, and at the appropriate time call upon the member concerned to ask for leave to move the adjournment of the House. If objection to leave being granted is taken, the Speaker will request those members who are in favour of leave being granted to rise in their places, and if not less than fifty members rise accordingly, he will declare that leave is granted. If, however, less than fifty members rise, the Speaker will inform the member that he has not the leave of the House.

(ii) Where the Speaker is satisfied *prima facie* that the notice of an adjournment motion is inadmissible, he will refuse his consent without bringing the matter before the House, and the member concerned will be informed of the Speaker's decision.

(iii) Once a member is informed of the Speaker's decision withholding his consent, no question shall be permitted to be raised in the House either on the subject matter of the notice or the reasons for disallowances thereof. If, however, the member would like to make a submission to the Speaker to reconsider his decision, the Speaker would be glad to see the member concerned in his Chamber later during the day, or consider any written representation the member may make.

(iv) In case the Speaker is satisfied on the submission of

[1] Lok Sabha Bulletin, part ii, 31 Aug. 1959.

9

the member that there are adequate grounds to bring up the motion before the House, he would either mention it or permit the member to raise it on the following day, irrespective of the fact that the notice had been given on the previous day.

(v) Where it is a border-line case, or the Speaker is not in possession of the full facts to decide the admissibility of a notice, he may mention the receipt of the motion from the Chair, and after hearing a brief statement from the member and/or the Minister concerned, give his final decision on merits.

(vi) A member of an organized party or group who desires to give notice of an adjournment motion would consult his group or party in the first instance. If the party or group felt that the matter sought to be raised by the motion is of sufficient urgency and public importance to be brought before the House, the member should have his notice supported either by the Leader, Deputy Leader, Secretary or Whip of his party or group. In any case, the Speaker's decision either to bring the matter before the House or to withhold his consent outside will be final.

In the Lok Sabha the Speaker, if he is satisfied that the debate has been adequate, can put the motion to vote on the expiry of two and a half hours from the commencement of the debate.[1] A time limit for the speech of a member is also prescribed.

Only one adjournment motion can be made at the same sitting of the House.

[1] Lok Sabha Rule 62.

CHAPTER VIII

RESOLUTIONS

IN the House of Commons a distinction is drawn between orders and resolutions. 'By its orders', as May expresses it,[1] 'the House directs its committees, its members, its officers, the order of its own proceedings and the acts of all persons whom they concern; by its resolutions the House declares its own opinions and purposes.' No such distinction is made in the Indian legislatures. All motions are expressed in the form of resolutions as ordinarily understood. But the term 'resolution' is used in respect of a certain kind of motion only. By a resolution, the legislature merely expresses its opinion with regard to the matter before it; by its nature, a resolution is only recommendatory and is not binding upon anybody.

In the Indian legislatures a resolution may be in the form of a declaration of opinion, or a recommendation, or formed in such a way as to record either approval or disapproval by the House of an act or policy of Government. It may convey a message, or commend, urge or request an action, or call attention to a matter or situation for the consideration of the Government; or it may be in such other form as the Speaker considers appropriate.

A resolution may be moved relating to any matter of general public interest; the matter, however, must not be one which does not primarily concern the particular Government. The resolution must raise some definite issue, and shall not refer to any matter which is under adjudication by a court of law[2], or to the conduct of any person except in his official or public capacity. A resolution recommending the amendment of an Act is admissible.[3]

No resolution which seeks to raise discussion on a matter pending before any statutory tribunal, or statutory authority performing any judicial or quasi-judicial functions, or any

---

[1] May, p. 413.
[2] I.P.D. 23 Nov. 1950, c. 543.
[3] W.B.L.A.P. 1951, vol. iii, no. 2, p. 91.

commission or court of enquiry appointed to enquire into or investigate any matter, is ordinarily permitted to be moved, but the Speaker may, in his discretion, allow such matters being raised in the House as are concerned with the procedure or subject or stage of enquiry, if he is satisfied that it is not likely to prejudice the consideration of such matters by the tribunal, authority or commission or court concerned.

NOTICE AND PRIORITY OF RESOLUTION

A period of notice is usually required for a resolution, but the Presiding Officer may, with the consent of the Minister to whose department the resolution relates, admit a resolution at shorter notice.

When there are a number of non-official resolutions the order of priority is determined by ballot as described in a previous chapter.[1] A member in whose name a resolution stands may, with the permission of the Speaker, authorize another member in whose name the resolution stands lower in the list to move it on his behalf; if a member is absent when called on, any other member authorized by him in writing may move his resolution if permitted by the Speaker. When a number of members tabled a resolution on identical terms the member who got priority intimated that he would not move the resolution, and when the Committee on Private Member's Bills and Resolutions did not allot any time for the resolution the Speaker declined to give permission to another member who had not given notice to move the resolution because he was lower down in priority.[2] (As to taking of resolutions out of turn see p. 72.)

A member when called upon may withdraw his resolution; but once moved, a resolution cannot be withdrawn without the leave of the House, and then the general rule that if there is a single dissentient voice a motion cannot be withdrawn will apply (see p. 111).

DISCUSSION ON RESOLUTION

Amendments can be moved to any resolution, and the general

[1] See p. 72.
[2] H.P.D. 1954, vol. iv, c. 6173.

rule as to amendments will apply (see p. 112). General rules applicable to motions, including rules against anticipation and repetition, are also applicable to resolutions.

The Presiding Officer has the authority to disallow any resolution which offends against any of the rules governing resolutions, e.g. if the matter sought to be raised is not the concern of the Government concerned,[1] or the resolution anticipates any matter of which notice has already been given. If the Presiding Officer disallows any resolution, his action cannot be criticized on the floor of the House. The member concerned may make a representation to the Presiding Officer in his chamber.[2]

Rules of some legislatures provide that a Minister may object to the discussion of a resolution before it is moved on the ground that it cannot be discussed without detriment to the public interest. If such objection is taken, no debate is allowed, but after brief explanatory statements have been made by the mover and the Minister the resolution is put to the vote of the House.

The Presiding Officer may, according to the rules of procedure of many legislatures, fix a time limit for the debate on any particular resolution, and also for the speeches of individual members.

No matter of general public interest can be discussed other than on a resolution in accordance with the rules applicable to it; the Presiding Officers are, however, authorized by the rules of legislatures to admit special motions in regard to such matters. (For special motions see p. 144).

In some legislatures, e.g. the Lok Sabha, when a resolution has been moved, no resolution or amendment raising substantially the same questions can be moved within one year from the date of the moving of the earlier resolution. If a resolution has been withdrawn with the leave of the House no resolution raising substantially the same question can be moved during the same session.

---

[1] W.B.L.A.P. 1952, vol. vi, no. 3, c. 1720.
[2] L.A.D. (Central) 3 Nov. 1944, p. 222.

CHAPTER IX

MISCELLANEOUS MOTIONS

MOTION FOR ADDRESS IN REPLY TO THE SPEECH OF THE HEAD OF THE STATE

THE Head of the State opens the first session of the legislature in each year and the first session after dissolution with a speech which outlines the policy of the Government, the legislative proposals and financial recommendations and the achievement of the Government during the previous year. The Constitution[1] lays down that the rules of procedure should provide for time for the discussion of the matters referred to in the speech. The Speaker fixes the time for the discussion of such matters. The Constitution originally expressly provided for the debate on the speech to be given precedence over other business of the House. But the provision has subsequently been amended, and although it is not compulsory to give precedence to the debate, precedence is in fact given over other matters of business except urgent and formal ones.

The debate on the speech is initiated, as in the House of Commons, by a motion for giving an address in reply expressing the thanks of the members of the House for the speech delivered. The motion usually takes the following form:

'That a respectful Address in reply be presented to the... as follows:

'Sir,

'We, the members of.......assembled in this session beg to offer our humble thanks to you for the most excellent speech which you have been pleased to deliver to this House.'

This motion is generally moved and seconded by two members of the Government party who are not in the Government.

Ordinarily the motion is moved immediately after each House assembles after the delivery of the speech to the Houses

[1] Arts. 87, 176.

assembled together. But the debate is usually adjourned to a later day in order to enable the members to table amendments if they desire to do so. The discussion may be adjourned on a motion made in favour of Government business or by an adjournment motion for the purpose of discussing a matter of urgent public importance.

Bills may be introduced, or motions for leave to introduce bills may be made, or other business of a formal character may be transacted on a day allotted for the discussion before the discussion commences.

Amendments are tabled in the form of adding words at the end of the address in reply, or in any other form that the Speaker may consider appropriate. The usual form of an amendment is to express regret at the policy enunciated in the speech or for the omission of reference to any matter which may be sought to be raised by the amendment.[1]

The usual form of an amendment is as follows:

'That the following be added at the end of the address in reply:- "But regret that no reference has been made in the speech to (the rehabilitation of refugees)." '

By such an amendment the question of the rehabilitation of refugees may be discussed.

An amendment for the addition of words expressing no confidence in the Ministers is admissible.[2]

Not only matters referred to in the address but those omitted from the address may be discussed.[3]

The Prime Minister or the Chief Minister or any other Minister, whether he has previously taken part in the debate or not, has a right of explaining the position of the Government at the end of the discussion.

(For scope of debate see Chapter III, p. 61).

PRESENTATION OF ADDRESS TO THE HEAD OF THE STATE

After the motion for an address in reply has been agreed to, the address is printed and sent to the Head of the State under the signature of the Presiding Officer. The Head of the State

---

[1] H.P.D. 19 May 1952, c. 87; see also ibid. 17 Feb. 1954, c. 151.
[2] H.C.D. 1924, vol. 169, c. 680.
[3] H.P.D. 1952, vol. i, c. 261; ibid. vol. i, c. 87.

sends a formal letter of thanks for the address which is usually read in the House.

MOTION OF NO-CONFIDENCE IN MINISTERS

A motion of no-confidence in the Ministry can be moved by any member subject to certain restrictions. The restrictions provided for by the rules of procedure of the Lok Sabha Rules are that leave of the House must be granted before such a motion can be moved. If the prescribed number of members support a motion of no-confidence when leave is asked for by rising in their places, leave is deemed to be granted; otherwise leave is deemed to be refused. No such restriction appears to be placed in regard to the motion of no-confidence against the Ministry in the House of Commons.

There is a convention in the House of Commons that when a demand is made by the Leader of the Opposition for the allotment of a day for the discussion of a motion of no-confidence in the Ministry, the Government always allots a day or more for the purpose. As May[1] says: 'This convention is due to the recognized and responsible position of the Leader of the Opposition as a potential alternative Government—a position which guarantees the legitimacy of such an interruption of the normal course of business. For their part the Government have everything to gain by meeting such a direct challenge to their authority at the earliest possible moment.'

The rules usually prescribe that leave must be asked for just after the questions are over and the business for the day is entered upon, and also that a notice of such motion must be left with the Secretary of the House before the commencement of the sitting.

As the Constitution[2] provides that the Ministry is collectively responsible to the Assembly, a motion of no-confidence can be moved against the Ministry as a whole and not against a particular Minister, although the action of a particular Minister can be the cause of the motion and his action can be criticized. This is so because the Ministry as a whole takes the responsibility of all actions of the Ministers.

[1] May, p. 305.
[2] Arts. 75, 164.

A motion expressing disapproval of the policy of the Government, but not expressing want of confidence in so many words, may not come within the rule regarding motions of no-confidence. Such a motion may be treated as a resolution. It is doubtful whether leave of the House would be necessary for moving such a motion, or whether such a motion can be moved on a day other than a non-official day. The effect of such a motion may in certain circumstances be tantamount to a vote of no-confidence although not expressed in so many words.

MOTION OF NO-CONFIDENCE MOVED IN THE UPPER HOUSE

The rules of the Rajya Sabha do not provide for the moving of any motion of no-confidence in the Ministry. Some legislatures in India have adopted that rule. In West Bengal, however, on 25 March 1958 a motion of no-confidence was allowed in the Upper House. The fundamental principle underlying modern parliamentary democracy is that the Ministry is responsible ultimately to the people; this principle has been succintly expressed by Herman Finer when he says that 'The Constitution is no longer parliamentary but plebiscitary.' The necessary corollary following from this principle is that the Ministry is proximately responsible to that House of the legislature which is directly elected by the people. This was accepted in England as long ago as 1850, when Lord John Russell, Prime Minister of England, declined to resign after a vote of censure was passed on the Ministry in the House of Lords. It is this principle which has been embodied in Article 164, clause (2) of our Constitution which lays down that 'the Council of Ministers shall be collectively responsible to the Legislative Assembly of the State'. It has, however, to be seen whether Article 164, clause (2) debars the Council from passing a motion of censure on the Ministry. There is nothing in this Article in regard to the passing of motions of censure. This Article only indicates the constitutional position of the Ministry *vis-a-vis* the Assembly. This Article of the Constitution in no way takes away the right of the Council to criticize the conduct of the Ministry or to show its disapproval of the policy of the Ministry. In fact there are provisions which envisage that the Council can show its disapproval of the policy of the Government, e.g. by rejecting the Appropriation Bill, or by adopting an amendment to the address in reply to the Governor's speech. Another method is to adopt a motion expressing in precise terms the disapproval of the policy of the Council of Ministers in any particular respect. Although technically the expression in terms of 'want of confidence' in the Ministry may not be a very happy form in which to put a motion censuring the Ministry in the Council, yet the result is the same. A vote of censure was passed in the House of Lords in 1850.[1] Sir Courtenay Ilbert in his book, *Parliament*, says in regard to the House of Lords: 'And, as the power of the executive government depends on the power of the purse, the whole range of executive government is placed beyond their (i.e., the House of Lords) effective control. They can criticize and their criticisms are often valuable and influential, but they cannot enforce their criticisms. The Ministry cannot afford to disregard a resolution or vote of the House of Commons expressing or implying condemnation of their policy or action. Such a resolution or vote must shake them, may destroy them. But they can afford to disregard a condemnatory resolution passed by the Lords.'[2]

It should also be mentioned that immediately after the House of Lords had passed the motion of censure on the Ministry in 1850, the Ministry obtained a vote of confidence in the House of Commons,[3] and this was a necessary measure to emphasize the constitutional ineffectiveness of such a motion of censure from the Upper House.

At a subsequent occasion on 8 August 1911, a motion of censure was moved in the House of Lords by no less a person than Lord Curzon of Kedleston against the King Emperor's Ministers, and it was passed.[4] It does not appear, however, that anything further was done in the House of Commons except the passing of the Parliament Bill, the introduction of which was the reason for this motion in the House of Lords. Thus it may be seen that the House of Lords is entitled to

[1] Parl. Deb. 3rd series, vol. iii, 17 June 1850.
[2] See 3rd edition, p. 182; see also W.B.L.C. Debates, vol. xiv, p. 267.
[3] Parl. Deb. vol. 112, June 28, 1850.
[4] Parl. Deb. Lords, 1911, vol. ix, c. 815.

pass a resolution condemnatory of the policy of the Government. If a motion of censure is allowed in the House of Lords, which is not an elected body at all but largely hereditary, the Council, which in a way is elected—although it may be by indirect election—seems to be entitled to discuss such a motion. But the reason why a no-confidence motion is not allowed in some of the Upper Houses in India may be traced to the fundamental distinction between the House of Lords and the Upper House in India. The House of Lords is not an elected body, and therefore the members do not have to look to the electorate for their acts. They can give their opinion independently of any popular support and in the national interest. Consequently their verdict carries a great weight. In India, however, the Upper Houses are elected bodies, and it may be said that they cannot have any greater value than the Lower Houses which are elected on adult franchise and are really representative of the people; it is the Lower House which can effectively control the Ministry. Besides, many channels have now been opened for the Council, e.g. moving for papers, half-an-hour debate, etc., whereby the Upper House can discuss or criticize the Ministry concerned. The absence of the right to move a no-confidence motion in express terms, therefore, does not affect the Upper House adversely in any way.

MOTION OF NO-CONFIDENCE IN THE PRESIDING OFFICER

The Constitution provides that a Presiding Officer can be removed by a resolution of the House, subject to certain conditions.[1] As there is a specific provision in the Constitution, it appears that a resolution in terms that so-and-so be removed from his office as the Speaker or other Presiding Officer, as the case may be, would be the proper form of such a resolution. Resolutions used to be moved in this form in the pre-Constitution period also.[2] After the Constitution came into force such motions have been moved in the Lok Sabha and some other State legislatures.[3]

[1] Arts. 90, 94, 179, 183.
[2] B.L.A.P. 1926, vol. xx, no. 1, p. 306.
[3] L.S.D. 18 Dec. 1954, vol. ix, cc. 3281-309, 3398-456; Or. L.A.D. 10 Apr. 1954; And. L.A.D. 17 May 1954; W.B.L.A.P. 20 Mar. 1959.

Fourteen days' notice of a resolution for the removal of the Presiding Officer must be given, and in order to be effective the resolution must be passed by a majority of all the then members of the House concerned.[1] Although the Constitution does not require that specific charges should be given in a motion for the removal of the Presiding Officer, in the opinion of Mr. Deputy Speaker of the Lok Sabha,[2] the principles of natural justice require that specific reasons or charges for the removal should be given, so that the Presiding Officer, who has a right under the Constitution to speak and take part in the debate, may refute the reasons or the charges in his reply if he chooses to do so.

Rules of some legislatures provide that leave to move a motion for the removal of the Presiding Officer must be granted by the House by a specified number of members rising in their seats before such a motion can be moved. In view of the clear provision in the Constitution that a Presiding Officer can be removed by a specified majority after notice for a specified period, it seems any further restriction on the right to move a resolution is *ultra vires*. The Constitution gives a right to any member to move a resolution for the removal of the Presiding Officer. The only restriction put upon his right is that he must give fourteen days' notice of his intention to do so; whether he would be able to carry the House by the required majority is to be decided when the vote is taken, and not at the time when he intends to move the resolution.

An amendment to the effect 'that this House expresses its full confidence in the Speaker of the House of Assembly etc.' was allowed to be moved to the main motion 'that this House disapproves of the manner in which Mr. Speaker discharges his function as Presiding Officer...etc.' in the House of Assembly (Union of South Africa).[3] A similar[4] amendment was allowed in the West Bengal Legislative Assembly, namely, 'that the House expresses its full confidence in the Speaker of the Assembly... etc.' to the main motion of no-confidence in the Speaker.

[1] Arts. 90, 94, 179 and 183.
[2] L.S.D. 1954, vol. ix, c. 3297.
[3] *Table* (1954), vol. xxiii, p. 90; see also *Votes and Proceedings*, pp. 494-7, House of Assembly (Union of South Africa).
[4] W.B.L.A.P. 20 Mar. 1959.

The Presiding Officer whose removal is under consideration cannot preside over the sitting of the House in which the discussion takes place. He is, however, entitled to speak or otherwise take part in the debate. He can also vote in the first instance on the resolution, or on any other matter during such proceedings, e.g. on an amendment. He cannot vote a second time if there is an equality of votes including his own first vote. The provision in the Constitution[1] is rather ambiguously expressed; but this seems to be the intention of the provision. There is an exception to the rule. The Chairman of the Council of States is not entitled to vote on any resolution for his removal, or on any other proceeding arising out of it; he is, however, entitled to speak.[2]

ACTION AGAINST PRESIDING OFFICER GUILTY OF UNPARLIAMENTARY CONDUCT

The question has sometimes been raised as to what steps can be taken against the Speaker if he is guilty of unparliamentary conduct or misconduct in the discharge of his duties.

So far as the House of Commons is concerned, there is no specific provision; but the House has the inherent right to take any action it likes against its own members including the Speaker, and, as it will appear later, it has exercised such a right.

In India, however, the matter is set at rest by the Constitution which provides for the removal of the Speaker from his office. Such a provision existed under the successive Government of India Acts beginning with that of 1919.

Apart from a resolution for the removal of the Speaker, it seems the House has an inherent power to censure the Speaker for his conduct. Such motions have been moved in the House of Commons, and the Indian legislatures, which have the same powers and privileges as the House of Commons, may have such a right. In 1925, when the Speaker granted a closure, although objected to by the Opposition, a motion was moved in the following terms:

'That, in view of the express provisions of Standing Order

---

[1] Arts. 96, 181, 185.
[2] Art. 92.

No. 26 for the protection of the rights of minorities, this House regrets the action of Mr. Speaker on the 25th May, 1925, when, contrary to recent precedents, he granted the Closure at 11–45 p.m. on the first day's Debate on the Motion for the Second Reading of the Finance Bill.'[1]

A similar motion was made in 1902 to the effect that the Speaker ought to have held a certain expression to be unparliamentary.[2]

On 16 February 1770, exception was taken to certain expressions used by the Speaker, and the words were taken down at the request of some members. There was a heated debate and a motion was moved 'that the words spoken by Mr. Speaker, from the Chair, are disorderly, importing an improper reflection on a member of this House, and dangerous to the freedom of debate in this House.' The motion was put to a vote and negatived.[3]

There is no recorded instance of the removal of a Speaker in the House of Commons. In 1694 a committee was appointed by the House to enquire into a charge of corruption against Sir John Trevor, the Speaker. The committee reported that the Speaker had been guilty of a high crime and misdemeanour in accepting a gratuity of 1,000 guineas after the passing of the Orphans Bill. On the next day the Speaker absented himself saying that he was suffering from colic. On the day after he was also absent, and the King sent a message that the Speaker had written to him that he, the Speaker, could not continue in his office owing to indisposition and asked the House to elect another Speaker. The House elected another Speaker. Two or three days later, the House expelled Sir John Trevor from membership of the House.[4]

Where it is alleged that the Speaker is guilty of unparliamentary conduct or misconduct in the discharge of his duties, two courses are open to the House: (i) to disapprove of the action of the Speaker if it is not proposed to remove him; or (ii) to remove him from his office under the Constitution in accordance with the procedure laid down there.

[1] H.C.D. 1925, vol. 184, c. 1591.
[2] Parl. Deb. 1902, vol. 107, c. 1031.
[3] Hansard, *Parl. History*, vol. xvi, p. 807.
[4] C.J. (1693-97) 274.

MOTION FOR DISCUSSION OF ANY MATTER

As has already been stated, in order to enable the House to discuss a matter, there must be a motion before the House. In the British House of Commons, if any debate is to take place on any matter for which no specific motion is provided, a motion is made that 'the House do now adjourn' and on that motion, a debate takes place (see p. 116).

Such a motion is not made in the Indian legislatures. Instead, if it is desired to have a debate, a direct form of motion is adopted that the matter be discussed or taken into consideration. When, for example, a Report of the Public Service Commission or Public Accounts Committee is laid before the House, a motion that the Report be discussed is moved if the House desires to take such Report into consideration.[1]

The Constitution[2] provides that the Report of the Auditor General and the Report of the Public Service Commission should be laid before the legislature. The obvious intention is that the legislature should have an opportunity to discuss them. If, therefore, when they are so laid, a member gives notice that he would move a motion for the discussion of the Reports or moves a motion forthwith, the Government would be bound to provide time for the discussion, and such time would not be counted as non-official time although the notice may be given or motion moved by a non-official member.

When statements of policy are made by Ministers, they are also debated by a motion either that the policy be approved or disapproved, or by a similar motion.[3]

DISCUSSION OF MATTER OF URGENT PUBLIC
IMPORTANCE FOR SHORT DURATION

A matter of urgent public importance may be discussed without a motion by a notice for a discussion on matters of urgent public importance of short duration.

A member who desires to raise a discussion on a matter of urgent public importance may give notice to the Speaker

---

[1] W.B.L.A.P. 1951, vol. iii, no. 3, p. 104; ibid. 1953, vol. vii, no. 3, c. 101.
[2] Art. 151.
[3] B.L.A.P. 1942, vol. lxiii, no. 1, p. 222; ibid. 1942, vol. lxiii, no. 2, p. 103; ibid. 1943, vol. lxvi, no. 2, p. 296.

specifying clearly and precisely the matter to be raised. The notice must be accompanied by an explanatory note stating the reasons for raising a discussion on the matter in question, and must also be supported by the signatures of at least two other members. If the Speaker is satisfied, after calling for such information from the member who has given notice and from the Minister as he may consider necessary, that the matter is urgent and is of sufficient importance to be raised in the House at an early date, he may admit the notice, and in consultation with the Leader of the House fix the date on which such matter may be taken up for discussion and may allow such time not exceeding two and a half hours as he may consider appropriate in the circumstances. He may refuse to admit the notice if an earlier opportunity is otherwise available for the discussion of the matter. No formal motion is moved before the House and no voting takes place. The member who has given notice may make a short statement, and the Minister is bound to reply briefly. Any member who has given previous intimation to the Speaker may be permitted to take part in the discussion.

CALLING ATTENTION TO MATTER OF URGENT PUBLIC IMPORTANCE

A member may, with the previous permission of the Speaker, call the attention of a Minister to any matter of urgent public importance, and the Minister may make a brief statement or ask for time to make a statement at a later hour or date. The proposed matter must be raised after the questions and before the list of business is entered upon, and cannot be raised at any other time during the sitting of the House. There can be no debate on the statement of the Minister at the time it is made. Not more than one matter may be raised at the same sitting. If more than one notice is received priority is given to the matter which is considered more urgent and important by the Speaker. In the Lok Sabha more than one matter may be raised and one question allowed to the member(s) giving notice.

SPECIAL MOTIONS

No matter of general public interest can be discussed except on a motion made with the consent of the Speaker. Such motions are known as special motions.

The motion for the discussion of a statement of policy by a Minister would seem to fall within the category of special motions. Special motions are sometimes moved for other purposes also, e.g. congratulatory messages on the termination of the war.[1]

MOTION FOR PAPERS

In the Rajya Sabha (Council of States), there is no adjournment motion, but in its stead there is a kind of motion known as the motion for papers. A motion for papers is moved in the following form:

'That there be laid before the House, papers in regard to.....', and thereafter the subject which is sought to be raised by the motion is specified. The subject matter must be a matter of urgent public importance, and must be clearly and precisely specified.

If the Chairman is satisfied that the matter is urgent and of sufficient importance to be raised at an early date, he may admit the motion and fix the date on which such motion may be taken up and allot such time for its discussion not exceeding three hours as he may consider appropriate. If an earlier opportunity is otherwise available for the discussion of the proposed matter, the Chairman may refuse to admit the motion. If at the end of the discussion the motion is not withdrawn, or the Minister states that there are no papers to be laid on the table, or that papers cannot be laid on the table on the ground that they are against the public interest, any member may move an amendment in such form as may be considered appropriate by the Chairman. Such an amendment if moved is, however, put to the vote of the House without discussion, unless the Chairman thinks fit to allot further time for the elucidation of any matter arising out of the amendment.

It appears that on two occasions notices of motion for papers were given in the Rajya Sabha, but discussion was

[1] B.L.A.P. 1941, vol. lix, no. 5, p. 201.

10

allowed on the subject matters sought to be raised and not on the motions as such.[1]

The procedure for motions for papers has also been adopted by the Upper Houses in many State legislatures.

In the House of Lords, when a member wishes to discuss any matter without asking the House to express any opinion thereon, he either gives notice of his intention to call attention to the subject 'and to move for papers', or gives notice of a question, adding at the end of the question the words 'and to move for papers'. He makes a speech on the day on which the motion or the question is taken up, and concludes by moving 'that there be laid before the House papers relating to the subject'. A debate then follows and the mover has a right of reply. Normally papers are not laid but they are merely a pretext for the debate. If a member wants a decision he puts down a resolution which the House approves or disapproves.

A motion for papers is also made use of in the House of Lords for the purpose of challenging delegated legislation and dividing the House upon the motion.

OBITUARY REFERENCE

Although there are no rules providing for obituary references, such references are in practice made to the deaths of persons whether members or not, whether eminent or otherwise. No definite policy can be ascertained as to whose deaths should be mentioned. There is also no definite rule as to who should make the reference. Sometimes the Presiding Officer does so, sometimes the Leader of the House, sometimes even the Leader of the Opposition.

In the House of Commons reference to the deaths of sitting members[2] began to be made from 1937.

If any death occurs the Speaker announces the death at the beginning of the sitting of the House, and expresses sympathy on behalf of the House to the members of the bereaved family.

No mention is made of the death of any persons other

---

[1] R.S.D. vol. 6, 1954, cc. 208, 440; ibid. vol. 22, 1958, cc. 110, 314.
[2] H.C.D. 1936-37, vol. 326, c. 3100.

than members, except the deaths of members of the Royal Family and Heads of foreign States in alliance with the British Government.

In the Lok Sabha obituary references are made on the passing away of the following:

(i) Sitting Members.

(ii) Ex-Members (including those who were members of the Old Central Assembly, Constituent Assembly of India (Legislative) and Provisional Parliament.)

(iii) Outstanding personages. In this category come Mahatma Gandhi, Shri Aurobindo Ghosh.

(iv) Heads of certain friendly foreign States. Obituary references were made on the death of His Majesty King George the Sixth of the United Kingdom, Marshal Stalin and His Majesty Bir Bikram Shah Tribhuvan, King of Nepal.

As a special case obituary references were also made in the Lok Sabha on the following occasions:

(i) On 15 February 1954, reference was made to those who died at Allahabad in the Kumbha Mela Tragedy.

(ii) On 16 August 1955, reference was made to those Satyagrahis who laid down their lives on 15th August 1955, for the liberation of Goa.

(iii) On 26 November 1956, reference was made to those who died on 23 November 1958, in the Madras Tuticorin Train Disaster.

(iv) On 9 May 1958, reference was made to the two airmen who died in the air accidents at Hoshiarpur and Safdarjang airport on the same day.

In regards to foreigners it may be noted that the State legislature can have no direct relation or communication with any foreign Government. It is the External Affairs Ministry of the Union Government which is concerned with communications with foreign States. The State legislature cannot send any message of condolence or sympathy directly. Besides, there may be questions of protocol and diplomatic practice. It is desirable to leave such reference to the Union Government.

References are also made to deaths by accidents. Two instances of reference to accidents will be of interest—one in the House of Commons and the other in the Lok Sabha.

When the steamship *Titanic* foundered on its maiden voyage, messages of condolence and sympathy were sent to the House of Commons from various legislatures in Europe and America. In the House of Commons, however, no formal reference to the deaths was made. In answer to a question the Prime Minister made a statement as to the facts[1], and in the course of his statement he paid a tribute to some persons for their 'willing sacrifices which were offered to give the best chance of safety to those who were the least able to help themselves', and expressed 'the warm and heartfelt sympathy of the whole nation to those who found themselves bereft of the nearest and dearest in their desolated homes.'[2] A note appears in the Hansard that 'Members in all parts of the House removed their hats during the Prime Minister's statement'.

In the Lok Sabha on 9 May 1958, the Minister concerned informed the House, in reply to a question, that an Enquiry Committee had been appointed to investigate into the air crash in which several Indian Air Force personnel lost their lives. In the course of the statement he paid a tribute to the gallantry of the Air Force personnel who could have saved themselves by parachuting, but risked their lives in an attempt to prevent the plane crashing into the city of Delhi. After the statement members stood up in silence—a rare tribute paid by the House which does not usually do so in this manner except in the case of the death of members.

[1] H.C.D. 1912, vol. xl, c. ...
[2] Ibid. vol. xxxvii, c. 193.

CHAPTER X

RULES OF DEBATE

WHENEVER it is necessary to obtain a decision of the House on any matter, a motion, as has already been explained, has to be made before the House. A motion may be moved by any member and also by the Presiding Officer. When a motion has been moved there is a 'question' before the House. Although a question may be and is sometimes decided without discussion, on a question being proposed, a discussion or debate in which the members take part is usually held. In order that the matter at issue may be properly discussed, there are certain rules of debate which are followed in all legislatures. These rules will be discussed in this chapter.

PROCESS OF DEBATE

There are three stages in the discussion of every motion: (a) a motion is moved by a member, and on the motion being moved the Presiding Officer proposes the motion before the House as a 'question'; (b) a debate follows and (c) after the close of the debate, the Presiding Officer puts the question to the vote of the House, and after ascertaining the opinion of the House declares the verdict.

Generally, a member formally moves the motion first and speaks after the question has been proposed by the Presiding Officer. But he may speak first and then at the end of his speech move the motion. In the latter case a member is allowed to speak on the distinct understanding that he will move the motion standing in his name.[1]

Seconding a motion is not necessary in the Indian legislatures except in the case of a motion of thanks to the Head of the State. In England the Select Committee of the House of Commons on Procedure[2] recommended that the seconding

---

[1] May, p. 406.
[2] *Report of the Select Committee on Procedure,* 1959.

of a motion should not be necessary except on ceremonial occasions, and under a change in Standing Orders in 1960 a motion now no longer requires a seconder, though on formal occasions this may be done if it is thought desirable.

After the speech of the mover of the motion other members may speak either in support of or in opposition to the motion. The mover of a motion has, subject to certain exceptions, a right of reply after the speeches of other members.

After a motion has been moved amendments may be proposed to the motion. If any amendment is proposed a new 'question' arises; the main question is for the time being put aside and the debate proceeds on the amendment. In some legislatures there is a practice of allowing the main motion and all amendments to be moved together and, after the mover of the main motion has spoken, of a general discussion taking place. The inconvenience of such a course has been pointed out in a previous chapter (see p. 114). The more satisfactory procedure is to clinch the debate to a particular amendment then before the House, and, after all the amendments are disposed of one by one, to take up the main motion.

MANNER OF SPEAKING

The Indian legislatures have adopted the practice prevailing in the House of Commons where the members make their speeches from their places and in doing so address the Chair. No rostrum is provided, and the member speaking does not address the assembly of members. A member has to make his speech standing except that a member disabled by sickness or infirmity may be permitted to speak sitting.

CATCHING THE SPEAKER'S EYE

If a member desires to speak on any motion before the House, he rises in his place and the Presiding Officer calls upon him to speak. If several members rise simultaneously, the Presiding Officer calls upon the member who first 'catches his eye'. In practice, however, the names of speakers on a particular subject are prearranged between the Whips of the different parties, and a list of the names is supplied to the Presiding

Officer. The Presiding Officer calls upon members from the list, and in order to give a lively and interesting turn to the debate going on usually calls upon members alternately from each party or group. The fiction of 'catching the Speaker's eye' is, however, maintained and the supply of the list of members is kept an open secret.

In 1872 Mr. Gladstone disclaimed the supply of any such list.[1] In 1911, when the practice of the supply of such a list seems to have been well-established, a member of the House of Commons, Mr. Ginnell, opposed the re-election of Speaker Lowther on the ground that Mr. Lowther as Speaker used to call upon members to speak from a list supplied by the Whips and was therefore unfair to back-benchers.[2]

It is also usual, in the absence of any agreed list, for members who wish to speak to submit their names to the Presiding Officer. The Presiding Officer, however, has absolute discretion[3] in the matter of calling upon members to speak, as has been observed in May:

'This practice (submission of names), while not fettering the discretion of the Speaker, affords to Members who avail themselves of it a better opportunity of "catching the Speaker's eye"; and to the Speaker a means of distributing the available time as equitably as possible between the various sections of opinion.'[4]

The Speaker has the right to decide the order in which members should speak.[5] Members of the Scheduled Castes and Scheduled Tribes were given priority when a debate was proceeding on the rights and problems of such communities.[6] Members coming from an area where rubber is produced were given priority when a bill relating to rubber production was being debated.[7] Members who had not spoken at any stage of a bill were given priority over those who had.[8]

---

[1] May, p. 446.
[2] H.C.D. 1911, vol. 21, cc. 8-10.
[3] L.A.D. 22 Mar. 1944, p. 1415; I.P.D. 7 Dec. 1950, c. 1318; H.P.D. 6 June 1952, c. 1316; ibid. 18 June 1952, c. 2033; ibid. 20 Dec. 1952, c. 2959; I.P.D. 10 Mar. 1951, c. 2127; ibid. 7 Apr. 1951, c. 6287; ibid. 9 Apr. 1951, c. 6343.
[4] May, p. 446.
[5] L.S.D. 1954, vol. viii, c. 825;
[6] H.P.D. 1952, vol. vi, c. 2228.
[7] L.S.D. 1954, vol. viii, c. 825.
[8] L.S.D. 1956, vol. iv, c. 7129; ibid. 1956, vol. v, c. 9881.

MAIDEN SPEECH

When several members rise to speak a new member who has not previously spoken is entitled to the courtesy of being called upon to speak in preference to others. This courtesy is extended only to a member who claims it in the first session of the Parliament to which he is returned.[1]

READING SPEECHES

There is no hard and fast rule in the Indian legislature prohibiting the reading of written speeches. In the British House of Commons written speeches are not permitted except on rare occasions when precision of statements is necessary, e.g. Budget statements, statements on foreign Policy,[2] etc. The reading of speeches detracts from the cut and thrust of debate, for the speech of a member reading a precomposed speech has often no relation to the arguments put forward by others, and such a course should be discouraged, except when important statements involving facts and figures have to be made.[3]

The reading of speeches is not encouraged in the Indian Parliament. Mr. Speaker Mavalankar said; 'Members will realize that if written speeches are permitted, it may mean that some other person writes a speech and the member reads it—of course, not in all cases; but then the speech read will have probably no reference to the speeches made by others in the debate. What is read would have been written previous to the starting of the debate. Therefore if we want really to have a debate with a life in it, without repetitions and with arguments addressed only to the points raised, then I am sure members will all agree with me that written speeches must be discouraged.'[4]

When a member persisted in reading a speech, although asked by the Speaker not to do so, he was asked to resume his seat.[5]

[1] May, p. 447.
[2] May, p. 445.
[3] H.C.D. 1944, vol. 400, c. 222; Con.A.L.D. 4 Dec. 1947, p. 1252.
[4] Con. A.L.D. 1947, vol. ii, c. 1252.
[5] L.S.D. 1955, vol. iii, c. 4031.

WRITTEN STATEMENT

Members not actually taking part in debate were allowed in the Lok Sabha to submit written statements containing their arguments and views afterwards, and the written statements were included in the proceedings as speeches made by the members.[1] This was done in special circumstances and should not be taken as a general rule but as an exception. A suggestion to incorporate written speeches in the Proceedings of the House was made before the Select Committee on Procedure 1959 where the Committee rejected the suggestion on the ground that the House would have no control through the Chair over the relevance or orderliness of the contents of the speeches.

SPEECH ALLOWED ONCE ONLY AND RIGHT OF REPLY

A member cannot speak twice on the same motion. The mover of a motion has, however, subject to certain exceptions, a right of reply, the exception being that the mover of an amendment to a bill or a resolution has no right of reply. The reply of the mover of a motion usually closes the debate on the particular motion. In the case of Ministers to whose department a motion relates, exceptions are made by the rules of the legislatures to the rule against speaking twice and also to the rule regarding the closure of debate. Such a Minister is allowed with the permission of the Speaker to speak after the reply of the mover, and he can do so even if he has already spoken once on the motion. The Speakers in India may allow a member to speak more than once, and may allow a right of reply to a mover of an amendment to a bill or a resolution, by way of exception to the general rule mentioned above.

PERSONAL EXPLANATIONS

When during a debate it appears that a member's speech has been misunderstood by another member or any comment is made against the character or conduct of a member, he is

[1] L.S.D. 1955, vol. x, c. 3144; cc. 4076, 4480.

allowed to offer an explanation even though he has spoken on the motion.[1] The time for giving an explanation is at the end of the speech of the member speaking at the time. But it is usual for the member offering an explanation to rise as soon as the statement requiring an explanation is made, and if the member in possession of the House gives way, he can explain himself then and there. But if the member speaking does not give way, the explanation can be given at the end of his speech.[2]

In giving the explanation a member must confine himself only to the relevant matter. He is not allowed to make another speech to elaborate his arguments or to make a reply to the arguments made by another member.[3] More latitude is, however, allowed when any imputation against the conduct or character of a member is made. If any statement is made regarding a member in his absence, he is allowed to offer a personal explanation even after the lapse of several days.[4] In the Indian legislatures a personal explanation may be given with the permission of the Speaker even though there is no question and therefore no debate before the House. But in such a case no debatable matter may be brought forward and no debate arises.

The Speaker has allowed in many cases a statement to be made by a member himself, but has not allowed any letter or comment of the gentlemen to be read by the member. A member must speak himself and give his own statement about the reference. References to past debates have also been taken exception to by the Speaker, but he has allowed reference in spite of the fact that the reference to a past debate would be irregular. In one case (see next page, footnote 2), it will be found that the Speaker has himself made a personal statement. There is no rigidity in the practice and it depends on how cleverly a matter is put in the House by the member.

Personal explanations are allowed on behalf of persons who are not members, whose conduct has been reflected on in

[1] Campion, 2nd ed., p. 193.
[2] L.A.D. 14 Sept. 1928, p. 777; ibid. 5 Apr. 1934, p. 3275; H.P.D. 22 May 1952, c. 354.
[3] Parl. Deb. 1862, vol. 165, c. 1032; ibid. 1862, vol. 167, c. 1216; ibid. 1864, vol. 175, c. 462; ibid. 1878, vol. 242, c. 1709.
[4] H.C.D. 1951-2, vol. 504, c. 1866; W.B.L.A.P. 1949, vol. v, no. 2, p. 107.

debate,[1] though permission to make an explanation of this nature has sometimes been refused by the Speaker.[2]

RIGHT OF MINISTERS TO TAKE PART IN DEBATES

A Minister who is a member of one House, has a right to attend, speak in, or *otherwise take part in the proceedings of* the other House.[3] Thus he has a right not only to address the House but also to move motions, etc. He has, however, no right to vote except in the House of which he is a member. A Minister can remain in office for a period of six months without being elected or nominated a member of the legislature. Such a Minister has also the right to address the legislature (both Houses where there are two Houses) and otherwise to take part (except voting) in its proceedings.

STATEMENT BY MINISTERS ON RESIGNATION FROM OFFICE

A member on resigning from the Ministry may, with the consent of the Presiding Officer, make a personal statement in explanation of his resignation. A Minister in office at the time such statement is made is entitled to make a statement pertinent to the matter in reply. No discussion is, however, permissible on such statements.[4] A Parliamentary Secretary has also been allowed to make a statement on resignation of his office.[5] In the House of Commons also, a member is allowed to make a statement on resignation of an office in the Government.[6] Whether anything occurring in Cabinet meetings can be divulged in such statements was raised in the House of Commons in 1952. Mr. Aneurin Bevan made a statement on resignation from office in which he referred to certain things which happened in a Cabinet meeting. The next day Mr. Attlee protested against this and said that there was a well-established rule inhibiting members of a Government

---

[1] *Case of Dr. Beke*—Parl. Deb. 1867-8, vol. 190, c. 422; see also *Case of Mr. Reed*, ibid. 1872, vol. 210, c. 403.

[2] See Parl. Deb. 1882, vol. 269, c. 1095; the Speaker himself has also made a personal explanation (H.C.D. 1947-8, vol. 445, c. 1205-6).

[3] Arts. 88, 177.

[4] B.L.A.P. 1943, vol. lxv, p. 37.

[5] B.L.A.P. 1944, vol. lxvii, no. 6, p. 183.

[6] May, p. 364.

from revealing what passed either in Cabinet or in confidential discussions. The following day, Mr. Bevan cited precedents[1] to show that Cabinet discussion had been referred to previously, and pointed out that if it were not so, no resigning Minister could say why he had resigned.[2]

In the Indian legislatures a copy of the proposed statement, or in the absence of a written statement the points or the gist of such statement, must be conveyed to the Speaker and the Leader of the House one day in advance of the day on which it is made. In the House of Commons the present practice is that a Minister resigning should inform the Speaker that he wishes to make a statement and should preferably furnish him with a copy although he is not obliged to do so.

QUESTION TO MEMBERS

If any member desires to ask any question of a member who is speaking, he can do so with the permission of the Presiding Officer. If the member speaking gives way, only then can such a question be put, but otherwise not.

POINT OF ORDER

If in the course of a debate any question arises as to the interpretation of any rule of debate, e.g. admissibility or relevancy, any member can submit the question for the decision of the Presiding Officer. Such a question is known as a point of order. A point of order must be raised at the earliest opportunity during the debate and not after business is over.[3] The member raising a point of order should first formulate his point and thereafter make his submission.[4] As soon as a point of order is raised the member in possession of the House at the time must give way and resume his seat. A point of order shall relate to the interpretation or enforcement of the rules of procedure or such Articles of the Constitution as regulate the business of the House, and shall raise a question which is within the cognizance of the Speaker in relation to the business

[1] H.C.D. 1931, vol. 256, c. 427.
[2] H.C.D. 1951-2, vol. 504, c. 1866.
[3] H.P.D. 1953, vol. vi, c. 447.
[4] H.P.D. 1952, vol. v, c. 329.

before the House at the moment. A point of order may be raised during the interval between the termination of one item of business and the commencement of another if it relates to maintenance of order in or arrangement of business before the House.[1] The member who raises such a point is entitled to make his submissions even though he may have spoken once during the debate, but he must confine himself to the specific point raised. The Presiding Officer may allow other members also to make their submission on the point of order raised. But no member, other than the member raising the point of order, is entitled to speak as of right. A point of order can be raised during a division if it relates to any matter concerning the division.

The decision of the Presiding Officer on a point of order is final, and no appeal is allowed to the House as is done in Canada or the United States.

Rulings of the Speaker of the British House of Commons are practically never questioned. It has been said that within living memory a ruling of the Speaker was only once questioned[2] in 1925, when a motion was put down to the effect:

'That, in view of the express provisions of Standing Order No. 26 for the protection of the rights of minorities, this House regrets the action of Mr. Speaker on the 25 May 1925, when, contrary to recent precedents, he granted the Closure at 11.45 p.m. on the first day's Debate on the Motion for the Second Reading of the Finance Bill.'

It will appear that even then there was no question of overruling the Speaker's decision.

A member may bring to the notice of the House any matter which is not a point of order by giving previous notice in writing to the Secretary stating briefly the point he wishes to raise together with reasons for wishing to raise it. If the Speaker gives his consent he can raise the point at such time and date as the Speaker may fix.

A ruling given by the Presiding Officer *pro tempo* cannot be revised by the Speaker.[3]

There cannot be any protest against a ruling on a point

[1] Lok Sabha Rules, Rule 376.
[2] H.C.D. 1925, vol. 184, c. 1591.
[3] Prov. Parl. Deb. 1951, vol. viii, c. 3196; L.S.D. 1954, vol. vii, c. 1656; ibid. vol. i, c. 729.

of order and the member must accept the decision. There cannot be a walk-out in protest against the ruling of the Chair.[1] But walk-outs in protest against the rulings of the Chair have become a common feature in Indian legislatures and the Presiding Officers do not seem to take any notice of them.

TIME LIMIT

The Presiding Officer has not the authority to impose a time limit other than in the case of a Finance Bill.[2] The limit of fifteen minutes for a speech applies only to non-official resolutions and resolutions for the removal of the Presiding Officer. In the case of adjournment motions the Speaker is under a duty to fix a time limit for a speech; but the length of time is not mentioned in the rules. The Speaker may fix a time limit in the case of discussion on matters of public importance of short duration and no-day-yet-named motions. There is no other time limit.

The only occasions when a time limit is placed on the speech of a member in the House of Commons are in regard to motions for leave to bring in bills and for the nomination of select committees at the commencement of public business and upon committal of bills[3]—Standing Orders Nos. 12 and 50. It should be noted, however, that these time limits are not hard and fast. The phrase used in the Standing Orders is 'brief explanatory statement', and ten minutes is in practice accepted as a resonable time limit.

CONTENTS OF SPEECHES: RELEVANCY

The speech of a member must have reference to the subject-matter under discussion. When a member wanders away from the subject, the Presiding Officer often calls him to order; members, however, often exercise considerable ingenuity in making their observations relevant, although on the face of them they might appear irrelevant.[4] It therefore devolves upon

---

[1] H.P.D. 1952, vol. ii, c. 2032; ibid. 1953, vol. vii, c. 1366; ibid. 1953, vol. ii, c. 1588.
[2] I.P.D. 21 Sept. 1951, c. 2994.
[3] *Table*, vol. 1 (1932), p. 67.
[4] B.L.A.P. 1944, vol. lxviii, p. 160.

the Presiding Officer to determine when a member is going to be irrelevant and to restrain him from being so.[1] If a member persists in irrelevance, he may be asked by the Chair to resume his seat.[2]

REFERENCE TO PRIOR DEBATES

Reference to prior debates on matters other than the matter then before the House is not ordinarily allowed.[3] Reference may, however, be made if a member wants to give any personal explanation or to complain of anything said in the course of the debate. Reference can also be made to prior speeches in order to show that the member is saying something different from what he said previously.[4] In that case only such portion of a prior speech as is relevant can be referred to. Disucssion in a Select Committee cannot be referred to in the House in any event.[5]

REFERENCE TO DEBATES IN THE OTHER HOUSE

It is one of the rules of debate in the British Parliament that no reference can be made in one House to debates held or speeches made in the other during the current session. The rule had its origin in the fact that previously the Houses did not allow their debates to be published, and therefore one was not supposed to know what was happening in the other House. Nowadays the debates are published daily, and the fiction of the prohibition of publication is invoked only in cases of breaches of privilege. Yet, the rule that no reference to any debate in one House may be made in the other is still followed, although not very strictly, for the reason that it prevents the two Houses from coming into conflict with each other and avoids mutual recrimination between the members of the two Houses in the absence of one or the other party.[6]

[1] H.P.D. 1952, vol. i, c. 678; ibid. vol. ii, c. 2529; ibid. vol. iii, c. 4121; ibid. 1955, vol. ix, c. 56; ibid. 1956, vol. viii, c. 6097; ibid. 1956, vol. x, c. 3576.
[2] L.S.D. 1955, vol. v, c. 9476; ibid. 1956, vol. viii, c. 6440.
[3] Parl. Deb. 1876, vol. 231, c. 749; ibid. 1878, vol. 238, c. 1403; H.C.D. 1933, vol. 283, c. 1258; ibid. 1942-3, vol. 385, c. 1319
[4] H.P.D. 1953, vol. i. c. 1470; ibid. vol. iii, c. 3561.
[5] H.P.D. 1952, vol. iv, c. 5022; ibid. vol. vi, c. 2017.
[6] Parl. Deb. 1893, vol. 15, c. 1781; see also L.A.D. 27 Feb. 1922, p. 2581.

Nowadays, however, Ministerial statements are often made in one of the Houses, and the members of the other House are allowed to refer to or criticize such statements.[1]

The above principle of the House of Commons has been embodied in the rules of Indian legislatures, which provide that no speech made in one House shall be quoted in the other unless it is a definite statement of policy by a Minister, except that the Presiding Officer may, on a request being made to him in advance, give permission to a member to quote a speech or make reference to the proceedings in the other House if the Presiding Officer thinks that such a course is necessary in order to enable the member to develop a point of privilege or procedure.

The principle enunciated above applies to debates in the House whether in respect of a motion or of a bill.[2] But it does not apply to the votes and proceedings of either House or to any reports of committees of either House.[3]

READING EXTRACTS FROM NEWSPAPERS OR BOOKS

There appears to be some misapprehension about the rule relating to the reading of extracts from newspapers or books in the course of a speech by a member. Sometimes objections are taken to the reading of extracts from newspapers, sometimes the member is asked to take responsibility for the facts stated, sometimes he is asked to lay the relevant paper before the House.

The rule so far as it is applied in the British House of Commons may be considered in two aspects, (i) reading of extracts from newspapers, pamphlets, etc., i.e. printed papers, and (ii) reading of extracts from other documents in the possession of the speaker.

The first can again be divided into two categories, (a) reading of speeches or proceedings of the House reported in the newspapers, and (b) reading of extracts relating to other matters.

---

[1] H.C.D. 1934-5, vol. 304, c. 1579; ibid. 1942-3, vol. 390. c. 373; H.P.D. 1953, vol. ii, c. 1674; ibid. 1953, vol. ii, c. 1855; ibid. 1954, vol. iii, c. 4393; ibid. 1954, vol. vii, c. 2870; ibid. 1956, vol. vii, c. 3591.

[2] H.C.D. 1876, vol. 228, c. 1183.

[3] May, p. 455.

READING OF SPEECHES OR PROCEEDINGS IN THE HOUSE FROM NEWSPAPERS

Reading of extracts from speeches made in the House, or referring to the proceedings of the House, as reported in newspapers, is not allowed. As Sir Robert Peel put it:

'It was irregular to refer to a report of a speech appearing in a newspaper, and purporting to have been delivered in the House; for of course hon'ble Members could not be held responsible for anything which they had not themselves formally authorized. Reports appearing in newspapers of speeches made in that House were undoubtedly matters which could not be referred to as authority.'[1]

OTHER MATTERS

But reference to other matters published in newspapers is not absolutely banned. In the course of the same speech Sir Robert Peel observed:

'Members, on account of the indecorum and the inconvenience that would result from such practice, should not be at liberty to read newspapers in the House which had no reference to the matter under consideration; but he doubted whether it would not be drawing the rule too tight to say that a member was not at liberty to read an extract from a newspaper as part of his speech. Suppose a public meeting had occurred, the resolutions of which were thought to be of sufficient importance to deserve the attention of the House, and that an hon'ble Member found reading from a newspaper to be the most convenient mode of putting the House in possession of those resolutions, were they to say that such a proceeding would be out of order? Could they establish a rule prohibiting such a reference?'

The discussion arose when a member of the House of Commons wanted to read an extract from the editorial remarks in a newspaper and the Speaker wanted to rule him out of order. Ultimately the member was allowed to read the extract.

The present practice was indicated by Lord John Russell when he said:

[1] Parl. Deb. 1840, vol. 52, c. 1064.

11

'If, however, an hon'ble Member made an extract, whether printed or written, whether from a newspaper or from a book, a part of his speech, be the strict rule what it might, the practice had of late been to leave such a matter to his own discretion.'[1]

Of course the extract must be relevant to the subject matter under discussion and must not be an extensive quotation.[2]

CITING DOCUMENTS

As regards citing documents, the rule observed in the case of Ministers is a little different from that observed in the case of private members. A Minister cannot quote from a despatch or other State paper unless a copy of such despatch or paper is laid before the House. This rule, however, applies only in the case of public documents, i.e. documents of the Government, and not private papers.[3] Even in the case of public documents, if the Minister declares that any document is of a confidential nature and cannot be disclosed without injury to public interests, the production of such a document cannot be insisted upon.[4] If a Minister summarizes the contents of a document without actually quoting from it, he is not bound to produce the document.[5] The following illustrations would make the position clear. In the course of a discussion on the cancellation of a proposed talk at the B.B.C., quotations were made from the script of the talk. On objection being taken that the document should be laid before the House it was ruled that the document was not an official document and quotations could be made without producing the document.[6] A Minister was allowed to summarize the proposals of an Enquiry Committee appointed by the Government, although the report of the Committee had not yet been presented to the House.[7]

The following observations of the Speaker of the House of Commons will be of interest:

'The general rule of the House is well understood, that if a

[1] Parl. Deb. 1840, vol. 52, c. 1064.
[2] L.A.D. 6 Sept. 1927, p. 4021; H.P.D. 1952, vol. iii, c. 3521.
[3] H.C.D. 1941-2, vol. 376, c. 2194.
[4] Parl. Deb. 1893, vol. 15, c. 1778.
[5] H.C.D. 1944-5, vol. 407, c. 1797.
[6] H.C.D. 1941-2, vol. 376, c. 2194.
[7] H.C.D. 1944-5, vol. 407, c. 1797.

Minister refers to public documents or Despatches he should lay them before the House; but confidential documents or documents of a private nature passing between officers of a Department and the Department, are not necessarily laid on the table of the House, especially if the Minister declares that they are of a confidential nature. It would be a precedent dangerous to the Public Service to say that they ought to be laid.[1]

Opinions given by law officers of the Government are deemed to be confidential, and their production cannot be insisted upon in the House of Commons. A Minister, however, can cite such opinions, if he thinks that the House should be informed.[2] But in the Indian legislatures, if in answer to a question or during debate a Minister discloses the advice or opinion given to him by any officer of the Government or by any other person or authority, he is required ordinarily to lay the relevant document or parts of the document containing that opinion or advice, or a summary thereof on the table.

A private member is in a somewhat privileged position in that he can cite from documents, whether public or private, in his possession without producing them before the House, and he cannot even be asked to disclose the source of the information. In the Indian Parliament a member cited passages from a correspondence between two highly placed Government officials. On objection being taken it was ruled that he could do so and that it was not open to the Government to ask how he had obtained them.[3]

In Indian legislatures, if a Minister quotes in the House a despatch or other State paper which has not been presented to the House, he shall lay the relevant paper on the table, but this rule does not apply to any documents which are stated by the Minister to be of such a nature that their production would be inconsistent with the public interest. It is also not necessary to lay the relevant papers on the table if a Minister gives in his own words a summary or gist of such despatch or State paper; whether a document is a privileged one which need not be laid on the table is for the Chair to decide. When a Minister contended that a report made to

[1] H.C.D. 1893, vol. 15, c. 1778.
[2] Parl. Deb. 1865, vol. 173, c. 354.
[3] Ruling of Deputy Speaker Ayyangar, 3 Mar. 1952; L.S.D. 20 Feb. 1958, cc. 1746-56; ibid. 3 April 1963; ibid. 6 May 1943; H.C.D. 28 Feb. 1945.

the President under Article 338 of the Constitution was privileged it was ruled that the report must be laid on the table.[1]

A document or any other paper intended to be laid on the table cannot be laid without its prior examination by the Chair.

A paper or document to be laid on the table must be authenticated by the member laying the same. All papers and documents laid on the table of the House are considered public.

If, in the course of his speech, a member wishes to lay a paper or document on the table without previously supplying a copy thereof to the Chair, he may hand it over at the table, but it will not be deemed to have been laid on the table unless the Chair, after examination, accords the necessary permission. If the Chair does not accord the necessary permission the paper or document shall be returned to the member and the fact indicated in the printed debate.[2]

Recently, on 26 February 1965, the Speaker of the Lok Sabha summarized the position thus:

   (i) A member can ordinarily quote from a document that is treated by Government as secret or confidential, and which Government have not disclosed in Public interest.

  (ii) Government are not obliged to lay such a document on the table of the House, and the Chair cannot compel them to do so, if they continue to hold the view that it is not in the public interest to do so.

 (iii) It is for the Government to consider whether a document, copies of which have been circulated among members or which have appeared in the press wholly or partially, shall still be treated as secret or confidential, and not laid on the table.

 (iv) While the Government cannot be compelled to admit or deny the correctness of any alleged copy of a document, which is classified as secret or confidential, it is necessary for the member who quotes from such a document, to certify that he has verified from his

---

[1] L.S.D. 1957, vol. x, c. 6248.
[2] *Directions by the Speaker*, Lok Sabha, 2nd. ed. Dir. No. 118.

personal knowledge that the document is the true copy of the original with the Government, and the member will do so on his own responsibility, and the Chair will permit him to proceed. In case the member is not prepared to give a certificate in these terms and he insists on quoting from such a document, the Chair may find out from the Government about the authenticity of such a document and the facts placed by the Government before the Chair will be final in determining whether such a document is genuine or not. Where Government decline to admit or deny the correctness of any alleged copy, the Chair will allow the member to proceed and it will be for the Government to give such answers as they think fit and the House possesses ample power to deal with the matter under the Constitution and the Rules.

(v) Normally a member is not expected to spring a surprise on the Speaker, the House and the Government by quoting from a document which is not public. In fairness to all, and in accordance with parliamentary conventions, the member should inform the Chair and the Government in advance so that they are in a position to deal with the matter on the floor of the House when it is raised. If this requirement is not complied with, the Chair may stop the member from quoting from such a document and may ask the member to make available to the Chair a copy before the Chair allows the member to proceed with any quotation therefrom.

(vi) It is a fact that a document, which is treated by the Government as secret or confidential, can be obtained through leakage or stealth or in an irregular manner, but the Chair would not compel the member to disclose the source from which copies have been obtained by the member.

(vii) The member has a right to quote from such a document subject to the conditions specified above. But there is an over-riding authority with the Speaker and under his inherent powers he can stop a member from quoting from a document in the national interest where security of the country is involved. Such cases shall be rare, but such a power exists in the Speaker and he can exercise it without assigning any reason.

CITING DOCUMENTS AND OFFICIAL SECRETS

Disclosures by members in the course of debates or proceedings in Parliament cannot be made the subject of proceedings under the Official Secrets Act. A disclosure made by a member to a Minister or by one member to another directly relating to some act to be done or to some proceeding in the House, even though it did not take place in the House itself, may be held to be part of the business of the House and consequently to be similarly protected. A casual conversation in the House, however, cannot be said to be a proceeding in Parliament, and a member who discloses information in the course of such a conversation would not be protected by privilege.

The above principles were laid down by a Select Committee of the House of Commons[1] on a question of privilege being raised by Mr. Sandys when he was asked to disclose the source of his information about certain confidential matters of which it appeared, from the draft of a question to be put by him in Parliament, that he had knowledge.

BRINGING IN EXHIBITS

Members are not allowed to bring in material exhibits to illustrate their arguments.[2] This rule seems, however, to be relaxed to a certain extent nowadays. In a recent ruling, the Speaker of the House of Commons observed:

'If it is really necessary for an honourable Member to produce an exhibit to illustrate his argument, I see no reason why I should prohibit it in advance. I hope, however, that honourable Members will respect the spirit of our usages which is that our Chamber should not be encumbered with matter from outside that is not relevant to the discussion.'[3]

[1] H.C. *Paper* 101 of 1939.
[2] L.A.D. 15 Feb. 1934, p. 850; H.P.D. 26 Nov. 1952, c. 1262.
[3] H.C.D. 5th series, vol. 498, c. 2751.

In Indian legislatures members often bring material exhibits in order to support their arguments.

SINGING OF SONGS

The singing of songs as a part of a member's speech is not permissible.[1] It appears, however, that in the Lok Sabha a member did in fact sing a song.[2]

REFLECTIONS

It has already been observed that utterances within the House of a legislature are absolutely privileged; but that does not mean that members have a licence to say whatever they please in the House. The legislatures are guided by their own rules of conduct, and although no action can be taken outside the House, the House of a legislature has always the power to enforce these rules, which are meant to check the abuse of the privilege of freedom of speech which members enjoy. Some of these rules observed in India are embodied in the Constitution, some in the rules of procedure and some in the practice and conventions followed which are similar to those followed in the British Parliament.

Reflections are unparliamentary conduct, and in a serious case may be visited with punishment for contempt of the House; and such punishment may range from admonition to expulsion from the House.[3]

REFLECTION UPON THE LEGISLATURE OR ANY OF ITS HOUSES

Reflections, that is to say, derogatory references to or criticisms of the legislature itself or any of its Houses are not permitted.[4] It is quite obvious that the legislature which makes laws for the people should not be brought into contempt by any utterance of its own members; it is also necessary that the two Houses, where they exist, should not be brought

---

[1] Bom. L.A.P. 1946, vol. 9, p. 1219; ibid. 1950, vol. xvi, p. 1443; Bih. L.A.D. 1951, vol. iii, p. 8.
[2] H.P.D. 24 Aug. 1953, vol. vii, 1953, cc. 1410-11.
[3] See cases cited in May, p. 124, *et seq.*
[4] Bom. L.A.D. 1953, vol. 24, p. 60.

into conflict by any derogatory references to the one in the other.

REFLECTION UPON STATUTES

Reference to a statute in derogatory or abusive terms e.g. Black Act,[1] is not allowed for that would bring the law into disrespect. Although an Act or a bill may be condemned during the debate on the repeal or the enactment thereof, abusive terms should not be used.

REFLECTION UPON MEMBERS

Reflections upon the conduct of members or use of abusive or derogatory epithets in regard to them are not allowed. Imputation of improper motives,[2] charges of uttering lies,[3] abusive or insulting language in reference to members, e.g. villain, hooligan, Churchill's jackals, are such reflections. (See Unparliamentary Expressions, p. 195). If the Speaker himself is guilty of making any reflection or of other unparliamentary conduct, the House can take action against him. In 1770 such a case happened when a motion that 'the words spoken by Mr. Speaker, from the Chair, are disorderly, importing an improper reflection on a member of this House, and dangerous to the freedom of debate in this House' was moved. The motion was however negatived.[4]

REFLECTIONS UPON JUDGES, PRESIDING OFFICERS ETC.

The Indian Constitution provides that there can be no discussion in any State legislature on the conduct of Judges of the Supreme Court or the High Courts in the discharge of their duties.[5] In the Indian Parliament no such discussion can take place except on a motion for the removal of a Judge. Judges of International Tribunals, e.g. the judges at the

---

[1] W.B.L.A.P. 1951, vol. iii, no. 3, p. 278, 11 Apr. 1951.
[2] See cases cited in May, p. 459.
[3] Ibid.
[4] Hansard, *Parl. History*, vol. xvi, c. 810-13.
[5] Arts. 121, 211; L.A.D. 26 Jan. 1926, p. 279; H.P.D. 1952, vol. iv, c. 4908; bid. 1955, vol. x, c. 2691.

Nuremburg Trials,[1] have been held to come within this rule.

No reflection is permitted against the President, the Governor, or any person whose conduct can be criticized only on a substantive motion. Under the foregoing rule no reflection is allowed to be made on the Presiding Officers of the legislatures.

No reflection can be made against a Sovereign or Ruler or the Government of a friendly State.

The rules of the Indian Parliament and some legislatures provide that a member cannot reflect upon the conduct of persons in high authority unless the discussion is based on a substantive motion drawn in proper terms. 'Persons in high authority' has been explained to mean persons whose conduct can or should, in the opinion of the Chair, only be discussed on a substantive motion drawn in proper terms. It is not understood what kind of persons are contemplated by the latter part of the definition as being persons in high authority.

MATTERS SUB-JUDICE

Debates or comments upon a matter which is *sub judice*, that is pending before a court of law, are not allowed in the House[2] on the same principles by which comments on pending proceedings are treated as contempt of court; the principle is that such comments may, or may tend to, prejudice the fair trial of the matter. As Lord Hardwicke put it, 'There cannot be anything of greater consequence than to keep the streams of justice clear and pure, that parties may proceed with safety both to themselves and to their character.' So far as parliamentary practice in regard to criticism of pending proceedings is concerned the following observations of Mr. Speaker Peel will be of interest:

'I am not aware that there has been any definite and distinct expression of opinion on the part of the House that pending trials should not be alluded to. Nor am I aware of any distinct and definite ruling from the Chair, though I

---

[1] H.C.D. 1947-8, vol. 445, c. 26.
[2] H.P.D. 1952, vol. i, c. 1064; ibid. 1952, vol. iii, c. 4215; ibid. 1953, vol. ii, c. 2150; ibid. 1954, vol. iii, c. 3309.

am aware of frequent expressions of opinions both from Ministers in this House and other Members with regard to the impropriety of alluding to pending trials in such a way as to prejudice a fair trial of the case. With these remarks I shall leave the subject in the hands of the House.'[1]

Because no contempt proceedings can be drawn up if comments are made in the House in regard to any matter pending before a court by reason of the privilege of freedom of expression, the House itself prohibits any such comments, for it is of paramount importance that 'the stream of justice must be kept clear and pure.' It seems, therefore, clear that only those comments which may amount to a contempt of court will not be allowed to be made in the House. A matter becomes *sub judice* as soon as a person is brought before a court, whether an actual trial is taking place or not.[2] A matter is *sub judice* when a writ petition is pending before the High Court.[3] However, a matter decided by a court but open to appeal is not *sub judice* unless an appeal has actually been filed.[4]

It is of the essence of contempt of court that the proceedings must be pending before a 'court'. What constitutes a court is a difficult question which has come up for decision in very many cases, but no positive test has been laid down for the determination whether a particular authority or tribunal is a court or not. It has however been said that if any authority has to act judicially in the sense that it has to act with fairness and impartiality, it is not necessarily a court.[5] Several such negative propositions have also been laid down in *Shell Co.* v. *Federal Commr.*[6] It is said:

'A tribunal is not necessarily a Court in the strict sense because (1) it gives a final decision; (2) nor because it hears witnesses on oath; (3) nor because two or more contending parties appear before it between whom it has to decide; (4) nor because it gives decisions which affect the rights of subjects; (5) nor because there is an appeal to a Court; (6)

---

[1] Parl. Deb. 1889, vol. 335, c. 1255.
[2] 51 C.W.N. 400.
[3] L.S.D. 1954, vol. iii, c. 4094.
[4] B.L.A.P. 1943, vol. lxvi, no. 1, p. 38; H.C.D. 1945-6, vol. 420, c. 303.
[5] 1842 Q.B. 431.
[6] 1931 A.C. 275.

nor because it is a body to which a matter is referred to by another body.'

In a Full Bench case of the Calcutta High Court[1] (*Khetsi Das* v. *Land Acquisition Collector*) it has been held that it is one of the fundamental characteristics of a court that its proceedings shall be public and the parties shall be heard, and that the authority in question must act in accordance with the established forms of judicial procedure. It was held in that case that the Land Acquisition Collector when acting under the Land Acquisition Act is not a court although he is required to act judicially, that is to say, with fairness and impartiality.

As regards Government departments such as the Sales Tax Department, the Income Tax Department or the Income Tax Commission, none of them will be considered to be a court judged by the above-mentioned tests, even though in making assessments they have to act with fairness and impartiality. They exercise administrative functions and not judicial functions. Labour Tribunals suffer from a further infirmity in that their awards have, of themselves, no binding force unless given effect to by the State government—thus lacking one of the fundamental attributes of a court of law.[2]

The purpose of the above discussion is to show that if a person criticizes or comments on any proceedings pending before any of the authorities mentioned above he cannot be proceeded against for contempt of court. If criticism or comment by the public cannot be prevented in such cases, there is no reason why discussion of such matters within the House should be prohibited.

In these days various Government departments are being entrusted with quasi-judicial work under statutory rules and administrative law. They lack those safeguards against arbitrary action which attach to courts of law such as public hearing, laws of evidence, right of audience and representation by lawyers. There is all the more reason, therefore, that their action should be open to criticism or scrutiny at least in the legislature.

[1] 50 C.W.N. 758.
[2] In West Bengal the Board of Revenue has been given the status of a High Court for the purpose of taking proceedings for contempt against itself by an Act, 'Bengal Board of Revenue (Amdt.) Act, 1953'.

CRITICISM OF STRANGERS

That there is absolute freedom of speech in the House of a legislature does not admit of any doubt; a member may say anything in the course of a debate, however offensive to the feeling or injurious to the reputation or character of particular individuals whether Government officials or members of the public, it may be, without being liable in law for libel or any other action. The debates of every legislature including the House of Commons abound in instances where attacks have been made on individuals. Indeed, the claim and the existence of the privilege of freedom of speech itself imply that such attacks can be made without fear of being liable to account for them. But the existence of the privilege which protects a member from being answerable outside the House does not, as Anson says, 'involve any unrestrained license of speech within the walls of the House'; and May[1] also has pointed out that cases in which members have been called to account and punished for offensive words spoken before the House are too numerous to mention. Some have been admonished, others imprisoned and some have even been expelled.

That there must be some restraint on attacks made within the House follows as a corollary of freedom of speech, not because the persons attacked are not before the House[2] to contradict the same but because no action can be taken outside the House for any statement made within. A member ought not to take advantage of his position as a member to make unfounded attacks upon persons outside, and it must be ensured that frivolous or scurrilous attacks are not made against persons under the cover of privilege.

But how such restraint is in practice to be applied is the question. It seems clear that no hard and fast rule can be laid down. It seems also clear that attacks cannot be prevented by shutting out references to outsiders. In the case of Government officials it has been the practice not to refer to the officials by name but by their official designation only. But this rule will not work in the case of members of the

---

[1] May, p. 53.
[2] H.P.D. 1952, vol. i, c. 1047; ibid. 1953, vol. ii, c. 2689; ibid. 1954, vol. v, cc. 65-97; ibid. 1955, vol. ix, c. 193; ibid. 1956, vol. vi, c. 1125.

public. For, unless names are mentioned, no specific allegations can be made. It appears, therefore, that if a member chooses deliberately to attack any particular individual by name, he must be allowed to do so, whatever consequences may follow afterwards. Indeed, it is much better that a member should make himself responsible for any charges that he may make and face the consequences and not indulge in irresponsible insinuations or innuendoes against unnamed individuals. If he acts *bona fide* he will not be liable to any action, even though the allegations may be unfounded, but if he acts *mala fide* or indulges in scurrilous attacks, the House has always the power to punish him. If this principle is followed, there may be occasional injustice to individuals, but as pointed out in *Wason* v. *Walter*, 'the nation profits by public opinion being thus freely brought to bear on the discharge of public duties.'[1]

REFERENCE TO PARTY MEETINGS

No reference can be made to what happens in a party meeting.[2]

MEMBER TO BE PRESENT TO HEAR REPLY

It is a rule of courtesy for a member making charges against the Government or any other member to be present to hear the reply.[3]

CLOSURE

When a motion is under discussion, any member, in order to put a stop to the debate, may move that the question be now put. Such a motion is known as a closure motion. It is within the discretion of the Presiding Officer to accept such a motion.[4] If he thinks that the motion has been sufficiently debated and the right of the minority to have a fair part in the dis-

[1] 4 Q.B. 94.
[2] I.P.D. 30 March. 1950, p. 2322.
[3] L.A.D. 5 Mar. 1929, p. 1543; H.P.D. 1952, vol. iv, c. 5463; ibid. 1953, vol. i, c. 305.
[4] H.P.D. 1952, vol. iii, c. 3361; ibid. 1952, vol. v, c. 1268; ibid. 1952, vol. vi, c. 1886.

cussion of the motion would not be infringed thereby, he may put the question that the question be now put to the vote of the House. There can be no discussion on a closure motion. If the question of closure is agreed to by a majority, the motion which was being discussed when the closure motion was moved must be put without further discussionf The Presiding Officer has a discretion under the rules o. Indian legislatures to allow the mover of a motion to reply to the debate. In the British House of Commons it is necessary for the passing of a closure motion that at least one hundred members must have voted for the closure (Standing Order 30). The closure has the effect of curtailing the debate and putting a stop to obstructive tactics by the Opposition. A closure motion cannot be put, although moved, in the middle of a speech.[1] There can be no discussion when a closure motion has been accepted by the Chair.

It will be seen that this type of closure motion can be effective only when a substantive motion is under discussion before the House. If there are a number of amendments to a substantive motion a closure will affect only the amendment which is before the House at the moment. In legislatures, when a substantive motion and all the amendments thereto are allowed to be moved and a debate follows, a closure motion will lead to confusion unless it is presumed that the amendment affecting the lattermost part of the motion is to be put. This is also one of the reasons why such a practice should not be allowed (see p. 114). In the House of Commons there is a form of closure known as the Contingent Closure. When a closure motion has been carried and the motion immediately before the House has been put and decided, any member may claim that a further question be put to decide the issue before the House. If such a claim is made the Speaker may put a further question forthwith without a closure motion being moved and carried. The rules of procedure of the Indian legislatures do not seem to contemplate any such power. Of course some of the rules, such as Rule 362 of the Lok Sabha, provide that if a closure motion is carried the Presiding Officer shall put the question *or questions* consequent thereon forthwith. This can be interpreted to mean that all

[1] H.P.D. 1952, vol. vi, c. 1885.

the amendments and the main motion shall be put forthwith without further debate if a closure motion is accepted at any stage during the debate.

In the House of Commons the application of the closure is not usually opposed when claimed at the end of a day's debate just before 10 P.M. At the Report and Committee stages of bills, however, the use of the closure could arouse strong controversy. Finance Bills were usually subjected to a lengthy Committee stage, during which the closure was normally invoked a number of times. An interesting example of the use of the closure arousing strong feelings in the House occurred in February 1963, when a Ways and Means Resolution connected with an increase in charges under the National Health Service Act was fiercely opposed by the Opposition, and the Government claimed a closure which the Chair granted. It is, in short, recognized as a necessary instrument, but one which occasionally stirs up strong party feeling.

SELECTION OF AMENDMENTS

There is another device for curtailing debate—selection of amendments. When there are a large number of amendments the Speaker, the Chairman or the Deputy Chairman in the British House of Commons is given the authority to select new clauses and amendments and to call those new clauses and amendments only. Such a power has been given to the Presiding Officers of Indian legislatures who can call upon members to give such explanation of the object of the amendment as may enable them to form a judgment upon it.

ALLOCATION OF TIME

There is yet another device for the purpose of curtailing debate and finishing business within a fixed time, which is known as the Allocation of Time Order. A fixed period of time is allocated for the consideration and passing of the different stages of a bill, e.g. consideration motion, clauses, third reading and so on, and other Government business. As soon as the time limit is reached, all questions necessary for the decision of the House are put forthwith without further debate. Such allocation of time is made by a motion carried in the House. In Indian legislatures such a motion is made on the recommendation of a committee known as the Business Advisory Committee (see p. 75). Such a motion can be made sometimes with agreement between the parties in the British Parliament.

When a debate becomes unduly protracted the Speakers in India can, of their own motion without any reference to the Business Advisory Committee and after taking a sense of the House, fix a time limit for the conclusion of discussion at any stage or at all stages of a motion or bill and put the question forthwith at the appointed hour.

PUTTING OF QUESTIONS

When the debate on a motion is finished the Presiding Officer puts the question to the vote of the House. The question is put in the form, 'The question before the House is that.... (then follows the text of the motion). Those who are in favour of the motion please say "Aye".' At this moment those in favour of the motion cry 'Aye'; then the Presiding Officer says, 'those who are against please say "No".' Then the dissentients cry 'No'. The Presiding Officer estimates by the volume of the response which group is in the majority and makes a preliminary announcement, 'I think the Ayes (or Noes, as the case may be) have it.' He pauses for a while and, if there is no challenge, he declares, 'The Ayes (or Noes as the case may be) have it.'

The estimate of the Presiding Officer can be challenged at the time of the preliminary announcement either by saying 'Division' or crying the contrary—if the Presiding Officer says, 'The Ayes have it', this can be challenged by crying 'No' or *vice versa*. The proper time for challenging the opinion of the Presiding Officer is just after the preliminary announcement is made; if the Presiding Officer proceeds to give his final verdict without a challenge his verdict stands.

If the estimate of the Presiding Officer is challenged the voting is recorded by the process known as Division. There are two lobbies adjacent to and on the two sides of the

Chamber—one is known as the Ayes lobby, the other as the Noes lobby. In some legislatures, the lobbies are not fixed as Ayes and Noes lobbies. Each lobby can be made the Ayes or the Noes lobby as circumstances require. For example, if the voting is on a motion sponsored by the Opposition, the lobby adjacent to the left portion of the Chamber where the opposition usually sits is made the 'Ayes' lobby and *vice versa* for Government motions. On a division being called a bell is rung for a fixed period, usually three minutes, in order to enable all the members who have been outside to assemble in the Chamber. After the expiry of the period the doors of the Chamber are closed and no one is permitted to enter the Chamber. The Presiding Officer again puts the question in the same manner as before, and if a division is again claimed on the preliminary announcement he directs the House to divide and asks the members to proceed to the respective lobbies, 'Ayes' and 'Noes', as they desire to vote. As the members pass the doors and proceed to the lobby the tellers take down the names of the members (usually ticks against the names in a printed list). When all the members have passed the doors, the doors are again closed and after a little time reopened. In the meantime the tellers have calculated the number of votes recorded and the result is announced by the Presiding Officer—Ayes so many, Noes so many. The Ayes or Noes, as the case may be, have it.

On 24 April, 1964 there was a division on a motion in the House of Commons, and the Speaker, on the statement of the Tellers, announced that the Ayes had it and the voting was shown as 76 for the Ayes and 68 for the Noes. The next day the Tellers came to the table and declared that a mistake had been made by them in reporting the votes and the correct voting was 68 for the Ayes and 76 for the Noes. The Speaker said, 'an appropriate correction will be made in the journal recording the numbers in the Division as being Ayes 68, Noes 76 with the result that on that occasion the Noes had it'. The Speaker then ruled that the subsequent proceedings were null and void and the bill was not in possession of the House, i.e. it had no existence.

Infirm members are usually allowed to record their votes without leaving the Chamber. As stated above, no one is

12

permitted to enter the Chamber after the doors are closed on the bell ceasing to ring. There have been occasions when members in their enthusiasm to record their votes have entered the Chamber forcibly after the doors have been closed. In such instances the votes of the offending members have been cancelled.[1]

If the Chair thinks that a division is unnecessarily claimed he can ask the members who are for the Ayes and those for the Noes respectively to rise in their places, and on a count being taken he may declare the determination of the House. In such a case names of voters are not recorded. It is open to the Chair to accept or not to accept the demand for a division.[2]

In certain Houses electrical voting apparatuses have been installed, and members can vote on a division without leaving the Chamber by pushing buttons fixed on their desks and recording their votes by means of lights (red for Noes, green for Ayes and yellow for neutrals) shown on the board fixed on the wall of the Chamber. A member can speak for a motion and vote against it; but he must 'vote according to voice', i.e. if after the question had been put he had said 'Aye', he must vote for the motion and *vice versa*.

PERSONAL OR PECUNIARY INTEREST

In the House of Commons it is a rule that no member who has a direct pecuniary interest in a question shall be allowed to vote on it. In theory this might be reckoned to be a topic bristling with difficulties, particularly as the House is made up of members who in most cases work for their living, who often direct companies engaged in contractual work for Government departments, and who frequently invest in Government securities. In fact the House has laid down such clear rules, members understand them only too well, and public opinion is so quick to strike down an offender that virtually no trouble arises in this potentially dangerous field. For example, it is a well-recognized convention that no member who is made a Minister may continue to hold any directorship or have any direct pecuniary interest in com-

[1] W.B.L.A.P. 1953, vol. vii, no. 2, c. 506.
[2] L.S.D. 1955, vol. v, c. 8390; ibid. 1956, vol. v, c. 8760.

panies which seek contracts from the Government, while
back-bench private members are expected to—and indeed
do—reveal their interest before speaking in the House on
any subject affecting their commercial activities. For example,
if a Minister holds shares in any industrial group his interest
might be so general and remote as not to be a matter of moment
either to him or to the House. And if a private member holds
shares in or directs a brewery, he may, provided it is a public
company, first declare his interest and then proceed to speak
and vote against a tax on beer. On 28 January 1960, a seemingly innocent question was put by a Labour Member asking
the Prime Minister 'what conditions govern the relationship
of Ministers with firms likely to obtain official contracts'. The
Leader of the House, Mr. Butler, answering as acting Prime
Minister during Mr. Macmillan's absence in Africa, said: 'The
general principle is that Ministers must so order their affairs
that no conflict arises, or appears to arise, between their private
interests and their public duties'. At this point the seemingly
innocent question was followed up by a loaded supplementary aimed at the new and alert Minister of Transport
(Mr. Marples) asking whether he was in fact the senior
partner of a firm of contractors which had obtained a
government contract worth £250,000, and whether the
Minister still held shares in the firm. At the end of Questions the Minister of Transport himself asked leave to make
a personal statement to explain his position:

'Before I became a junior Minister, in November 1951,
I was managing director of Marples, Ridgway and Partners,
and I held a controlling interest in that company. As soon
as I became a junior Minister I resigned my directorship
and ceased to take any active part in the business.

'When I became Minister of Transport, last October,
I realised that there was a risk of a conflict of interest appearing
to arise in consequence of my holding a controlling interest
in the company. I immediately took steps to effect a sale of
my shares. It has taken some time to arrange this as the company is a private one engaged in long-term contracts in
civil engineering, but I hope that it will be completed very
soon. Then I shall have no financial interest in the company.'

Disallowance of a vote on the ground of personal interest

is restricted to cases of pecuniary interest only, and has not been extended to other occasions when the dictates of self-respect and of respect due to the House might demand that a member should refrain from taking part in a division.[1]

In the Indian legislatures, if the vote of a member in a division is challenged on the ground of personal, pecuniary or direct interest in the matter to be decided, the Speaker may, if he considers it necessary, call upon the member making the challenge to state precisely the grounds of his objection and the member whose vote had been challenged to state his case, and shall decide whether the vote of the member should be disallowed or not.

The interest of the member whose vote is challenged must be direct, personal or pecuniary, and separately belong to the person whose vote is questioned and not in common with the public in general or with any class or section thereof or on a matter of state policy.[2] But voting against a reduction of a Minister's salary or in connection with members' salaries has been allowed.[3]

The same principle applies to the case of voting in Committees.[4]

In India objection can be made to the inclusion of a member in a committee on the ground of personal, pecuniary or direct interest. If any such objection is taken, the Speaker decides the matter and his decision is final.

ERRORS IN DIVISION

If a member finds that he has voted by mistake in the wrong lobby, he is allowed to correct his mistake if he brings it to the notice of the Chair before the result of the voting is announced.[5]

If there is any confusion or irregularity in the voting the Chair has the right to put the question again and direct a division *de novo*.[6]

[1] May, p. 443.
[2] Parl. Deb. 1811, vol. 20, c. 1001.
[3] Parl. Deb. 1889, vol. 334, c. 732; H.C.D. 1911, vol. 29, c. 79.
[4] H.C. *Paper* 72, of 1929-30; Standing Committee Debates 1929-30, Committees A & B; & ibid. 1933-4, Committee D.
[5] L.S.D. 1955, vol. iii, c. 4153.
[6] H.C.D. 1937-8, vol. 337, cc. 1092-93; C.J. 1946-47, p. 51, cf. p. 101.

CASTING VOTE

If the numbers in a division are equal, the Presiding Officer has to give the casting vote. In the performance of this duty he can give his vote like any other member without assigning any reason. But, according to May,[1] 'in order to avoid the least imputation upon his impartiality, it is usual for him when practicable to vote in such a manner as not to make his decision final and to explain his reasons.'

The principle which guides a Presiding Officer in giving his casting vote was thus explained by Mr. Speaker Addington. On 12 May 1796, on the third reading of the Succession Duty on Real Estates Bill, there having been a majority against 'now' reading the Bill the third time, and also against reading it that day three months, there was an equality of votes on a third question, that the Bill be read the third time tomorrow, when the Speaker gave his casting vote with the Ayes saying, 'that upon all occasions when the question was for or against giving to any measure a further opportunity of discussion, he should always vote for the further discussion, more especially when it had advanced so far as a third reading; and that when the question turned upon the measure itself—for instance that a Bill do or do not pass—he should then vote for or against it, according to his best judgment of its merits, assigning the reasons on which such judgment would be founded.'

Similarly, on 24 February 1797, the voices being equal on the question of going into committee on the Quakers Bill, Mr. Speaker Addington cast his vote with the Ayes.

The course adopted by successive Speakers, in giving their casting vote, can be traced in the following examples.

On 10 May 1860, the numbers being equal upon an amendment proposed to a bill, on report, Mr. Speaker Denison stated that as the House was unable to form a judgment upon the propriety of the proposed amendment, he would best perform his duty by leaving the bill in the form in which the committee had reported it to the House, and accordingly gave his vote against the amendment. A similar course has

[1] May, p. 435.

generally been taken on stages in the progress of bills—often without stating any reasons.

Upon the division on the motion on 1 July 1864, that the Tests Abolition (Oxford) Bill be read a third time, the numbers were equal. Under these circumstances Mr. Speaker Denison said that he would afford the House another opportunity of deciding upon the merits of the bill, by declaring himself with the Ayes; ultimately the question that the bill do pass was negatived by a majority of two.

On 3 April 1905, the numbers being equal upon an instruction to the Committee on the London County Council (Tramways) Bill to omit certain tramways, Mr. Speaker Gully stated that in order that the matter might be considered by the committee and that the House might have a further opportunity of coming to a more decisive conclusion he gave his voice to the Noes.

On 12 April 1938, the numbers being equal upon the question of leave to bring in a bill to extend Palestinian nationality under Standing Order No. 12 (at that time No. 10) Mr. Speaker FitzRoy stated that he thought he ought to vote for the introduction of the bill so that the House could deal with it as the House thought fit.[1]

On 16 September 1938, the President of the Central Legislative Assembly ruled that although in giving a casting vote the maintenance of the *status quo ante* is a good rule in ordinary cases, it is not an invariable rule. The question arose when in a motion for the omission of a clause in a bill the President cast his vote in favour of the motion. He said that in giving his vote he took into consideration not only the clause and the amendment proposed but also the existing law as embodied in the Criminal Procedure Code which was sought to be modified.[2] In the Indian legislatures after Independence, the Presiding Officers 'have exercised their casting votes to maintain the *status quo ante*.'[3]

PAIRING

When a member finds it necessary to absent himself, and

[1] May, p. 436; *See* also H.C.D. 2 June, 1965.
[2] Debates of the Central Assembly, 16 Sept. 1938.
[3] Andhra State Bill, And. L.A. 21 July 1953; Hyderabad Abolition of Cash Grants (Amdt.) Bill, Hyd. L.A. 12 Apr. 1954.

it is anticipated that divisions might be called which would render his vote essential, it is customary to find another member on the other side who may also be under the necessity of being absent, and to agree that the two do absent themselves so that the two votes may be neutralized. This is ordinarily arranged by the Whips of the different parties.

OTHER RULES OF CONDUCT

There are certain other rules of conduct which have to be observed by all members who are present in the House.

MEMBERS TO KEEP TO THEIR PLACES

Members should keep to their respective places and should not unnecessarily move about. If they have occasion to leave their places or take their seats it is customary to make obeisance to the Chair. A member desiring to speak or to interrupt a debate should do so from his usual place and not from any other place where he may be at the time. Members should not leave or enter the Chamber while the Presiding Officer is on his feet. When leaving or entering the Chamber they should do so with decorum.

Members sometimes walk out of the House in protest against something said or done about which they feel aggrieved. Walking-out has become an almost parliamentary form of protest in India, and unless accompanied by other unparliamentary conduct, such as tumultuous behaviour, is not considered unparliamentary. It appears from a newspaper report[1] that the Poujadist members of the French National Assembly walked out of the Assembly as a mark of protest. But a walk-out as a protest against a ruling of the Chair would seem to be unparliamentary.[2] As pointed out by May, 'It is absolutely necessary that the Speaker should be invested with authority to repress disorder and to give effect promptly and decisively to the rules and orders of the House.' This is the reason why the Speaker's rulings cannot be criticized in debate and must be obeyed. Even if a ruling given by the

---

[1] *The Statesman*, 23 Apr. 1956.
[2] H.P.D. 1953, vol. ii, c. 1588.

Speaker is wrong, the ruling must be obeyed for the time being, for, unless this is done, no deliberation can proceed smoothly. If a point of order is submitted for the decision of the Speaker, and a decision is given, it is the duty of the members to submit to the ruling even if it goes against the member raising the point. No question of protest should arise, and a walk-out in protest would seem to be an unbecoming way of making a protest although such walk-outs are not uncommon in India.

CROSSING BETWEEN THE PRESIDING OFFICER AND A MEMBER SPEAKING

A member should not pass between the Presiding Officer and a member who is speaking.

READING OF BOOKS ETC.

The reading of books, newspapers, etc. is not allowed unless connected with the business of the House, e.g. preparing speeches.

SILENCE

Silence is observed in the sense that, if a member has to carry on a conversation with his neighbours, he should do so in a subdued voice so that there may not be any noise or disturbance during a debate.[1]

INTERRUPTIONS

Members are not to interrupt the business of the House by hissing, booing or making other kinds of noise.[2] But often there are disorderly scenes and uproars in the legislatures. Some kinds of interruption in mild form such as the crying of 'hear, hear', 'divide', 'order, order', etc. are tolerated.[3] Although cries of 'shame, shame' are considered unparliamentary, the

[1] L.S.D. 1956, vol. iv, c. 7325.
[2] H.P.D. 1952, vol. i, c. 241; ibid. 1952, vol. ii, c. 2052; ibid. 1952, vol. i, c. 1358; ibid. 1953, vol. i, c. 1302.
[3] W.B.L.A.P. 1949, vol. v, no. 2, p. 99.

rule against such cries is frequently disregarded even in the British Parliament.

The above-mentioned rules of conduct are expressly prescribed by rules of the Indian legislatures, as follows:

Whilst the House is sitting, a member:

(i) shall not read any book, newspaper or letter except in connection with the business of the House;

(ii) shall not interrupt any member while speaking by disorderly expression or noise or in any other disorderly manner;

(iii) shall bow to the Chair while entering or leaving the House, and also when taking or leaving his seat;

(iv) shall not pass between the Chair and any member who is speaking;

(v) shall not leave the House when the Speaker is addressing the House;

(vi) shall always address the Chair;

(vii) shall keep to his usual seat while addressing the House;

(viii) shall maintain silence when not speaking in the House;

(ix) shall not obstruct proceedings, hiss or interrupt and shall avoid making running commentaries when speeches are being made in the House;

(x) shall not applaud when a stranger enters any of the Galleries, or the Special Box;

(xi) shall not while speaking make any reference to the strangers in any of the Galleries.

When the Speaker is on his feet a member cannot remain standing. If he does so, he may be asked to leave the Chamber even though he may be a Minister.[1] A member should not stand with his back to the Chair.[2]

SMOKING

Smoking is not allowed either in the House or in committee. There is no objection, however, to the taking of snuff; as a matter of fact, snuff is provided in a box at the entrance of

---

[1] H.P.D. 1952, vol. iii, c. 4081; ibid. 1953, vol. ii, c. 1581; ibid. 1953, vol. iii, c. 3445.

[2] H.P.D. 1953, vol. ii, c. 2349; ibid. 1955, vol. ix, c. 1731.

the House of Commons.[1] There seems to be no objection to the chewing of *pan* ((betel) if done unostentatiously and spitting is not indulged in. The Speaker of the Jammu and Kashmir Legislative Assembly admonished a Deputy Minister for chewing *pan* and asked him to go out and come back after cleaning his mouth.[2]

STICKS, UMBRELLAS, BAGS, ETC.

Neither sticks nor umbrellas may be brought into the House except when any member requires the help of a stick on account of bodily infirmity. No attache cases or boxes are allowed, but nowadays wallets or portfolios may be brought in. In the British House of Commons the general rule is that no member is permitted to bring in an attache case; exception is, however, made in the case of Ministers who can bring their papers in despatch boxes. A question arose whether lady members could bring handbags, and Mr. Speaker Morrison ruled that ladies not being provided with pockets in their dress could bring handbags of sizes which were left to the good sense of such members.[3]

POWERS OF THE PRESIDING OFFICER

The Presiding Officer must have the authority to enforce the rules of debate and order in the House. For that purpose the rules of all legislatures confer certain powers upon the Presiding Officer. If a member offends against any rule of conduct the Presiding Officer calls him to order. But if he still persists in such conduct and disobeys the directions of the Presiding Officer, the Presiding Officer can ask him to withdraw from the House. In the Indian legislatures the Speaker may either ask a member to withdraw or name him for grossly disorderly behaviour. The consequence of the first course is that the member is suspended for the remainder of the sitting of that day; and of the second that a question is forthwith put by the Speaker that the member be sus-

---

[1] Guy Eden, *The Parliament Book*, p. 107.
[2] J & K. L.A.D. 13 Mar. 1954.
[3] *Table*, vol. xxi, p. 159; Hansard, vol. 498, 5th series, cc. 2749-52.

pended for the remainder of the session.[1] The House has
the power to recall the order of suspension.[2] In the British
House of Commons the Speaker has the authority to direct
the Sergeant-at-Arms to remove a contumacious member
forcibly provided that the necessary preliminary steps have
been taken under Standing Order Nos. 21 or 22 to suspend
the member. There is no such express power conferred by
any rules of the legislatures in India. In one instance, the
Marshal (corresponding to the Sergeant-at-Arms) of the
Lok Sabha was asked by the Speaker to remove a member.[3]
The power has also been used subsequently.[4] In the Uttar
Pradesh Assembly three members were forcibly removed by
the Police by order of the Speaker. Thereafter two of them
were suspended for the remainder of the session (which,
however, meant only half an hour by which period the session
was extended).[5] In the Rajasthan Assembly also a member
was forcibly removed by the Sergeant-at-Arms.[6]

If there is grave disorder in the House the Speaker has
authority to suspend the sitting of the House. Such a situation
arose on 25 May 1944 when a member of the Bengal Legislative Assembly attempted to carry away the Mace in order
to stop the business of the House which was under strong
attack from the Opposition—as Cromwell did on 20 April
1653 when he ordered the Mace of the House of Commons
to be taken away. There were also two other similar incidents
in the West Bengal Legislature.[7]

The House has, however, undoubted authority to deal
in any way it likes with a contumacious member and would
appear to have the same powers as the British House of
Commons. The punishments that may be inflicted are (a)
reprimand and admonition, (b) suspension and it seems also
(c) expulsion. In the British House of Commons the punishment of expulsion is nowadays, as stated by May,[8] 'reserved

[1] H.P.D. 1952, vol. iv, c. 5328; ibid. 1953, vol. ii, c. 1991; ibid. 1955, vol. vi,
c. 11331.
[2] L.S.D. 1955, vol. vi, c. 11467.
[3] H.P.D. 1952, vol. iii, c. 4086.
[4] H.P.D. 1953, vol. ii, c. 1585.
[5] U.P.L.A.P. 4 Mar. 1953.
[6] Raj. A. P. 21 May 1954.
[7] W.B.L.A.P. 27 Mar. 1958; W.B.L.C.P. 14 Dec. 1960.
[8] May, p. 105.

for the punishment of persons convicted of grave misde-
meanours, whose seats are not, as in the case of Members
convicted of treason or felony, automatically vacated.'

In India, under the Representation of the People Act, a
person convicted of any offence and sentenced to any term
exceeding two years becomes disqualified from retaining a
seat in any legislature. Therefore the punishment by expulsion for any other cause would seem to be too drastic. In
Mudgal's Case a motion was made for his expulsion, but as
the member resigned before the motion could be passed the
motion was amended in the form that he deserved to be
expelled.[1]

A question may arise as to what steps should be taken
when members in a body obstruct the business of the House.
Should the Speaker remove all opposition members when
they *en bloc* oppose the business of the House and create
disturbances in the House disregarding the appeal from the
Chair? Should the Chair enforce the penal provisions and
remove all the members of the Opposition, or should he
adjourn the House in such an instance considering it to be a
case of grave disorder?

The disciplinary power of the Speaker to punish disorders
is exercised in the following cases:

(i) irrelevance and tedious repetition;

(ii) minor breaches of order;

(iii) use of disorderly or unparliamentary expressions;

(iv) obstruction of business of the House otherwise than by
disorderly conduct or persistence in irrelevance;

(v) grossly disorderly conduct;

(vi) grave disorder.

Instances of naming a member for grossly disorderly conduct, disregarding the authority of the Chair or abusing
the rules of the House by persistently and wilfully obstructing
the business of the House are not rare. There are also instances
where several members have been jointly named for having
jointly disregarded the authority of the Chair. But there has
hardly been any occasion before a legislature of naming all the
members of the Opposition when opposing business simultaneously and *en bloc*, disregarding the appeal from the Chair

[1] H.P. Proceedings, 25 Sept. 1951.

asking them to be orderly. The Chair, no doubt, has the authority to enforce penal provisions upon all the offending members. But the question is, should he do so? There is a rule in the rules of procedure of all the legislatures in India empowering the Presiding Officer to adjourn the House or suspend any sitting for a time named by him if he thinks it necessary to do so in the case of a grave disorder arising in the House. The meeting may be suspended for a period of time at the first instance, and if the disorder continues even after the House has reassembled the meeting may be adjourned until the next working day. The representative character of a House in a democratic setup will be lost if all Opposition members are asked to withdraw.[1]

A sitting of the House of Commons was suspended owing to grave disorder, and Mr. Speaker observed:

'I have to inform the House that if it will not listen to me, I shall suspend the sitting [Hon. Members: Hear, Hear.] That appears to some honourable members to be a desirable course. I am certainly not going to have the Chair put in the position of not being heard in this House of Commons. The Sitting is suspended for half an hour.'

Mr. Speaker thereupon suspended the sitting for half an hour and later said:

'...But I have to say to the House quite frankly that my sense of responsibility is so great that if disorder of this kind persists—I am sure that it will not now—I shall have no option but to adjourn the House.'[2]

EXPUNGING

In the Indian legislature rules the Chair is authorized to expunge expressions which are in the opinion of the Chair defamatory, indecent, unparliamentary or undignified. The portions so expunged are marked by asterisks, and an explanatory footnote is inserted in the printed proceedings. On 22 May 1956, during the debate on the Life Insurance Corporation Bill, the Minister of Finance (Shri C. D. Deshmukh) made certain references to the Comptroller and

[1] See also p. 108. But see Proceedings of Bihar Assembly, 11 Aug. 1965.
[2] H.C.D. 1955-6, vol. 558, cc. 1619-26.

Auditor General, and those references were not objected to by any member in the House. Immediately after the session, the Comptroller and Auditor General made a representation to the Speaker that those references were derogatory to the dignity and office of the Comptroller and Auditor General. The Speaker considered the matter and ordered expunction of certain expressions as being derogatory to the dignity and office of the Comptroller and Auditor General. On 13 August 1956 a point of order was raised whether any person could make a representation to the Speaker for the expunction of any portions of a debate after a debate had actually taken place. The Speaker ruled that any person, especially if the remarks were made about a dignitary mentioned in the Constitution, could bring such matters to his notice. Such a representation should be made immediately, and not long after the relevant debates had been held. In such instances the Speaker exercises his discretion on the merits of each case.[1]

In the House of Commons it has not been possible to find any instance in which (a) the Speaker has directed the expunction of anything without an order from the House, or (b) anything has been ordered to be expunged (either by the Speaker or the House) from the Parliamentary Debates (Hansard) which contain the full reports of proceedings of the House.

The House has directed matters to be expunged from the journal, but the words objected to appear in full in the debates. For instance:

(i) A resolution containing an imputation against Sir Robert Peel was moved and negatived. A motion for expunging the resolution from the journal was moved and carried. But the full text of the resolution and the debate thereon appeared in Hansard.[2]

(ii) A member was expelled for using unparliamentary language (liar). A motion for expunging the entry in the journal was moved and carried. But everything, including the unparliamentary expression, appeared in Hansard.[3]

---

[1] L.S.D. part ii, 22 May 1956, c. 9223 and 13 Aug. 1956, c. 3087.
[2] Parl. Deb. 1833, vol. 17, c. 1324; ibid. 1854-5, vol. 137, c. 202.
[3] Parl. Deb. 1909, vol. vii, cc. 2174-5, 2181.

On the other hand, it has been ordered that unparliamentary expressions and reflections (even of the Speaker) be taken down so that they may form part of the proceedings. When a member utters any unparliamentary expression or reflection a specific motion is made that the words be taken down, and if the Speaker thinks that the expression or reflection is unparliamentary he directs the clerk to take it down. The reason for taking down words is that unless they form part of the record, no disciplinary action can be taken against the member because there would be no evidence as to what the member had said. It is probably for this reason that no part of the proceedings appears to have been expunged.[1]

The House can always order the expunging of anything from the records. In that case also a motion for expunging is a very unusual one and is seldom resorted to except under extraordinary circumstances.[2] May has cited only five instances during the period from 1769 to 1909 where it was ordered that entries from the journal be expunged.[3]

It may be pointed out that the question of expunging can only arise if words or expressions sought to be expunged are out of order, i.e. fall within the following categories:

(i) if they are filthy, obscene and unprintable;

(ii) if they are considered to be unparliamentary;

(iii) if they cast reflection upon anybody on whom reflection cannot be cast.

As regards filthy, obscene and unprintable words or expressions there can be no doubt that such words or expressions should be excluded altogether from the proceedings in the interest of public morality.

As regards expunging words or expressions which are considered unparliamentary or which cast any reflection, the following matters call for consideration in deciding whether the Presiding Officer should exercise such power:

(a) If words or expressions are expunged, no disciplinary

---

[1] Parl. Deb. 1879, vol. 247, c. 1380; ibid. 1882. vol. 270, cc. 310-1 (the expression 'infernal speech' was objected to and withdrawn, but it appears in the Report); ibid. 1877, vol. 235, c. 1806; ibid. 1882, vol. 272, cc. 1561-72 (Reflection against the Chair).

[2] H.C.D. 1909, vol. vii, c. 2481.

[3] May, p. 268.

action can be taken against the member, for there will be no
record as to what has been said by him.[1]

(b) There will be no record for future guidance as to what
words are considered unparliamentary.

(c) Whether the Presiding Officer should pass an order for
expunging in the House or can do so privately without the
knowledge of the House. In the latter case any action of the
Speaker, although justified, may be open to unmerited criticism in the House that he has done something without the
knowledge of the House.

It may be pointed out that in the House of Commons
unparliamentary expressions and reflections have never been
expunged from the proceedings of debates. What have been
expunged are entries in the journal. The debates appear in
full, but action has been taken against members for using
unparliamentary expressions or casting reflections. Members
have been asked to withdraw the expressions and apologize.
On their refusal they have been asked to withdraw from the
House or they have been suspended. The Indian legislatures
possess these powers and they may be used in suitable cases.
The possibility of disciplinary action being taken against
members is more likely to be effective in checking unparliamentary or scurrilous attacks than expunging their utterances.
For a member may make scurrilous attacks knowing full well
that his remarks may ultimately be expunged and no action
taken against him, and that his purpose will have been served
by simply making the attack.

The reason why words which are merely ruled as unparliamentary and not vulgar or indecent should not be expunged
has already been stated. A statement which contains a charge
against a person may amount to defamation if uttered outside. But such statements are privileged under the Constitution. The intention is quite clear; one cannot criticize a
person or say anything against him if one is constantly under
the fear of being hauled up for defamation. If defamatory
statements were expunged the scope of free criticism in the
House would be diminished. If reckless statements are made
the House, as has already been stated, can take action. 'Undignified' is a vague term, and the test of dignity varies with

[1] Parl. Deb. 1879, vol. 247, c. 1380.

the time and the individual. A member's conduct may be undignified without actually being unparliamentary.

There is another question as to when, if at all, an order for expunction may be made. The publication of any expression which has been ordered to be expunged is considered a breach of privilege. The Press Commission[1] raised the point that if an order of expunction is made after the report has already been sent to a newspaper office, a breach of privilege would unwittingly be committed, and the Commission recommended that in such cases no action should be taken against the newspaper concerned. It seems also proper that the Chair should not direct the expunction of any word or expression without the knowledge of the House.

SECRET SESSION

During World War II, it had been the practice both in India and England to hold secret sessions of the legislature when it was considered that members should be taken into full confidence with regard to the prosecution of the war, but that information which might be given in the debate should not be available to the enemy.

A motion was made in England in the form 'that the proceedings be held in secret session'. In the Indian Assembly, however, no motion was made. The Leader of the House made a suggestion that the proceedings of a particular day on which the war situation would be discussed might be held in secret session. The President ascertained the wish of the House, and thereafter on the day fixed after the question hour he directed the galleries, except that of the members of the Council of the State, to be cleared.[2] He also directed that the proceedings should not be taken down.

A note in the proceedings was made to the following effect: 'The remainder of the sitting was in secret session and the Assembly discussed the following motion moved by the Hon'ble Mr. M. S. Aney: "That the War situation be taken into consideration." '

In the British House of Commons also a similar report of

---

[1] *The Report of the Press Commission*, part i, 1954, para. 1101.
[2] Cent. L.A.D. 23 Feb. 1942 and 27 Feb. 1942.

13

the proceedings in a secret session appeared. When a division took place a division list showing the names of members and how they voted and the form of the question was published.[1]

. The Indian legislature rules provide for the holding of a secret session, as follows:

(i) On a request made by the Leader of the House, the Speaker shall fix a day or part thereof for the sitting of the House in secret.

(ii) When the House sits in secret no stranger shall be permitted to be present in the Chamber, Lobby or Galleries:

Provided that members of the Council may be present in their Gallery:

Provided further that persons authorized by the Speaker may be present in the Chamber, Lobby or Galleries.

(iii) The Speaker may cause a report of the proceedings of a secret sitting to be issued in such manner as he thinks fit, but no other person present shall keep a note or record of any proceedings or decisions of a secret sitting, whether in part or full, or issue any report of, or purport to describe, such proceedings.

(iv) The procedure in all other respects in connection with a secret sitting shall be in accordance with such directions as the Speaker may give.

(v) When it is considered that the necessity for maintaining secrecy in regard to the proceedings of a secret sitting has ceased to exist, and subject to the consent of the Speaker, a motion may be moved by the Leader of the House or any member authorized by him that the proceedings in the House during a secret sitting be no longer treated as secret.

(vi) On adoption by the House of the motion under subrule (v), the Secretary shall cause to be prepared a report of the proceedings of the secret sitting, and shall, as soon as practicable, publish it in such form and manner as the Speaker may direct.

(vii) Subject to the provisions of these rules, disclosure of proceedings or decisions of a secret sitting by any person in any manner shall be treated as a gross breach of privilege of the House.

It is a breach of privilege to divulge matters discussed in

[1] H.C.D. 1942-3, vol. 388, cc. 200-204.

a secret session to outsiders.[1] Whether such a matter can be revealed to a member who was not present during the secret session was discussed in the House, and it appears that, although it can be done, it should not be done in such a way as to make the information available to others.[2]

The members of one House can be present in the other while a session is being held in secret. But the principle of keeping matters secret equally applies to them.

UNPARLIAMENTARY EXPRESSIONS

Although the subject dealing with 'The Rules of Debate' is somewhat technical, the debate in itself is no doubt the life blood of a Parliament. In England, until the mid-eighteenth century, members insisted that they could speak on any subject at any time, but obviously this right proved so disruptive of the business of the House that the right had to be curtailed. A member had complete freedom to express himself subject to the rule of relevancy, but he was not to abuse the right by the use of unparliamentary expressions or immoderate language. Members were to remember that they had the privilege of freedom of speech, but that could not be allowed to degenerate into licence. Speeches and actions in Parliament may thus be said to be unquestioned and free. But this freedom is based on a basic rule that a member must not use words or expressions calculated to provoke such rage as to result in physical combat. If a member uses such an expression the Chair directs him to apologize to the member thus insulted and to the House.

Expressions which may be ruled out of order cover a wide range, and the Speaker is often required to make a quick decision as to whether he can allow such expressions. What is allowed in one period of parliamentary history is not necessarily allowed in another.

The following is a by no means exhaustive list of expressions which have been held to be unparliamentary. The expressions will, of course, have to be read with reference to the context in which they were spoken.

[1] H.C.D. 1939-40, vol. 355, c. 1210.
[2] H.C.D. 1941-2, vol. 376, c. 2246.

'Abominable lie', (425 Com. Hans. 615).

'Absolutely and basically false', (Queensland Hans. pp. 178-9).

'Abuse', (74 Union Assem. Hans. 107).

'Abysmal depths', (H.P.D. 12 May 1953).

'Accusing another member of a plain lie', (H.C.D. 1950-51, vol. 485, c. 1943).

'Accusing members of bribery', (74 Union Assem. Hans. 1479).

'Accusing the Opposition of causing a revolution', (63 Union Assem. Hans. 3554).

'Accusing the Opposition of murder', (63 Union Assem. Hans. 3554).

'Acts of dishonesty', (H.P.D. 4 Aug. 1953).

'Adventurism', (L.S.D. vol. xiv, 1 Apr. 1958).

'A friend of an enemy of this country', (H.C.D. 1945-46, vol. 425, c. 1873).

'A gang', as applied to the Opposition, (1925, Queensland Assem. Hans. 32).

'Agents of Pakistan', (H.P.D. 5 Dec. 1952).

'All India Cowards Committee', applied to All India Congress Committee, (H.P.D. 22 July 1952).

Alluding collectively to members as a 'bundle of robbers', grossly disorderly, (H.C.D. 1938-39, vol. 348, c. 210).

'Amusement', with reference to the speech of a member, (15 Bom. L.A. Hans. 874).

'Anyone who will support a thing like that has no respect for his mother or for womanhood', in reference to a particular member, (L.A.D. 3 Feb. 1932, p. 432).

'Apology for a Chairman', (1929 Queensland Assem. Hans. 2056).

'Arrant nonsense', (12 Bom. L.A. Hans. 20 March 1948, p. 979).

'Arrogant and completely false', (Can. Com. Hans. 26 June 1958, p. 1639).

'Arrogant ways', with reference to a member, (10 Bom. L.A. Hans. 19 Mar. 1947, p. 1516).

'A source of infection', referring to Deputy Speaker, (H.C.D. 1945-46, vol. 421, p. 1375).

'A tissue of lies', (L.A.D. 26 Mar. 1946, p. 2929).

'Aurat hakim ghazab khuda'—A woman administrator is a curse of God. (L.S.D. Part ii, vol. vii, no. 29, cc. 4275-76, 24 Aug. 1956).

'Babbling tongues', (L.S.D. part ii, 30 Aug. 1955).

'Barbarous', (L.S.D., part ii, vol. x, no. 30, c. 4089, 22 Dec. 1956).

'Barefaced steal', in regard to Government's action, (262 N.Z. Hans. 218, 219, 220).

'Baseless', (124 U.P.L.A.P. p. 213; 139 ibid. 42).

'Bastard', (H.C.D. 1948-49, vol. 469, c. 72).

'Behaving like a jackass', (291 Com. Hans. 2097).

'Bestial', (H.P.D. 1 May 1953).

'Big-bellied', 'flat-nosed', 'Yankee-speaking pilot-fish', (1951-2 Trinidad Hans. 578).

'Biassed cheapjack', to describe a University Professor, (178 C'th Hans. 1597).

'Big head', (H.C.D. 27 Feb. 1957, vol. 565, c. 1216).

'Blackguardly', (Council of States Debates, 9 Aug. 1952, vol. i, c. 3707).

'Blackguards', (H.C.D. 1922, vol. 153, c. 1500).

'Blackmail', (483 Com. Hans. 1794).

'Blackmailed', (398 Com. Hans. 1394; 435 Com. Hans. 1211).

'Blessed', (9 Bom. L.A. Hans. 109).

'Bloke who was sacked', (1952 S. Rhod. Hans. 684).

'Bloody', (478 Com. Hans. 2756).

'Bloody bastard', (71 U.P. Hans. 42, 1950).

'Bloody lie', (514 Com. Hans. 1574).

'Bloody swine', if said with Mr. Speaker's knowledge, (320 Com. Hans. 599).

'Bluebird', (303 N.Z. Hans. 137).

'Bluff', (78 U.P. Hans. 94).

'Bogus', as applied to information furnished by Government, (19 Bom. L.A. Hans. 982); (see also L.S.D. 12 Mar. 1958).

'Born to a foreigner', applied to a member, (H.P.D. 19 Feb. 1953).

'Bribe, it has become the trade and profession of members to take—', (4 Bih. L.A. Hans. no. 16, p. 36).

'Bribes', to accuse another member of accepting, (435 Com. Hans. 1233).

'Brute majority', (9 Bom. L.A. Hans. 986).

'Buffoon', to call another member a—, (L.A.D. 16 Nov. 1932, p. 2221).

'Bunch of robbers', grossly disorderly—alluding collectively to members as a—, (348 Com. Hans. 210).

'Butcher', as applied to Government, (10 Bom. L.A. Hans. 1520).

'Cad', to call another member a—, (L.A.D. 11 Apr. 1934, p. 3613).

'Cads', (516 Com. Hans. 395).

'Calculated, wilful, malicious and deliberate act', (1953-4 Trinidad Hans. 1661).

'Callous', as applied to Government held to be unparliamentary, (16 Bom. L.A. Hans. 1043).

'Cant', (504 Com. Hans. 150).

'Cant and hypocrisy', (72 Union Assem. Hans. 6545).

'Can they (the party opposite) deny that they had dealings with the enemy?' (64 Union Assem. Hans. 634).

'Cesspool methods', (1953 Can. Com. Hans. 65).

'Chameleon politicians', as applied to a member, (H.C.D. 1923, vol. 165, p. 1564).

'Chaps, these', referring to other members, (1954 Fed. Rhod. and Nyas. Hans 435).

'Charged with misappropriation', (L.S.D. 1959, vol. 27, 3062).

'Cheat', if applied to individuals, (414 Com. Hans. 794; 23 Bom. L.A. Hans. 144).

'Cheeky young pup', (522 Com. Hans. 623).

'Chiding', as applied to a Minister, (18 Bom. L.A. Hans. 2313).

'Chief Goonda of the State', with reference to the Commissioner of Police held not in order, (17 Bom. L.A. 1121).

'Childish attempt', (1936 S. Rhod. Assem. Hans. 929).

'Choke him off', referring to a member, (1951 S. Rhod. Hans. 1576).

'Class-room regulated by a stern schoolmaster' (of the House and the Chair), (L.S.D., part ii, 30 Aug. 1955).

'Cock-crowing', (1951-2 Trinidad Hans. 1470).

'Commonsense', or 'want of commonsense', attributing to a member held not proper, (20 Bom. L.A. Hans. 370, 382).

'Complete distortion of the facts', (75 Union Assem. Hans. 6582).

'Conspiracy' is unparliamentary, (23 Bom. L.A. Hans. 1170).

'Contemptible', (1952 Can. Com. Hans. 1792).

'Corrupt', (Parl. Deb. (1908), 184, p. 1462).

'Corruption', (L.S.D. 1 Sept. 1954).

'Could not imagine anything lower in the political life of the country', (298 N.Z. Hans. 1384).

'Courts of law rode to orders', (297 N.Z. Hans. 614).

'Coward', (84 Union Assem. Hans. 849).

'Cowardice', to describe the attitude of a member as smacking of—, (L.A.D. 18 Mar. 1936, p. 2798).

'Cowardly', (85 Union Assem. Hans. 5113; 1954 Aust. L.A. Hans. 1337; 9 Bom. L.A. Hans. 99).

'Cowardly insinuations', (78 S. African Assem. Hans. 3673).

'Crabs in a barrel', (1952-3 Trinidad Hans. 445).

'Crafty', applied to the Report of a Committee, (1953 S. Rhod. Hans. 1715).

'Criminal', to use the word in expressions like 'It should be criminal on the part of Hon'ble Members...' (L.A.D. 5 Apr. 1939, p. 3390; 1952-3 Trinidad Hans. 835; Punjab Leg. Council, vol. ii, no. 4, p. 21).

'Criminals', (H.P.D. 22 July 1952; Parl. Deb., 1902, vol. 105, c. 1072).

'Crypto-Communists on the other side', (79 Union Assem. Hans. 6154).

'Culture of gangsterism', (C.S.D. 17 Dec. 1952, vol. ii, c. 2224).

'Cunning', 'Cunningly misrepresent the truth', (R.S. Deb., 13 Feb. 1958; 1958, N.Z. Hans., no. 9, p. 558 and no. 14, p. 854).

'Cut down the enormous amount of bumph', (1951 S. Rhod. Hans. 876).

'Damn', held to be unparliamentary, (17 Bom. L.A. Hans. 2255).

'Damned', (350 Com. Hans. 1880; 35 N.I. Com. Hans. 526).

'Damned days' work in his life', (493 Com. Hans. 764).

'Damned lie', (518 Com. Hans. 1430).

'Damned wrong', (W. Nigeria Hans. 19-29 Jan. 1953, 175).

'Damn good thing too', (494 Com. Hans. 1773).

'Daniel come to judgment', applied ironically to Chair, (L.S.D. 25 Mar. 1954).

'Deaf and Dumb institution', with reference to any part of the House, (16 Bom. L.A. Hans. 136).

'Deafness of Treasury benches', (H.P.D. 5 Mar. 1953).

'Deceive', with reference to the Planning Commission's Report held to be unparliamentary, (19 Bom. L.A. Hans. 1253).

'Deceiving', (303 N.Z. Hans. 673; 130 U.P.L.A.P. 616; H.C.D. 19 Nov. 1956, vol. 560, c. 1377).

'Declared traitor', (456 Com. Hans. 969).

'Definite deliberate mis-statements', (303 N.Z. Hans. 53).

'Definite untruth', (78 Union Assem. Hans. 5486; 81 Union Assem. Hans. 92).

'Degrade himself', of a Minister, (H.P.D. 11 Mar. 1953).

'Deliberate misrepresentation', (71 Union Assem. Hans. 4119; H.C.D. vol. 478, c. 2764).

'Deliberately concealed', (527 Com. Hans. 307).

'Deliberately misleading', (1934 S. Rhod. Assem. Hans. 333).

'Deliberately mislead the House', (298 N.Z. Hans. 2084-5; 299 N.Z. Hans. 110).

'Dens of perjury', (H.P.D. part ii, 5 May 1954, c. 6597).

'Designed to mislead', (H.C.D. 1953-54, vol. 527, c. 300).

'Despicable', (75 Union Assem. Hans. 4932; 1958 N.Z. Hans. no. 7, 417).

'Devil quoting scripture', (23 Bom. L.A. Hans. 1374).

'Dingo', as applied to a member, (1932 Q'ld. Assem. Hans. 917).

'Dirty accusations', (303 N.Z. Hans. 323).

'Dirty dog', (478 Com. Hans. 2034).

'Dirty, low, mean attacks', (54 Union Assem. Hans. 582).

'Dirty remark', (84 Union Assem. Hans. 1089).

'Disgraceful conduct', (75 Union Assem. Hans. 4932).

'Disgraceful performance', (CCLXVIII, Can. Com. Hans. 2394).

'Disgraceful replies', (486 Com. Hans. 632; H.C.D. 457, c. 118).

'Disgrace to Saskatchewan', applied to a member, (1952 Can. Com. Hans. 1603).

'Disgusting completely', (1954 S. Aust. L.A. Hans. 980).

'Dishonest', (524 Com. Hans. 1914; 525 ibid. 2007; 303 N.Z. Hans. 853; 1953-4 Trinidad Hans. 1656; 510 Com. Hans. 1395; 75 Union Assem. Hans. 5033; H.C.D. 142, c. 988; with reference to provisions of a Bill—L.S.D. 25 Aug. 1956).

'Dishonest argument', (453 Com. Hans. 1450).

'Dishonest evasion', (410 Com. Hans. 29).

'Dishonesty', (386 Com. Hans. 143; P.L.C.D. vol. ii, no. 4, p. 34).

'Disown their British inheritance', (298 N.Z. Hans. 1869).

'Distort', 'distortion', (77 Union Assem. Hans. 2816; 78 ibid. 3649).

'Distortions', (84 Union Assem. Hans. 454; 1952-3 Trinidad Hans. 947).

'Divine jewel', if used satirically, (xli Bom. Council Hans. 829).

'Dogs, etc.', (III U.P. Hans. 29).

'Double dealing', (78 Union Assem. Hans. 5219).

'Downright lie' is unparliamentary, (11 Bom. L.A. Hans. 1275).

'Downright untruth', (529 Com. Hans. 1463).

'Drivel'—an hon. member accusing another of talking, (262 N.Z. Hans. 687).

'Dunderhead', (H.C.D. 1958-59, vol. 599, c.c. 837-38).

'Duped', that it is disrespectful to the House to say that it has been—into doing anything (xxxvii Bom. L. Council Deb. 944).

'Fabrication', (24 Bom. L.A. Hans. 1185-6; 304 Com. Hans. 1608).

'False', as applied to a statement of a member, (81 Uttar Prad. Hans. 292; 23 Bom. Hans. 663; 18 Bom. L.A. Hans. 1117).

'False', as applied to information by Government, (10 Bom. L.A. Hans. 248).

'False', as applied to a statement by the Government, (Rajya Sabha Deb. 24 Dec. 1954, vol. viii, c. 3313).

'False accounts', (1952 Mysore L.A. Hans. vol. vii, 950).

'False statements', (4 Bihar L.A. Hans. no. 32, p. 18; 1959, N.Z. Hans. 1051, 1209).

'Farce', as applied to the Wage Board not proper, (22 Bom. L.A. Hans. 819).

'Fascist', as applied to a foreign Government, (465 Com. Hans. 2094).

'Fat head', (H.C.D. 17 Feb. 1957, vol. 565, c. 1216).

'Fellow', as applied to a member of the House, (Rajya Sabha Deb. 26 Sept. 1955, vol. x, c. 4685).

'Fifth column', in reference to M.P. (361 Com. Hans. 751; 22 Bom. L.A. Hans. 822).

'Filibuster', (496 Com. Hans. 1454).

'Filibustering', (514 Com. Hans. 1205).

'Filthy statement', (298 N.Z. Hans. 922).

'Financial sharks', (L.S.D. 16 Apr. 1958).

'Fleas on the workers', (1932 Q'ld. Assem. Hans. 2083).

'Foolish fellow', (25 Bom. L.A. Hans. 190).

'Fools of themselves', (cclxvii Can. Com. Hans. 1663).

'Foreign King', (35 N.I. Com. Hans. 26-7).

'Foul tongue', (W. Nigerian Hans. 2nd Sess, 1954, p. 72).

'Fraud', (78 Union Assem. Hans. 5176).

'Frauds', to describe hon. members opposite as a lot of frauds in a personal sense, (H.C.D. vol. 424, c. 2072).

'Free-lance demagogue', (463 Com. Hans. 554).

'Friend of an enemy of the country', (425 Com. Hans. 1873).

'Futile', as applied to an answer by a member of the Government, (1921 India C. of S. Hans. vol. i, p. 50).

'Gadarene swine', if used against an individual, (484 Com. Hans. 2612).

'Gang', used for Ministers or for members, (H.P.D. part ii, 5 Aug. 1953, c. 128).

'Gang', as applied to the Opposition, (1925 Q'ld Assem. Hans. 32).

'Gentleman', asserting that another member is not a, (lxxxvi Can. Com. Hans. no. 113, 5760).

'Get back to the gutter', (299 N.Z. Hans. 179).

'God forbid', (H.C.D. 1959-60, vol. 615, c. 739).

'Government are following a madman's path', (15 Bom. L.A. Hans. 1720).

'Government influenced by minority and influential bodies', (1951-2 Trinidad Hans. 1849).

'Government protected financial crooks', (N.S.W. 1930 Assem. Hans. 7878).

'Government receives dictation from an outside body', 'has done something at the dictation of a group of people', (297 N.Z. Hans. 888; 298 ibid. 917-9).

'Greedy swine', (1950 S. Rhod. Hans. 2573).

'Grin like a Cheshire cat', (297 N.Z. Hans. 573).

'Gutless wonders', (1953 S. Aust. L.A. Hans. 611).

'He called upon his supporters to contravene the law', in reference to an hon. member, (63 Union Assem. Hans. 3314).

'He made a despicable speech', (73 Union Assem. Hans. 9311).

'He was nothing but a tool for the Nazis', (1949 Union Sen. Hans. 3741).

'Henchman', to describe a member as being a—of another member, (L.A.D. 18 Mar. 1932, p. 2239).

'His brains could revolve inside a peanut shell for a thousand years without touching the sides', (285 N.Z. Hans. 429).

'Hitler and Goebbels', applied to members, (Bih. L.A.D. 19 Mar. 1953).

'Holy and pious member for...', (1883 Q'ld Assem. Hans. 194).

'Hon. member is a political lawyer', (72 Union Assem. Hans. 629).

'Hon. Minister is improving, even at this time of day', (1951 S. Rhod. Hans. 1082).

'Hon. Ministers, even if they were in the House, would be sleeping', (1952 Mysore L.A. Hans. vol. viii, p. 333).

'Hoodwink', (14 Bom. L.A. Hans. 1827).

'Hoodwinking or duping', (4 Bih. L.A. Hans. no. 32, p. 9).

'House indifferent to human life', (454 Com. Hans. 1297).

'Humbug', (313 Com. Hans. 2157).

'Hypocrisy', 'Hypocritical', 'Hypocrites', (499 Com. Hans. 1769; 500 ibid. 1854; 297 N.Z. Hans. 474, 480; 78 Union Assem. Hans. 3730).

'I am merely mentioning this to question the sincerity of ...', to say in the course of a speech, (L.A.D. 17 Aug. 1938, p. 688).

'I am not a liar like the Minister', (1936 N.S.W. Assem. Hans. 1037).

'I believe him but thousands would not', (70 Union Assem. Hans. 129).

'I cannot give the Hon'ble Member the intelligence to understand', to suggest that any other member has no intelligence, (L.A.D. 16 Mar. 1927, p. 2324).

'Idiot', (476 Com. Hans. 2249).

'Idiotic obstinacy', (Rajya Sabha Deb. 18 Dec. 1954, vol. viii, c. 2583).

'I do not like the smell of this section', (1952 S. Rhod. Hans. 387).

'I do not care a damn about "order"', (355 Com. Hans. 422).

'If the hyena opposite would give his attention', (310 Com. Hans. 923).

'If the Minister has not got the guts to order an inquiry', (L.A.D. 24 Mar. 1950, p. 2108).

'If you (an hon. member) said that outside you would get six months', (54 Union Assem. Hans. 2040).

'Ignorance', (297 N.Z. Hans. 885).

'Ignorance—abysmal', 'ignorance—colossal', ignorance-gross', were held unparliamentary when applied to members, (Madras L.A.D. vol. ix, pp. 784 and 787).

'Ignorance of the members', (25 Bom. L.A. Hans. 492).

'I have no time to read it out to a lunatic', (71 Union Assem. Hans. 3835).

'I'll make you do it outside', (Q'ld Assem. Hans. 2nd Sess. 38).

'Imbecile', to describe the Assembly as—(L.A.D. 28 Jan. 1925, p. 397).

'Immoral', 'immoral motives', (1954 S. Aust. L.A. Hans. 1339; 4 Bihar L.A. Hans. 22 Mar. 1954).

'Impertinent', (ccxvii Can. Com. Hans. 3717).

'Implying that an hon. member was a demagogue', (ccxxxvi Can. Com. Hans. 2450).

'Impudence', (H.C.D. 1948-49, vol. 460, c. 857 and U.P. L.A. Deb., vol. 196, pp. 67-68).

'Impudent', (92 Parl. Deb. c. 968, and Bom. L.A. Deb. 17 Mar. 1939, vol. v, p. 1731).

'In a scandalous way he mis-stated the facts', (1949 Union Sen. Hans. 2643).

'Inciter', (79 Union Assem. Hans. 6312).

'Incompetence of the Government', (1935 S. Rhod. Assem. Hans. 929).

'Incorrect', (297 N.Z. Hans. 17, 19; 298 ibid. 1154, 1263).

'Incorrect and you know it', (299 N.Z. Hans. 304).

'Incorrect, you know that is', (303 N.Z. Hans. 169, 489).

'Indecent', in connection with speeches, (L.A.D. 24 Sept. 1924, p. 4071).

'Indifference of this House to human life', (H.C.D. 1947-48, vol. 454, c. 1297).

'Infamous lie', (78 Union Assem. Hans. 5486).

'Infection, you are the source of', (421 Com. Hans. 1375).

'Informers', applied to members of public service, (49 Kenya Leg. Cou. Hans. 1430).

'Insinuation of a dishonourable nature', (75 Union Assem. Hans. 6608).

'Insulting'—with reference to the speech of the Chancellor of the Exchequer, (74 H.C.D. c. 1947).

'Insulting dog', (H.C.D. 1930-31, vol. 245, c. 1655).

'Intentionally misleading', to describe a member's speech as—(L.A.D. 17 Feb. 1925, p. 1131).

'Intentions of Government are not honourable', is not proper, (22 Bom. L.A. Hans. 1998).

'Intoxicated' is objectionable under certain circumstances, (10 Bom. L.A. Hans. 525).

'In view of the impertinent nature of the reply', (502 Com. Hans. c. 1198).

'Irresponsible Member', (vii W.B. Hans. no. 1, p. 518).

'Is this...honesty?', (63 Union Assem. Hans. 2750).

'It (a tax) is a damned scandal', (H.C.D. 1940-41, vol. 370, c. 1378).

'It is a deliberate untruth', (70 Union Assem. Hans. 176).

'It is a lie', (347 Com. Hans. 401, 402).

'It is definitely a "wonkie" name', (1951 S. Rhod. Hans. 905).

'It is most unfair', used towards Mr. Speaker, (388 Com. Hans. 1923).

'It was a scandal that (an Hon. Member) was sent out', (78 Union Assem. Hans. 3728).

'I will see you outside', (H.C.D. 1957-58, vol. 591, c. 485).

'I wish you had that sense of honour and you would be a better man', (1949 Union Sen. Hans. 3960).

'Jiggery-pokery', (55 Kenya Hans. 135).

'Jobbery political', (W. Nigeria Hans. 2nd Sess., p. 19).

'Jolly good fellow', as applied to the head of the administration not proper, (16 Bom. L.A. Hans., pp. 268-9).

'Just hated the sight of Khaki', an hon. member referring to the members on the Government side as, (263 N.Z. Hans. 527).

'Justice', member for...incapable of, (1933 Ceylon Hans. 565).

'Kicked out', (Beng. L.A. Proc. 10 Aug. 1937, vol. li, no. 2, p. 104).

'King of goondas', (L.S.D. 24 Apr. 1956).

'Lack of guts', (485 Com. Hans. 913).

'Laughing jackass', (297 N.Z. Hans. 892).

'Law is so badly formulated', not proper, (12 Bom. L.A. Hans. 919).

'Leaderless rabble', 'Leaderless group of politicians'— with reference to Opposition, (Beng. L.A. Proc. 28 Nov. 1940, vol. lviii, p. 79).

'Liar', (269 Com. Hans. 939; 380 Com. Hans. 189).

'Liar', 'Lie', 'Lying', (H.C.D. 1957-58, vol. 584, c. 536).

'Liar', 'Damned liar', (315 Com. Hans. 834, 837).

'Libertine males', (L.S.D. part ii, 16 Sept. 1954, c. 2092).

'Lie', (525 Com. Hans. 1223; 303 N.Z. Hans. 727, 728, 729; 11 Madras L.A. Hans. 405; W. Nigerian Hans. 2nd Sess. p. 108; 315 Com. Hans. 836; 313 Com. Hans. 2157; 441 Com. Hans. 2166; 399 Com. Hans. 1120; Punjab Legis. Council Deb., vol. ii, no. 3, p. 31 and vol. ii, no. 4, p. 34).

'Lie down dogs', (260 Com. Hans. c. 1911).

'Lie, Lies', (498 Com. Hans. 660; 505 ibid. 1338; 297 N.Z. Hans. 209; 77 Union Assem. Hans. 1935; Pakistan Const. Assem. Hans. vol. ii, no. 5, p. 294; no. 10, p. 580 and no. 11, p. 608; 1951-2 Trinidad Hans. 1804).

'Lie, 'Lying', (517 Com. Hans. 73; 1953; Can. Com. Hans. 4226).

'Light-hearted levity', (L.S.D. 24 Apr. 1956).

'Light-hearted vote', (L.A.D. 27 Feb. 1937, p. 1154).

'Locusts from Pakistan', (H.P.D. 4 Mar. 1953).

'Look at the face of so-and-so', with reference to Minister or member, (18 Bom. L.A. Hans. 2167).

'Loot', (L.S.D. 25 Apr. 1956).

'Low', (75 Union Assem. Hans. 4427).

'Lying', (393 Com. Hans. 142).

'Machination', (1950 W.B. Hans. 336).

'Made common cause with the enemy', in reference to a member, (62 Union Assem. Hans. 310).

'Malevolently', (73 Union Assem. Hans. 7755).

'Malignant attack', (Parl. Deb. 1915, 74, c. 1947).

'Malignant slander', (Parl. Deb. 1902, 105, c. 579).

'Manoeuvering or sleight of hand', held to be not proper, (10 Bom. L.A. Hans. 1821).

'Mastery at misrepresentation', (1953 S. Aust. L.A. Hans. 614).

'Matter for regret', to say that the way in which debate has been going on is a matter for, held to amount to reflection on Chair, (1947 Madras L.A. Hans., iv, 965).

'Mean', imputation to Chair, (H.P.D. 2 Aug. 1952).

'Mean advantage of', to say that a certain member has taken a—, (L.A.D. 3 Oct. 1931, pp. 1472-73).

'Mean insinuation', (75 Union Assem. Hans. 6608).

'Medieval pantomime', (H.C.D. 23 Jan. 1957, vol. 563, c. 212).

'Member is not true to his conscience', (16 Bom. L.A. Hans. 871).

'Member not to accuse other hon. members of lying', (H.C.D. 1938-39, vol. 289, c. 1566).

'Members were Nazis', (74 Union Assem. Hans. 3242).

'Members would like to see the workers on the bread line all the time', (1954 S. Aust. L.A. Hans. 1731).

'Member was inspired by something else', (xxxvii Bom. C. Hans. 944).

L.'Menace to Parliament', (1953 Can. Com. Hans. 4219).

'Mendacity', 'Mendacious', (297 Com. Hans. 1665).

'Ministers have repeatedly come to the House and have d', (409 Com. Hans. 237, 239-43).

lie'Mischievous', as applied to speech or statement of a member, (10 Bom. L.A. Hans. 192; 18 ibid. 1809).

'Misleading', (P.L.C.D. vol. ii, no. 4, p. 34).

'Misleading and lying statements', (262 Com. Hans. 611).

'Misleading the country', (75 Union Assem. Hans. 5325).

'Mislead the House', with reference to a statement, (H.C.D. 1940-41, vol. 367, c. 392).

'Misled us deliberately', (84 Union Assem. Hans. 1992).

'Misrepresentation', (75 Union Assem. Hans. 5038).

'Monkey', (H.P.D. 13 Mar. 1953).

'Monkey House', to describe the Assembly as—(L.A.D. 12 Mar. 1935, c. 2220).

'Monsters', (H.P.D. 29 Feb. 1952).

'Most deceitful man in the House', (303 N.Z. Hans. 674).

'Mr. Speaker unduly anxious to intervene and interrupt speech', (410 Com. Hans. 1947).

'Mug', (1932 Q'ld Hans. 2189).

'Mulish tactics', (125 U.P.L.A.P. 166, 213).

'Murdered or killed people, the British authorities have', (454 Com. Hans. 1311-3).

'Murderer', (Parl. Deb. 1923, vol. 165, c. 2382; H.C.D. 1 Nov. 1956, vol. 558, cc. 1745-6).

'Name will go down as our South African Quisling', (1949 Union Sen. Hans. 587).

'Nefarious', (84 Union Assem. Hans. 545).

'Negotiated with the enemy', in reference to an hon. member, (62 Union Assem. Hans. 3107).

'Neither fish nor fowl nor good red herring', (64 U.P. Hans. 292).

'Never had a conscience', in reference to an hon. member, (xli Bom. Hans. 1282).

'Nobody but a knave or fool', in allusion to a member, (1934 S. Rhod. Assem. Hans. 210).

'No language is in order which can be reasonably said by Senator to be offensive to him', (1913 Aust. Sen. Hans. 4127).

'Nonsense', (1952-3 Trinidad Hans. 433; 22 Bom. L.A. Hans. 767).

'Nonsense' or 'utter nonsense', (H.P.D. part ii, 18 Mar. 1950, p. 1749).

'Nosey parker', (H.C.D. 15 Nov. 1955, vol. 546, c. 186).

'Not a damned one of you opposite', (423 Com. Hans. 107).

'Not game', (303 N.Z. Hans. 680, 821).

'Not got the guts to order an inquiry', (Parl. Deb. 24 Mar. 1950, part ii, p. 2108).

'Not true', (303 N.Z. Hans. 59, 60, 869; 298 N.Z. Hans. 174, 1265, 1600).

'Now the hon. Minister of Justice comes along and he abuses his powers', (1949 Union Sen. Hans. 724).

'Obstructing', (77 Union Assem. Hans. 2464).

'Obstruction', member charging other members with, (413 Com. Hans. 152-3).

'Offensive', epithet must not be used about other members, (318 Com. Hans. 618).

'Offensive lie', (443 Com. Hans. 2004, 2010).

'One-man tribunal', casting aspersions on a High Court Judge, (L.S.D. 9 Mar. 1954).

'One of those who were prepared to sell their souls', to characterize another member as—, (L.A.D. 5 Apr. 1929, p. 2892).

'One standard for the Congress and another for the Opposition', (H.P.D. 2 Aug. 1952).

'Only a Mussulman by name', (L.A.D. 11 Sept. 1929, p. 654).

'Only one actual rat', (441 Com. Hans. 2102).

'Opposition is opposing for the sake of opposition', not proper, (22 Bom. L.A. Hans. 1623).

'Order be damned', (274 Com. Hans. 1307).

'Organized mendacity', (299 N.Z. Hans. 20).

'Organized obstruction', (309 Com. Hans. 923).

'Ought to be ashamed of themselves', (297 N.Z. Hans. 573).

'Outraged maiden', referring to a Minister, (H.P.D. 5 Dec. 1952).

'Outrageous', (418 Com. Hans. 292).

'Outrageous lie', (70 Union Assem. Hans. 1490).

'Outside body real parliament of N.Z.', 'Outside political body influencing the Government', (297 N.Z. Hans. 900; 298 ibid. 916).

'Owl', (4 Bih. L.A. Hans. 16 Mar. 1954).

'Parliament is a farce', (1949 S. Rhod. Hans. 1046).

'Past master of underhand campaigns', (1952 Can. Com. Hans. 1792-3).

14

'Perverter of the truth', (262 Com. Hans. 611).

'Personal experience of the police', with reference to a member, (H.P.D. 30 Mar. 1953).

'Pig', calling another member a—, (488 Com. Hans. 1267).

'Plain lie', accusing anohter member of, (485 Com. Hans. 1958).

'Playing to the gallery', (23 Bom. Hans. 503).

'Plunder and rob', (W. Nigeria Hans. 19-29 Jan. 1953, 193).

'Poisonous atmosphere these methods are creating', (302 Com. Hans. 1119).

'Pecksniffian cant', (H.C.D. 1928, vol. 215, c. 1932).

'Political courtier', with respect to High Court Judges, (L.S.D. 25 Sept. 1958).

'Political dishonesty', (299 N.Z. Hans. 197).

'Political probity of the Huggins Government is impugned', (1950 Rhod Hans. 375).

'Political rogue', (78 Union Assem. Hans. 3838).

'Pompous brass hats', in reference to Defence Force Staff, (ccxxx Can. Com. Hans. 2002).

'Prepared to sell their souls', (L.A.D. 5 Apr. 1929, vol. iii, p. 2892).

'Preposterous', as applied to bills which the House passes, (13 Bom. L.A. Hans. 1620).

'Pretentious behaviour', but only when applied to a member, (125 U.P. Hans. 27).

'Public tripe', (298 N.Z. Hans. 1632).

'Pumping from behind', (Council of States Deb. 19 Dec. 1952, vol. ii, c. 2500).

'Puppet', as applied to a member of the Bombay Delimitation Advisory Committee, (17 Bom. L.A. Hans. 2254).

'Quisling', when applied to Minister or M.L.A. (v. 1947 Madras L.A. Hans. 586).

'Quite maliciously', to describe a certain member as repeating, (L.A.D. 27 Feb. 1936, p. 1720).

'Rabble', (H.C.D. 1950-51, vol. 484, c. 404; 1958, N.Z. Hans. no. 18, p. 1116).

'Ragged rabble', (298 N.Z. Hans. 1921).

'Rats', reference to other members as, (441 Com. Hans. 2504).

'Raving' or 'Thundering', use in respect of member's speech (H.P.D. part ii, 2 Sept. 1953, cc. 1987-8).

'Raving of the Hon. Gentleman', (475 Com. Hans. 1997).

'Reflections on colour or matters of a personal nature', (v. Madras L.C. 2303).

'Renegade', (85 Union Assem. Hans. 3880).

'Retardate worm', an Hon. Member describing another as a—, (262 N.Z. Hans. 696).

'Ribald', (H.C.D. 1958-59, vol. 607, c. 1038).

'Ridiculous', (vii W.B. Hans. no. 3, p. 135).

'Road of revolution on which he led his supporters', (63 Union Assem. Hans. 3314).

'Robbery' (alleged against a public servant), (L.S.D. 1959, vol. 30, c. 13942).

'Rogue and scoundrel', (L.S.D. part i, S.Q. no. 1576, 8 Oct. 1955).

'Rotten lie', to use the expression, (L.A.D. 1 Mar. 1927, p. 1561).

'Rt. Hons. Gent. has directly falsified the facts', (497 Com. Hans. 2059).

'Running of blood', (1951-2 Trinidad Hans. 1477).

'Sacked for incompetence', (1953 S. Rhod. Hans. 1305).

'Sanctimoniously hypocritical', (H.C.D. vol. 548, c. 2387).

'Scandal-mongers', (ccxvii Can. Com. Hans. 3750).

'Scandalous', (75 Union Assem. Hans. 6570).

'Selfishness', (22 Bom. L.A. Hans. 1174).

'Sermon', as applied to the speeches made by the Members in the House held to be objectionable, (22 Bom. L.A. Hans. 1173).

'Shabby moneylenders', (441 Com. Hans. 1985).

'Shame', (W. Nigerian Hans. 2nd Sess. p. 52; 1950 W.B. Hans. 72; 9 Bom. L.A. Hans. 975).

'Shame, shame'—to cry when a Party leaves the House, (Beng. L.A. Proc. 10 Mar. 1938, vol. lii, no. 4, p. 127).

'Shameful', not to support a bill, (23 Bom. L.A. Hans. 483).

'Sheer fraud and hypocrisy', (75 Union Assem. Hans. 6519).

'Show-boys of the Treasury Benches', (O.L.A.P. 1 July 1952, p. 71).

'Showed a rather extraordinary concern for the black-marketeers', (77 Union Assem. Hans. 1952).

'Shrimp', (1932 Q'ld Hans. 1435).

'Shut up', (vii W.B. Hans. no. 1, pp. 451, 585; 297 N.Z. Hans. 675).

'Silly', (1950 W.B. Hans. 179).

'Silly and stupid', (1951-2 Trinidad Hans. 1257).

'Silly ass', (419 Com. Hans. 216).

'So-called mother of Shri Aurobindo Ashram', (H.P.D. 11 June 1952).

'Some unprincipled blackguards', (312 Com. Hans. 1995).

'Sordid', applied to ministerial methods, (78 Union Assem. Hans. 5200).

'Speaking on the authority of his ignorance', (22 Bom. L.A. Hans. 2650).

'Spies' applied to members of public service, (49 Kenya Leg. Council Hans. 143).

'Stealing funds', as applied to a Minister, (18 Bom. L.A. Hans. 1731).

'Steam-rollered through Parliament', (72 Union Assem. Hans. 6290).

'Steam-rollering tactics', (73 Union Assem. Hans. 7467).

'Stolen', (303 N.Z. Hans. 339).

'Stooge', (493 Com. Hans. 362; 498 ibid. 1583).

'Stooge, question', (513 Com. Hans. 1416).

'Strategy', with reference to getting a bill passed in the House, (22 Bom. L.A. Hans. 1578).

'Stupid', (1952-3 Trinidad Hans. 857).

'Stupid' and 'foolish fellow', (25 Bom. L.A. Hans. 190).

'Sub-standard County', (1953 S. Aust. L.A. Hans. 616).

'Sucking the bones of the poor', (130 U.P.L.A.P. 192).

'Surreptitious', with reference to Government, (17 Bom. L.A. Hans. 450).

'Swine', as referring to a Member, (313 Com. Hans. 437, 438).

'Take him out—he is drunk', (416 Com. Hans. 1472).

'Talking out of the back of his neck', (1950 S. Rhod. Hans. 2258).

'Talking rot', (H.P.D. 19 Dec. 1952).

'Talking shop' and 'Gas Chamber', (H.P.D. part ii, 4 Mar. 1953, c. 1405).

'Tax is a damned scandal', (370 Com. Hans. 1378).

'Throat cut', member should have his, (494, Com. Hans. 1430).

'That is a lie', (417 Com. Hans. 674; 75 Union Assem. Hans. 4698; 350 Com. Hans. 2505; 383 Com. Hans. 1454).

'That is cowardly', in reference to the Prime Minister's course of action, (65 Union Assem. Hans. 2976).

'That is not true', (478 Com. Hans. 753).

'That long-distance calls were made to Hitler', (64 Union Assem. Hans. 636).

'Their (Government's) unholy hands', (1949 S. Rhod. Hans. 785).

'There should be a public enquiry into the mental attitude of a member', (24 Bom. L.A. Hans. 1185).

'There you lie', (71 Union Assem. Hans. 2657).

'These are illegal steps', insinuation that the Minister took, (65 Union Assem. Hans. 3335).

'They are misleading', (P.L.C.D. vol. ii, no. 4, p. 34).

'They are Nazis', (75 Union Assem. Hans. 5287).

'Thief', (127 U.P.L.A.P. 252).

'Thieves', applied to Ministers, (H.P.D. 25 July 1952).

'This is not a meeting of the Carlton Club', (385 Com. Hans. 2133).

'This obnoxious Bill', (1950 S. Rhod Hans. 2742).

'Throw him out by the neck', (131 U.P.L.A.P. 535-6).

'To cheat', (23 Bom. L.A. Hans. 144).

'To hell with the English', (446 Com. Hans. 14).

'To hell with the Government', to use the expression of, (L.A.D. 13 Mar. 1939, p. 1945).

'Tool in the hands of', in relation to a member, (1931 Ceylon Hans. 549).

'To pursue a personal vendetta against someone', (485 Com. Hans. 982).

'Totalitarian', Minister (418 Com. Hons. 1109).

'Totally untrue', (490 Com. Hans. 1676).

'Traitor', (423 Com. Hans. 1604; L.A.D. 9 Oct. 1936, p. 2804).

'Treachery', (L.S.D. 1959, vol. 26, c. 3062).

'Treason', (96 Com. Hans. 2482).

'Treating Parliament with contempt', (1953 Can. Com. Hans. 4219).

'Twisting', (78 Union Assem. Hans. 3623; 82 Union Assem. Hans. 844).

'Twisting certain passages', (75 Union Assem. Hans. 6554).

'Twisting good at', (1954 S. Rhod. Hans. 970).

'Ulterior motive', use of expression—while referring to the act of State Government, (H.P.D. part ii, 28 June 1952, c. 2776; 16 Bom. L.A. Hans. 1683).

'Unfit to be the Leader of the House', (L.S.D. 1959, vol. 37, c. 5382).

'Ungentlemanly method', to use the expression—with reference to another member, (L.A.D. 15 Feb. 1933, pp. 718-19).

'Unmitigated lie', (403 Com. Hans. 1212).

'Unscrupulous', in motion or in question, (Ceylon, 1933, Hans. 1307).

'Unspeakable blackguard', (403 Com. Hans. 44).

'Untrue', (500 Com. Hans. 1854; 297 N.Z. Hans. 118, 517, 298; ibid. 1183, 1265; 80 Union Assem. Hans. 8883; 303 N.Z. Hans. 727, 728, 729, 784; 304 ibid. 1599; 86 Union Assem. Hans. 6724).

'Untrue', 'Untruths' (512 Com. Hans. 1560; 299 N.Z. Hans. 20, 248, 255; 1952-3 Trinidad Hans. 740).

'Untrue statement', (425 Com. Hans. 614).

'Untruth', telling the House an, (432 Com. Hans. 732).

'Untruth', charging another member with telling an, (432 Com. Hans. 732).

'Unworthy', (H.P.D. 28 Apr. 1953).

'Unworthy of position...of supposedly responsible Minister', (1953 Can. Com. Hans. 3035).

'Useless talk', (136 U.P.L.A.P. 148).

'Vindictive', (W. Nigerian Hans. 30 Jan. and 6 May 1953, 415).

'Wangle', (436 Com. Hans. 1387).

'Wasting time', use words like—against a member, (H.P.D. part ii, 10 June 1952, c. 1498).

'Weak and cowardly', as applied to Government, (1932 Q'ld Hans. 1709).

'We have too much to do in trying to restrain the effects of the wicked and crooked legislation of this Government', (N.S.W. Assem. Hans. 1930, c. 7862).

'What a fool', (74 Union Assem. Hans. 2984).

'Whatever we said the non-member would trust it', (65 Union Assem. Hans. 3388).

'What have you been drinking?' an undesirable remark, (297 Com. Hans. 662).

'What is the attitude of the Chair I do not know', (L.A.D. 17 Nov. 1938, pp. 3137-8).

'When a Minister gets upon that Box and states a deliberate untruth, he ought to be told that he is not telling the truth and that he is lying', (315 Com. Hans. 836, 837).

'Whole conception was a lie', (399 Com. Hans. 1120).

'Whose policy he now so warmly and for so many golden reasons supports', (1949 Union Sen. Hans. 1400).

'Why the hell', (Pakistan Const. Assem. Hans. vol. ii, no. 10, pp. 581-2).

'Wicked act', (W. Nigerian Hans. 2nd Sess. p. 52).

'Wicked mis-statement of the truth', (498 Com. Hans. 278).

'Will betray South Africa', in reference to a non-member, (63 Union Assem. Hans. 3234).

'Wily old bird', only looked upon as a facetious remark, (276 Com. Hans. 2109).

'Work in league', (23 Bom. Hans. 1258).

'Wowser', (1911-12, Q'ld Assem. Hans. 3095).

'Wrong', Member knows his statements to be completely—, (303 N.Z. Hans. 540).

'You are a lot of hypocrites', (1932 N.S.W. Assem. Hans. 222).

'You are jumping from one branch to another like monkeys', (1952 Mysore Leg. Council Hans. vol. i, p. 62).

'You are the rottenest', (77 Union Assem. Hans. 2607).

'You did not', addressed to the Chair, (498 Com. Hans. 1982).

'Zoological approach to a human problem', (L.S.D. 11 Apr. 1958).

CHAPTER XI

LEGISLATION

ALL proposals for legislation are initiated in the form of bills which, when passed by the legislature and assented to by the Head of the State, become Acts. Where the legislature consists of two Houses, legislation can be initiated in either of the Houses, except that Money and Financial Bills can be introduced only in the Lower House and all bills (other than Money Bills) must be passed or deemed to be passed by both the Houses.[1] If bills are introduced in the Lower House of a State legislature (the Assembly), they can become law without the concurrence of the Upper House (the Council). But bills introduced in the Upper House must be concurred to by the Lower House; otherwise they cannot become law. (For a discussion of the respective powers of the two Houses see p.244).

Bills may be classified into Government bills and Private Members' bills. But the procedure for both the classes is the same.

Bills originating in either of the Houses are considered in three stages—Introduction, Consideration and Passing. The procedure followed in the two Houses is the same (except in the case of Money Bills). We shall now discuss the procedure common to both the Houses and then take up the discussion of the procedure relating to the transmission of bills from one House to the other.

INTRODUCTION.

When it is proposed to introduce a bill, the member who wishes to do so gives notice of a motion that he will ask for leave to introduce a bill. The period of notice varies in different legislatures.

The procedure of giving notice of motion for leave to introduce a bill is usually dispensed with in the case of Govern-

[1] Arts. 107, 196.

ment bills. The rules of some of the State legislatures provide
that the Head of the State may direct any bill to be published
in the Official Gazette, although no motion for leave to
introduce the bill has been made, and that if a bill is so published it is not necessary to move for leave to introduce the
bill.[1] This procedure is resorted to by the Government.

In the Indian Parliament and in some State legislatures
the Presiding Officer and not the Head of the State may,
on a request made to him, direct the publication of any bill,
and on such publication being made no leave of the House
is necessary for the introduction of the bill. It appears that
the authority of the Presiding Officer is not confined to Government bills; he may direct the publication of Private Members'
bills also.

A notice to a motion for leave to introduce must be accompanied by a Statement of Objects and Reasons and by a
certain number of copies of the bill; when a bill is published
in the Official Gazette without prior leave of the House,
a Statement of Objects and Reasons must also be published
along with the bill.

Two further statements are also required to be submitted
in addition to the Statement of Objects and Reasons. If
the bill involves expenditure, a financial memorandum
drawing attention to the relevant clauses and containing an
estimate of the recurring and non-recurring expenditure
involved, proposals for delegation of legislative power, and a
memorandum explaining such proposals, drawing attention
to their scope and stating whether they are of normal or
exceptional character, must also be submitted.

In the case of Private Members' bills, the sanction or recommendation of the President, if previous sanction or recom-

---

[1] The origin of the rule is as follows: One of the principles that was followed
in framing the rules of procedure was that full opportunity for discussion and
consideration of every legislative measure should be afforded to the Legislative
Council and to the public. Accordingly there was a rule that when leave was
given to introduce a bill, the bill should be published in the Official Gazette
and that a period of eight, and in some cases twelve, weeks should intervene
before the bill could be taken up for consideration. It was felt that this rule
should be so changed as to enable the Council to consider a bill without undue
delay, and at the same time to ensure that the public should be afforded sufficient
time to offer their criticisms. The Lieutenant Governor was therefore authorized
to publish a bill beforehand so that the public might have an opportunity to
examine and discuss the bill.

mendation is necessary, must also be annexed to the notice. In other cases, the order of the President granting or withholding the sanction or recommendation must be communicated to the Secretary in writing by the Minister concerned.

If a bill is introduced to replace any ordinance, the rules require that there shall be placed before the House along with the bill a statement explaining the circumstances which had necessitated immediate legislation by ordinance. When an ordinance embodying wholly or partly or with modifications the provisions of a bill pending before the House is promulgated, a statement explaining the circumstances which had necessitated immediate legislation must be laid on the table at the commencement of the session following the promulgation of the ordinance.

Government bills are, as stated above, usually published in the Official Gazette without asking for leave of the House and no leave of the House is, therefore, necessary for the introduction of such bills. If a notice is received from the Minister-in-charge of such a bill that he will introduce the bill, it is placed in the list of business for the day allotted to it by the Government.

At the time of giving notice of introduction a member may simultaneously give notice of motions he would like to move after introduction, e.g. that the bill be taken into consideration and be passed or that the bill be referred to a Select Committee, etc.

When a Government bill which has been previously published in the Official Gazette is called on, the Minister-in-charge does not ask for leave but merely says that he begs to introduce the bill. The Secretary thereupon reads out the long title of the bill and the Minister-in-charge proceeds to move the motion of which he has given notice, e.g. motion for consideration or reference to Select Committee.

In regard to bills which have not been previously published in the Official Gazette the member who has given notice of a bill asks for leave of the House to introduce the bill. The introduction of a bill is not usually opposed.[1] But there are

---

[1] B.L.A.P. 1937, vol. li, no. 4, p. 1503; ibid. 1946, vol. lxxi, no. 1, p. 102; ibid. 1939, vol. liv, no. 5, p. 385; L.A.D. 1 Feb. 1927, p. 366.

precedents when the introduction of such bills has been opposed.[1]

If the introduction of a bill is opposed, the rules of all legislatures provide that the Presiding Officer may, after permitting the member who seeks to introduce the bill and the member who opposes to make a short explanatory statement, put the question forthwith without debate; although under such a rule the Presiding Officer has discretion to allow a discussion in the case of any bill. The rules, however, expressly provide that the Speaker may permit a full discussion in the case of bills the introduction of which is opposed on the ground of legislative incompetence.

Where no leave of the House is necessary for the introduction of Government bills, copies of such bills are made available to the members. But where leave is necessary bills are published in the Official Gazette only after leave is given by the House to introduce the bill. Copies of such bills are therefore not circulated (unless the member-in-charge himself takes steps to have copies printed and circulated) to members before leave is given. Copies of the bill must, however, be available to members before the bill can be taken into consideration.[2]

MOTIONS AFTER INTRODUCTION

When a bill has been introduced a motion may be made: (a) that the bill be circulated for eliciting opinion; or (b) that the bill be referred to a Select Committee or a Joint Select Committee of the Houses where the legislature consists of two Houses; or (c) that the bill be taken into consideration.

When any of the motions mentioned above is made, the general principles of the bill are discussed. No amendments to the clauses are allowed at this stage. Only amendments which are relevant to the motion then before the House, e.g. if it is a motion for consideration of the bill, an amendment that the bill be referred to a Select Committee and so on,

---

[1] W.B.L.A.P. 1953, vol. vii, no. 3, cc. 348, 357; H.P.D. 1952, vol. iii, c. 3445; ibid. 1952, vol. iii, c. 3925; ibid. 1954, vol. viii, c. 690; ibid. 1956, vol. iv, c. 5637; ibid. 1957, vol. viii, c. 1939.
[2] B.L.A.P. 1937, vol. li, no. 4, p. 1503; L.S.D. 1956, vol. i, c. 46.

may be moved. The above mentioned motions can be made as a substantive motion only by the member-in-charge of the bill. A member-in-charge of a bill means in the case of a Government bill any Minister, Deputy Minister or Parliamentary Secretary,[1] and in the case of a non-official bill, the member who has introduced the bill, or in the case of a bill transmitted by the other House, the member who has given notice of his intention to move that the bill be taken into consideration.

Any member may move any such motion which is relevant by way of amendment to any other such motions.

If the member-in-charge of a bill is unable, for reasons which the Speaker considers adequate, to move any motion after introduction, he may authorize another member to move such a motion with the approval of the Speaker. The member who has introduced the bill, however, remains the member-in-charge of the bill (For such amendments see under relevant motions).

MOTION FOR CIRCULATION

When the member-in-charge of a bill makes a substantive motion that the bill be circulated for eliciting opinion, it is clear that the member does not desire the House to take the bill into consideration immediately. The rules of all legislatures provide that a motion that a bill be taken into consideration can be made only by the member-in-charge of the bill, i.e. the member who has introduced the bill. No amendment to the effect that the bill be taken into consideration can therefore be made to such a motion for circulation. But there is no bar to an amendment being moved to a motion for circulation that the bill be referred to a Select Committee. (For motions for reference to a Select Committee, see p. 222).

A motion that the bill be circulated for eliciting opinion may also be moved as an amendment. (For when such a motion can be moved see p. 225).

A date is fixed by which the opinions are to be received.

[1] H.P.D. 1952, vol. v, c. 517; ibid. 1955, vol. vii, c. 12376; ibid. 1955, vol. ix c. 1523; ibid. 1957, vol. vi, c. 10912; ibid. 1955, vol. ix, c. 254.

When several circulation motions (as amendments) fixing different dates are tabled, all the motions are moved, and the debate conducted on them simultaneously. But when putting the motions to the vote it is convenient to split one of these motions into two portions: first, that the bill be circulated for eliciting opinion leaving out the date and then, if that motion is carried, the portion relating to the date. If the first portion is negatived all the motions for circulation fall through. If the first motion is carried, then each motion relating to the date is put before the House until a verdict as to the date is obtained. If the House agrees to a particular date all the other motions fall through.[1]

As a substantive motion for circulation of a bill can be made even in the case of a Government bill,[2] it is evident that a motion for circulation (whether as a substantive motion or as an amendment) is not considered a dilatory motion, and if carried is not accepted as a virtual rejection of the bill. It may be mentioned that in England an amendment that the bill be read a second time *six months hence* instead of *now* is proposed when it is desired that the bill should not be considered by the House. If the Chair is of the opinion that a motion for circulation or recirculation of a bill, after a Select Committee or a Joint Committee has reported thereon, is in the nature of a dilatory motion in abuse of the rules of the House, in as much as the Select Committee or the Joint Committee has dealt with the bill in proper manner, or that no unforeseen or new circumstances has arisen since the bill emerged from such a Committee, the motion for circulation is considered to be dilatory.[3] In such a case the Chair may forthwith put the question or may decline to put the question.

After the expiry of the period of circulation a motion may be made that the bill be referred to a Select Committee. In an exceptional case, if the Presiding Officer permits, a motion may be made that the bill be taken into consideration. If a motion is made for reference to a Select Committee, an amendment for the recirculation of the bill is in order.[4]

---

[1] B.L.A.P. 1940, vol. lviii, p. 296.
[2] Hindu Marriage and Divorce Bill, 1952; C.S.D. 20 Dec. 1952, c. 2649.
[3] Lok Sabha Rule 341; L.S.D. 1954, vol. v, c. 6985; ibid. 1955, vol. iv, c. 6548.
[4] B.L.A.P. 1938, vol. lii, no. 3, p. 96.

If a motion is allowed to be made for the consideration of the bill, an amendment for reference to a Select Committee, or for the recirculation of the bill would be in order.[1]

MOTION FOR REFERENCE TO SELECT COMMITTEE

A motion may be made by the member-in-charge of a bill that the bill be referred to a Select Committee. It is usual to find in the rules of many of the legislatures that the Minister-in-charge of the Department concerned and the mover of the motion (if he is not the Minister-in-charge, e.g. if the motion is made as an amendment) shall be named as members of the Select Committee. It is also necessary that the consent of the members proposed to constitute the Committee must be forthcoming before the motion can be moved.[2] No one can be appointed to a Select Committee if he is not willing to serve on the Committee, and the member proposing the name of any member must ascertain that he is willing to serve on the Committee.

MODE OF CHOOSING, AND MAXIMUM NUMBER OF MEMBERS

There is no hard and fast rule on how the members of a Select Committee are to be chosen. In some legislatures[3] there is a convention that all parties in the legislature should be represented in the Select Committee. In the British House of Commons, members of Standing Committees are so chosen as to reflect the composition of the House,[4] but no such procedure is followed in the case of Select Committees.[5]

A question may arise whether a bill, in respect of which a motion that it be taken into consideration has been passed and several clauses have been adopted as parts of the bill, can be referred to a Select Committee.

The stages in which a bill is considered in the legislatures in India are, as stated above, three, (i) Introduction, (ii)

---

[1] B.L.A.P. 1938, vol. lii, no. 3, p. 96.

[2] L.A.D. 22 Feb. 1921, pp. 327-28; H.P.D. 1952, vol. iv, c. 4936; ibid. 1954, vol. viii, c. 19; ibid. 1956, vol. ix, c. 1064; ibid. 1953, vol. ix, c. 426; ibid. 1953, vol. x, c. 1669.

[3] B.L.A.P. 1943, vol. lxvi, no. 2, p. 379; H.P.D. 1952, vol. vi, c. 2904.

[4] May, p. 646.

[5] Ibid. p. 612.

LEGISLATION 223

Consideration, and (iii) Passing, corresponding to (i) first reading, (ii) second reading, Committee stage and consideration by the House on report from the Committee, and (iii) third reading of a bill, in the British House of Commons. At the second, i.e. consideration stage, a motion that the bill be referred to a Select Committee can be made either in the alternative or as an amendment to a motion that the bill be taken into consideration. If the motion that the bill be taken into consideration be passed, the bill is considered clause by clause. There is a difference at this stage between the procedure obtaining in the Indian legislatures and the House of Commons. In the House of Commons, as soon as a motion is adopted that a bill be read a second time, the bill is automatically referred to a Standing Committee or, if the House so directs, to a Select Committee, or a Committee of the Whole House. That is, a Committee stage (at which the bill is considered clause by clause) always intervenes between the passing of a motion for a second reading and the consideration of the bill as a whole by the House when amendments to clauses may also be offered. Therefore, no precedent exactly applicable to the question raised can be available in the practice of the House of Commons. But the procedure which obtains there for the recommittal of a bill to a Committee after it has once been reported may be of some help by way of analogy. In India, if a bill has been reported by a Select Committee, a motion that the bill be recommitted is ordinarily made by way of an amendment to a motion that the bill as reported be taken into consideration. It appears that in the House of Commons a motion for recommital may be made either at the beginning or the end of the consideration stage but not during the proceedings on consideration.[1] That is to say, a motion that the bill be recommitted to a Select Committee may be made even after (in fact, must be made after, if not made at the beginning) the entire bill has been considered by the House on report from the Committee. Then again, such a motion can be made after the House has ordered the bill to be read the third time; the order for a third reading is discharged and the bill is recommitted.[2] In either

[1] May, p. 574.
[2] Ibid. p. 576.

case, a bill can be recommitted as a whole or only in part. If a bill can be recommitted to a Select Committee after the bill has been adopted by the House on report from a Committee, or even at the third reading stage by discharging the order for a third reading, it seems a bill can be committed to a Select Committee in the circumstances envisaged above, subject to a limitation discussed later on.

It may be argued that in the consideration stage, once a motion has been adopted that a bill be considered, or some clauses have been adopted, it amounts to a decision of the House which cannot be altered on the principle that a decision once taken by the House cannot be altered during the same session. That principle is applicable to the House of Commons also; but it appears from the practice referred to above that a decision that a bill be read a second time or a third time can be discharged and the bill recommitted. It also appears that if a bill is referred to a Standing Committee, the order of reference can be discharged and the bill referred to some other committee, e.g. a Select Committee.[1] This practice can be supported on the basis that the general principle that a decision once taken by the House cannot be altered during the same session applies only to a final decision. The order of the House that a bill be read a second time or be referred to some committee is only a stage in the process of consideration of the bill, and it cannot be said that a final decision has been taken by the House until the motion that the bill be passed has been adopted.

It will have been seen that no motion for recommittal can be made during the proceedings on consideration. If the practice of the House of Commons is followed, it seems a motion that a bill be committed to a Select Committee cannot be made at the stage when only certain clauses of the bill have been adopted, but it can be made at the end of the consideration stage.

Standing Order No. 50 of the House of Commons provides that if a motion for recommittal of a bill is opposed, the question must forthwith be put to the House without debate after a preliminary explanation from the mover and the opposer. It has, however, been held that Standing Order No.

---

[1] May, p. 536.

50 applies only to the recommittal of a bill as a whole and to such a motion made at the beginning of the consideration stage but not otherwise.[1]

AMENDMENTS

To a motion for reference to a Select Committee, the following amendments may be moved:

  (a) that the bill be circulated for eliciting opinion;

  (b) that the bill be referred to a Joint Select Committee of the two Houses, (where the legislature consists of two Houses);

  (c) that names of certain proposed members be omitted or certain other names be added either as addition to or in substitution of proposed names.[2] (For motions for circulation see p. 220.)

COMMITTEE OF THE WHOLE HOUSE

No motion for the reference of a bill to a Committee of the Whole House is now made in India. For, if a bill is not referred to a Select Committee, the House proceeds to consider the bill clause by clause after the motion for consideration is passed (see p. 237), and in effect performs the function of a Committee.

JOINT SELECT COMMITTEE OR JOINT COMMITTEE

A motion may be made either substantively or by way of amendment that a bill be referred to a Joint Select Committee of the two Houses. Such a Committee can only be appointed with the concurrence of the two Houses.

BRITISH PRACTICE

A Joint Committee composed of an equal number of members of each House is appointed at the instance of one House or the other.

[1] May, p. 575.
[2] L.A.D. 5 Apr. 1932, p. 3003.

15

If either House considers it expedient that a Joint Committee should be appointed to consider a bill, it passes a resolution to the effect 'that it is expedient for the bill to be committeed to a Joint Committee of the Lords and Commons' and sends the resolution to the other House for concurrence. The other House thereupon passes a resolution 'that this House concurs in the Resolution communicated by the... viz. that it is expedient etc.'

After the message of concurrence of the other House is received, the originating House appoints a 'Select Committee to be joined by a Committee to be appointed by the other House', and sends a message stating that a Select Committee has been appointed of a certain number of members and requesting the other House to appoint a Committee of equal number of members. The names of proposed members are not sent.

The other House thereafter appoints a Select Committee to join with the Committee of the originating House.

To appoint a Select Committee straightaway and ask the other House to appoint members to the Committee is considered discourteous to the other House. The Joint Select Committee elects its own Chairman (who may be a member of either of the Houses) and its procedure is guided by the rules of procedure of a Select Committee of the House of Lords where the rules differ from the procedure of a Select Committee of the House of Commons.

The Report of a Joint Select Committee upon the bill is presented to both Houses by the Chairman to the House to which he belongs and by a member of the other House appointed by the Committee to that House.[1]

When a bill is reported from a Joint Committee to the House in which the bill originated, the bill is always recommitted to a Committee of the Whole House.[2]

After the bill has been considered clause by clause by a Committee of the Whole House, it is again considered by the House (that is known as the Report stage), and then a motion is made that the bill be read a third time.

When a bill reported by a Joint Committee is passed by

[1] May, p. 665.
[2] Ibid. p. 568.

the House in which it originated, it is sent to the other House for concurrence. And the other House considers the bill in the same way as it would in the case of any other bill. The bill is considered on a motion for second reading and is as a rule committed to a Committee of the Whole House.[1]

It therefore appears that the House, by concurring in the appoinmtent of a Joint Select Committee, is not committed to the principles of the bill. In fact, when a bill is committed by the House to a Committee, the Committee is bound by the principles of the bill and not the House. The House can always negative the bill at any stage. This was also the view taken by the Chairman of the Council of States in India when the Preventive Detention Amendment Bill (introduced in the House of the People) was referred to a Joint Select Committee. He observed:

'So far as that (discussion of the principles of the Bill) is concerned, we will have ample opportunities when the House of the People refers this Bill back to us to enter into complete detail, to consider whether an Act like this is necessary at all and whether particular details required to be modified or not—all these questions we will have at a later stage when the House of the People refers this matter to us.'[2]

INDIAN PRACTICE

A bill may be referred to a Joint Select Committee of both Houses with the concurrence of the two Houses. The practice appears to be to appoint a Committee of a certain number of members of the House in which the bill has originated, to fix the number of members to be appointed by the other House and to ask the other House to concur in the appointment of a Joint Select Committee and to name its members. The proportion of the number of members from the House of the People and the Council of States is fixed by convention as 2 : 1.[3] Such a procedure is, as already stated, not allowed in the British Parliament. No motion for reference to a Joint Committee can be made in respect of Money Bills. When

[1] May, p. 500.
[2] C.S.D. vol. i, p. 1876.
[3] *The Indian Parliament*, ed. by A. B. Lal, p. 108.

a bill is taken into consideration on a report from a Joint Select Committee, an amendment may be moved that the bill be recommitted or be circulated or recirculated for opinion.

When a bill originating in one House is sent to the other House, the bill is not referred to a Select Committee if it has already been considered by a Joint Committee. Also no amendment that the bill be circulated for opinion is allowed.

The procedure would therefore be as follows. A motion is moved in the House in which the bill has been introduced that the bill be referred to a Joint Select Committee of the two Houses. The motion names the members (of the House in which it is moved) who should be the members of the Joint Committee, and usually specifies the number of members of the other House who should be joined. The motion if carried is sent to the other House for concurrence. The other House then concurs in the motion, names its own members and sends back the motion to the originating House. The bill then stands referred to the Joint Select Committee. The procedure followed in the Joint Select Committee is the same as that of a Select Committee (see p. 229). The Chairman to preside over the deliberations of the Joint Select Committee, unless otherwise provided by the rules of any legislature, is elected by the members of the Joint Select Committee.

AMENDMENT TO A MOTION FOR REFERENCE TO A JOINT SELECT COMMITTEE

To a motion for reference of a bill to a Joint Select Committee of the two Houses the following amendments are in order: (a) motion for circulation of the bill (see p. 220); (b) motion for reference to a Select Committee of the House in which the motion is moved (see p. 222).

ADDITION OR SUBSTITUTION OF NAMES

When an amendment is moved for the addition or substitution of the name of a new member, his consent must be forthcoming before the amendment can be moved.[1]

[1] B.L.A.P. 1938, vol. liii, no. 1, p. 138.

EFFECT OF ACCEPTANCE OF MOTION FOR REFERENCE TO COMMITTEE

When a motion is made for reference to a Select Committee or a Joint Select Committee of the two Houses, the general principles of the bill are discussed. The clauses can be discussed only in so far as they are relevant in elucidating the general principles of the bill. If such a motion is carried, the general principles of the bill are taken to have been accepted by the House and are binding on the Committee;[1] the Committee cannot go beyond the principles of the bill as accepted by the House. In the case of a Joint Select Committee, however, the House in which the bill is not pending but which has only concurred in the appointment of a Joint Select Committee is not bound by the decisions of the originating House because of the appointment of the Committee.[2] It can discuss the general principles of the bill when the bill actually comes before it after being passed by the originating House.[3]

PROCEDURE IN SELECT COMMITTEE: CHAIRMAN

The rules of legislatures in India provide that the Speaker shall nominate the Chairman. The Deputy Speaker is to be nominated as the Chairman if he is appointed a member of the Select Committee. In a Joint Select Committee the members elect a Chairman.

QUORUM

A quorum for a meeting of the Select Committee is fixed by the rules of procedure (one third of the number of members). A quorum must be present throughout the sitting of the Committee.

The rules provide that if a quorum is not present on two successive days fixed for a meeting of the Committee, the Chairman should report the fact to the House.

[1] L.A.D. 4 Feb. 1925, p. 745; ibid. 19 Feb. 1926, p. 1541.
[2] C.S.D. vol. 1, c. 1876; H.P.D. 1953, vol. x, c. 2427.
[3] The Calcutta Municipal Bill, 1951, West Bengal.

The rules also provide that if a member is absent from a meeting on two or more successive occasions a motion may be made in the House for the discharge of the member from the Committee.

SITTINGS OF SELECT COMMITTEE

A Select Committee can sit while the House is sitting. There are rules which require that a Select Committee should suspend or adjourn its sitting if a division is called in the House.

There is no bar, as there is in England, to a Select Committee sitting when the House is not in session.[1] But a Committee cannot sit during question hour.[2]

SITTING BEYOND THE PRECINCTS OF THE HOUSE

In England a Select Committee cannot, without the leave of the House, sit in any place beyond the precincts of the House. In India the same rule is followed except that a meeting can be held elsewhere with the permission of the Speaker. There are instances in some legislatures in which Select Committees have at the instance of the Committees held their sittings in places other than the House.

DATE AND ADJOURNMENT OF MEETING

The date of the first meeting of a Select Committee is usually fixed by the Chairman of the Committee, and the officer who acts as the Secretary to the Committee issues the notices to members.

POWERS OF THE SELECT COMMITTEE

A Select Committee is a Committee of the House and has such authority only as is conferred upon it by the House. When a bill is committed to a Select Committee the Select Committee has authority to consider the bill clause by clause and amendments relevant to the subject matter of the bill.

[1] L.S.D. 1956, vol. vi, c. 984.
[2] Ibid. vol. v, c. 7992; ibid. vol. vi, c. 362.

A Select Committee is bound by the decision of the House given at the time of reference as regards the principles of the bill, and cannot go into the question of principles; nor can it amend the bill in a manner which is opposed to such principles. There is, however, no limitation to the power of the Select Committee to amend a bill in such a way as to make it a new bill altogether, provided the amendments made are within the scope of the bill. In such cases the Select Committee makes a report that the bill should be republished. The rules provide that a Select Committee, when reporting a bill, should state whether or not in its opinion, the bill has been so altered by it as to require republication.

The rules also provide that if a bill is altered by the Select Committee the Select Committee may make a recommendation to the member-in-charge of the bill that his next motion should be one for circulation, or when the bill has already been circulated, for recirculation. Instructions may be given to a Select Committee to make some particular or additional provisions in the bill, and if necessary or convenient to consider and report on amendments which may be proposed to the original Act which a bill seeks to amend.

The House can also give instructions to consider amendments to the sections of the parent Act when an amending bill does not seek to amend such sections.[1]

POWER OF A SELECT COMMITTEE TO RECOMMEND THE DROPPING OF A BILL

A Select Committee to which a bill has been referred has no power to put an end to the bill itself. In the British House of Commons Select Committees have sometimes negatived all the clauses and the preamble of bills, and have made a special report to that effect to the House. If a Select Committee is of the opinion that a bill should be dropped, it may make a special report that the bill should not be further proceeded with. If such a report is made, ordinarily the bill is dropped. A bill can, however, be recommitted or referred back to a

---

[1] H.P.D. 1952, vol. iii, c. 4107; ibid. 1952, vol. iv, c. 4998; ibid. 1952, vol. v, c. 325; ibid. 1953, vol. iii, c. 4716.

Committee after the Committee has reported that it is not expedient to proceed further with the bill.[1]

In West Bengal, recommendations that the bill should not be proceeded with were made and accepted by the House in the case of the following bills: (i) Bengal Municipal Amendment Bill, 1934; (ii) Bengal Moneylenders Amendment Bill, 1937; (iii) West Bengal Special Powers (Second Amendment) Bill, 1947.

EXAMINATION OF WITNESSES

The rules of all legislatures authorize the Select Committee to take expert evidence and hear representatives of special interests affected by the bill. Whether a Select Committee can summon a witness and compel his attendance or can compel the production of any paper depends upon the powers given to the Committee by the House. The rules also expressly authorize a Select Committee to do so. The legislatures in India enjoy the powers and privileges of the British House of Commons, and therefore have the power to summon a witness and compel the production of any paper. A default on the part of any person in complying with the directions of the Committee would be a breach of privilege and would be liable to be visited with penalty.

The Government, however, may decline to produce any document on the ground that its disclosure would be prejudicial to the safety or interest of the State.

Witnesses are summoned by an order signed by the Secretary. It is doubtful whether a witness appearing before a Select Committee can be put on oath or affirmation. In England there are statutes (Parliamentary Witnesses Act, 1858 and Parliamentary Witnesses Oaths Act, 1871) which authorize Parliament and its Committees to administer oaths to witnesses before Parliament. But in practice witnesses are not ordinarily examined on oath except in cases of judicial or exceptional character.

Under the Constitution the Houses of legislatures in India have inherited the powers of the British House of Commons; whether they can claim not only the powers which are parts

[1] May, p. 644.

of the privilege of the House of Commons, but also any power which is conferred by statutes upon the House of Commons is a question of some difficulty. The language of the Constitution seems to warrant the wider view. Under the Indian Oaths Act, 1873, 'persons having by law or consent of parties authority to receive evidence' are authorized, by themselves or by any officer empowered by them, to administer an oath or affirmation. A House of a legislature or any committee thereof is not authorized under any 'law' to receive evidence unless the provision of the Constitution is interpreted to attract the powers conferred by the Parliamentary Witnesses Oaths Act, 1871.

Authority to receive evidence by consent of parties contemplates arbitration tribunals and not committees or Houses of legislatures where there are no parties at all.

It appears that the Committee of the House of the People, which was appointed in 1951 to enquire into the conduct of a member[1] (H. G. Mudgal), was authorized by a resolution of the House to receive evidence and the Committee itself decided to take evidence on oath. The course may be open to objection. The matter is not merely of academic importance and should be put on a surer footing. For, any witness giving false evidence before a Committee cannot be prosecuted for perjury if he is not on oath or is on an oath which is unauthorized. There is now a rule which empowers a Committee to administer the oath.

REPORT

A Select Committee after considering the bill and making amendments, if any, makes a report to the House. If any member disagrees with the report he can submit a minute of dissent. The practice in the British Parliament is different —no minute of dissent or separate report is allowed to be presented.[2] The majority report is the only one which is presented to the House.

A Select Committee may make an interim or special report to the House if it has not been able to finish its deliberations

---

[1] *Mudgal's Case*, published by the Parliament Secretariat, 1951.
[2] May, p. 636.

within the time fixed by the House, and may ask for an extension of time. The rules provide that a Select Committee must make a report to the House within three months if no time is fixed by the House.

PUBLICATION OF PROCEEDINGS OF SELECT COMMITTEE

The proceedings of a Select Committee are treated as confidential and cannot be disclosed. What happens in the Select Committee cannot be disclosed or referred to even in the House when the bill comes up for discussion.[1]

The Report of the Select Committee or its recommendations cannot be disclosed until and unless the Report has been presented to the House.[2]

The evidence taken by a Select Committee cannot also be discussed until presented to the House or made available to members. This rule may, however, often be relaxed, and evidence may be disclosed confidentially in the interest of convenience or advantage in the enquiry, e.g. when the evidence of a witness is disclosed to another witness. It is, however, the practice in the British Parliament to ask leave of the House to report the minutes of evidence from time to time if it is intended to make the evidence available generally to witnesses and parties.[3]

In the British Parliament usually no objection is taken to the publication of the evidence of witnesses examined in public before Committees, provided the report is fair and accurate.[4]

ADMISSION OF STRANGERS

When a Select Committee is deliberating no stranger is allowed to be present. When evidence is being taken strangers may be present but may be excluded by order of the Committee. A member of the House which has appointed a Committee is entitled to be present during the sitting of a Committee even when the Committee is deliberating, but he is

[1] May, p. 628; L.A.D. 29 Mar. 1941, p. 2161; Parl. Deb. 1950, vol. v, c. 2187.
[2] I.P.D. 27 Mar. 1950, p. 2187.
[3] May, p. 627.
[4] Ibid.

not entitled to take any part in the proceedings of the Committee. A member can only be excluded by an order of the House.[1]

SUB-COMMITTEES

A Select Committee cannot divide itself into sub-committees without the authority of the House unless authorized by the rules. When a Select Committee is authorized to appoint sub-committees it can delegate to sub-committees only such functions as are authorized by the House to be delegated. If so authorized, a sub-committee may include persons outside the Select Committee.[2] A Select Committee can, however, appoint one of their members or some of them to assist the Committee for the purpose of its business, e.g. drafting the Report which does not involve delegation of authority.[3] Rules in India expressly provide for the appointment of sub-committees by a Select Committee.

PRESENTATION OF REPORT

The Chairman of a Select Committee or any member authorized by the Select Committee is authorized to present the Report to the House. When presenting the Report, the Chairman or the member makes a short explanatory statement. No motion is made at the time of presentation. Subsequently a motion is made that the bill as reported by the Select Committee be taken into consideration.

CONSIDERATION OF BILL REPORTED BY A SELECT COMMITTEE

Subsequent to the presentation of the Report of a Select Committee, the member-in-charge of the bill may make a motion:

(i) that the bill as reported by the Select Committee be taken into consideration; or,

(ii) that the bill be recommitted either (a) without limit-

---

[1] Parl. Deb. 1849, vol. 102, c. 1183.
[2] C.J. 1917-18, p. 170; ibid. 1918, pp. 13, 72, 204; ibid. 1920, p. 94.
[3] May, p. 631.

ation, or (b) with respect to particular clauses or amendments, or (c) with instructions to make some particular or additional provision in the bill.

Rules of legislatures provide that a motion may also be made by the member-in-charge for the circulation or recirculation of the bill. Such a course may be adopted when a bill has been so altered by the Select Committee as to be unacceptable to the member-in-charge, and he may avoid the passing of such a bill by making a motion for circulation or recirculation. There are instances where the member-in-charge did not make any motion for consideration of the bill as reported by the Select Committee, and the bill was automatically dropped.[1]

When a motion is made for the consideration of a bill as reported by a Select Committee, any member may move an amendment for the recommittal of the bill. Rules provide that an amendment may also be moved for the circulation or recirculation of the bill.

An amendment for the recommittal of a bill cannot be moved after the motion for consideration has been adopted, and the bill is taken into consideration clause by clause. The practice in the British Parliament is otherwise. A motion for recommittal may be made there either at the beginning or end of the consideration stage, between the consideration and third reading and also on the third reading, although it appears that a motion for recommittal of a Government bill by a private member has been disallowed by the Speaker.[2]

A motion for the recommittal of a bill as a whole is regarded in certain circumstances as obstructive in the British Parliament, and a Standing Order[3] provides that if a motion for the recommittal of a bill *as a whole* is opposed the Speaker, after allowing the mover of the motion and the member who opposes to make explanatory statements, must forthwith put the question. Such is not the position in India.

A bill may be recommitted to the same Select Committee.

[1] Bengal Secondary Education Bill, 1942.
[2] H.C.D. 1920, vol. 132, c. 1359.
[3] S.O. no. 50: 'If a motion to recommit a bill as a whole be opposed, Mr. Speaker shall permit a brief explanatory statement of the reasons for such recommittal from the Member who moves and from a Member who opposes any such motion respectively, and shall then without permitting further debate put the question thereon.'

In the British Parliament a bill reported from a Select Committee is always recommitted to a Committee[1] of the Whole House. Motions are also made for the recommittal of a bill reported by a Standing Committee to a Select Committee.[2] In India there are no Standing Committees on bills. Whether a bill reported by a Select Committee can be recommitted to another Select Committee is an open question. The rules of procedure do not bar such recommittal, although some may consider such a course discourteous to the Select Committee reporting the bill. It has also been ruled in the House of the People that recommittal of a bill to a new Select Committee is permissible.[3]

When a bill is recommitted with respect to particular clauses or amendments, or with any particular instruction, only those matters and amendments relevant to those that have been referred are considered by the Committee. When a bill is recommitted as a whole the entire bill is before the Committee, and the Committee can make such further or other amendments as it desires.

A bill may be recommitted as many times as the House pleases.

CONSIDERATION OF CLAUSES

When a motion for consideration is accepted without referring the bill to a Committee or on a report from a Committee, the House considers the bill clause by clause, and any member can propose amendments to the clauses of the bill. There is some difference in this respect between the procedure of the British House of Commons and the legislatures in India. In the House of Commons bills are invariably committed to Committees—either to the Standing Committees or Committees of the Whole House. The Committees consider the bill clause by clause. The House never considers a bill clause by clause but considers it as a whole. Consequently, there are certain restrictions as well as liberties as regards amendments that can be proposed to a bill under consideration by

---

[1] May, p. 568.
[2] C.J. 1928, p. 256; ibid. 1929-30, p. 336; see also May, p. 575.
[3] I.P.D. 4 Sept. 1951, c. 1902.

the House. For instance, no amendment which purports to
impose a tax or a charge upon the public revenue can be
proposed in the House. On the other hand, an amendment
to leave out a clause or several clauses is in order because
no question is put for each clause to stand part of the bill.[1]

In the Indian legislatures, however, the House, when
considering a bill on second reading, acts, as has already been
stated, more or less as a Committee. And the rules which
govern the procedure in a Committee of the House of Commons
are applied when a bill is being considered by the House
clause by clause.

Each clause is called out by the Presiding Officer. If there
are amendments proposed, the amendments are put to the
vote. Then the question is put that the clause (or the clause
as amended) do stand part of the bill. If there is no amendment to any particular clause, and no member desires to
speak on the clause, the question is put forthwith. Sometimes
for convenience and in order to save time several clauses
are put *en bloc*, unless any member desires to speak on any
particular clause. Schedules are treated in the same manner
as clauses.

The consideration of the preamble is postponed until
after the clauses have been considered, because it may be
necessary to amend the preamble in consequence of amendments made in the clauses. Consideration of particular clauses
also can be postponed if thought convenient.

In the Lok Sabha the consideration of clause 1 is also
postponed. After all the clauses, schedules, etc. are disposed
of, clause 1, the enacting formula, the preamble and the title
of the bill are taken up and put to the House.

Clauses and schedules can be amended, clauses or schedules
omitted or new clauses or schedules added by way of
amendment.

AMENDMENTS

Notices of amendments have to be given, and the period of
notice is prescribed by the rules of the respective legislatures.
The Presiding Officer is empowered to accept amendments

[1] May, p. 572.

at short notice, even on the floor of the House when a bill is under consideration.

An amendment must be relevant to and within the scope of the bill, and when offered to a clause must be relevant to the subject matter of the clause.[1]

Whether an amendment is within the scope of a bill or not has to be judged from the Statement of Objects and Reasons, the preamble and the provisions of the bill.[2] No single one of these is conclusive. Each is a factor to be taken into consideration.

The scope of a bill has to be decided on the merits of each case and the facts of each case, and it is the function of the Chair to say whether a particular amendment is within the scope of a bill.[3]

An amendment which is dependent upon amendments which have already been negatived is inadmissible. In practice such amendments are not put as having fallen through.

An amendment which is inconsistent with any decision of the House on any clause or part of the bill or a previous amendment is inadmissible.[4]

An amendment which is unintelligible, vague or offered 'in a spirit of mockery' is inadmissible.[5]

An amendment which would be unintelligible without subsequent further amendments is inadmissible if no notice of such further amendments has been given.

An amendment to leave out a clause is out of order[6] as it has the effect of a negative vote, and the same result can be obtained by voting against the clause. An amendment to omit the only effective word or words of a clause, upon which the rest of the clause is dependent, or any amendment which is a negative of the clause as it stands, is out of order.[7]

An amendment to substitute an alternative clause is allowed in the Indian legislatures; in England the practice is to

[1] L.A.D. 15 Jan. 1923, p. 1035; ibid. 19 Mar. 1925, p. 2655; ibid. 28 Mar. 1934, p. 2901; ibid. 6 Feb. 1923, p. 2005; ibid. 29 Sept. 1937, p. 2675.

[2] B.L.A.P. vol. li, no. 4, p. 1639; ibid. vol. liv, no. 7, p. 241; ibid. vol. liv, no. 5, p. 202.

[3] L.S.D. 1954, vol. viii, c. 709; ibid. 1956, vol. viii, c. 6095; ibid. 1956, vol. iv, c. 7448; ibid. 1956, vol. vii, c. 2389.

[4] Ibid. 8 Sept. 1955, c. 12797.

[5] May, p. 556.

[6] I.P.D. 21 Dec. 1950, c. 2213.

[7] May, p. 555.

negative the clause and offer the alternative as a new clause.[1]

When a clause contains several sub-clauses, an amendment to omit any sub-clause is not in order if the sub-clause is dependent upon another which is not sought to be omitted or any amendment to do so has been negatived.

An amendment which purports to impose any charge or which involves expenditure from the public funds is inadmissible unless recommended by the Head of the State. Under Articles 117(1) and 207(1), no amendment which imposes any tax or involves withdrawal of money from the Consolidated Fund, or contains any provision which is of the nature of a provision of a Money Bill can be moved without a recommendation from the Head of the State. Under Articles 117(3) and 207(3) any amendment which, if passed, would involve expenditure from the public funds, cannot be passed without such recommendation although such amendments can be moved. The effect is that such amendment cannot be put unless recommended by the Head of the State.

The effect of this provision of the Constitution is that an amendment which would involve a higher expenditure than that provided for in a Government bill is inadmissible unless recommended by the Head of the State.[2]

AMENDMENTS TO AMENDING BILLS

When a bill seeks to amend an Act the question of the scope of amendment often arises in the form of whether amendments to the provisions of the Act which are not sought to be amended are admissible or not. In such a case, if the amending bill has what is known as an open preamble, i.e., if the amending bill seeks to amend the parent Act without any limitation, all the provisions of the parent Act are open to amendment. But if the preamble is a restricted one, as is often the case, i.e., if the amending bill seeks to amend the parent Act 'in the following manner and for certain purposes', only provisions which are sought to be amended are open to amendment. The other provisions of the parent Act cannot be

[1] May, p. 555.
[2] B.L.A.P. vol. li, no. 3, p. 427.

touched.[1] There are rulings of the House of Commons which appear to hold that when a bill seeks to amend only certain sections of an Act, amendments to other sections are out of order.[2]

In the case of the Preventive Detention (Second Amendment) Bill, it was ruled by the Speaker of the House of the People that amendments to the provisions of the parent Act which were not sought to be amended would be admissible if they were within the scope of the amendments which were before the Committee.[3]

When it is sought to continue an Act after the expiry of the date mentioned in the Act by an amending bill, an amendment seeking to amend the provisions of the Act is inadmissible.[4] It has been the practice in the House of Commons that in the case of Expiring Laws Continuance Bills, amendments to the provisions it is sought to continue are ruled out of order.[5]

BILL TO CONFIRM AGREEMENTS

When a bill is introduced to ratify or give effect to an agreement, the agreement is appended as a schedule to the bill. No amendment to the schedule embodying the agreement can be made. The House may reject the agreement as a whole; no alteration of the terms of the agreement is possible.[6]

TITLES, MARGINAL NOTES AND HEADINGS OF PARTS

Marginal notes, headings of chapters or parts of a bill are not put to the House and no amendment of these is admissible. If by reason of amendments any change in the marginal note or heading is neeessary it may be made by the secretariat.

The long title of the bill is also not put for standing part of the bill. The long title can be altered, if necessary, by the

---

[1] B.L.A.P. vol. li, no. 4, p. 1639; H.P.D. 11 July 1952, c. 3609; I.P.D. 8 Feb. 1951, c. 2573.

[2] H.C.D. 1917, vol. 99, c. 817; ibid. 1903, vol. 122, c. 1886.

[3] H.P.D. 1952, vol. 3, part 2, c. 4209; L.S.D. 3 Dec. 1954.

[4] W.B.L.A.P. 1953, vol. vii, no. 1, p. 622; L.S.D. 13 Dec. 1954.

[5] H.C.D. 1925, vol. 188, c. 240; ibid. 1948-9, vol. 469, c. 815.

[6] W.B.L.A.P. 1951, vol. iv, p. 137.

16

secretariat if the bill as amended makes such a course necessary.

In the British Parliament an amendment of the long title is made in the Committee although no question that the long title do form part of the bill is put.[1]

In the Indian Parliament, however, the long title and the enacting formula also are put to the House for standing part of the bill.

THIRD READING

When the clauses and the schedules and the preamble, if any, and the enacting formula and the title of the bill where necessary have been agreed to, a motion is made that the bill as settled in the House be passed. The debate on such a motion is commonly known as a third reading, although no motion in terms that the bill be read a third time, as in the House of Commons, is made in India. There is a rule incorporated in the rules of procedure of all legislatures that if a bill has been amended in the House any member may object to the third reading of the bill on the same day, and such objection if raised should prevail. This is a salutary rule (but often not observed in practice, the Presiding Officer having authority to suspend the rule and often doing so), particularly when a bill has been extensively amended, because it allows some time to consider the effect of amendments and to see whether any inconsistencies have crept in. Such a course would also help the members to participate in the debate on the third reading of the bill more profitably.

A bill may be amended during the course of the third reading, but to a motion that the bill may be passed the only amendments that are permissible are those of a formal or verbal character or consequential upon any amendment having been made to the bill during the consideration stage.[2]

The debate on the third reading of a bill is of a restricted character, limited to the matters contained in the bill;[3] the rules provide that the discussion must be confined to submis-

---

[1] May, p. 564.
[2] Ibid, p. 578.
[3] L.A.D. 24 Feb. 1932, p. 1154; ibid. 28 Feb. 1946, p. 1691; ibid. 29 Feb. 1952, c. 1551.

sion of arguments either in support or rejection of the bill, and the details of the bill cannot be referred to further than is necessary for the purpose of such arguments which should be of a general nature.[1]

The motion is then put and voted upon.

After a bill has been passed, no alteration in the bill is permissible; the rules of procedure for all legislatures, however, authorize the Presiding Officer or the Secretary (as in West Bengal) to correct patent errors and make such other changes in the bill as are consequential on the amendments accepted by the House, e.g. renumbering of clauses and correcting references to sections in the clauses necessitated by such renumbering.

After a bill has been passed and is in the possession of the Lok Sabha, the bill is sent to the draftsman, Ministry of Law for scrutiny. Where an amendment to a clause has been moved and adopted by the House and the official draftsman, while scrutinizing the bill as passed, has subsequently suggested any correction which is accepted by the Speaker as valid, such a correction is incorporated in the body of the amendment itself without any footnote in the printed debate. Where the Speaker accepts a correction suggested by the official draftsman relating to a clause and *not* to an amendment to a clause which has been adopted by the House, such a correction is indicated with an appropriate footnote in the printed debate. For instance, extensive changes were made to the Companies Bill 1956, after the Bill had been passed by both the Houses.

SENDING OF BILL FROM ONE HOUSE TO THE OTHER

Where there are two Houses of the legislature, the next step is to transmit the bill as passed by the House in which the bill originated to the other for its concurrence.

A message from the originating House signed either by the Presiding Officer or the Secretary, and accompanied by a certain number of copies of the bill also similarly signed, is sent to the other House. The message is read in the House

---

[1] L.S.D. 1955, vol. ix, c. 251; ibid. 1956, vol. ix, c. 893; ibid. 1953, vol. ix, c. 110.

and copies of the bill are laid on the table. Thereafter, any Minister, in the case of a Government bill, or any member in the case of a Private Member's bill, may give notice that the bill be taken into consideration. The period of notice is provided by the rules of procedure, and short notice may also be given with the consent of the Presiding Officer. The subsequent procedure of discussion and amendment is the same as in the originating House discussed above except in the case of Money Bills. After the bill is passed by the receiving House, it is sent back to the originating House with amendments, if any.

DISAGREEMENT BETWEEN TWO HOUSES: INDIAN PARLIAMENT

If a bill (except a Money Bill) passed by and transmitted from one House is amended by the other House, the bill as amended is sent back to the originating House. If the originating House does not agree to the amendments or makes further amendments to which the other House does not agree, the President may summon a joint session of the two Houses.[1] If the President notifies his intention to summon a joint session by message the Houses are precluded from proceeding further with the bill. The bill is considered by the two Houses in the joint sitting, and is deemed to be passed by the two Houses in the form in which it is passed by a majority of the total number of members of both Houses present and voting.

At a joint sitting, (a) if the bill, having been passed by one House, has not been passed by the other House with amendments and returned to the originating House, no amendments can be proposed to the bill other than such amendments, if any, as are made necessary by the delay in the passage of the bill, and (b) if the bill has been so passed and returned, only such amendments as mentioned above and such other amendments as are relevant to the matter with respect to which the Houses have not agreed, may be proposed. The decision of the Presiding Officer as to the admissibility of such amendments is final.

A joint session may also be summoned if a bill passed by one House is rejected by the other, or if more than six months

[1] Art. 108.

elapse from the date of the reception of the bill by the other House without the bill being passed by it.

A curious procedure appears to have been adopted in the Lok Sabha with regard to the Manipur State Hill Peoples (Administration) Regulation (Amendment) Bill, 1954, on 30 May 1956. This bill was passed by the Rajya Sabha on 21 September 1954, and was transmitted to the Lok Sabha on 23 September 1954. When a bill is transmitted by the Rajya Sabha to the Lok Sabha, a Minister or a member, under the Lok Sabha Rules, has to give notice of a motion that the bill be taken into consideration. It is not clear whether such notice was given or not. On the other hand, it appears that a motion seeking the concurrence of the Rajya Sabha to leave being granted by the Lok Sabha to withdraw the bill was adopted by the Lok Sabha on 11 May 1956, and was transmitted to the Rajya Sabha for its concurrence. The Rajya Sabha having concurred, a motion for leave to with-draw the bill was placed on the order paper on 30 May 1956, and was thereupon adopted.[1]

This seems to be a rather strange procedure to adopt. If the Lok Sabha was not willing to pass the bill, it could have rejected the bill or laid it aside. There are instances in the British Parliament when either the House of Lords or the House of Commons has laid aside the bill transmitted by the other. Of course, under the Indian Constitution there is provision for a joint session in such cases. If the Government was not eager to proceed with the bill the President, who acts on the advice of the Ministers, might not have called a joint session, and the bill would have been laid aside with-out any further action. Then again, what was the necessity of seeking the concurrence of the Rajya Sabha? For the concurrence of the Rajya Sabha to a motion in the Lok Sabha to withdraw a bill is absolutely unnecessary. The Lok Sabha itself might have given the leave. And what is the effect of the granting of leave by the Lok Sabha? The effect is that the bill is withdrawn from the Lok Sabha but *not from the Rajya Sabha*. The leave of the Lok Sabha has no effect on the Rajya Sabha. The bill remains where it was, that is to say, the bill has been passed by the Rajya Sabha, has

[1] L.S.D. 30 May 1956.

been transmitted to the Lok Sabha and remains laid on the table of the Lok Sabha.

The Speaker of the House of the People presides over a joint sitting, and in his absence the Deputy Speaker, and in the absence of both the Speaker and the Deputy Speaker the Deputy Chairman of the Council of States presides.

In regard to Money Bills, the House of the People may or may not accept the recommendations of the Council of States for amendments (see below). In either case a Money Bill is deemed to be passed by both the Houses in the form it emerges from the House of the People after the bill is passed a second time.[1]

The Council of States is bound to return a Money Bill with or without recommendations within fourteen days of the receipt of the bill. If it does not do so, the bill is deemed to be passed after the expiry of fourteen days in the form in which it was passed by the House of the People.[2]

STATE LEGISLATURES

There is no provision for any joint session in the State legislatures. There is some difference of procedure when a bill (other than a Money Bill) is amended by the receiving House, dependent upon whether the receiving House is the Upper or the Lower House. If a bill transmitted by the Lower House has been amended by the Upper House the bill is sent back to the Lower House. The Lower House again considers the bill and may or may not accept the amendments made by the Upper House. If the Lower House accepts the amendments the bill is passed by the Lower House in the amended form. If it does not accept the amendments made by the Upper House, or if a bill passed by the Lower House is rejected by the Upper House, or if more than three months elapse from the date on which the bill is laid before the Upper House without the bill being passed by it, the Lower House may again pass the bill with or without amendments, if any, suggested by the Upper House and send it back again to the Upper House for concurrence. If, after a bill has been

---

[1] Art. 109.
[2] Ibid.

passed for the second time and transmitted to the Upper House, the Upper House (a) rejects the bill, or (b) does not pass it within one month from the date on which the bill is laid before it, or (c) makes any amendments to which the Lower House does not agree, the bill is deemed to be passed by both the Houses in the form in which it was passed for the second time with such amendments as may have been made by the Upper House and agreed to by the Lower House.[1]

In the case of a bill originating in the Upper House the bill is sent to the Lower House. If the Lower House amends the bill it is sent back to the Upper House. If the Upper House accepts the amendments the bill is deemed to be passed. But if the Upper House does not accept the amendments made by the Lower House it can again send back the bill to the Lower House. But unless and until the bill is agreed to by both Houses it cannot become law.

In regard to Money Bills the Upper House is bound to return a Money Bill within fourteen days of the receipt of the bill. If it does not do so the bill is deemed to be passed by the two Houses after the expiry of fourteen days in the form it was passed by the Lower House. If the Upper House makes any recommendations for amendments the Lower House may or may not accept the amendments. In either case, the bill is deemed to be passed by the two Houses in the form it is passed by the Lower House on the second occasion.[2]

MONEY AND FINANCIAL BILLS

There are two classes of bills which may contain financial provisions, (a) Money Bills as defined in Articles 110 and 199 of the Constitution, and (b) other bills containing financial provisions which may be called Financial Bills.

A bill is deemed to be a Money Bill when it contains only provisions dealing with all or any of the following matters:

(i) The imposition, abolition, remission, alteration or regulation of any tax;

(ii) the regulation of the borrowing of money, or the giving

[1] Art. 197.
[2] Art. 198.

of any guarantee by the Union or the State, or the amendment of the law with respect to any financial obligations undertaken or to be undertaken by the Union or the State;

(iii) the custody of the Consolidated Fund or the Contingency Fund of the Union or the State, the payment of moneys into or the withdrawal of moneys from any such fund;

(iv) the appropriation of moneys out of the Consolidated Fund;

(v) the declaring of any expenditure to be expenditure charged on the Consolidated Fund, or the increasing of the amount of any such expenditure;

(vi) the receipt of money on account of the Consolidated Fund or the public account of the Union or the State, or the custody or issue of such money, (and in the case of the Union) the audit of the accounts of the Union or of a State;

(vii) any matter incidental to any of those specified above.

It should be noted that in order to be deemed a Money Bill, a bill should contain *only* any or all of the matters enumerated in Articles 110 and 199. If any other matter is included in a bill containing any or all of the aforesaid matters, the bill will not be considered a Money Bill.[1] This definition substantially follows the definition of a Money Bill in the English Parliament Act of 1911. And such an interpretation has been put upon the relevant section of that Act.[2]

An Appropriation Bill which does not impose any tax or divide the amount sought to be drawn from the Consolidated Fund is not a Money Bill.[3]

Three other classes of bills involving financial matters have been excluded from the category of Money Bills:

(a) bills which provide for the imposition of fines or other pecuniary penalties;

(b) bills which provide for the demand or payment of fees for licenses or fees for services rendered;

(c) bills which provide for the imposition, abolition, remission, alteration or regulation of any tax by any local authority or body for local purposes.[4]

---

[1] L.S.D. 1955, vol. viii, c. 15810.
[2] May, p. 820.
[3] L.S.D. 1957, vol. x, c. 5617.
[4] Arts. 110, 199.

RESTRICTION AS TO MONEY BILLS

There are two restrictions in regard to Money Bills: (i) they cannot be introduced in the Upper House, and (ii) they cannot be introduced without the recommendation of the Head of the State.[1]

The power of the Upper House is also limited in regard to Money Bills. A Money Bill after it has been passed by the Lower House is transmitted to the other House for its consideration and recommendation. The Upper House has no right to amend a Money Bill; but it can recommend to the Lower House that certain amendments be made.[2] This provision of the Constitution has been adopted from the practice which obtains in Australia and is known as 'the process of suggestion.' The practice had its origin in the South Australian Parliament in 1857, when the two Houses agreed that it would be 'competent for this Council to suggest any alteration in any such Bill,' viz. Money Bills. Such a provision was subsequently embodied in Section 53 of the Commonwealth of Australia Constitution, 1900.

The procedure adopted is as follows. After a Money Bill has been transmitted to the Upper House, the Minister-in-charge of the bill makes a motion that the bill be taken into consideration. After the motion for consideration is adopted, a motion may be made in the following form: 'That the Council recommends that in Clause such and such, the following words be added or substituted' as the case may be. The motions for recommendations are taken clause by clause. The recommendations may be for specific amendments in the clause or in general terms. It is more convenient if recommendations are in the nature of specific amendments of clauses as in that case drafting motions for amendments is obviated in the Lower House.

If the motions for recommendations are accepted, the bill is sent back to the Lower House with the recommendations in the form of a schedule. If no recommendations are made the bill is sent back without any recommendations.

There is no necessity for putting the clauses to the vote or

[1] Arts. 109, 117, 198, 207.
[2] Arts. 109, 198.

for making any motion that the bill be passed. Although in certain legislatures questions are put that the clauses do stand part of the bill and also that the bill be passed, the procedure is not warranted by the Constitution. There does not seem to be any scope for the Upper House to pass a Money Bill although the words 'shall be deemed to have been passed by both Houses' in clauses (3), (4) and (5) of Article 198 seem to imply that passing by the Upper House is also necessary in the case of Money Bills. It is difficult, however, to see in what form a motion for a third reading would be made in the Upper House when recommendations have been made for amendments in the bill. The motion cannot be in the form that 'the Bill be passed' because the House is not willing to pass the bill as transmitted by the Lower House. It cannot be that 'the Bill be passed with the recommendations made,' because that would carry no meaning. It seems therefore that the only duty of the Upper House is to take up a Money Bill at the consideration stage, to have a general discussion, and if the consideration motion is passed, to propose recommendations (either in general terms or in the form of specific amendments to the clauses of the bill), and after the recommendations are adopted to send back the bill to the Lower House with the recommendations, and if no recommendations are proposed, to send the bill after the consideration motion is passed to the Lower House with a certificate that no recommendations are made. Of course, if no recommendations for amendments are made the Upper House may pass a motion that the bill be passed. But it does not seem logical that two different procedures should be adopted in respect of the same class of bills.

It is instructive to note here the procedure adopted by the Irish Senate, because analogous provisions obtained there in respect of Money Bills. Mr Hugh Kennedy, the Attorney-General, who afterwards became Chief Justice, was of the opinion that the functions of the Upper House in regard to Money Bills were strictly limited to the making of recommendations. But the Senate drew up its standing orders in accordance with the view that Money Bills should be dealt with so far as possible on the same basis as other bills. Every Money Bill was given a second reading when a general discussion might take place; a third (Committee) stage and a fourth (Report) stage when recommendations (instead of amendments) might be passed; and a fifth stage when the bill was finally passed. It was then duly certified and returned with a list of recommendations, if any, that had been made or with a certificate that no recommendation had been made.[1]

As has been stated above, it is difficult to formulate the form of a motion for a third reading when recommendations for amendments in the bill have been accepted by the Upper House. In the case of bills other than Money Bills, a motion may be made that the bill be passed because the Upper House may pass a bill in a different form than that passed by the Lower House, although such a bill would not become law unless some other formalities are gone through. But a motion, in the case of a Money Bill when recommendations have been made, that 'the Bill be passed' or that 'the Bill be passed with recommendations' seems singularly inappropriate. If at all necessary, the motion may be that 'the Bill be sent back to the Lower House with or without recommendations'.

In the Upper Houses in India a motion that the bill be returned is made. In West Bengal, previous to the adoption of new rules in 1961, no motion was made after the consideration motion was passed. The bill was returned with a message that no recommedations had been made or that recommendations had been made, as the case might be.

Financial Bills cannot be introduced without the recommendation of the Head of the State and cannot be introduced in the Upper House, but they can be amended by the Upper House because Articles 109 and 198 appply only to Money Bills defined under Articles 110 and 199. (As regards amendments see p. 238)

When a Money Bill is transmitted to the Upper House from the Lower House a certificate that the bill is a Money Bill has to be subscribed by the Speaker. The certificate is conclusive on the question whether a bill is a Money Bill or not. The Upper House has no right to question the certificate. This is also the view taken in the British Parliament

[1] Donal O'Sullivan, *Irish Free State and its Senate*, 1940 ed. p. 546.

where the Speaker has to certify a Money Bill under the Parliament Act, 1911.[1]

There was some discussion in the Indian Parliament as to the meaning of the expression 'if any question arises' in clause (3) of Article 110 (a similar expression occurs in Article 199), which lays down that the decision of the Speaker shall be final if any question arises whether a bill is a Money Bill or not. It was contended that the Speaker's certificate appended under clause (4) could not be conclusive, but that if a question is raised in the House (whether the Lower or the Upper) the Speaker would be called upon to give a decision and such decision would be conclusive. But the contention did not prevail.[2]

(For Appropriation Bills, see Financial Procedure)

ULTRA VIRES BILLS

Questions often arise as to whether a bill is within the legislative competence of the legislature in which it is introduced and as to the function of the Presiding Officer if such questions are raised. The competence of the legislature is determined by various factors. Certain bills (e.g. bills regulating trade and commerce) require the previous sanction of the President if they are to be introduced in State legislatures; certain bills, e.g. Money Bills, require the recommendation of the Head of the State before they can be introduced. Legislative competence also depends upon the subject matter of legislation—whether a particular subject matter is within the Union List or the State List of Schedule VII of the Constitution. Such a question can arise not only when a particular bill relates to a matter not within the legislative list giving the legislature the authority to legislate, but also when a bill is *prima facie* within the relevant legislative list but may incidentally encroach on a matter not within the competence of the legislature. Different questions of law arise in such circumstances, and reports of decided cases show to what extent even the law courts may differ in their views.

The following principles should therefore be borne in mind

[1] May, p. 818.
[2] C.S.D. 30 Apr. 1953, vol. iii, c. 4455.

when any question of legislative competence is raised. If a bill is on the face of it inadmissible, e.g., if it is sought to introduce a bill which requires the previous sanctions or recommendation of the Governor without such sanction or recommendation, the Presiding Officer will rule such a bill to be out of order and inadmissible unless such sanction or recommendation is forthcoming. But if the competence of the legislature depends upon the construction of the Constitution or any question of law upon which different views may be held, the Presiding Officer would not take upon himself the responsibility of deciding such a question and prevent the bill from being introduced or passed. The question of whether such a bill is *ultra vires* would have to be decided, if occasion arises, in a court of law. In short, if the admissibility of a bill depends upon some question of procedure, the Speaker will decide the point and give his ruling either for or against the bill; but if it depends upon some substantive question of law, the Speaker would not decide the question so as to prevent the bill being introduced or passed. As has been expressed by Bourinot: 'The Speaker will not give a decision upon a constitutional question, nor decide a question of law though the same be raised on a point of order or privilege.'[1]

In a case in West Bengal a question arose whether the President's prior sanction was necessary to a bill. The Government obtained legal opinion that it was not necessary. The Speaker, although he felt some doubt as to the soundness of the opinion, allowed the bill to proceed in view of the fact that the defect, if any, might be cured by the subsequent assent of the Preisdent.[2] In Madhya Bharat, however, in a similar case, a bill was not allowed to proceed without the President's sanction.[3]

---

[1] Bourinot, *Parliamentary Procedure*, p. 180; Hatsell, vol. ii, p. 227; Redlich, vol. i, p. 31; ibid. vol. ii, p. 159; Beauchesne, *Paliamentary Practice and Procedure*, p. 825; Parl. Deb. 1858, vol. 150, c. 2104; B.L.A.P.vol. liv, no. 2, p. 223; ibid. vol. liv, no. 5, p. 326; ibid. vol. lviii, p. 289; W.B.L.A.P. vol. i, 1947-8, p. 185; W.B.L.A.P. 1953, vol. viii, c. 253; L.A.D. 17 Feb. 1942, p. 283; L.A.D. 25 Mar. 1942, p. 1533; Con.A.L.D. 9 Dec. 1947, p. 1568; H.P.D. 25 Nov. 1952, c. 1148; L.S.D. vol. iii, 15 Apr. 1955, c. 5324; I.P.D. 1951, vol. viii, c. 2607; ibid. 1951, vol. xi, c. 7366; L.S.D. 1955, vol. v, c. 9042; ibid. 1955, vol. x, c. 2483; ibid. 1956, vol. viii, c. 5292; ibid. 1957, vol. viii, c. 390; ibid. 1957, vol. x, c. 7134.

[2] W.B.L.A.P. 1955, vol. xii, no. 2, p. 31.

[3] Ruling of Deputy Speaker, 12 Apr. 1956.

ASSENT

When a bill is passed or deemed to have been passed by both Houses the bill is sent to the Head of the State for his assent. The Head of the State may assent to the bill or may withhold his assent, and may in the case of bills passed by State legislatures reserve the bill for the consideration of the President.[1] If a bill is, in the opinion of the Head of the State, of such a nature that if it became law it would so derogate from the powers of the High Court as to endanger the position which the High Court is designed to fulfil under the Constitution, the bill must be reserved for the consideration of the President.[2]

If a bill which a State legislature is competent to enact under the Concurrent List contains any provision inconsistent with the provision of any law made by the Parliament or any existing law, then, in order that such provisions may have validity, the bill must be reserved for the consideration of the President and must receive his assent.[3]

There are certain other classes of bills, such as bills for the acquisition of any 'estate' or property, which also require the assent of the President.[4]

There has been no occasion since 1947 of any bill being refused assent by the Head of the State. In England also there has been no occasion of any bill being refused assent by the Crown since 1707. There has been some difference of opinion among constitutional lawyers regarding the question whether the Head of the State in assenting to a bill should act at his own discretion or on the advice of his Ministers. It may be argued that, as all legislation must have been initiated or supported by the Ministry, the Ministry can have no occasion to advise against the giving of assent by the Head of the State, and if the Head of the State is to act on the advice of his Ministers his assent is a mere formality. Circumstances may, however, be conceived in which the Head of the State, e.g. a Governor, may have to withhold his assent on the direction of the President to any bill which has been passed by a State

[1] Arts. 111, 200.
[2] Art. 200.
[3] Art. 254.
[4] Art. 31.

legislature, but which is against the policy of the Central Government. A constitutional crisis may arise, but it cannot be said that the Governor would be acting unconstitutionally if he withholds his assent in such circumstances. This is, however, a matter of constitutional propriety and not of procedure, and we can leave the question at that.

The Head of the State may also send a bill back for reconsideration either as a whole or with respect to any specified provisions thereof, and may also suggest amendments to the bill. The House, or where there are two Houses of legislature, the Houses, must then reconsider the bill, and may or may not accept the amendments suggested by the Head of the State. The bill, after being reconsidered and passed, has to be presented again to the Head of the State for his assent. This time the Head of the State is bound to give his assent.[1]

The President may also direct the Head of any State to send back a bill (other than a Money Bill), which has been reserved for his consideration, for reconsideration by the legislature which had passed the bill. The legislature must reconsider the bill within six months, and present it to the President for his assent. The President may then assent to the bill; he may also withhold his assent.[2]

PROCEDURE OF RECONSIDERATION

When a bill is returned for reconsideration the procedure in regard to bills in general applies *mutatis mutandis* to the consideration of the bill as a whole, or of the amendments suggested by the Head of the State. Amendments suggested by the Head of the State are treated as amendments to clauses and are moved and put accordingly.

The question whether the President or the Governor can return a bill with a message that the bill be 'dropped' arose in the Bihar Legislative Assembly on 18 January 1951. It appears that the President sent a message to the Bihar Legislature recommending the dropping of the Bihar Black Marketing Bill, which had been reserved for his assent. The Speaker ruled, and it seems he was right in ruling, that the

[1] Arts. 111, 200.
[2] Art. 201.

message was not inconsistent with the provisions of the Constitution. The real difficulty lies in the form of the motion to be moved. In such cases the usual motion is that the bill as returned by the Governor be taken into consideration, and amendments, if any, suggested by the Governor or the President are either accepted or rejected. In this case a motion was moved that the bill be 'dropped'. The proper motion would have been, after the consideration of the bill as returned by the Governor, to move that the decision of the House that the bill be passed be rescinded or discharged.

PENDING BILLS

A bill pending in the legislature (in any of the Houses where there are two Houses) does not lapse on prorogation of the legislature or of any of the Houses of the legislature.[1] A bill will be deemed to be pending when it has been introduced, and not when only notice of an intention to introduce (in the case of Government bills) and to move for leave to introduce (in the case of Private Members' bills) is given. The rules of legislatures, however, provide that bills of which only notice has been given, but which have not been actually introduced, would not lapse.

When a bill has been partly gone into in one session, it can be proceeded with in the next session from the stage in which it was left in the previous session.[2] The practice in the House of Commons is quite different. All proceedings pending at the date of prorogation are quashed. Every bill has to be renewed after prorogation as if it were being introduced for the first time. Proposals were made for the continuance of bills from one session to another but did not find favour.[3]

All bills pending in that House, as also all bills which have been passed by the Lower House but are pending in the Upper House, lapse[4] on the dissolution of the Lower House.

However, bills pending in the Upper House, except bills

---

[1] Arts. 107, 196.
[2] Bengal Secondary Education Bill, 1940, (order of Speaker, 18 Sept. 1941).
[3] May, p. 280.
[4] Arts. 107, 196.

transmitted by the Lower House, do not lapse on the dissolution of the Lower House.[1]

MORE THAN ONE BILL WITH THE SAME PURPOSE IN THE SAME SESSION

There is no bar to the introduction of more than one bill relating to the same subject and containing similar provisions during the same session. But if the House has given a decision on one of such bills, e.g. if the House has taken one bill into consideration or committed it to a Select Committee or has circulated the bill for opinion, the other bill cannot be proceeded with in the same session.[2] If, however, a bill has been withdrawn, another bill with the same object may be proceeded with. If a part of a bill refers to a subject on which the House has already come to a decision in another bill, the subsequent bill may be proceeded with in Committee (e.g. can be referred to a Select Committee), for it would then be open to the Committee to strike out the offending clause.[3]

AMENDMENT OF ACT IN THE SAME SESSION

In England, formerly, an Act could not be amended in the same session in which it had been passed on the ground of repetition. But this is now allowed by the Interpretation Act, 1889. There is no statutory provision either way in India, though it seems that the principle of the Interpretation Act would be followed in India, and amendment of an Act in the same session in which it is passed would be allowed.

DELEGATED LEGISLATION

The grant of rule-making powers to the executive Government has been a feature of legislative practice from the very beginning of the functioning of legislatures in India. There is no constitutional impropriety in the delegation of powers to the executive, since, as in England, the doctrine of the

---

[1] Arts. 107, 196.
[2] May, p. 522.
[3] Parl. Deb. 1870, vol. 203, c. 563.

17

separation of powers is not the basis of the Indian Constitution. Although at one time the Supreme Court had viewed such delegation with abhorrence,[1] there has been a change in outlook, and the recent trend of the decisions of that Court is in favour of holding such delegation as valid.[2]

The usefulness of the delegation of rule-making powers cannot be questioned. In these days of extensive legislation, minute procedural or technical details can be left to be worked by rules rather than by taking up the time of the legislature for such matters, provided definite principles are laid down and there is scope for proper parliamentary control.

Statutory instruments as they are known in England, or rules or regulations as they are known in India, fall into the following classes:

(i) Rules that are not laid before the legislature; these relate to minor procedural matters which may safely be left to the executive without any provision for parliamentary control.

(ii) Rules that are laid before the legislature for information only without any further provision for parliamentary control.

(iii) Rules that are laid before the legislature and are liable to modification by the legislature within a prescribed period of time.

(iv) Rules that are liable to be annulled by the legislature.

(v) Rules that require the approval of the legislature before they can come into operation.

Classes (iv) and (v) do not appear to have come into existence in India. Class (iii) exists in India but does not exist in England. The Select Committee of the House of Commons on Delegated Legislation, however, disapproved the proposal for the introduction of this class of rules on the ground that:

'If a procedure were introduced whereby amendments to the statutory instruments could be moved, debated and decided, then Parliament instead of being relieved of the burden of attending to detail, would find itself engaged more than ever in disposing of matters of detail.'[3]

---

[1] *Jatindra's Case*, 1949, F.C.R. 595.
[2] *In re Delhi Laws Act* S.C.R. 1951 (110, 747).
[3] H. C. *Paper* 310 of 1953.

Parliamentary control over delegated legislation, that is to say, over statutory rules framed under statutes, may be exercised in various ways. The legislature may empower the authority delegated to frame rules without any reference to the legislature. In such a case parliamentary control can only be exercised by the legislature as the supreme legislative authority by either repealing or amending the rules by legislation.

Parliamentary control can also be exercised in any of the following ways:

(a) by retaining a power of scrutiny, without any power of annulment or confirmation;

(b) by retaining the right of annulment by simple resolution; or

(c) by retaining the right of confirmation by simple resolution.

In the first case, a statute may prescribe simply that the rules framed thereunder shall be laid before the legislature. In such a case the House has no authority to amend or annul the rules (except of course by legislation). The House cannot take into consideration such rules unless there is a motion before the House. As the Government would be under no necessity to allot any time for the consideration of such rules, they may be considered only on a non-official resolution on a non-official day.

In England any matter relating to statutory rules which are simply laid before the House of Commons can be raised either by question to the Minister concerned or on a motion for adjournment at the end of business. It is also possible to canvass such a rule on a substantive motion; but if such a motion were agreed to, it would have no binding legal effect, being merely the expression of the opinion of the House.

It should be noted that the validity or the coming into operation of such rules does not depend upon the laying thereof before the legislature if the statute simply says that rules shall be laid before the legislature. The only consequence is to make the Minister responsible to the legislature. Even if the rules are laid after inordinate delay, no consequence follows. In 1944 a point of order was raised in the Bengal Legislative Assembly whether rules made under the Motor

Vehicles Act, which it was proposed to lay before the House long after they were made, should be allowed to be laid. Mr. Speaker Nausher Ali ruled that he could not disallow the laying. The Chief Minister pointed out that the House might censure the Government, but there was no defect in the laying.[1] The enabling statute may of course provide that the rules would not be operative unless laid before the House.

In the British House of Commons a curious incident happened some time ago. Under the Fire Services Emergency Provisions Act, 1941, it was provided that regulations made under the Act should be laid before Parliament, and that either House would have the power to annul any regulation within twenty-eight sitting days after the regulation had been laid. It was discovered about three years after the regulations were made that the regulations were not laid in time. The regulations were laid again before Parliament after the discovery, and an Act (National Fire Service Regulations Indemnity Act, 1944) indemnified the Secretary of State from all consequences of not laying them in due time. It does not appear that any objection was raised as to the validity of the regulations[2].

When a right of annulment is retained by the legislature the statute ordinarily provides that the rules shall be laid before the legislature and shall be liable to annulment within a specified period. That is what is known as the method of control by negative resolution.

In the case of confirmation—known as the method of 'positive resolution'—the rules must be confirmed by the House before they can come into operation.

In either of the above cases a right of amending the rules may also be retained.

In the case of a positive resolution, it is the Government which must come before the House and allot time for discussion. In the case of a negative resolution, if a member gives notice of any such resolution or gives notice of any amendment when a right of amendment has been retained, it seems it would be the duty of the Government to allot time for the discussion. In the British Parliament proceedings

[1] B.L.A.P. vol. lxvii, no. 1, p. 425.
[2] See Herbert Morrison, *Government and Parliament* pp. 321-23.

for annulment of statutory regulations are 'exempted business', and do not interfere with the programme of daily
business. But as pointed out by May,[1] in the case of exceptionally controversial orders or regulations, the Government
may find it necessary to set apart some of their own time for
debating motions for disallowance. The procedure of 'prayers'
for the annulment of statutory rules is not known in India.

When any statute prescribes that rules can be amended or
annulled within a specified time, and the legislature is prorogued or adjourned before the expiry of the period, a question
may arise on how the requirements of the statute are to be
satisfied. The English Statutory Instruments Act, 1946,
provides for the contingency, and lays down that in computing the period no account is to be taken of time during
which Parliament is dissolved or prorogued or during which
both Houses are adjourned for more than four days. The
rules of all legislatures provide that where rules are required
to be laid before the House for a specified period, and such
period is not completed on or before the day of the last sitting
of the session in which they are laid, the rules shall be relaid
in the succeeding session or sessions until the said period is
completed in one session.

The Presiding Officer may allot time for the consideration
of amendments to such rules of which notice may be given
by any member.

Rules provide that when a bill contains proposals for the
delegation of legislative power, a memorandum explaining
such proposals and drawing attention to their scope and
stating also whether they are of normal or exceptional character
must accompany the notice of the bill.

The Indian Parliament and most of other legislatures set
up committees to scrutinize and report to the House whether
the powers delegated by the legislatures have been properly
exercised within the framework of the statute delegating such
powers. When rules are laid before the House, it is the duty
of the committee to examine such rules and report to the
House after considering the following matters:

(i) whether it is in accord with the general objects of the
Act pursuant to which it is made;

[1] May, p. 306.

(ii) whether it contains matter which in the opinion of the committee should more properly be dealt with in an Act of Parliament or the State legislature;

(iii) whether it contains an imposition of taxation;

(iv) whether it directly or indirectly bars the jurisdiction of the courts;

(v) whether it gives retrospective effect to any of the provisions in respect of which the Act does not expressly give any such power;

(vi) whether it involves expenditure from the Consolidated Fund or the Public Accounts;

(vii) whether it appears to make some unusual or unexpected use of the powers conferred by the Act pursuant to which it is made;

(viii) whether there appears to have been unjustifiable delay in the publication or laying it before the legislature;

(ix) whether for any reason its form or purport calls for any elucidation.

Many of the statutes of Indian legislatures provide that rules are to be made after previous publication. If such be the case, a draft of the rules has to be published in a manner prescribed by the Government (ordinarily in the Official Gazette), and time has to be given for submitting objections to the rules, and the rule-making authority has to take into consideration objections if any are submitted.

CHAPTER XII

SYSTEM OF COMMITTEES

THERE are various matters for which the House is not a suitable forum of discussion or action. If, for example, an enquiry is to be held, it must be made by a small committee rather than a House containing hundreds of members. Such tasks are often entrusted to committees constituted *ad hoc*, e.g. select committees or standing committees such as the Committee of Privileges. The committees take evidence, if necessary, investigate or deliberate upon the matter referred to them and make a report containing their conclusions and findings. No committee can, however, bind the House by their report. It is for the House to take any action on the report. Very often reports are made only for the purpose of information of the House and no action is taken.

Certain general rules govern the procedure of committees. The members of the committees are often elected on a motion, but some of them are formed by nomination by the Presiding Officer. In some of the committees, the composition of the House party-wise is reflected, e.g. the Committee of Public Accounts which is elected on the principle of proportional representation. The Committee of Privileges is nominated by the Presiding Officer.

The following are the classes of committees which are common in the legislatures:

(i) Committee of the Whole House. The House may resolve itself into a committee but this is not usual in India.

(ii) Business Advisory Committee. This committee is nominated by the Presiding Officer. The function of this committee is to recommend the time that should be allocated for the discussion of the stage or stages of such Government bills and other business as the Presiding Officer in consultation with the Leader of the House may direct to be referred to the committee. (See p. 75).

(iii) The Committee on Petitions is also nominated by the Presiding Officer, and its function is to examine all petitions submitted to the House and direct the circulation of such petitions if they are in order.

(iv) The Estimates Committee and the Committee on Public Accounts are two financial committees through which the House keeps a check on expenditure. For detailed discussion see Chapter xiv.

(v) The Committee of Privileges is, as stated above, nominated by the Speaker and examines all questions of breach of privilege which are referred to it.

(vi) The Committee on Subordinate Legislation. All rules to be laid before the House are examined by this committee, and the function of the committee is to consider:

(a) whether the rules are in accordance with the general objects of the Constitution or the Act pursuant to which they are made;

(b) whether they contain matters which should be properly dealt with in an Act;

(c) whether they contain the imposition of any tax;

(d) whether they directly or indirectly bar the jurisdiction of the courts;

(e) whether they give retrospective effect to any of the provisions where the Act or Constitution does not confer such authority;

(f) whether they involve expenditure from the Consolidated Fund or the public accounts;

(g) whether they appear to make any unexpected or unusual use of the powers conferred;

(h) whether there have been unjustifiable delays in the publication of the rules or in laying them before Parliament;

(i) whether for any reason they call for any elucidation.

(vii) The Committee on Government Assurances scrutinizes the assurances, promises, undertakings, etc. given by Ministers from time to time on the floor of the House, and reports on the extent to which such assurances etc. have been implemented; and where implemented, whether such implementation has taken place within the necessary minimum.

(viii) The Committee on Absence of Members from the Sittings of the House considers all applications for leave of absence from members and may, it seems, report against granting leave. It also considers whether a member's seat should be declared vacant when a member has been absent for more than sixty days.

(ix) The Rules Committee considers whether any amendment or modification of any such rules is necessary and reports its opinion. The amendments proposed are promulgated as rules unless any member gives notice of any amendment. By virtue of this provision rules in the Indian legislatures are always in a fluid state and may be amended very easily.

(x) The Committee on Private Members' Bills and Resolutions decides on the priority of Private Members' bills having regard to their importance, and classifies them as category A and category B and allocates the time to be allotted to such bills and resolutions.

(xi) The Committee on Public Undertakings. A committee has been constituted in the Lok Sabha to investigate into the working of public undertakings. The committee consists of ten members of the Lok Sabha and five members of the Rajya Sabha elected on the principle of proportional representation. The functions of the committee are:

(a) to examine the reports and accounts of the public undertakings specified in the Schedule;

(b) to examine the reports, if any, of the Comptroller and Auditor General on the public undertakings;

(c) to examine, in the context of the autonomy and efficiency of public undertakings, whether the affairs of public undertakings are being managed in accordance with sound business principles and prudent commercial practices; and

(d) such other functions vested in the Public Accounts Committee and the Estimates Committee in relation to the public undertakings specified in the Schedule by or under the Rules of Procedure and Conduct of Business of the House as are not covered by clauses (a), (b) and (c) above and as may be allotted to the committee by the Speaker from time to time.

Provided that the committee shall not examine and investigate any of the following matters, namely:

(a) matters of major Government policy as distinct from business or commercial functions of public undertakings;

(b) matters of day-to-day administration;

(c) matters for the consideration of which machinery is established by any special statute under which a particular public undertaking is established.

(xii) Besides these, there are other committees—the General Purposes Committee, the House Committee and the Library Committee. The function of the General Purposes Committee is to consider and advise on such matters concerning the affairs of the House as may be referred to it by the Speaker. The House Committee deals with matters of accommodation, food and medical aid of members. The Library Committee's function is (a) to consider and advise on such matters concerning the Library as may be referred to it by the Speaker, (b) to consider suggestions for improvement of the Library and (c) to assist members in fully utilizing the services provided by the Library.

PROCEDURE IN COMMITTEES

The Chairman of a committee is nominated by the Presiding Officer, but if the Deputy Presiding officer is a member of the committee he has to be nominated as Chairman.

The quorum is fixed at one-third of the number of members of a committee. There is provision for the discharge of a member from the committee if he is absent from two or more consecutive meetings of the committee. Committees are authorized under the rules to appoint sub-committees to take evidence and send for persons and papers. Proceedings before committees are considered confidential, and any premature publication of its proceedings is considered a breach of privilege. The committees may sit during the sittings of the House and may also sit during the period of prorogation. The committee may sit only within the precincts of the House unless authorized by the Speaker to do otherwise.

There is no provision for any minority report except in the case of Select Committees on Bills. There is a time limit of three months, unless extended by the House, for making a report. Any report submitted by a committee may be made available by the committee to the Government before its presentation to the House.

These are the general rules of procedure and, as already stated, the Presiding Officer is authorized to give directions regarding procedure to any committee.

CHAPTER XIII

FINANCIAL PROCEDURE

THE Indian Constitution has adopted the fundamental principle governing the British financial system, namely parliamentary control over the receipt and expenditure of public money. It took centuries of struggle between the King and Parliament in England to achieve the supremacy of Parliament in matters of finance. In India, however, although the supreme control over the finances of the country was never vested completely in the legislature before Independence, the Indian financial system was essentially based on that of the United Kingdom, and when the Indian Constitution came to be framed it was an easy step to confer such control on the legislature.

GROWTH OF THE INDIAN FINANCIAL SYSTEM

An idea of the various changes undergone by the Indian financial system from a State with no control to one of full control by the legislature may be had from the brief history of the growth of the system outlined below.

There was hardly any properly organized system of financial administration at the time of the East India Company. By the Regulating Act of 1773, the Governor-General of Bengal and his Council were required to transmit to the Court of Directors reports of all transactions and matters relating to the revenues or interest of the Company. By Pitt's India Act of 1784, a Board of Control acting through a Minister responsible to the British Parliament was created to function in addition to the Court of Directors, but no appreciable change was made in the system of financial administration. By the Charter Act of 1833, the Governor-General of Bengal in Council was designated the Governor-General in Council of India, and the superintendence, direction and control of the revenues in India were vested in him. The financial powers of provincial governments did not rest on any statute but were derived from executive arrangements. By the Charter Act of 1853, a Legislative Council for the Governor-General was established, but the Council had no opportunity to say anything in matters of finance except in connection with bills for levying taxes. The Government of India Act, 1858, transferred from the hands of the Company to the British Crown the control of Indian affairs, to be exercised by a Secretary of State in concert, in certain cases, with a Council. In effect this Act applied almost solely to the Government in England, and the Government in India was carried on as before.

So far as matters of finance or financial administration were concerned, powers in varying degrees were exercised during this period by different authorities, namely the British Parliament, the Secretary of State in Council, the Governor-General in Council and the provincial governments. Section 2 of the Act of 1858 declared: 'And all the territorial and other revenues of or arising in India and all tributes and other payments in respect of any territories which would have been receivable by, or in the name of the said company, if this Act had not been passed, shall be received for, and in the name of, Her Majesty, and shall be applied and disposed of for the purposes of the Government of India alone, subject to the provisions of this Act.' Section 41 of the same Act provided that the expenditure of such revenues was placed under the control of the Secretary of State in Council, no grant or appropriation being allowed to be made without the concurrence of the majority of votes at a meeting of the Council of the Secretary of State. Under section 53, the accounts of each financial year were required to be placed before Parliament. The powers of the Governor-General were enlarged by delegation. The position of the provincial governments remained as before. It is noticeable that during this period, following the tradition of the Company, there was taxation with as well as without legislative sanction. The land revenue, which formed about half of the income of the Government of that time, revenues from forests, post offices, telegraphs, and tributes from Chiefs of native states were realized without any legal sanction. It may be mentioned here that Parliamentary control over Indian finance was nominal. It will be relevant to note here that the submission of accounts of the

Government of India before the British Parliament continued until India attained independence. The estimates of revenue and expenditure of the Government of India used to be laid before Parliament until the commencement of the Government of India Act, 1935, but the Finance Accounts continued to be laid there until 1947. The laying of the Accounts and the Estimates was in terms of the successive Government of India Acts beginning with that of 1858 as already mentioned.

At the time when the Act of 1858 came into force the finances of the Government of India were in a deplorable condition because of the 'Mutiny' which was then just over. There was a heavy addition to the public debt and the revenues were insufficient. No reforms were more urgent than the establishment of an efficient system of public accounts and strict financial control throughout India. This work was begun in 1860 by Mr. James Wilson, the well-known Secretary to the Treasury in England, and the first financial member of the Governor-General's Council under the Crown, and it was afterwards actively continued and completed. In carrying out these reforms it was perhaps inevitable at the outset that the Central Government should retain for itself a larger measure of financial control than would ultimately be expedient for it to exercise. In its anxiety to prevent extravagance it imposed rules of such stringency that no financial authority remained except its own. The whole of the revenues from all the provinces of British India were treated as belonging to a single fund, expenditure from which could be authorized only by the Governor-General in Council. The provincial governments were allowed no discretion in sanctioning fresh charges. For the first time in India income tax was levied at the instance of Mr. Wilson. Another step towards the improvement of financial administration made by Mr. Wilson was the preparation of the Budget and its presentation before the Legislative Council of the Governor-General. Mr. Wilson was appointed Finance Member in 1859, and within a few months of his appointment presented the first Budget on 18 February 1860, with a speech in the traditional style of the British Chancellor of the Exchequer. The legislature, however, did not discuss the Budget. The submission of the Budget was not enjoined either by any Act or by the rules of the Council. During this period, that is between 1853 and 1861, the Indian legislature was modelling itself on the procedure of the House of Commons. Much of the 'inconvenient degree of independence' on the part of the legislature was drastically curtailed by section 19 of the India Councils Act of 1861, but the presentation of the Budget was somehow not affected. Mr. Wilson died before the presentation of the next Budget in 1861, and his successor in the British Treasury, Mr. S. Laing, was appointed the Finance Member of the Governor-General's Council. He presented the Budget on 27 April 1861. In his speech Mr. Laing referred to the necessity of making provincial Budgets and their presentation before the provincial legislatures. Nothing, however, was done until 1871. Still, ever since 1860 the Budget was presented to the legislature in the Centre every year, except in 1873 and the three following years, when the Budgets were published in the Gazette.

The India Councils Act, 1861, remodelled and enlarged the Council of the Governor-General of India and also established Councils for the Presidencies. This Act provided that no legislative measure, affecting public debt and public revenue and creating charge on revenue, should be introduced, without the previous sanction of the Governor-General or the Governor, as the case might be. Up to this time the administration of Indian finance was vested in the Government of India, a task which they found difficult and performed inefficiently. A policy of decentralization was intiated by Lord Mayo's Government in 1870, and the 'Provincial Contracts' came into existence. The resolution of the Government of India effecting decentralization was considered in some quarters to have vested the provincial Legislative Councils with the power of passing the Budget by means of an Appropriation Bill. The 19th paragraph of the decentralization Order, was as follows:

'Each Local Government will publish its own yearly estimates and accounts in the Local Gazette, together with a financial exposition (which should, where possible, be made before the Local Legislative Council) analogous to that annually made in the Legislative Council of the Governor-General. The several estimates and accounts will be compiled, and a general statement for all India published as a supplement to the imperial estimates and accounts.'

In Madras, at any rate, in 1871, the executive government, under the guidance of Mr. (subsequently Sir) Alexander Arbuthnot, claimed the right of having their Budget passed by the local Legislative Council, but the Government of India subsequently disabused them of that impression. Provincial finance, on the whole, remained under the constant check and supervision of the Central Government, and was only a part, and not independent, of central finance. This position continued until the commencement of the Government of India Act, 1935.

It will be worthwhile mentioning in some detail the features of the Provincial Contracts or Settlements, as these Settlements have formed the basis of the finances of the Governments in India even after the Constitution of India came into force, though with many necessary changes. According to the Settlement, the Government of India directly administered the obviously common services, viz. the Army, Foreign Relations, Home Charges, Railways, Posts and Telegraphs. The services appertaining to the internal administration of the country viz. General Administration, Registration, Law and Justice, Police, Jails, Education, Medical, Stationery and Printing, Provincial Civil Works and Forests, were under the caıe of the provincial governments. The Central Government received the incidental revenue yielded by the expenditure heads under its control, while the provincial governments took the receipts from the provincial heads of expenditure. Of the great revenue heads Opium, Salt, Customs, Mint, Railways, Posts and Telegraphs, and Tributes from native States were Central; Forests were entirely provincial; Land Revenue, Excise, Stamps and Assessed Taxes were shared between the Centre and the provinces generally in equal proportions.

So far as the legislatures were concerned, they could under section 19 of the Act of 1861 meet only for legislative purposes. There was no obligation imposed on the executive to present the Budget or to allow its discussion. The legislature could and did discuss the position of finance or financial matters if any bill imposing fresh taxation was brought before it.

Though not regularly, it did also discuss the Budget on several occasions. The position was improved by the India Councils Act of 1892 which authorized the Governor-General in Council to make rules permitting the Legislative Council to discuss the annual Financial Statement of the Governor-General in Council, subject to certain conditions and restrictions.

Similar provisions were enacted for the provincial Legislative Councils also, and under these provisions the Budget prepared by the Comptroller and Auditor General and approved by the Finance Member with such changes as he considered necessary was passed by the Governor-General in his Executive Council. On the basis of this a Financial Statement was made by the Finance Member to the Legislative Council. After an interval of at least a week, the members delivered speeches which generally ranged over the whole field of administration. The President of the Legislative Council wound up the debate with a speech of his own. No vote was taken and no amendments were allowed. A similar course was followed in the provincial Councils. But these provisions of the Act of 1892 were not mandatory. This was effected by the India Councils Act of 1909 which made it compulsory for the executive to make rules permitting the discussion of the Annual Financial Statements of the Governments by the respective Legislative Councils. Detailed rules were framed for such discussion both at the Centre and in the provinces. Under the rules the discussion was in stages. A distinction was made between the 'Financial Statement' and the 'Budget'. The former might be described as the preliminary Budget. The Financial Statement of the Centre was ordered to be presented with an explanatory memorandum. An interval was then allowed and a day fixed for the first stage of discussion. Members had the opportunity of moving any resolution relating to any alteration in taxation, any new loan or any additional grant to local governments. The resolutions might be voted on. After all the resolution on these three matters had been discussed and disposed of, the Council entered upon the second stage of the discussion. The Financial Statement contained about thirty-six heads of revenue and about fifty-three heads of expenditure. At the second stage of discussion those heads

18

(barring about nine heads of revenue and about thirteen heads of expenditure which were not open to discussion) were to be discussed head-wise, the consideration being introduced by the member-in-charge of the Department concerned and resolutions could be moved, discussed and voted on at this stage also. After the discussions were closed, the Budget was decided on by the executive government— after giving due weight to the resolutions that might have been passed by the Council, but on the responsibility of the executive only, and presented to the Legislative Council by the Finance Member—and it was followed subsequently by the usual general discussion. It may be mentioned here that the President was empowered to prescribe a time-limit for speeches at every stage of discussion.

So far as the provincial Legislative Councils were concerned the procedure for discussion of the Budget was somewhat different. A Draft Financial Statement prepared by the executive government was at the first stage considered by a Finance Committee under the chairmanship of the Finance Member, and composed of six members nominated by the Governor and six members elected by the non-official members of the Council. The Committee submitted its report to the Local government which embodied its own conclusions and referred the Statement thus amended to the Government of India. The Draft Financial Statement as approved (provisionally) by the Government of India was then known as the Revised Financial Statement. Copies of the Draft as well as of the Revised Statement were supplied to members. Subsequent stages of discussion, moving of resolutions and finalization of the Budget were on the lines of the Central Budget. In the provinces, too, certain heads of revenue and expenditure were not open to discussion. These were known as 'allotted heads', the others as 'unallotted heads'. It must be noted that the ultimate right to determine the Budget rested with the executive which was, under the constitution of India at that time, permanent and unalterable. It could not afford to have its hold over the purse weakened by an adverse vote of the Legislative Council. This situation continued until the commencement of the Government of India Act (1919).

The Act established a bicameral legislature at the Centre,

known as the Council of States and the Legislative Assembly. The legislatures in the provinces were unicameral and were called Legislative Councils. At the Centre the Governor-General had his Executive Council, appointed by the Crown, which was not removable by the legislature. In the provinces, the Governors had their Executive Councils, similarly appointed as well as their Ministers. The Ministers were in charge of certain specified subjects known as transferred subjects. They were, as a matter of fact, removable by the legislature. The 'estimated annual expenditure and revenue' was known as the Budget. A large number of heads and items of expenditure was not subject to vote by the legislature. Discussion of the Budget was permitted at two stages, first a general discussion after the presentation and next when demands for grants for the voted items were moved. At the Centre only the Legislative Assembly could vote supplies, although the Budget was laid before both the chambers. The rules of procedure prescribed that no demand could be made except on the recommendation of the Governor-General or the Governor, as the case might be. The rules also permitted the moving of cut motions, as the Act empowered the Assembly and the provincial Councils to reduce or refuse any grant. After the demands were voted the Budget was to be submitted to the Governor-General or the Governor, as the case might be. In the event of any refusal or reduction of grant, the Governor-General, if he was satisfied about the essentiality of the requirement, was empowered to act as if the demands had all been granted. In the Provinces, the Governor could similarly act in the case of reserved subjects, while in the case of 'transferred subjects' he could authorize such expenditure as he thought necessary. The rules of the legislatures provided that supplementary, additional and excess grants were to be discussed and voted upon as in the case of demands for grants on annual estimates. As regards taxation both Chambers of the Indian legislature had equal rights. If they refused to pass any bill, the Governor-General had the power to override the decisions of the legislature. A bill refused by both the Chambers could be enacted if it received the assent of the Crown. Similar provisions were made for the provinces where the legislature was unicameral. The Act further provided that no bill imposing any tax (except certain taxes exempted for the purpose) affecting the public debt should be considered except without previous sanction of the Governor-General. Another matter which deserves mention is that under the rules of legislatures under this Act, Public Accounts Committees, composed partly of non-official members of the legislature and partly of members nominated by the executive, were constituted both at the Centre and in the provinces to deal with the appropriation accounts of the respective Governments.

Further advancement was made by the Government of India Act, 1935, which created bicameral legislatures in some of the provinces, known as the Legislative Assembly and the Legislative Council. It must be mentioned here that, so far as the Centre was concerned, the provisions of the Act relating to the Centre were not applied as the Federation contemplated in the Act was not established. The Centre continued to be governed by the Government of India Act, 1919, until India attained independence. But so far as the provinces were concerned the Act was operative. The Act abolished the Executive Councils, and the Governor was to be aided and advised by his Council of Ministers. Though the Act did not expressly mention that Ministers were responsible to one or both Chambers of the legislature, they were removable by the legislature. The Act, for the first time, created separate Public Accounts for the Centre and for each of the provinces. It provided that the 'Statement of estimated receipts and expenditure', known as the Budget, was to be presented to the Chamber or both the Chambers of the legislature. Expenditure was classified as expenditure charged on the revenues and expenditure to be voted by the Legislative Assembly. The discussion on the Budget was held in two stages. First a general discussion, which was permitted even in respect of items of charged expenditure, and secondly a discussion by the Legislative Assembly alone when demands for grants on voted items were moved. The Assembly had the right to assent to, refuse or reduce any grant. So motions for reduction of grants were permitted. After the grants were voted, the Governor was to authenticate a schedule of expenditure, both charged and voted. In the event of any refusal or reduction of grant, the Governor could restore the grants if in his opinion the discharge of his special responsibilities would be affected. The Act also made provision for presentation of supplementary estimates, and these were dealt with as in the case of annual estimates. The Act further provided that bills of a financial nature, that is to say those imposing taxation, regulating, borrowing or financial obligations, declaring any expenditure as charged on the revenues, were not to be introduced in the Council and would require the recommendation of the Governor before introduction in the Assembly. Bills entailing expenditure were also not to be passed by any Chamber without the recommendation of the Governor. The power of the Governor-General to enact into law any bill rejected by the legislature was withdrawn, but the legislature was under an obligation to consider a bill returned to them for their consideration. The Crown had the right to disallow any Act passed by any legislature. These, no doubt, weakened to some extent the application of the principle of no taxation without consent.

With the passing of the Independence of India Act, 1947, the Government of India Act, 1935, was adapted with the result that the Governor or the Governor-General had no special responsibilities entrusted to him. Consequently the power of certifying expenditure not assented to by the legislature was withdrawn. Lastly, with the commencement of the Constitution of India, full rights in financial matters were vested in the legislature, particularly in the Legislative Assemblies in the States and the Lok Sabha at the Centre.

FUNDAMENTAL PRINCIPLES

The fundamental principles of the system can be outlined in the form of four propositions:

(i) Parliamentary or legislative control over taxation; no tax can be imposed except with the authority of the legislature.

(ii) Parliamentary or legislative control over expenditure; no expenditure can be incurred except with the sanction of the legislature.

(iii) Financial initiative of the executive government; no tax can be imposed or expenditure sanctioned unless asked for by the executive government.

(iv) Principle of annuality; all expenditure except that specifically charged by any enactment requires to be sanctioned on an annual basis.

(1) *No tax can be imposed except with the authority of the legislature.*

Article 265 of the Indian Constitution provides that 'no tax shall be levied or collected except by authority of law'.

All tax proposals of the executive government would therefore have to be presented before the legislature in the form of bills to be passed into law. And unless an Act is passed authorizing the levying of any tax, no tax can be levied.

A question arose whether taxation can be made under an Ordinance under the Ordinance-making power of the executive government. An Ordinance has the same effect as that of an Act of the legislature. Strictly speaking, therefore, an Ordinance is also law under the authority of which any tax can be levied or collected. But having regard to the fundamental constitutional principle that there can be no taxation without representation, such a course would seem to be at least unconstitutional. It may be said that an Ordinance must be laid before the legislature and would expire unless enacted into law by it. Therefore no permanent taxation can be imposed by an Ordinance. But it would be possible to levy an *ad hoc* tax without any sanction of the legislature. There are instances where taxes have been so imposed and collected under Ordinances, and the provisions of the Ordinances have not been renewed under any Act.[1]

(2) *No expenditure can be incurred except with the sanction of the legislature.*

As has been said, 'The most ancient, as well as the most valued, prerogative of the House of Commons is the right of supreme control over taxation, to which the right to control issues is a natural corollary.'[2]

This principle has been adopted by Article 266 of the Constitution which lays down that all revenues received, all loans raised and all moneys received in repayment of loans by the Union or the State shall be paid into the Consolidated

[1] U.P. Terminal Tax Ordinance, Central Ordinance no. 1 of 1954.
[2] Durell, p. 3.

Fund of the Union or the State, as the case may be, and that no money can be withdrawn out of that fund except in accordance with law and for the purpose and in the manner provided for in the Constitution.

All moneys received by the State (except certain deposits in the Public Accounts, see p. 282), therefore, find their place in the Consolidated Fund, and once they get there no money can be withdrawn except under appropriation made by law.[1]

A question arises whether appropriation can be made under an Ordinance. It may be contended that an Ordinance is a temporary law and as such appropriation may be permitted by such law. But Article 266 categorically provides that no moneys out of the Consolidated Fund shall be appropriated except in accordance with law and for the purposes and in the manner provided in the Constitution. Further, Articles 114 and 204 provide that no money shall be withdrawn from the Consolidated Fund except under appropriation made by law passed in accordance with the provisions of those Articles, that is, on introducing a bill after grants have been made by the Lok Sabha or the Legislative Assembly, as the case may be, and necessarily completing all subsequent stages involved in the passing of the bill and its assent by the Head of the State. The Constitution, however, has made an exception in Article 357 (1) (c) under which, during an emergency, the President is empowered to authorize expenditure from the Consolidated Fund of a State, pending the sanction of such expenditure by Parliament. Such power can be exercised by the President only on the failure of the constitutional machinery in the State, the powers of the State legislature being exercised by or under the authority of Parliament and the Lok Sabha not being in session at the time.

In other cases, appropriation by Ordinance promulgated by the President or by the Governor will not, it appears, be warranted by the Constitution. There have, however, been instances of such appropriation having been made by means of Ordinance in some States.[2]

Before going into the matter further, it will be profitable

[1] Arts. 114, 204.
[2] Assam Ordinances No. 1 & 2, 1960.

at this stage to discuss what is meant by appropriation. To put it succinctly, appropriation is the application of money for expenditure on a service specifically named, the issue of the money being legally authorized by the law which also specifies the optimum limits of expenditure and issue for such service. Now, the circumstances under which an Ordinance was made to effect appropriation were as follows.

The Assam Ordinance was promulgated at a time when the Contingency Fund was exhausted, and there was no surplus in the head of account from which money could be paid to the Contingency Fund, but the need for incurring some unforeseen expenditure was pressing. The Governor promulgated two Ordinances simultaneously. By one, the Contingency Fund was paid a specified amount out of the Consolidated Fund, it being provided in the same Ordinance that the amount would be retransferred to the Consolidated Fund before the expiry of the year. By the other Ordinance, money to an equal extent was provided for appropriation to the head of account to enable transfer therefrom to the Contingency Fund. Immediate expenditure was met from the Contingency Fund thus replenished. Before the expiry of the year Supplementary Demands were voted and an Appropriation Bill passed in respect of the services provisionally met out of advances from the Contingency Fund, and the transactions and cross transactions were regularized by transfer through books.

(3) *No tax can be imposed or expenditure sanctioned unless asked for by the executive government.*

The British Parliament has imposed upon itself 'some self-denying restrictions' in that it does not impose any taxation or sanction any expenditure which is not asked for by the Crown. This principle has been adopted in the Indian Constitution. The initiative for taxation or expenditure lies with the executive, and the legislature cannot act in these matters *suo motu.*

No bill for imposing any tax can be introduced in the legislature except on the recommendation of the President or the Governor,[1] i.e., the President or the Governor as

[1] Arts. 117, 207.

advised by his Ministers and, therefore, the executive government. In giving notice of such bills, the Minister-in-charge states in the notice that the President or the Governor, as the case may be, recommends the introduction of the bill. For obvious reasons no such bill can be introduced by a private member.

Similarly, no demands for grant of any money for expenditure can be made except on the recommendation of the President or the Governor.[1] When moving the demands for grants the Minister-in-charge states that he is doing so on the recommendation of the President or the Governor, as the case may be. No formal communication of the recommendation as in the case of Money and Financial Bills is made (see p. 249).

(4) *All expenditure except that specifically charged by any enactment requires to be sanctioned on an annual basis.*

Expenditure of public money has been classified under two heads, charged and voted. The distinction between the two is that in the case of charged expenditure, no demands for grants need be made to the legislature and no sanction of the legislature is necessary for incurring such expenditure; but in the case of voted expenditure, demands for grants have to be made to, and sanctioned by, the legislature. Certain expenditures, e.g. salaries of High Court Judges, have been made charged expenditure by the Constitution itself. The legislature can also, by law, make any expenditure a charged one.[2]

Under Articles 112 and 202 the estimate of expenditure for any financial year, which in India is the period between 1 April in one year and 31 March in the next, has to be presented to the legislature. The estimate contains both the charged and the voted expenditure. But no sanction of the legislature is necessary for the charged expenditure, and the legislature has no power to interfere in any way with such expenditure. The estimate of charged expenditure which will ultimately be incorporated in the Appropriation Bill has to

[1] Arts. 113, 203. The financial initiative of the Crown was expressly adopted in India in 1856 by a resolution of the House of Commons. See Parl. Deb. 1856 vol. 153, c. 1107.
[2] Arts. 112, 202.

be shown for information of members, and members have the right to discuss although they have no power to disallow such expenditure.

The voted expenditure, however, is entirely within the control of the legislature. But, as will have been seen, what is to be presented is an annual estimate, and sanction of the expenditure is given on that basis, that is to say, on an annual basis. Moneys are granted for payment coming in the course of the year and the amount unspent at the end of the year lapses.

CONTROL OVER EXPENDITURE

The control over expenditure therefore is exercised through the provision of the Constitution under which an annual estimate of the receipts and expenditure has to be presented to the legislature; money required has to be granted under demands and withdrawal of money out of the Consolidated Fund and appropriation for the various services have to be authorized by an Act.[1] Further control is exercised by the legislature when the accounts audited by the Comptroller and Auditor General come before the legislature[2] and are examined by the Public Accounts Committee.

PUBLIC ACCOUNTS

Apart from the money which is paid into the Consolidated Fund, certain other moneys are received by the Government, such as Suitors' Deposits, etc. These are not paid into the Consolidated Fund but are kept distinct in a Public Account, and no authorization of the legislature is necessary for the purpose of withdrawal of any money out of this Account.

CONTINGENCY FUND

Circumstances may arise in which it may be necessary to incur expenditure in an emergency or in excess of money granted for any service in anticipation of the sanction of the

[1] Arts. 113, 114, 203, 204.
[2] Art. 151.

legislature by a supplementary grant. There is a provision in the Constitution[1] for creating a Contingency Fund out of which the executive government is authorized to spend money pending the sanction of the legislature. Such a Contingency Fund is created by an Act of the legislature, and a certain amount of money is transferred from the Consolidated Fund to this Fund in the form of an imprest out of which money is spent, and the amount spent is reimbursed when sanction for the expenditure is accorded by the legislature. All moneys, whether in the Consolidated Fund, the Public Account, or the Contingency Fund, are held by the Reserve Bank of India in accounts in the name of the Central or the State Government. All Governments, Central or State, are bound to deposit all cash balances free of interest in the Reserve Bank; Governments, however, may hold such cash balances as may be necessary at any place where there is no branch of the Reserve Bank.[2] The exception authorizes Governments to keep treasuries in the mofussil where there is no Reserve Bank in which moneys are received and payments made. Under agreements between the Reserve Bank of India and the various Governments, the Reserve Bank of India agrees to make ways-and-means advances up to a certain limit to Governments.

ANNUAL ESTIMATES: FORM OF THE BUDGET

The form in which the Annual Estimates, or the Budget as they are commonly called, is drawn up is dependent upon the form in which the accounts of the State are kept. The form of the accounts is determined by the Comptroller and Auditor General with the approval of the President.[3] In order to achieve uniformity in accounting, the Comptroller and Auditor General has prescribed the same form of accounts throughout India, whether for the Union or for the States. It may be that certain items of receipt or expenditure may not be relevant for any State and may not appear in the account of the State at all.

[1] Art. 267.
[2] Reserve Bank of India Act, sec. 21.
[3] Art. 150.

The main items of receipts and expenditure are divided into different sections, and are distinguished by letters of the alphabet, the same letter being used both for receipt and expenditure, e.g. C for Administrative Services, D for Social and Developmental Services, and so on.

Capital and Revenue Accounts of the same subject-matter are kept distinct by using one letter for the Revenue Account and double-letters for the Capital Account, e.g. D for Social and Developmental Services, DD for Capital Account of Social and Developmental Services.

A section is again divided into major heads of receipts, indicated by Roman numerals, and of expenditure, indicated by Arabic numerals; but the numbers of major heads do not necessarily correspond, e.g. under section F on the receipt side No. XXXVII is Public Works, No. XXXVIII Bombay Development Scheme, and so on, while on the expenditure side No. 50 and No. 51 denote the same subjects.

There are about 19 sections from A to N (including double-letters) and about 134 major heads.

Besides the above, there are also the sections O to X dealing with Debts, Deposits, etc. which have no major heads of account.

The major heads are again subdivided into minor heads according to the different nature of the expenditure involved under the same major head.

Under Articles 113 and 203 of the Constitution, so much of the Estimates as relates to charged expenditure is not subject to any vote of the legislature, but so much of the Estimates as relates to other expenditure has to be submitted to the Lok Sabha or the Legislative Assembly, as the case may be, in the form of demands for grants. These demands correspond to the votes of the House of Commons; but there is no class division as obtains there. The demands are consecutively numbered. The same nature of expenditure is ordinarily included in one demand, and the major heads under which such expenditure is classified in the accounts are indicated. It may be that several major heads are included under one demand; it may also be that one major head may be split up and appear in more than one demand. It is usually for the Finance Department of the State to determine the nature of demands. For the convenience of members, the classification of demands should be made in consultation with the House. In the Lok Sabha the demands are classified after consulting the Estimates Committee. In the House of Commons, although the Estimates Committee is not asked to give specific sanction every year to the form of the Estimates, it is consulted when any major change in the form of the Estimates is proposed.

Something must be said about the arrangement of the demands in the printed Budget which is presented to the House. In most legislatures the Budget demands are printed consecutively in accordance with the number of the major heads and not with those of the demands. Consequently, when a demand includes major heads of widely differing numbers, the grants appear on different pages resulting in a great deal of inconvenience to the members in finding out the total demand and the details of expenditure. It may be suggested that the Budget should be printed in accordance with the numbers of the demands and all major heads included in one demand should be put together.

Another suggestion which may be put forward is that the expenditure for a particular service which may be included in different demands may be indicated in a note, as is done in the Estimates presented to the House of Commons. For example, the salaries and other expenditure relating to the House of Commons appear under one vote; but in a note under that vote, the costs of maintenance of the buildings, etc. which appear under different votes, are shown, and the total expenditure for the House of Commons can be ascertained from that note.

In the Estimates of the House of Commons, in all votes, an increase or decrease in the number of the staff and corresponding increases or decreases in the expenditure are shown. The system can be very usefully adopted in India also.

Every demand for grant in the printed Budget includes the major head or heads comprising the grant. The major heads are again subdivided into minor heads, the minor heads are subdivided into sub-heads and those again subdivided into primary units which in turn are subdivided into secondary units showing the details of expenditure.

PREPARATION OF THE BUDGET AND ITS PRESENTATION

The expenditure for any financial year, which in India is the period between 1 April of one year and 31 March of the next, must be sanctioned either totally or in part (for vote on account see p. 297) before the expiry of the previous financial year, that is to say, a Budget has to be passed whether totally or in part before 31 March of each year. The Budget is ordinarily presented in the month of February each year. The Finance Department prepares the Budget by the end of December. The Budget is presented along with an Explanatory Memorandum. The Budget contains the estimates of receipt and expenditure with other figures mentioned hereafter. The Memorandum contains a comparative statement of such receipts and expenditure for the current year and the next year and reasons for any increase or decrease in the amounts. The Memorandum also furnishes other information relating to the Estimates, e.g. actuals of recent years, nature of receipts and expenditure, progressive expenditure in the case of projects the financing of which is spread over a number of years. In England the Annual Estimates contain comparative statements of two years only, viz. the year for which the estimates are presented and the preceding year. In England a daily statement of accounts is available and it is possible to give an almost complete statement of expenditure for the current year. In India as the accounts of a year are not completed before the expiry of the year, the usual procedure is as follows. The Budget Estimates of the coming year is given, the revised Budget Estimate for the current year on the basis of actual expenditure during the first eight months of the year, figures for which are available when the Budget is prepared, is given, and the actual expenditure for the previous year is also given. In the Centre, since 1924, following a resolution of the legislature, the Budget for the Railways is presented, discussed and voted upon separately. An abstract of the Budget, however, is incorporated in the main Budget which under the Constitution must be a comprehensive annual statement. To allow for the separate treatment of the Railway Budget, the rules of procedure of the Houses of Parliament have prescribed that the Budget can be presented in parts and dealt with separately. Most of the States have made similar provisions in their rules although this rule is rarely applied.

APPROPRIATION FROM ONE HEAD TO ANOTHER

While on the subject of grants and major heads included in one grant, it would be profitable to discuss the principles of appropriation or expenditure of money for any particular purpose. It is one of the fundamental principles of legislative control of the finances of the State that no money can be spent for any service or purpose other than that for which the money is granted. Each grant is deemed to be a distinct service, and by an Appropriation Act (see p. 291) the sum voted on a particular grant is appropriated to that grant. Consequently, money granted under one grant cannot be appropriated to another grant. It has already been stated that the expenditure under one grant may contain more than one major head, and that the major heads are divided into minor heads showing the details of expenditure. Although money is granted in a lump under particular grants in the Appropriation Act, the grants are made on the basis of the Budget which shows the details of expenditure under major and minor heads. Though it would not be illegal to reappropriate money from one major head to another included in the same grant, or from one minor head to another within the same major head, it would be against the principle of financial control that such reappropriation should be made. But the legislature cannot exercise control over details, and control at this stage is exercised by the Finance Department. No money can be reappropriated by any department without the sanction of the Finance Department, and in sanctioning reappropriation the Finance Department is guided by certain principles. These principles have been succinctly laid down by the Public Accounts Committee of the British House of Commons in the following words:

'The Public Accounts Committee agree that there is nothing unconstitutional in the practice of applying savings of one sub-head of a vote to meet the deficiency under another sub-head, as the formal vote of the House of Commons applies only to the total amount of each estimate; but at the same time it is of opinion that even here the Treasury should exercise care that the money is not spent in any way which seriously differs from the details presented to Parliament. It is, however, doubtful as to the correctness of sanctioning transfers between sub-heads if they are not clearly of the same kind. So far as civil votes are concerned, this is agreed to by the Treasury, which never sanctions transfer unless the sub-heads are closely allied.'[1]

BUDGET PROCEDURE

After the Budget has been presented, money has to be asked for as demands for grants. The Budget is dealt with in two stages—a general discussion, and the demands for specific grants. No motion is made for a general discussion, as is done in the British House of Commons when the general discussion of expenditure takes place on a motion that Mr. Speaker do now leave the chair, on each of the four main branches of the estimates. Usually about four days are allotted for the general discussion, and it is also customary for the leader of the opposition to initiate the discussion. As there is no motion before the House, no amendments are called for. The Finance Minister has a right of reply.

After the general discussion is over, the Ministers concerned make their demands, and the form of the motion is that so much money (stating the total amount of the grant) be granted under Grant No.... At this place it will be relevant to state that in India the demand for grant is for the gross amount required for expenditure. In the United Kingdom certain kinds of expected departmental receipts are allowed to be used by the department concerned to defray part of its expenditure. These receipts are known as Appropriation-in-Aid; they are separately shown as a distinct sub-head in the vote relating to the department and also set out in the Appropriation Act. The demand for grant in the case of a vote having an appropriation-in-aid sub-head as for the net amount, that is the gross amount of expenditure as reduced by the amount of appropriation-in-aid. In India appro-

[1] Quoted by Durell, p. 299.

priations-in-aid are not recognized, and consequently all receipts are credited in the corresponding head of receipt and the demand for grant is for the gross sum estimated to be expended. And as the principle of the financial initiative of the executive government has been adopted by the Indian constitution, the Ministers when moving their motions state that they are doing so on the recommendation of the Head of the State.

To such motions amendments are allowed for the reduction of the amount demanded or for the omission or reduction of any item in any grant. But on the principle mentioned above no amendment can be moved for the increase of any amount or the alteration of the destination of any grant, that is to say, the transference of any amount from one grant to another or from one item to another within the same grant.

In the British Parliament the demands for grants are made not in the House (theoretically) but in the Committee of Supply which is nothing but a Committee of the Whole House in which certain restrictions as to debate do not apply. The Committee stage in its origin was intended for the scrutiny of the proposals for expenditure from the financial point of view. But gradually, with the expansion of the House and the growth of party government, the Committee of Supply lost its significance as a financial committee, and the consideration of the demands by the Committee has ceased to be a scrutiny of the financial reasons for the demand, and discussion in the Committee has now become only an occasion for criticizing government policy. In consequence, amendments for only token reductions (of £100) are moved and are made the peg on which to found a debate on government policy.

In India, however, Budget demands are considered in the House itself. But the system of proposing amendments for token reductions has been adopted, and the form of amendment is that the grant be reduced by a fixed sum. A maximum number of days is fixed for the debate on the Budget—general discussion as well as demands for grants—by the procedure rules of the legislatures. And the executive government allots a number of days not exceeding such maximum for the purpose. As already mentioned, four days are usually allotted for general discussion and the remaining days for debate on the demands for grants. Usually the rules provide that not more than two days shall be taken up for the debate on any particular grant. On the last of the allotted days all demands which have not been passed by the House are guillotined, that is, put to the vote without any debate. If the rules provide that one demand shall not be debated for more than two days, and a demand is not finished on the day it is moved, the demand is also guillotined on the second day.

AMENDMENTS TO MOTION FOR DEMAND

As in the House of Commons, amendments to the motion for the demand of any grant is made in the form that the demand be reduced by a specified sum on which a discussion on the policy underlying the demand is criticized.

The Indian legislatures have, by their rules of procedure, defined three kinds of amendments, known as 'Cut Motions'. These are Economy Cuts, Policy Cuts and Token Cuts. The Economy Cuts are directed to reduce the demand by such amounts as the members want to effect an economy. The amounts of reduction vary accordingly. By means of Policy Cuts, the amount of the demand is sought to be reduced to Re 1 to raise a discussion of policy underlying the grant, and by means of Token Cuts, the amount of the grant is sought to be reduced by a fixed sum (generally Rs. 100) to raise a discussion on some grievance. The number of cut motions is generally heaviest under the category of Token Cuts. Usually a number of such amendments are tabled specifying the subject matter on which discussion is sought to be raised. A practice prevails in the Indian legislature[1] of putting all such amendments, or 'cut motions' as they are called, involving the same amount to the vote. This practice is erroneous. The specifying of the subject matter for discussion is not a part of the motion. Once a verdict is given either way on the motion that the demand be reduced by a specified amount, no further motion involving the same amount can be put. In the House of Commons the original motion for demand is withheld from

[1] L.S.D., part ii, 1 Mar. 1956, c. 776.

the decision of the House by proposing reductions of the various amounts or by omission of particular items.[1]

APPROPRIATION BILL

After the demands for grants have been passed by the House, an Appropriation Bill is brought in. The bill authorizes the withdrawal of the total amount of the Budget from out of the Consolidated Fund, and in a schedule specifies the amount which has been granted under each grant. The principle of the financial initiative of the executive government applies to the case of Appropriation Bills also. The Constitution[2] itself provides that no amendment shall be proposed to any such bill (Appropriation Bill) which will have the effect of varying the amount or altering the destination of any grant. The scope of amendment in an Appropriation Bill is, therefore, very limited. Amendments may be moved for the circulation of the bill for eliciting opinion or for reference of the bill to a Select Committee. But such a dilatory course can be evaded by means of a law as contemplated by Article 119 or 209 of the Constitution. The rules of procedure of the respective Houses have also empowered the Speaker to disallow such a course if he considers it necessary. The Constitution further provides that amendments cannot be moved for the reduction of any grant or of any item in any grant, but it appears that an amendment to omit an item altogether is admissible.[3] The Appropriation Bill supplies another occasion for the criticism of government policy, but as the entire administration will have been criticized during the debate on the demand for grants, subjects which cannot be touched upon during the debate are usually discussed during the debate on the Appropriation Bill.[4]

The relevancy of debate and amendments on the Appropriation Bill has been stated thus in May:

'Debate and amendment on the stages of these bills must be relevant to each bill and must be confined to the conduct or action of those who receive or administer the grants speci-

[1] May, p. 733.
[2] Arts. 114, 204.
[3] H.C.D. 1884, 292, c. 588.
[4] Rule 237 of the Rules of Procedure of the Lok Sabha.

fied in the bill.... In general terms, any questions of administrative policy may be raised which are implied in such grants of supply. Thus, whereas the field of debate on the main Consolidated Fund Bill of the year and upon the Appropriation Bill is normally commensurate with the whole range of administrative policy, debate upon a Consolidated Fund Bill introduced for the express purpose of providing funds for some newly undertaken service is limited to that service. Debate on these bills is thus limited to relevant questions of administration, and, as in Committee of Supply, questions of taxation and legislation cannot be discussed.'[1]

SUPPLEMENTARY ESTIMATES

It may be found that the money granted for any service will not be sufficient to meet the actual expenditure involved, or that it is necessary to incur expenditure on a new service for which money was not provided in the Budget. In such cases a supplementary estimate is presented to the House, and the same procedure as applies to the main estimate is followed. There is a general discussion and demands for grants, and an Appropriation Bill has also to be passed.

The term 'new service' appearing in Articles 115 (1) (a) and 205 (1) (a) of the Constitution means the service or services 'not contemplated in the annual financial statement for the year'.

A 'new service' has been described by Sir Frederic Gauntlet, formerly Auditor General of India as follows:

'A new form of service or a new instrument of service. It is desirable to explain by a concrete illustration the difference between these two. If in a province there is no Borstal Institute and one is inaugurated that undoubtedly is a new form of service. In every province there are jails. If it is decided to build a new jail this is not a new form of service because jails already exist. It is, however, a new instrument of service because it is a new jail additional to those already in existence. When expenditure is to be incurred on a new form of service, then in all such cases, theoretically, it should be held that the expenditure is to be incurred on a new service within the

[1] May, p. 746.

meaning of the Act. A new instrument of service, however, may be a new University, if there is already a University in the province, or it may be an additional Chowkidar. The former may cost over a crore of rupees with very considerable recurring expenditure, while the Chowkidar may cost perhaps Rs. 60 a year recurring expenditure. It is not practical politics to insist that an additional grant shall be obtained to meet expenditure of Rs. 60 per annum on a new Chowkidar when there are already thousands in existence. It is, however, obviously essential to obtain an additional grant if the new instrument of service is to be of the importance of a University and to entail very considerable expenditure.'[1]

NEW SERVICE

The term 'new service' has not been defined in any precise form, anywhere. Each case has more or less to be decided on its merits as and when it arises. Primarily it is the Government which takes a decision whether a particular proposal involves expenditure on a new service or whether it is a continuation or an extension of an existing service provided for in the Budget Estimates. Normally a demand for grant is composed of certain heads of expenditure—major, minor, sub-head, or primary unit—under which the amount of the demand is distributed. If any new proposal involving expenditure during the course of a year arises, an important question to be considered is whether the expenditure has been contemplated in the annual Budget or forms part of a demand and can be covered by any of the existing heads under the demand. If the proposal is entirely outside the scope of the demand or has not been contemplated in the annual Budget presented to the legislature, it is clearly a new service for which a demand for supply has to be placed before the legislature. It may be, in some cases, that the extra expenditure on the new item can be met by savings within the demand from other heads. Still, expenditure cannot be incurred on the item as it will constitute a new service, and it is necessary that a supplementary demand for a token sum should be

[1] *Memorandum on the Work of the Public Accounts Committee in India,* by Sir Frederic Gauntlet.

brought before the legislature. The essence of this requirement is that, without a vote of the legislature, money shall not be spent beyond the scope of the demand granted by the legislature. To put it in another way, the purpose is to see that Government does not and will not attempt to 'smuggle' new items of expenditure into the original estimates.

Beyond what has been stated above, it will be advisable not to attempt a precise definition of the technical expression new service, but to leave it to be regulated by experience and the evolution of a body of case law. Further the expression 'new service not contemplated in the annual financial statement for that year', has been incorporated in the Constitution [see Articles 115 (a) and 205 (a)], and legal interpretation of the term can only be given in keeping with Article 367. This would make inappropriate any attempt to give a precise definition. It might, however, be possible to enunciate certain fairly definite propositions which may be taken as a guide. Thus, a new item of expenditure is not necessarily a 'new service'. In the term 'new service' both the words have special significance. If there has been provision in the current or previous years for a particular expenditure, a 'new service' is not involved. Expenditure, before it can be said to be incurred on a 'new service', must involve the adoption of a new policy, the provision of a new facility or the alteration in character of an existing facility.

As regards the distinction between a 'new service' and a 'new instrument of service', the latter has, in actual practice, normally been treated in the same manner as the former in cases where the amount of expenditure involved is relatively large. It may be argued from a strictly logical point of view that the amount of expenditure is not a relevant consideration, and attention should be confined to the term actually used in the Constitution, viz., 'new service not contemplated in the annual financial statement for that year.' But there is a practical justification for this distinction, as will be evident from the following examples. An important extension of a previous specific commitment or facility such as the provision of a new jail, the doubling of a railway line, or the provision of like for like—for instance the substitution of a new naval ship or aircraft, even of identical specification, for an existing one that is to be scrapped—may constitute examples of 'new instruments of service', and it is but proper for the Government to take the prior consent of the legislature specifically on such items where the amount involved is relatively large, so that due respect is paid to the authority and responsibility of the legislature in the matter of financial control.

No specific monetary limit has been made in this regard. Nor will it be practicable to set a limit. As observed at the outset, each case will have to be decided on its merits, as it is not always the magnitude of the amount that matters.

SCOPE OF DEBATE ON SUPPLEMENTARY ESTIMATE

The scope of the debate on the supplementary estimate is, however, restricted. The general policy of the administration in regard to matters for which a supplementary estimate is presented cannot generally be discussed. The policy can be discussed only in so far as it is involved in the increase of the expenditure.

The following ruling of the Speaker of the House of Commons lays down the scope of the debate on a supplementary estimate:

'Of course it is quite obvious it would be improper, as a general rule, to raise on a Supplementary Estimate the whole question of policy involved in the original Estimate, but, as I have stated, the discussion is properly confined to the items of the Supplementary Estimate. I think, however, that I ought to state that items of Supplementary Estimates may raise in themselves questions of policy, but the interpretation whether they do raise questions of policy or not must clearly be left to the Chairman of Committees. If I may be allowed to illustrate what I mean, I would say the question of the draining of any particular house in Constantinople would clearly not raise the whole question of Foreign Embassies. But on the other hand, a Vote which would largely increase the Vote for a railway to Uganda might raise the whole question of the policy involved in the original Vote for Uganda.'[1]

---

[1] Parl. Deb. 1893, vol. 9, c. 975; I.P.D. 27 Mar. 1950, p. 2194; Con. A.L.D. 31 Mar. 1948, p. 2841; I.P.D. 20, Feb. 1951, c. 3196; H.P.D. 8 Dec. 1952, c. 1830; ibid. 12 Dec. 1952, c. 2156; L.S.D. 27 Sept. 1955.

On the same subject May observes as follows:

'If the sum demanded by a supplementary estimate is of the same order of magnitude as the original estimate, the chairman has allowed questions of policy to be raised upon it which would have been in order if it had been an original estimate; but if the supplementary estimate is merely to provide additional funds of a relatively moderate amount required in the normal course of working of the services for which the original vote was demanded, only the reasons for the increase can be discussed and not the policy implied in the service which must be taken to have been settled by the original vote.'[1]

It is worthwhile to mention here that the above procedure was in vogue in the House of Commons so long as the debate on supplementary estimates was not subject to guillotine. Since 1960, by a change in the Standing Orders, the supplementary estimates having been made subject to guillotine, the limitations to debate have been removed. But in Indian legislatures the limitations continue to apply by virtue of provisions in the rules of procedure.

A supplementary estimate for a new service, that is to say, for a service for which no money was provided in the original estimate, raises the whole question of the policy implied in the service in the same way as an original estimate.[2]

The question sometimes arose in former times that a supplementary estimate should not be presented after expenditure had actually been started. Such a question cannot arise now. For the Government can now spend money out of the Contingency Fund in anticipation, or pending authorization, of the supplementary estimate.[3]

It sometimes happens that a supplementary estimate is presented for expenditure which is likely to be incurred if a certain Act is passed by the legislature but before the Act has actually been passed. Such a practice has been deprecated by the Public Accounts Committee of the British House of Commons. In any event, it has been the practice to state in a note to the estimates that the expenditure is subject to further

---

[1] May, p. 738.
[2] L.A.D. 27 Mar. 1935, p. 2859; H.P.D. 24 Feb. 1954, c. 592.
[3] Art. 267.

statutory authority and the necessary bill becoming law before the additional expenditure can be authorized by an Appropriation Act.[1]

VOTE ON ACCOUNT

As no money can be withdrawn from the Consolidated Fund without legislative sanction, and as sanction is given on an annual basis, the Budget must be passed and the necessary money granted before the expiry of a financial year so that expenditure can be incurred in the next year. The practice that was followed and prescribed by the Government of India Acts was to have the Budget of the financial year passed before 31 March of the previous year. In the British Parliament, however, the Appropriation Bill cannot be passed before 31 March (that is also the date of expiry of the financial year there), and what is done to regularize expenditure is to vote in lump a portion of the estimates so that the administration can be carried on. This procedure is known as a Vote on Account. The estimates in England are divided into four branches, the Army, the Navy, the Air, and the Civil and Revenue Estimates. Each branch is divided into a number of votes corresponding to grants in India. The procedure is to sanction a portion of money on each vote of the Civil and Revenue Estimates; in the case of the other estimates, to vote the entire amount of a few votes in each branch. The reason for the difference is this; the Army, the Navy and the Air Ministries have the power of 'virement' under authority of the Treasury, that is to say, they can spend the surplus of any vote for expenditure under any other vote, whereas the Civil Departments have no such power. The amount which would be necessary for expenditure for about three to four months, i.e. up to the probable date of the final passing of the Appropriation Act, is usually taken on a vote on account. A vote on account may also be necessary in the case of a dissolution of the legislature before the Appropriation Act can be finally passed.

This procedure of taking a vote on account has now been authorized by the Indian Constitution.[2] The procedure is,

[1] May, p. 749.
[2] Arts. 116, 206.

however, a little different. In India no department has any right of 'virement'. It is, therefore, necessary to sanction a portion of each demand for grant sufficient to carry on until the entire Budget is passed. In England no appropriation is made on a vote on account, but a lump sum is authorized to be paid out of the Consolidated Fund by an Act known as the Consolidated Fund Act; appropriation of the amount of the entire votes (including the amount voted on account) is made by the Appropriation Act after the final passing of all supply votes. The Indian Constitution, however, requires that an Appropriation Act should be passed even on a vote on account.[1]

The form of motion of a vote on account is generally to move a motion for the grant of a consolidated amount, and to show the amount of each grant in a schedule. Amendment may be moved for the reduction of the whole grant or of any of the grants in the schedule.[2] As the Budget can be criticized when the time for finally passing it comes, a vote on account is taken as more or less a formal affair. As Mr. Speaker Mavalankar of the Indian Parliament put it:

'In this procedure, as full discussion follows, the grant of supply for the interim period on the Motion for Voting on Account is always treated as a formal one just like a Motion for leave to introduce a bill or the introduction of a bill. I trust honourable members will appreciate this position and treat voting on account as a formal affair as they would have a full opportunity to discuss the demands for grants in a detailed manner later.'[3]

EXCESS GRANT

It sometimes happens that money is spent by a department in excess of the amount granted by the legislature. When it is anticipated that the expenditure will go beyond the amount sanctioned, a supplementary estimate is ordinarily presented, but if there is no time to take a supplementary vote, excess expenditure may be unavoidable. Excess expenditure, however, is always considered a serious matter and a financial

[1] Arts. 116, 206.
[2] H.P.D. 26 Feb. 1952, c. 1283.
[3] Ibid. 12 Mar. 1951, vol. 9, part ii, c. 4350.

sin—so much so that the British House of Commons recorded its disapproval of excess expenditure in a resolution on 30 March 1849 in the following language:

'When a certain amount of Expenditure for a particular Service has been determined upon by Parliament, it is the bounden duty of the Department, which has that Service under its charge and control, to take care that the Expenditure does not exceed the amount placed at its disposal for that purpose.'[1]

If, however, an excess expenditure has in fact been incurred, such expenditure has to be regularized by the legislature. The Indian Constitution[2] has, therefore, provided that demands for such excess shall be made in the same way as for an ordinary grant.

The question of regularizing, however, arises after the accounts of the year in which the excess expenditure has been incurred have been audited, and the exact amount ascertained, and the Public Accounts Committee, if any, has reported on it.

The procedure is the same as that for an ordinary grant, including the passing of an Appropriation Act.

VOTES OF CREDIT

The Indian Constitution[3] provides that the legislature can make a grant for meeting an unexpected demand upon the resources of India when, on account of the magnitude or the indefinite character of the service, the demand cannot be stated with the details ordinarily given in the annual financial statement. Such a grant is known in England as a vote of credit and was taken during great wars. The form of a vote of credit is, as stated by May, 'a demand for a lump sum with the objects stated in very general terms'.[4] Under the Indian Constitution an Appropriation Act is necessary also in the case of a vote of credit.

EXCEPTIONAL GRANTS

The Indian Constitution[5] provides that the legislature can

---

[1] C.J. 1849, p. 190, quoted in May, p. 718.
[2] Arts. 115, 205.
[3] Arts. 116, 206.
[4] May, p. 720.
[5] Arts. 116, 206.

make an exceptional grant which forms no part of the current service of any financial year. Such exceptional grants are known in England and have been divided by May into three classes:[1]

(i) Demands for pecuniary aid for the maintenance of the dignity or well-being of the Crown (e.g. Civil List or a grant of marriage portion for any member of the royal family) or for the reward of distinguished public service.

(ii) Novel and non-recurrent expenditure, e.g. grant of money for abolition of slavery.

(iii) Grants for national purposes, e.g. monuments for a deceased statesman.

Expenditure under such classes has, however, on occasions been sanctioned on any ordinary estimate and not on an exceptional grant.

The procedure for the main estimate, including the passing of an Appropriation Bill, is necessary under the Indian Constitution for exceptional grants also.

REVISED ESTIMATE

If it is necessary to revise the estimate once presented, a revised estimate can of course be presented before the original estimate is voted; the original estimate is withdrawn and a revised estimate is presented. If the revised estimate is for an increased amount, it is usual nowadays in England, as May[2] points out, not to present a revised estimate but to present a supplementary estimate. In West Bengal, however, during the Budget session, 1952, a revised Budget on certain grants for an increased amount was presented. The original Budget was not formally withdrawn, but it was taken as if a revised estimate as a whole had been presented.

TOKEN VOTES

When money is available from the sum already sanctioned on a grant or from some other source (e.g. a loan by the Central Government), but it is necessary to obtain legislative

---

[1] May, p. 720.
[2] May, p. 711.

sanction for expenditure, it is customary to demand a nominal sum of Re 1 which is known as a token grant. When money has been granted for a particular purpose included in a grant, but it is proposed to spend the saving, for some other purposes also within the grant though not similar, it is usual to acquaint the legislature about such appropriations and obtain legislative sanction by means of a token grant on a supplementary estimate. In England token votes are also taken when the expenditure is to be met totally from appropriation-in-aid. But as has already been stated, there is no provision for appropriation-in-aid in India, and that question does not therefore arise.

SCOPE OF DEBATE ON THE BUDGET

In the British House of Commons the general discussion on each main branch of the Estimates is, as has already been stated, initiated by a motion 'that Mr. Speaker do now leave the Chair', and amendments are proposed to the motion. There is no such procedure in India. The general discussion of the Budget takes place without any motion. The entire administration is open to critcism, but in practice only questions of general policy are debated, leaving the criticism of the departments individually to be made at the time when the demand for grant for each department is made.

When motions for demands for grants are made for each grant relating generally to a particular ministry or department, motions for a token reduction are proposed in order to raise a discussion on the general policy of the ministry or department concerned, or on particular aspects of the administration of the ministry or department. The motion for reduction and the subject to be discussed on such motion must relate to the specific object of the grant.[1] A service for which there is a specific grant cannot be discussed on the demand for grant of a department which may include the salary of the Minister concerned. In India the grant for general administration includes the salaries of all Ministers and all the officers at the Headquarters, but the policy of a Minister in regard to

[1] L.A.D. 15 Mar. 1924, p. 1857; ibid. 26 Feb. 1927, p. 1401; ibid. 9 Mar. 1934, p. 1915; ibid. 22 Feb. 1935, p. 1227.

the department for which he is responsible or of a particular department cannot be discussed on the grant for general administration if there is a specific grant for that department.[1] A discussion on the demand for grant for a particular service must not travel beyond that service.

Where two or more votes are concerned with any particular service, a method has been devised in England whereby the entire service may be considered at one and the same time. A token amount of each vote is included in a schedule, and a token vote in regard to the whole amount is taken, and on that vote criticism of all the departments concerned may be made.[2]

UPPER HOUSE AND THE BUDGET

We shall now consider the rights of the Upper House in relation to the Budget. The Budget is considered in the Lower House in three stages: (i) Presentation and general discussion, (ii) Demands for Grants, and (iii) Appropriation Bill sanctioning the withdrawal of money and its appropriation to the various purposes for which the grants are made.

Under the Indian Constitution the Budget has to be presented to both Houses of the legislature. The Upper House, therefore, has the right to discuss the Budget, and the rules of procedure of all Upper Houses provide for a general discussion of the Budget. In England, however, the Estimates are not presented to the House of Lords. But the Lords can debate the Estimates and express their opinion thereon by means of a question and a formal motion of 'moving for papers'.

As to whether a statement of financial policy should be made in the Upper House also, as is done in the Budget speech of the Finance Minister in the Lower House, the practice does not appear to be uniform. In the Council of States the Budget was laid on the table by the Leader of the House, in 1952, but no statement or speech appears to have been made. In West Bengal the Finance Minister makes a speech in the Council giving a short *resume* of the policy

---

[1] H.C.D. 1927, vol. 204, c. 1726; ibid. 1931, vol. 255, c. 2128; ibid. 1931, vol. 252, c. 1627; ibid. 1932, vol. 265, c. 1449.
[2] May, p. 737.

which he had outlined in the Budget speech in the Lower House.

Demands for grants are not made to the Upper House. It is the exclusive privilege of the Lower House to grant money demanded by the Government.

In the general discussion that follows the presentation of the Budget, a criticism of the general financial policy of the Government is made; but no motion is proposed before the House and ordinarily the Finance Minister replies. In the Lower House particular departments come in for criticism when demands for grants are made for those departments. The Upper House is at a disadvantage in this respect. As no demands for grants are placed before the Upper House, questions on the administrative policy of particular departments can only be raised either during the general discussion of the Budget or the debate on the Appropriation Bill. But as in neither case is there any specific motion before the House, the debate tends to be discursive, there is no knowing what subjects will be raised in the debate, Ministers have no notice and are not always present to reply. If the debate is to be fruitful, all the Ministers should be present during the debate on the Budget as also on the Appropriation Bill.

A method has been evolved in the South African Parliament to give an opportunity to the Upper House to criticize individual departments. The Minister for a particular department makes a motion that 'this House takes into review the policy pursued by the Minister of....' A debate follows either on this motion or on any amendment that may be proposed to it. If such a motion is made, the Senate, i.e. the Upper House, does not go into Committee on the Appropriation Bill, and does not require the presence of all the Ministers during the debate on it.

A debate on any particular subject can also be raised during the consideration of the Appropriation Bill by arrangements through what are known as 'the usual channels', that is to say, by arrangement between the Whips of the Opposition and the Government. But in the absence of an organized single Opposition, it is not always possible to adopt this course.

Another course may be suggested. An amendment for the omission of any item in the Appropriation Bill may be tabled, and although such an amendment would be out of order it may be used as a means of giving notice as to the matter which it is proposed to raise. Such a procedure is not entirely unknown. In the House of Commons an amendment to leave out a clause of a bill is out of order; but such amendments are tabled, and although never called, are allowed to remain on the Order Paper for the purpose of indicating that the member desires to speak on the question that the clause stand part of the bill.

UPPER HOUSE AND APPROPRIATION BILL

The Appropriation Bill has to be sent to the Upper House, and as it is a Money Bill the procedure relating to Money Bills has to be followed (see p. 000). In the case of the Appropriation Bill, however, there is practically no scope for making any recommendation for amendment. For, under the Constitution, no amendment can be proposed to the Appropriation Bill which would have the effect of varying the amount or altering the destination of any grant. It has been ruled that an amendment seeking to omit any item would also be out of order. The debate on the Appropriation Bill is therefore confined to the second reading or consideration of the bill. In this debate all questions of the administrative policy of the Government involved in the grants are relevant.

CHAPTER XIV

FINANCIAL COMMITTEES

EFFECTIVE financial control involves scrutiny into the details of estimates and accounts, but the House itself is not a suitable organ for going into such minute details. It has neither the time nor the facilities for such detailed examination, and accordingly it has necessarily to delegate such duties to Select Committees which are in a position to discharge these functions efficiently, while their reports keep the House informed as to the result of the investigation, and enable it to take action thereon, where action is necessary.

These investigations are carried on for the purpose of safeguarding public economy either (i) with a view to ensuring economy in expenditure or (ii) with a view to securing regularity, legality and propriety in the matter of financial administration.

The Estimates Committee of the legislature is concerned with the duties of the former kind, while the Public Accounts Committee is concerned with those of the latter kind. Committees of this nature have, however, no executive power. They merely report to the House their findings and recommendations, and it is the duty of the administration to consider their propositions, to subject them in turn to careful scrutiny and to decide, upon their own responsibility, to what extent and in what way the reforms can be carried out.

ESTIMATES COMMITTEE

Estimates Committees are of recent origin in India. An Estimates Committee was set up for the first time in 1950 by the House of the People. Thereafter the Legislative Assemblies of all the States have appointed Estimates Committees. The functions of an Estimates Committee are similar to those of the Estimates Committee of the House of Commons. Indeed, the rule of the House of the People which provides for the appointment of an Estimate Committee follows the language of the resolution of the House of Commons appointing such a Committee, namely, 'to examine such of the estimates as may seem fit to the Committee and to suggest economies consistent with the policy underlying the estimates'.[1] It will presently be seen that the term of reference was subsequently enlarged. (see p. 311).

ESTIMATES COMMITTEE OF THE HOUSE OF COMMONS

It will therefore be profitable to discuss the origin and function of the Estimates Committee of the British House of Commons. It is well known that the Estimates in the House of Commons are first considered by a Committee of the Whole House known as the Committee of Supply. In its origin, the Committee of Supply was intended to be something like a Select Committee to scrutinize the financial aspects of the Estimates. But gradually, with the enlargement of the House and the growth of party government, the Committee lost its significance as a Financial Committee, and its consideration of the Estimates has ceased to be a scrutiny of the financial reasons for the demands, and has now become an occasion for criticizing government policy.

A Select Committee on National Expenditure was appointed by the House of Commons in 1902, and the appointment of a small committee for the purpose of examining the estimates presented to the House was one of the recommendations it made. The Report of the Committee contains the following observations:

'But we consider that the examination of Estimates by the House of Commons leaves much to be desired from the points of view of financial scrutiny. The colour of the discussions is unavoidably partisan. Few questions are discussed with adequate knowledge or settled on their financial merits. Six hundred and seventy Members of Parliament, influenced by party ties, occupied with other work and interests, frequently absent from the Chamber during the 20 to 23 Supply days, are hardly the instrument to achieve a close and exhaustive examination of the immense and complex Estimates now

---

[1] Lok Sabha Rule 243; C.J. 167, p. 109.

annually presented. They cannot effectively challenge the smallest item without supporting a Motion hostile to the Government of the day; and divisions are nearly always decided by a majority of members who have not listened to the discussion. Your Committee agree in thinking that the Estimates are used in practice—perhaps necessarily by the Committee of Supply—mainly to provide a series of convenient and useful opportunities for the debating of policy and administration, rather than to the criticism and review of financial method and of the details of expenditure. We are impressed with the advantages, for the purposes of detailed financial scrutiny, which are enjoyed by Select Committees, whose proceedings are usually devoid of party feeling, who may obtain accurate knowledge collected for them by trained officials, which may, if so desired, be checked or extended by the examination of witnesses or the production of documents; and we feel it is in this direction that the financial control of the House of Commons is most capable of being strengthened....

'We consider that if the portion of the Estimates selected were not unduly large the temporal difficulties incidental to their examination would be removed, and that as the Committee would have no power to disallow any expenditure, but only to report thereon, there could be no question of any interference either with ministerial responsibility or with Parliamentary control.

'Your Committee are therefore prepared to recommend that such a Select Committee be appointed, and that it be called "The Estimates Committee".'[1]

No steps were, however, taken to implement the above recommendation until 1912 when a Select Committee was appointed in the following terms: 'That a Select Committee be appointed to examine such of the Estimates presented to this House as may seem fit to the Committee and to report what, if any, economies consistent with the policy implied in those Estimates should be effected therein.'

Such a Committee has since been appointed every year on the same terms—although during the two great wars the

---

[1] *Report of the Select Committee of the House of Commons on National Expenditure*, 1903.

Committee was known not as the Estimates Committee but as the Committee on National Expenditure.

A question was raised in 1921 on the motion for the appointment of the Estimates Committee as to what was to be done in the House itself with recommendations of the Committee. It was suggested that if the Committee recommended that a certain economy was desirable the vote on that recommendation should be a free vote and not taken under the compulsion of the party whips. But that suggestion was never accepted on the ground that such a position would be a complete abandonment of the ministerial responsibility for the finance of the country.[1]

FUNCTIONS OF THE ESTIMATES COMMITTEE

It therefore appears that the recommendations of the Estimates Committee are purely advisory and have no relation to or influence upon the voting of the demands in the House. The Committee has no power to disallow any expenditure; it can only recommend what economies can be effected in government departments. The recommendations of the Estimates Committee do not necessarily precede the consideration of the estimates by the Committee of Supply. In fact the voting on the estimates is over when the recommendations of the Committee are generally presented to the House.

The entire estimates are not examined by the Estimates Committee but subjects are chosen for examination and the Committee takes evidence from departmental officials and outsiders and considers and makes its recommendations on the subjects in reports submitted from time to time to the House. The reports are considered by the House and the usual motion that is made is in the form, 'That this House takes note of the Report of the Select Committee on Estimates.'[2]

The recommendations may or may not be accepted by the Government, and replies by the various departments concerned dealing with the recommendations are sent to the committee in the form of minutes and are made part of the subsequent report by the Committee.[3]

[1] Parl. Deb. 1921, vol. 143, c. 1496, 1506.
[2] C.J. 1950-51, p. 297.
[3] L.S.D. 21 May 1954, c. 7988.

Although there is some probing and check on departmental expenditure by the Estimates Committee and although there is a necessity for the setting up of machinery to secure due economy in expenditure, it seems to have been the opinion of the Committee on National Expenditure of 1943-4 that, for a variety of reasons, the Estimates Committee was not considered as providing a satisfactory solution to the main problems. The Committee in its Eleventh Report said that although the House had been successful in setting up machinery capable of securing that money was spent only upon the objects for which it was voted (i.e. by the Public Accounts Committee), the House had not succeeded in devising satisfactory permanent machinery to secure due economy in the national expenditure.

The causes which impaired the usefulness of the Estimates Committee were pointed out by the Select Committee in 1918, and the view of that Committee was endorsed by the Committee on National Expenditure of 1943-4 as follows:

(i) The task imposed is too large for one body working as a single unit; when the estimates of a particular department had been considered, a period of from seven to ten years would probably elapse before those estimates were again considered.

(ii) The handicap imposed by the form in which estimates are presented—one of probable cash requirements only and not of the actual cost of any particular scheme.

(iii) The Estimates Committee has no professional assistance.[1]

Durell observes as follows regarding the utility of an Estimates Committee:

'Although, then, the Estimates Committee in theory secures parliamentary control over the estimates—so far as it can be secured by any body other than the House itself—the apparent advantages and the possible results of its work are reduced to a minimum, because of the proportion of similar ground covered by the Public Accounts Committee and by the Treasury....

'Even in the case of the advantage which is nominally secured by the examination of the Estimates Committee of

[1] *Eleventh Report of the Select Committee on National Expenditure*, 1943-4.

a particular year's estimates, two years before the Public Accounts Committee examine the expenditure of the money provided on those estimates, the benefits are more apparent than real; for the expenditure of any department is, as a rule, of the same type from year to year and the review by each committee must be mainly a review of the application of continuing principles. It would therefore be only in the case of new classes of expenditure that the examination in this respect by the Estimates Committee would be actually in advance of that of the Public Accounts Committee, and the probable results to be achieved in such cases would be proportionately small, as it is these very items which would have been most recently approved and therefore scrutinized by the Treasury.'[1]

A Comptroller and Auditor General of India says: 'In recent years, however, the Committee's contribution has been more impressive. It has interpreted the word "estimates" to mean "current activities" and has undertaken a selective review of governmental activity on the ground that these would, in any case, be reflected in the estimates under examination. While the Committee refrains even now from openly criticizing the policy implicit in the estimates, its examination does often indirectly reflect on the manner in which a particular policy has been evolved or is being implemented. There has also been considerable improvement in the organization of the Committee and in its technique, which has better equipped it to fulfil its responsibilities. Even though it works within the limitations inherent in a democratic form of government, its contributions are tending to become more and more effective in economizing national expenditure.'[2]

In India the functions of the Committee were initially not dissimilar from the functions entrusted to the U.K. Committee. The Committee, however, complained that its scrutiny was circumscribed and its usefulness curtailed by the exclusion of examination of policy from its terms of reference. Sometime in 1953 the scope of the Committee's examination was extended so as 'to suggest alternative policies in order to bring about efficiency and economy in administration'.

[1] Durell, p. 153.
[2] Chanda, *Indian Administration*, p. 186.

The Speaker issued a directive to the Committee, explaining the connotation of the term 'policy'. 'The term "policy",. he explained, 'relates only to policies laid down by Parliament by statute or by specific resolutions passed by the Committee from time to time and that it will be open to the Committee to examine any matter which may have been settled as a matter of policy by the Government, in the discharge of its executive functions.' The Committee should not, he said, question approved policies, but it was nevertheless the duty of the Committee to comment on a particular policy, if it was evident that it was not fulfilling its purpose or that it was leading to a waste of public funds.

The Committee has put a liberal interpretation on its terms of reference in accordance with the Speaker's instructions. The Committee pays a great deal of attention to the organizational aspect and to measures which would, in its opinion, provide that the money voted by Parliament is better spent. In its very first report it discussed the efficiency and organization of the ministry which it had taken up for examination. The second report was entirely devoted to the reorganization of the secretariat of the departments of government.[1]

LINE OF ACTION

The Committee is not required to consider all the estimates of the different departments or ministries. At the beginning of each financial year it makes a selection of subjects concerning any part of the estimates of a ministry or ministries to be examined during the year under review. The department (ministry) or departments are asked sufficiently in advance to collect all relevant information relating thereto for submission to the Committee. They are required to furnish full information regarding the organization, functions and volume of work of the respective ministry and its attached and subordinate offices, together with broad details on which estimates are based, schemes or projects undertaken by them, actual expenditure incurred under each sub-head of estimates during the preceding three years, reasons for variations, if any,

[1] See also Chanda, p. 191-192.

between the actuals of the past years and the current estimates and reports, if any, issued by the department. They are also to furnish any other information that the Committee may call for. Questions are framed by members on the basis of the information furnished. On the date or dates when the estimates are examined by the Committee, the secretary or head of the department and the accredited representative of the Ministry of Finance are required to attend to explain the details of the estimates and to furnish such information as the Committee may ask for. Questions are put and eluci- dations obtained. Minutes are prepared and decisions arrived at, and the report containing the recommendations of the Committee is finalized.

The Committee may enquire about the justifiability of rates of pay given for the work done and the size of the staff allowed for a particular work. It may also go on to suggest reorganization of the ministries or departments. The Committee is also authorized to consider questions of the arrangement and structure of the estimates and the advisability of dividing up sub-heads or giving more detailed information about them. Questions of this kind relating to the form of estimates are settled by the Finance Minister in consultation with other bodies or authorities, e.g. the Public Accounts Committee and the Auditor General, when the importance of the question so demands.

In the House of Commons the Chairman of the Estimates Committee is always a member of the Government party. The Committee nowadays appoints several sub-committees to each of which a liaison officer belonging to the Treasury is attached. It has been found that the Estimates Committee is able to put forth a greater amount of work by reason of the fact that a number of small sub-committees can deal with a larger number of subjects or ministries than can one single large committee.[1] The same practice is followed in the Lok Sabha in India.

PUBLIC ACCOUNTS COMMITTEE

The origin of the Public Accounts Committee in India dates

[1] Chubb, *Control of Public Expenditure*, p. 223.

back to 1923. Although in the Government of India Act, 1919, there was no provision for laying the Audited Accounts and Audited Report thereon before the legislature, the rules framed under that Act authorized the constitution of such committees for the Centre as well as for the provinces to examine the accounts of the respective Governments. Such committees were not wholly committees of the legislature, as their members were partly elected by members of the legislature and partly nominated by the executive, and it was the duty of the Public Accounts Committee so constituted to bring to the notice of the legislature any irregularity in the accounts of the State. In the provinces such affairs continued until the Government of India Act, 1935, came into force in 1937. This Act required the submission of Accounts and Audit Report before the legislature, and since then the committees have been constituted by the rules of procedure of the House.

Under the provisions of the Constitution[1] the Reports of the Comptroller and Auditor General relating to the acccounts of the respective Governments are to be laid before the respective legislatures. The accounts are also appended to the reports. It is implied that the legislature has the right to discuss the report, but in practice the House does not take up the discussion until the Public Accounts Committee has first reported thereon.

In regard to economy and scrutiny, the influence of the Committee is more regular and efficient than that which is or could be exercised by the House. The Committee is designed to guarantee financial regularity and audit, and exercises great influence over the departments (of the Government), although it possesses no direct power other than the power to call for documents and to require witnesses to attend. Its power is indirect and lies nominally in the potential results of its reports. Actually its power lies in the publicity which it is able to give to the question it investigates, and in the normal effect of its criticism on the departments.

The Committee functions under certain technical limitations. One of the limitations is that there is no obligation on the part of the executive to adopt the reports of the Committee. In such cases the executive, in its minutes upon the

[1] Art. 151.

reports of the Committee, is required to state the reason for any difference of opinion it may hold, and the question is reserved for reconsideration by the Committee in the next session. In the case of eventual disagreement the House is there, and its attention may be specially directed to the fact by those who represent that department when any matter over which differences have arisen is under consideration. In spite of these limitations, the influence of the Committee is admittedly effective. 'The fear of the Public Accounts Committee, and the very searching examination that takes place there, does a great deal to keep in the path of rectitude the members of the civil service.'[1]

ADVANTAGES OF THE COMMITTEE OVER THE HOUSE

The Committee is so constituted as to represent all parties of the House, and in the matter of representation of different parties of the House those members who evince interest in public economy and accounts are usually nominated. The special feature of the Committee is that its proceedings, unlike the proceedings of the House, are usually devoid of party feelings. The question of public accounts is recognized as a national question and not one of party politics and, as such, investigation is made in the public interest from a financial and not a political point of view. The advantage of the Committee is that it contacts directly executive officers, administrators and those who spend money. Questions can be thrashed out fully and promptly by direct elicitation of information from these officials or by summoning further witnesses and calling for documents. If necessary, evidence may be taken on oath, but in practice that is not adopted by any select committees except in very special cases. Such examinations—although *post mortem*—are effective. Finally, the Committee possesses the great advantage of being served regularly and continuously by the public department under the Comptroller and Auditor General, whose assistance is further intensified by the personal attendance at the meetings of the Committee either of the Auditor General himself or of the Accountant-General or of both. A principal permanent

---

[1] Durell, p. 112; Chubb, *Control of Public Expenditure*, p. 190.

officer of the Finance Department (usually the Finance Secretary himself) also attends every meeting. The Committee is thus able to obtain accurate information from trained officials. The Comptroller and Auditor General has been described as to a large extent the acting hand of the Committee. He guides the Committee in its labours, he detects the points of questions, presents it with available information and leaves the Committee to pursue its investigations and to report on them. His assistance is able and thorough, and the Committee naturally attaches great importance to his views.

A question has sometimes been raised that the Public Accounts Committee's term should be coextensive with the term of the Assembly, but that one third of the members should retire annually, so that continuity may be maintained. The main objection to this course is that at the subsequent elections it would be difficult to have proportional representation. In practice, the majority of old members are re-elected, so that continuity is maintained in fact.

Another question is whether the Finance Minister or any other Minister should be a member of the Committee. In some legislatures the Finance Minister or any other Minister is a member of the Committee, and when the Finance Minister is on the Committee he is in practice made Chairman of the Committee. The Lok Sabha Rules specifically prohibit a Minister from being chosen as a member of the Public Accounts Committee. In England a Junior Minister is invariably selected a member of the Public Accounts Committee, but he does not now attend its sittings or take part in its deliberations because the criticism of the Committee may cause him embarrassment.

Another question relates to the Chairmanship of the Committee. In England a member of the Opposition, preferably a person in the position of a Minister in the last Government having experience in the Treasury, is elected Chairman. The question of the election of a member of the Opposition as Chairman was first raised before the Public Accounts Committee in Bengal in 1931 by Dr. Haridhan Dutt and again in 1939 by Dr. Nalinaksha Sanyal.

In the Lok Sabha the Speaker nominates a Chairman,

but if the Deputy Speaker is elected a member of the Committee, he acts as the Chairman. The State legislatures also have similar rules. In some of them a member of the opposition is appointed Chairman.

FUNCTIONS OF THE PUBLIC ACCOUNTS COMMITTEE

Placed as the Committee is with its limitations and limited powers as well as its advantages and influence, it is worthwhile examining its procedural methods and functions as well as its scope and ambit.

It is appointed for the examination of accounts showing the appropriation of the sums granted by the House to meet public expenditure. In scrutinizing the Appropriation Accounts and the Audit Report thereon it must satisfy itself that the moneys shown in the accounts as having been disbursed were legally available for and applicable to the service or purpose to which they have been applied or charged, that the expenditure conforms to the authority which governs it, and that every reappropriation has been made in accordance with the provisions made in this regard in the Appropriation Act or under rules made by competent authority lawfully empowered in this behalf. The term of reference also includes the examination of any trading, manufacturing and profit and loss accounts and balance sheets of Government concerns run on commercial lines, together with their Audit Reports and any other audited accounts of receipts or of stores and stocks or other matters in respect of which the executive may have required the accounts to be prepared and audit conducted.

The functions of the Committee are, however, considerably wider than those suggested by the bare terms of this reference. It is not merely a duplication or verification of the Comptroller and Auditor General's work. Although in practice the Committee works on the Auditor General's brief, any member may raise any relevant question on his own initiative, and although the Committee is primarily guided in its line of investigation by the Comptroller and Auditor General's report, so far as the subjects it selects for consideration are concerned, it is not necessarily restricted to the ground covered by that report.

From the accounting point of view, the Committee necessarily reviews the Comptroller and Auditor General's report
and investigates any irregularities brought to notice in that
report. The examination amounts to an enlarged revision
of the report, supplementing it by oral examination both
of the accounting officer and of other officers concerned in
the expenditure.

It deals with cases of expenditure in excess of the grants
made which may necessitate an excess vote by examining
the causes of, and jurisdiction for, such expenditure. The
attention of the House is invariably directed to all such cases,
and the very first report of the Committee to the House must
contain its recommendations and findings on all such cases.
'It is an unwritten law and the universal practice that no
excess vote can be taken without having been previously
submitted to this Committee.'[1] 'No alternative remains at
this stage but to recommend that an excess vote be taken;
but if it can be shown that the probabilities of an excess
were known in sufficient time for a supplementary estimate to
have been put forward, the department would be severely
censured. The known fact that the Committee does not deal
leniently with excess, exercises the strongest deterrent effect on
the departments against willingly or knowingly exceeding
parliamentary provision.'[2]

In dealing with the accounts the Committee's function
is not restricted to mere formalities of expenditure so far as
irregularities or excesses are concerned. Its function extends
to the 'wisdom, faithfulness and economy' in matters of
expenditure. It acts not only as a check upon extravagant,
irregular or unauthorized expenditure, but also within limits
upon unwise methods of management.

It may be mentioned in this connection that the Committee is not concerned with questions of policy, which are
the domain of the Cabinet and the House. This is because a
discussion on the question of policy might imply a right,
whether exercised or not, or approving or disapproving of
that policy, and an expression of opinion on points of policy

[1] Durell, p. 117; Willoughby, Willoughby and Lindsay, *System of Financial
Administration of Great Britain*, p. 128; Higgs, *Financial system of the United Kingdom*
p. 75; Campion, *Introduction to the Procedure of the House of Commons*, 2nd ed. p. 266.
[2] Durell, p. 117; Chubb, *Control of Public Expenditure*, p. 195.

either by way of approving or disapproving is likely to be set up as such by a department in its defence. Furthermore, there should be no intervention between the Minister and the House in the matter of policies. The amounts of estimate or of grants are also outside the scope of the Committee, even when the policy is common knowledge, as sometimes items of an estimate are based on policies resting on confidential documents which in the national interest even the House does not require to be divulged. The Committee, therefore, does not attempt any enquiry into every matter determined by the settled policy of the Government. The powers of the Committee are also limited in regard to changes of policy during the year of expenditure, even if such changes may have a very material effect on the expenditure as compared with the parliamentary appropriation. If excess expenditure is attributed to a change of policy it must be accepted. But the Committee is right in ascertaining whether such change of policy could have been foreseen and schemes worked out and decisions given in time to admit of provision being made in the estimates or at least in a supplementary estimate. No department should be allowed to take shelter under an excuse of 'a change of policy' to evade parliamentary control of expenditure through scrutiny by the Committee. Furthermore, the Committee is in its own field when, leaving aside the question of policy underlying an expenditure as well as the economic results of such policy, it restricts itself to the merit of such expenditure only so far as the administration is involved, although it is sometimes very difficult to determine its extent. Again the Committee is within its rights in considering the purpose—apart from the amount or the policy in respect of a grant so as to see that the expenditure conforms to the purpose.

In this way the Committee deals with the accounts of different departments and makes reports thereon, taking one or more or all at a time according to circumstances.

The reports made by the Committee contain its views and findings on the accounts of different departments of the Government, expressing its satisfaction in some cases, and recording its disapproval of unsatisfactory expenditure in cases involving financial irregularities. The Committee will point out the abuses in the management of public finances, suggest remedies, and report after proper investigation its opinion on disputed points of account between departments or between agencies and departments. The Committee may also offer suggestions regarding the form or arrangement of the estimates or of its number of grants. It may also formulate or suggest principles for the improvement or growth of the existing system of accounting. On rare occasions it also reports on cases of non-compliance with the law and cases where the function of the legislature has been usurped, giving sufficient allowance for the circumstances of the case.

Some remarks are needed to describe the impersonal attitude that is all along maintained by the Committee. In matters of fraud and proved negligence resulting in loss it does not require to know the name of a delinquent, but sees whether the head of the department has promptly enquired into the origin of the affair and taken suitable steps to bring the delinquent to book as also to prevent a recurrence. It may express its opinion on the adequacy of steps taken and of the punishment meted out. It possesses the power to intervene in order to examine the systems under which the departments work, and acts as a check on unwise methods of expenditure; but it does not think it advisable to interfere in administration but merely calls attention to the weak points in the system, leaving the department to remedy them.

The manner in which the Committee discharges its functions, combined with its impersonal attitude, enables it to exercise an increasingly effective and salutary influence on the administration of public finances.

UPPER HOUSE AND THE PUBLIC ACCOUNTS COMMITTEE

The accepted convention of the British Parliament is that it is the elected House, the House of Commons, which grants the money to the Crown for expenditure, and it is that House which has the right to scrutinize expenditure and see that the money has been spent for the purposes for which it was granted. It is therefore the House of Commons which appoints the Public Accounts Committee to examine the accounts. In fact the accounts are not laid before the House of Lords.

In the British Parliament the House of Lords does not appoint[1] any committee to scrutinize the Public Accounts; nor are any members of the House of Lords associated with the House of Commons. On two occasions it appears that the House of Lords tried to appoint some additional members of their own to be associated with the Standing Committee of the House of Commons to scrutinize the Public Accounts, but the attempts failed. The claim of the House of Lords was based on the ground that the Accounts were to be laid before both Houses.

In India, however, the Upper House, the Council of States of the Indian Parliament and the Legislative Councils of State legislatures, have claimed a right to discuss the Comptroller and Auditor General's Report and the Accounts on the ground that 'under the Constitution, the Reports and the Accounts are to be laid before the Legislature'; the Upper House also claims the right to scrutinize and discuss the accounts.

It does not seem that the claim is very well justified. Theoretically, of course, it can be said that the Upper House has the right to discuss the Accounts and the Auditor General's Reports because these are laid before the House. But what would be the result of discussion? The Upper House has no control over the finances of the State. It cannot withhold the grant of any money, for no demands for grants are made to it. It has no control over the Appropriation Bill, for the Appropriation Bill can become law without the concurrence of the Upper House. It is the Lower House which grants the money and which can withhold the money from the executive, if the money is spent in a manner of which it disapproves. It stands to reason, therefore, that it is the Lower House only which has the right to call for explanation from the executive government.

Then again, if there are two Public Accounts Committees of the two Houses, government departments would be at a great disadvantage. They would have to appear twice before the two Committees, and if the two Committees differed in their views in any particular matter, they would not know whom to hearken unto, the voice of Delphi or the voice of Dodona.

[1] Durell, p. 108.

On 10 May 1954, the Lok Sabha adopted a motion to associate seven members of the Rajya Sabha with the Public Accounts Committee of the Lok Sabha. Although the Speaker said, after the motion was adopted, that so far as the deliberations, voting and every other matter were concerned members of the Council who were associated with the Committee would have the same status as other members of the Committee, yet it was emphasized that the Committee was a Committee of the Lok Sabha and the associated members would be under the control of the Speaker.[1] State legislatures have also followed this practice.

DISCUSSION OF THE REPORT OF THE PUBLIC ACCOUNTS COMMITTEE

Although there is no specific rule for the discussion of the Report of the Public Accounts Committee, there are rules which provide that no discussion on the Accounts of the State shall take place until the Public Accounts Committee has reported its findings. It is usual to have the Report of the Public Accounts Committee discussed on a motion that the Report of the Public Accounts Committee be taken into consideration.

In the House of Commons the Reports of the Public Accounts Committee are not generally discussed unless some important point with political repercussions or of a scandalous nature is involved. Such discussions took place in 1942 and 1947. There is, however, a feeling extant that the Reports of the Public Accounts Committee should be discussed, and the Select Committee on Procedure recommended:

'Your Committee approve Sir Gilbert Campion's suggestion that provision should be made for securing discussion in the House of the Reports of the proposed Public Expenditure Committee [combining the Estimates Committee and the Public Accounts Committee] by giving them precedence on not more than two of the days allotted to supply[2] (See also Miscellaneous Motions, p. 143).

Since the amendment of Standing Order No. 16 in 1947,

---

[1] Proceedings of the House of the People, 10 May 1954, c. 6959.
[2] *Report of the Select Committee on Procedure*, 1946, H.C. 189.

21

it has been possible to consider reports from the Public Accounts Committee or from the Estimates Committee on a day allotted to the business of supply.[1]

CONTROL OVER CORPORATIONS

A new form of undertaking which affects parliamentary control of finances has recently come into existence, viz. state-owned or state-controlled corporations or companies. The following observations of Mr. Narahari Rao, Comptroller and Auditor General of India, deserve careful consideration:

'I refer to the formation of private companies under the Indian Companies Act for the management of Government industrial undertakings from the Consolidated Fund. These private limited companies are, in my opinion, a fraud on the Companies Act and also on the Constitution, because money cannot be taken away from the Consolidated Fund for the establishment and transformation of certain concerns into private companies in the name of the President and Secretary to Government.... To convert a government concern into a private company solely by executive action is unconstitutional. While recognizing that the management of industrial and business concerns differs from the normal day-to-day duties of administration and that special organization and delegation of authority more in accordance with speedier business practices may be necessary, the Government should have the backing of suitable Parliamentary enactment for the setting up of Corporations.

'There is another important point involved in this procedure of creating a private company under the Companies Act. Private companies are to be audited by auditors nominated by the Board of Directors. The Comptroller and Auditor General will not, therefore, have any automatic right to audit such a company.... It is true that the company may request him to be the auditor, if necessary by incorporating suitable provisions in its Articles of Association, but this would be neither proper nor binding, as the Comptroller and Auditor General's duties and functions are prescribed

[1] May, p. 739.

by Parliament and cannot be regulated by the Articles of Association of a company. Furthermore, even if he undertakes audit on a consent on payment of fees, he can only submit his audit reports to the company and not to the Parliament through the President. The Parliament cannot watch through the Public Accounts Committee the regularity of the operations and the financial results of such company.'[1]

It may, however, be worthwhile to state here that there is another class of corporations created by *ad hoc* statutes. Some of these corporations are kept outside the purview of the Comptroller and Auditor General of India, e.g. the Reserve Bank of India, the State Bank of India, and the Life Insurance Corporation. The Public Accounts Committee has accordingly no function with regard to them. In some cases the statutes creating autonomous bodies have made provisions that their accounts will be audited by the Comptroller and Auditor General and his report placed before the respective legislature, e.g. the Damodar Valley Corporation. In such cases the Public Accounts Committee is within its rights to examine the financial position of the Corporation as in the case of a government department.

A Committee known as the Committee on Public Undertakings has now been constituted to investigate into the working of public undertakings (See p. 265).

CONCLUSION

In conclusion it may be stated that time has shown that the Financial Committees of the legislature have done useful work which has been recognized by Parliament and by the Press of the country. In a free atmosphere the Committees have taken a dispassionate and objective view of matters coming before them, and have contributed in their own way to the growth on sound lines of parliamentary democracy in India.

---

[1] Statement of Mr. Narahari Rao before the Union Public Accounts Committee; quoted in *The Indian Parliament*, ed. by A. B. Lal, p. 163. But see sec. 619, Companies Act, 1956, which authorises the Comptroller and Auditor General to appoint auditors for Public Companies. *see* also p. 337.

CHAPTER XV

THE COMPTROLLER AND AUDITOR GENERAL OF INDIA

THE Constitution[1] provides that there shall be a Comptroller and Auditor General of India who shall be appointed by the President by warrant under his hand and seal, and shall not be removable from office except on an address by the two Houses of Parliament for removal on the ground of proved misbehaviour or incapacity. The Constitution[2] also provides that the Comptroller and Auditor General, after ceasing to hold that office, shall not be eligible for reappointment in any capacity either by the Union or by the State Government, and that the administrative expenses of his office, including all salaries, allowances and pensions payable to or in respect of persons serving in that office, shall be charged upon the Consolidated Fund of India. The object of these provisions is to secure the independence of the Comptroller and Auditor General from executive control so that he can discharge his duties without fear or favour.

DUTIES OF THE COMPTROLLER AND AUDITOR GENERAL

The duties of the Comptroller and Auditor General as prescribed by the Constitution are:

(i) to prescribe, with the approval of the President, the form in which the accounts of the Union and of the States are to be kept;

(ii) to perform such duties and exercise such powers in relation to the accounts of the Union and the States and of any other body or authority as may be prescribed by any law made by Parliament; and

(iii) to report to the President or to the Governors of the States on the accounts of the Union or the States, as the case may be.[3]

[1] Art. 148.
[2] Ibid.
[3] Arts. 149, 150, 151.

Article 149 further prescribes that until law, as aforesaid, is made by Parliament, the Comptroller and Auditor General is to perform such duties and exercise such powers as the Auditor General of India was doing immediately before the commencement of the Constitution in relation to the accounts of the Dominion of India and of the provinces.

No law has yet been passed by Parliament, and the Comptroller and Auditor General is exercising his powers as heretofore which were prescribed by the Audit and Accounts Order, 1936, and the Initial and Subsidiary Accounts Rules made by the Governor-General under that order.

The Constitution has further provided in Article 279(1) that the Comptroller and Auditor General is to ascertain and certify the net proceeds of any tax or duty mentioned in Chapter I or Part XII of the Constitution, or of any part of such tax or duty in or attributable to any area. (For the duties of the Comptroller and Auditor General in connexion with State enterprises see p. 337).

FORM OF ACCOUNTS

The Comptroller and Auditor General is authorized, as mentioned above, to prescribe with the approval of the President the form in which the accounts of the Union and the States are to be kept. (For a discussion of the form of accounts see p. 283). It appears to have been accepted that the power to prescribe the form includes the power to give any direction with regard to the methods or principles in accordance with which any accounts are to be kept. Under this power the Comptroller and Auditor General has prescribed a uniform form of accounts for the Union and the States.

The Comptroller and Auditor General is, in pursuance of the Audit and Accounts Order, 1936, continuing to be responsible for the keeping of accounts of the Union and the States, except the accounts relating to Defence and to Railways and accounts relating to transactions in the United Kingdom. There is, however, a proposal for the separation of Accounts from Audit. The proposal is being given a trial on an experimental basis in some of the departments of both the Union and the States. The Comptroller is, however, relieved of keeping the initial accounts in the treasuries and departmental offices. The treasurers and these officers are liable to render accounts to the Comptroller and Auditor General in such form as he may prescribe, and consequently it is the Comptroller and Auditor General who prescribes the form in which initial accounts are to be kept.

DUTIES AND POWERS OF THE COMPTROLLER AND AUDITOR GENERAL IN REGARD TO AUDIT

Paragraph 13 of the Audit and Accounts Order, 1936, as adapted, contains the fundamental provisions relating to audit, and runs as follows:

'13 (1) It shall be the duty of the Auditor General:

(i) to audit all expenditure from the revenue of the Dominion and of the Provinces and to ascertain whether moneys shown in the accounts as having been disbursed were legally available for and applicable to the service or purpose to which they have been applied or charged and whether the expenditure conforms to the authority which governs it;

(ii) to audit all transactions of the Dominion and of the Provinces relating to debt, deposits, sinking funds, advances, suspense accounts and remittance business;

(iii) to audit all trading, manufacturing and profit and loss accounts and balance sheets kept by order of the Governor-General or of the Governor of a Province in any department of the Dominion or of the Province; and in each case to report on the expenditure, transactions or accounts so audited by him.

(2) The Auditor General may, with the approval of, and shall, if so required by, the Governor-General or the Governor of any Province, audit and report on:

(i) the receipts of any department of the Dominion or, as the case may be, of the Province;

(ii) the accounts of stores and stock kept in any office or department of the Dominion or, as the case may be, of the Province.

The Governor-General or the Governor of a Province

may after consultation with the Auditor General make regulations with respect to the conduct of audits under this sub-paragraph.'

The phraseology employed in clause (1) of the paragraph of the Audit and Accounts Order, quoted above, follows closely the wording of the Exchequer and Audit Department Act of the United Kingdom, the duty of the Audit Department being stated as that of auditing certain specified accounts and of reporting upon them. No attempt has, however, been made to define 'audit' itself, for such a definition might limit the authority and discretion which the Audit Department ought rightly to exercise.

REPORT OF THE COMPTROLLER AND AUDITOR GENERAL

Article 151 of the Constitution prescribes that the Report of the Comptroller and Auditor General relating to the accounts of the Union and each State shall be presented to the President or the Governor of the State, as the case may be. The duty of making a report is, however, imposed on him by the Audit and Accounts Order, 1936, which contemplates a report on the expenditure, transactions and accounts audited by him. The Reports so made, along with the accounts of the Union or the States, as the case may be, have to be laid before the respective legislatures. It is on the basis of these Reports that the Public Accounts Committees scrutinize the accounts.

The Reports and the Accounts are made in two parts, the Finance Accounts and the Appropriation Accounts. The Finance Accounts show the accounts of actual receipt and expenditure during the year; and the Appropriation Accounts show the appropriation of the money granted by the legislature to the various grants and heads of expenditure, i.e. whether the money granted for specific purposes has been spent for those purposes or not, and whether there is a surplus or an excess expenditure over the amount granted.

It will have been seen that the Comptroller and Auditor General's duties and powers cover both the audit and accounting of all the financial transactions of the Union and the States. In the matter of accounting, his responsibilities are well defined and conform to the traditional functions of an accountant, except that the form in which the accounts of the Union and the States are to be maintained is prescribed by him with the approval of the President.

As an auditor, his functions and authority are wider and more comprehensive than those exercised by professional auditors. A public auditor, responsible for the audit of commercial enterprises, is primarily concerned with the certification of the profit and loss account and the balance sheet. For this purpose he undertakes the audit of vouchers, cash book and other related books and documents. So long as any expenditure incurred is covered by a sanction of the appropriate authority, and so long as it does not contravene the provisions of the Company Law, he is precluded from commenting on the propriety of the sanction or on the discretion by these authorities. Quite apart from these legal limitations, he may also be influenced in his work by the fact that his appointment is made annually by the board of directors, and any expression of opinion which comes into conflict with the board may jeopardize his continuance as the auditor of the concern.

Audit by the Comptroller and Auditor General is not restricted by any such limitations. He is free to bring to the notice of Parliament or State legislature, as the case may be, the impropriety of any executive action, even when its legality is not in question. Nor does his continuance in office depend on the will or convenience of the administration. The special provisions incorporated in the Constitution do not merely underline his position as a servant of the people; they also endow him with appropriate authority in that conception to review the financial administration of the country as a whole.[1]

AUDIT OF APPROPRIATION ACCOUNTS

The audit of appropriation accounts involves scrutiny from different points of view. These may be summed up as, (i) audit from the point of view of accountancy, (ii) audit from the point of view of classification, (iii) audit from the point

[1] See Chanda, *Indian Administration*, pp. 245-6.

of view of authority and (iv) audit from the point of view of propriety.

AUDIT OF ACCOUNTANCY

With regard to audit from the point of view of accountancy, the auditor of public accounts has to perform the same duties as an auditor of private commercial accounts. The object is to be satisfied as to the accuracy and completeness of accounts, to see that all revenue and receipts collected are brought to account under the proper head, that all expenditure and disbursements are authorized, vouched for and correctly classified, and that the final account represents a complete and true statement of the financial transactions it purports to exhibit. Fraud and technical errors are also to be checked and detected. Part of the work in connexion with the scrutiny of expenditure is entrusted, for the sake of convenience and economy, to the officers of the spending departments. In such cases, as well as in cases of disbursements made by officers of departments other than the Indian Audit and Accounts Department, the audit officer has to rely upon or accept certificates furnished by the spending departments. Cases of suppression of expenditure are against the interest of the spending authorities, but there may be cases of fraud either by way of payments being made to payees not legally entitled or of claims being entertained which are not in accordance with facts. On the receipt side, too, it is not possible for the auditor to be by the side of the men receiving cash, and thus to ascertain that in every instance the amount payable to the Government has actually been recorded, or to state that all persons liable at law have been duly charged. The audit officer has necessarily to accept and rely upon departmental returns and the documents accompanying them. A thorough audit in respect of all items both on the receipt side and the payment side is impracticable with the limited establishment of the audit office. It is also not incumbent upon audit to conduct a thorough wholesale audit. Recently, however, the Union Government and some of the State Governments have required thorough audit of receipts under some specified tax heads.

So far as the detection of fraud is concerned, most of the frauds are checked and detected in the course of scrutiny by executive officers. The audit officers render valuable assistance in indicating directly or indirectly to the executive officers defects or irregularities which require their attention. The checks prescribed in the financial rules and treasury rules for executive officers, supplemented by occasional local audit by the officers of the Audit Departments and continuous central audit, sufficiently provide for the detection of fraud.

The number of technical errors detected in the course of scrutiny is considerable, and the defects are remedied by reference to the spending departments by way of audit objections.

In commercial accounts cases of errors of principle are also detected in the course of audit. In Government audit there is little scope for detection of such errors of principle in the system of accounts adopted. This is because the responsibility for the determination of or advice as to the form in which accounts should be kept devolves upon the Comptroller and Auditor General himself.

The Government audit in India is continuous, and as far as possible proceeds *pari passu* with cash transactions. It does not wait until the year is over and the accounts of the year are completed. It is also prompt. Although all transactions of public moneys are not thoroughly audited, the system of financial administration requires the executive to lay down rules, regulations and procedures sufficient to secure a proper and effective check upon the due assessment and collection of revenue and payment of dues from the Government, and in the test-audits the auditor must satisfy himself that there are such rules, regulations and procedures and that these have been enforced by the department. Results of such tests are communicated to the departments concerned and also included in the reports on the appropriation accounts.

Besides cases of fraud detected in the course of audit, all cases of loss of revenue, whether by way of remission by competent authority on the ground of irrecoverability or otherwise, as also cases of writing off of losses by competent authorities, are included in the Report so that the House is apprised of the actual position. It is incumbent upon the departments to notify to the Audit all cases in which payments have been waived or claims abandoned or losses written off, so that the Audit may incorporate the facts with its views in the Audit Report.

AUDIT OF AUTHORITY

'Closely allied to appropriation audit, and necessarily bound up with it, is the audit of authority or administrative audit: the examination or expenditure with a view to seeing that it is supported by the requisite authority in each case.'[1] The Audit and Accounts Order makes it incumbent upon the Comptroller and Auditor General to ascertain whether the expenditure conforms to the authority which governs it. 'The House appropriates the grants, but the expenditure, even though made on the service for which it is appropriated, is not valid unless incurred under proper authority. The provision made by Parliament (Legislature) for a service detailed in the estimates is not in itself any authority for carrying out that service, if it is a service for which treasury authority is required. The audit of authority is therefore an important function of the Comptroller and Auditor General, and it is his duty to report to the House any unauthorized expenditure for which treasury sanction is unobtainable; and he would normally recommend it for disallowance, but in special circumstances he would use his discretion as to admitting charges which are unauthorized, subject to the review of the Public Accounts Committee, whose attention would be drawn to them in his report.'[2]

The Constitution is the basis of all audit and all authorities. It is the duty of Audit to see and satisfy itself that all expenditure incurred should conform to the relevant provisions of the Constitution and of the laws made thereunder, and should also be in accordance with the financial rules and regulations framed by competent authority, and that there should exist sanction, either special or general, accorded by competent authority authorizing the expenditure. 'In con-

---

[1] Durell, p. 186.
[2] Ibid. p. 188; Chubb, *Control of Public Expenditure, pp.* 58-9.

ducting the audit in respect of the audit of authority the auditor performs quasi-judicial functions, in that he has to apply the rules and orders as they stand, irrespective of the position of the person against whom they are enforced. He may not relax or waive the rules, except where he is specially empowered to do so.'[1]

'In order to enable this audit of authority to be properly conducted, it is essential that regulations should be as explicit as possible. Anything like a wide discretion renders the action of the audit department nugatory, and the Public Accounts Committee deprecates the insertion in regulations of warrants (Orders) of such phrases "as a rule"; such a limitation obviously does not extend to the delegation of power to be exercised in special cases, for it is impossible to legislate in advance for every case that may arise. For audit purposes it is essential that the regulations should make it clear who the approving authority is and the limit of his powers. The discretion is then specially defined, and the exercise of it is a matter of administration.'[2]

The result of the audit of authority in cases where expenditure has been incurred without the approval of the competent authority, together with cases of excesses in subheads as a result of such expenditure, should be included in the Audit Report for the attention of the Public Accounts Committee and of the House.

AUDIT OF APPROPRIATION

The most important part of the obligatory audit is the audit of appropriation. It is incumbent upon the Auditor to see that the grants are spent for the purpose for which they are provided. 'The appropriation of the grants to specific purposes is the expression of the will of Parliament, which becomes law on the passing of the Appropriation Act. Deviations therefrom consequently diminish parliamentary control, even though specially legislated for in certain cases, because Parliament can only be able to give an *ex post facto* sanction

---

[1] *Introduction to the Indian Government Accounts and Audit Published by Govt. of India,* 1954.

[2] Durell, p. 188; Chubb, *Control of Public Expenditure,* p. 53, footnote.

to them. The strictness with which appropriation is applied is the measure of parliamentary control. No grants may be exceeded without fresh parliamentary authority accorded by a supplementary estimate or an excess grant, except in those special cases in which the Treasury [Finance Ministry/Department] is empowered to exercise, temporarily, modified powers of virement [reappropriation], subject to final approval by the House. The money must be spent within the time for which it was granted, and no sums are chargeable against the grants which do not actually come in course of payment within the financial year, a natural sequence of this condition being that any unspent surplus must be surrendered. Every amount charged in the account must be supported by proof of payment, the Comptroller and Auditor General being the sole judge of the sufficiency of evidence of payment.'[1]

The importance of the appropriation audit does not permit a test audit to be substituted for a thorough audit. It must be a detailed and complete audit. Every payment is cheked into the books to its right head of service so as to secure that the intentions of the House are duly carried out. These intentions are expressed in the estimates as finally granted. The estimates consequently form the basis for the appropriation audit.[2] The audit functions, however, vary with different parts of the estimates. The appropriations specifying the total amount voted for each grant are the primary concern. The major heads of account come next in order of importance, and next come the minor heads and sub-heads, and last of all come the detailed heads. The Comptroller and Auditor General holds and always has held that the estimates (including the parts) are put before him as a whole; that although they are divided into three parts, yet, inasmuch as Parliament grants the money on the understanding that it is going to be spent in that manner, the department presenting those estimates to Parliament cannot repudiate the responsibility for the divisions under which it presents them, and upon faith of which Parliament grants the money. Therefore, the Comptroller and Auditor General holds that the estimates are put before him as a whole; that he is entitled, if he thinks proper,

---

[1] Durell, p. 182-3; Higgs, *Financial System of the United Kingdom*, p. 73.
[2] Ibid. pp. 183-4.

to question any deviation from the estimates as shown by
the figures giving details of expenditure.[1] The audit records
expenditure against the appropriation grant and the respective head. Expenditure that exceeds the grant or appropriation or does not seem to fall within its scope is treated as
unauthorized expenditure, unless regularized by further
provisions. Hence, in the appropriate audit, the audit of
provision of funds and the audit of classification are two
essential factors. With these are closely connected the form
of the estimates, the form of the accounts and the authority
of classification. Durell says, 'Considerations connected with
the form of the estimates affect the Comptroller and Auditor
General to a limited extent since they form the basis of the
form of accounts with which they are closely bound up.'[2] The
authority for the form of the estimates is derived from the
procedure rules of the respective legislature, and it is left to
the Finance Ministry/Department to prescribe the form with
such suggestions as the Estimates Committee may offer; the
authority for the form of the accounts is derived from Article
150 of the Constitution, and the form is left to the Auditor
General to be prescribed; the ultimate authority for classification rests with the executive in consultation with the
Auditor General, under the Audit and Accounts Order. In
matters of classification the executive is the final authority;
audit, however, has the right to criticize the validity of any
such classification which is inconsistent with the Budget
provisions, or which makes the accounts an incorrect or misleading representation of facts. 'Having regard to all these,
the Comptroller and Auditor General in his dual capacity
as keeping and as auditing the accounts of Government is
responsible for securing that entry of financial transactions
in the accounts conforms to such forms and directions.'[3]

It must also be remembered that under the provisions
of the Constitution[4] the expenditure charged upon the Consolidated Fund should be shown distinct from that which
has been voted, and also that expenditure on revenue account
should be shown distinguished from capital expenditure.

[1] Durell, p. 184.
[2] Ibid. p. 186.
[3] *Audit Code.*
[4] Arts. 112, 202.

'It is, therefore, an important function of Audit to verify that no expenditure is classified as "charged on the Consolidated Fund" except in accordance with the terms of the Constitution and conversely that no expenditure is classified as voted which should be "charged".'[1]

In the matter of classification of expenditure allocation between capital and revenue is very important, as otherwise the financial picture will be entirely misleading. 'It should be borne in mind that the decision whether expenditure shall be met from current revenues or from borrowed moneys rests with the executive subject to the approval of the legislature. It is, however, the duty of Audit to bring to notice occasions on which the classification of expenditure between revenue and capital or its distribution between current revenues or loan funds appears to be contrary to the dictates of sound and prudent financial administration. The financial and accounting conception of capital expenditure is imported from commercial theory and practice and an essential feature is that expenditure of a capital nature is not met from the revenue or profits of a concern. The essential purpose of the opening of capital heads of account is to facilitate the exhibition of financial results of any special undertaking on the basis of generally accepted commercial principles or in some more simple conventional manner, either that the cost of a service may be ascertained or that the full financial implication of any policy may be made clear.'[2] Capital expenditure may also be financed from revenue accounts when so decided by the executive, but that too should be properly recorded. The purpose of recording capital expenditure within the revenue account as separate and distinct from revenue expenditure is almost always to enable accounts to be prepared according to commercial principles.

'With regard to audit of accounts of transactions pertaining to Reserves or Reserve Funds it may be stated that any device of rendering grants non-lapsing by withdrawing amounts to a fund is contrary to the strict theory of Parliamentary financial control. But if such a course is adopted with the cognizance and approval of the legislature, the audit should classify

[1] *Audit Code.*
[2] *Audit Code.*

such accounts having regard to the procedure followed in budgeting for these transactions and the principles specially enunciated for the purpose.'[1]

AUDIT OF PROPRIETY

From the point of view of regularity, an expenditure may be in order when it satisfies all the foregoing tests, namely, that it is a properly vouched expenditure, sanctioned by a competent authority, the sundry rules being duly observed both by the disbursing and the sanctioning officers, and that it is met from the allotment of funds provided for in the estimates passed by the legislature and recorded under the relevant head of account. In spite of all such formalities being regularly observed, there may be cases of expenditure involving extravagance or waste. Such expenditure may be termed as improper expenditure. Similarly there may be improper waste of stores. Principles of sound financial administration warrant a review of the expenditure from this point of view, and audit being an instrument of financial control it devolves on audit to call the attention of the House to all such cases of extravagance and waste. But the functions of the Comptroller and Auditor General in this regard have not been precisely defined. According to Durell, such functions of the Comptroller and Auditor General fall within the range of the 'discretionary review,' and the limits of such review are governed more by usage and precedent than by enactment. 'This practice of drawing attention to cases of extravagance is a good instance of a development of procedure arising out of the system provided by Parliament, but not specifically legislated for.'[2] The Comptroller and Auditor General may be required to investigate the methods of expenditure involved in the consideration of the purpose thereof, and therefore to investigate the questions of extravagance, and he is also required to report on the accounts 'The words "report on the accounts" probably do not legally confer a right to point out such cases to the Public Accounts Committee; but the practice is recognized by all departments, and no department has ever com-

[1] *Audit Code.*
[2] Durell, p. 192; Chubb, *Control of Public Expenditure*, p. 61.

plained of attention being drawn to questionable expenditure even when regularly vouched.'[1]

'This accepted view of the practice which has grown up is a wise one in the interests of national finance, if not carried too far. If, however, the Comptroller and Auditor General were to set up as the central authority for reviewing expenditure generally, and its necessity, it would create friction, and in the end do more harm than good. If he reports on a matter of administration from the point of view of its effects on the public purse, it will be for the purpose of bringing before Parliament something which would otherwise pass unnoticed. It is impossible to deny that it is always his right, and will often be his duty, to take this step; but it is equally obvious that the occasion and manner of such report must be matters of discretion. The success of the practice, and its consequently beneficial results, are due to the moderation and tact with which it has hitherto been applied.'[2]

It is thus obvious that in this field of discretionary review the duties of an Audit Officer cannot be regulated by laying down precise rules. The Auditor General's rules made under the Government of India Act, 1919, laid down some 'canons of financial propriety'. 'There are no such statutory canons now and hence audit may challenge an expenditure—otherwise regular, not on the basis of any such canon but as transgressing a universally accepted standard of official conduct or financial administration.'[3]

POWERS AND DUTIES OF THE COMPTROLLER AND AUDITOR GENERAL IN RELATION TO AUTONOMOUS CORPORATIONS

As already observed, a new form of undertaking affecting parliamentary control of finance has recently come into existence, viz. State-owned or State-controlled corporations or companies. These enterprises are either registered as companies under the Company Law or incorporated as corporations by special legislation.

The Company Law defines 'a Government Company' as a

---

[1] Durell, p. 192; Chubb, *Control of Public Expenditure*, p. 61.
[2] Ibid.
[3] Pinto, *System of Financial Administration in India*, p. 264.

company in which not less than fifty-one per cent of the share capital is held by one or more Governments, in India. The law provides that in respect of such a company the appointment of an auditor shall be made on the advice of the Comptroller and Auditor General, who shall have power to direct the manner in which the company's accounts shall be audited and also to give instructions to the auditor so appointed in any matter relating to the audit of the said accounts. The Comptroller and Auditor General shall also have power to have a supplementary or test audit of the accounts done by any person authorized by him, and have the right to comment upon or supplement the report of audit made by the auditor so appointed. These are laid before Parliament and the State legislatures concerned under the Company Law. (See also chapter XII—the Committee on Public undertakings).

So far as the corporations incorporated by *ad hoc* statutes are concerned, whether or not the Comptroller and Auditor General shall have any function in regard to them, they are governed by the provisions of the respective statutes creating the bodies. There are different categories of such bodies. In some cases, e.g. the Reserve Bank of India, the State Bank of India and the Life Insurance Corporation of India, the finances and the accounts are outside the purview of the Comptroller and Auditor General. In some other cases, e.g. the Damodar Valley Corporation, the Comptroller and Auditor General has the same relation as he has in connexion with the examination of the accounts of a government.

CHAPTER XVI

FINANCE DEPARTMENT

A sound control over public finance is not and cannot be a discontinuous process. The ultimate control lies, of course, with the legislature but that control is of a political character; the control exercised by the Finance Committees of the House, the Estimates and the Public Accounts Committees, is also indirect and that of the Comptroller and Auditor General retrospective. But, as remarked by Durell, 'the public and the Parliament should be satisfied that somewhere or other in the Government there is a guarantee for financial order; that there is some authority that will watch the progress of public expenditure, the obligations which the different departments are incurring, and will give timely warning if that expenditure or those obligations are either outrunning the revenue provided for the year, or engaging the nation too deeply in future years.'[1] Such a continuous and concurrent control is vested in the Finance Ministry or Finance Department of the Government. Even when the executive government was not responsible to the legislature, there were Finance Departments both in the Centre and in the provinces to watch over the financial transactions of the respective Governments.

The position of the Finance Department is analogous to that of the Treasury in the United Kingdom. There are, however, substantial differences between the structure and functions of the Treasury in the United Kingdom and those of the Finance Ministry or Finance Department of a Government in India. These arise from the historical evolution of the administration in the two countries. The Treasury in the United Kingdom is much more than an organ of financial control; it has other traditional responsibilities. In India, though the Finance Department (Ministry) was originally constituted on the pattern of the financial wing of the Treasury with analogous functions, it has not absorbed the changes

[1] Durell, p. 242.

instituted subsequently in the United Kingdom and has evolved on its own lines.[1]

The function of the Treasury has been stated by Durell to be 'to control, to authorize and to advise, apart from its duty of having to secure that the money required is available. It is responsible for seeing that the Consolidated Fund is always in a position to meet the demands made upon it.'[2] The functions of the Finance Ministry or the Finance Department of a Government in India are, broadly speaking, of the same nature, and it has to discharge the same responsibility in respect of the Consolidated Fund of the Government concerned.

FUNCTIONS OF THE FINANCE DEPARTMENT

After the commencement of the Constitution the Finance Ministry or the Finance Department of a Government derives its authority from the Rules of Business made by the President or the Governor in pursuance of Article 77(3) or 166(3) of the Constitution, as the case may be. The functions of the Ministry (Department) are also broadly outlined by these rules.

The powers and functions of the Department were also defined in earlier times. The Devolution Rules made under the Government of India Act, 1919, prescribed the functions of the Finance Department. And although modifications have been made to suit the changed circumstances after Independence, that Department still exercises substantially the same functions.

They are as follows:

1. It shall be in charge of the account relating to loans granted by the Government and shall advise on the financial aspect of all transactions relating to such loans.

2. It shall examine and report on all proposals for the increase or reduction of taxation.

3. It shall examine and report on all proposals for borrowing on the security of the Consolidated Fund or for giving guarantees, shall take all steps necessary for the purpose of

[1] See Chanda, *Indian Administration* pp. 204-5.
[2] Durell, p. 242.

raising such loans as have been duly authorized and shall be in charge of all matters relating to the service of loans or the discharge of guarantees.

4. It shall be responsible for seeing that proper financial rules are framed for the guidance of other departments and that suitable accounts are maintained by other departments and establishments subordinate to them.

5. It shall be responsible during the year for watching the state of the Government's balances.

6. It shall prepare a statement of estimated revenue and expenditure to be laid before the legislature in each year and any supplementary statements of expenditure; it shall also prepare the demands for excess grants, vote on account, votes of credit and exceptional grants, if any, required to be submitted to the legislature.

7. For the purpose of such preparation, it shall obtain from the departments concerned materials on which to base its estimates and it shall be responsible for the correctness of the estimates framed on the materials so supplied.

8. It shall examine and advise on all schemes of new expenditure for which it is proposed to make provision in the estimates, and shall decline to provide in the estimates for any scheme which has not been so examined.

9. It shall be responsible for the preparation of Appropriation Bills to be introduced in the legislature.

10. On receipt of a report from an Audit Officer to the effect that expenditure for which there is no sufficient sanction is being incurred, it shall require steps to be taken to obtain sanction or that the expenditure shall immediately cease.

11. It shall cause the Report of the Comptroller and Auditor General of India relating to the appropriation accounts to be laid before the legislature, and shall bring to the notice of the Committee on Public Accounts such other matters as should be referred to the Committee.

12. It shall advise departments responsible for the collection of revenue regarding the progress of collection and the methods of collection employed.

It will have been seen that the Finance Department has been invested with a certain priority over other departments. The Finance Department, however, does not possess any power of final decision on any matter; for questions of policy are the concern of the Ministry. Any disagreements between the Finance and other departments are resolved by the Cabinet whose decision is of course final.

POWERS OF THE FINANCE DEPARTMENT

The powers of the Finance Department are as follows:

1. No department shall without previous consultation with the Finance Department authorize any orders (other than orders pursuant to any general delegation made by the Finance Department) which,

(i) either immediately or by their repercussion, will affect the finances of the Government concerned, or which, in particular, (a) involve any grant of land or assignment of revenue or concession, grant, lease or licence of mineral or forest rights or a right to water power or any easement or privilege in respect of such concession; or (b) in any way involve any relinquishment of revenue; or

(ii) relate to the number of grading or cadre of posts or the emoluments or other conditions of service or posts.

2. No proposal, which requires the previous consultation of the Finance Department under the Rules of Business, but in which the Finance Department has not concurred, may be proceeded with unless a decision to that effect has been taken by the Cabinet.

3. No reappropriation (virement) shall be made by any department other than the Finance Department, except in accordance with such general delegation as the Finance Department may have made.

4. Except to the extent that power may have been delegated to the departments under rules approved by the Finance Department, every order of an administrative department conveying a sanction to be enforced in audit shall be communicated to the audit authorities by the Finance Department.

IMPORTANCE OF FINANCE DEPARTMENT

The importance of the Finance Department in connexion with public finance has been very ably dealt with by Durell, and the following passage will show the principles under which the Treasury acts and the manner in which the Treasury is treated in the United Kingdom.

'It is the Department on which Parliament mainly relies for the prevention of financial irregularities on the part of the accounting Departments. Its control commences with the preparation of the estimates and continues throughout the various processes of expenditure, accounting and audit, until the final report of the Public Accounts Committee has been dealt with.'[1]

Not being a spending department itself, it is in a good position to judge the requests that come from other departments.

The functions of the Treasury are wide; for, as the department responsible for financial order, there can be no question on the financial bearings of which it will not have the direct or potential right to express its views. However, it ought not to be, and cannot be, an authority on extremely scientific or technical proposals. In criticizing, for instance, the professional expenditure of the Army and the Navy, the Treasury would soon be infringing upon that criticism of policy which it is not its duty to exercise. Its functions are necessarily limited in such directions by the practicability of their exercise. On the other hand, its control is not limited to seeing that the money is spent according to appropriation and under authority but also to seeing that it is wisely and needfully spent. In the case, therefore, more particularly of the manufacturing departments and cognate concerns and services, the Finance Department is entitled to ask a department to show cause for the work that is done and whether what is being done is still needed.

Nor again must it intervene too much in administration. Though it is a department having control over other departments the word 'control' implies not that it is its duty to watch them and act the part of a detective towards them, but that, whenever charges are made and difficulties occur and scandals are detected, it is its duty to devise regulaions for meeting, correcting or remedying them. In this sense only does it control. It is impossible that it ever should, or that it ought to, watch over and inquire into the expenditure of the other departments; it has no machinery for doing so.

[1] Durell, p. 244.

The control of the Finance Department by the Legislature is effected, firstly, through the control of the House over the Finance Minister, and secondly, through the Financial Committees. The Finance Department is under obligation to be present before the Financial Committees of the House and to write minutes on the reports of the Committees, even though it may not agree with the views of the Committees on some cases. These minutes provide a valuable insight into the policy of the Finance Department in relation to principles and practice.

In conclusion it may be said that, as a central financial authority, it is the Finance Department which promotes financial order, secures uniformity of system, exercises a valuable influence in advising departments as to organization and similar general questions, compels a department to justify its proposals, and acts as an impartial critic on the departments' proceedings generally. Moreover, the existence of such a factor both relieves and strengthens the control of the legislature. Consequently the Finance Department has been authorized to decide whether expenditure not authorized by the House may be incurred in exceptional circumstances and to authorize reappropriations.

CONTROL OF FINANCE DEPARTMENT

The general control of the Finance Department over public finance may be classified mainly under three heads, (i) Control over estimates, (ii) Control over details and (iii) Control over expenditure.

(i) *Control over Estimates:* this is anterior control and it terminates with the presentation of the estimates to the House. This question has been considered in an earlier chapter in connection with the Annual Financial Statement.

(ii) *Control over Details:* in respect of the expenditures of the various departments, the Finance Department must have previous cognizance from the estimates which are sent up to it as a matter of rule. The smooth working of the financial system of the Government largely depends upon the responsibility of respective departments with overall control by the Finance Department. The general control of the

Finance Department is exercised by according previous approval to the general objects of contemplated expenditure and to the limits within which it must be carried out. The detailed financial administration works mostly on the basis of financial rules framed under the authority of the Rules of Business of the respective Governments, and also under the rules framed under Article 283 of the Constitution. Government departments and various authorities under them are largely invested with powers delegated by the Finance Department in matters of details of expenditure. As a matter of rule, no department can without previous consultation with the Finance Department authorize any orders which may directly or indirectly affect the finances of the State. Even in the case of a new item of recurring expenditure of small amount the previous approval of the Finance Department is necessary. As has been expressed by Durell:

'It is a fundamental and constitutional rule that the sanction of the Treasury is necessary to increase expenditure, not only in regard to additions to establishments but also as regards rates of pay, extra and special pay and allowances: and herein lies a valuable part of Treasury control, for such supervision "stops the constant leakage of public money in items of outlay, trivial perhaps in themselves but amounting in the mass to a heavy demand upon the taxpayer".'[1]

As will have been seen from the outlines of the powers and functions of the Finance Department described above (see p. 340) the sanction of the Finance Department is necessary, for, among others, the following matters:

(a) Increase of the staff of any department, even though provision may have been made in the Budget for such increase.

(b) Increase of the rates of pay or allowance or the granting of any special pay or allowance.

(c) Purchase of land or houses, sale or exchange of land or houses.

(d) Grants-in-aid to public bodies.

(e) Writing off of losses, abandonment of claims.

(f) Deficiencies or over-issues.

[1] Durell, p. 328; see also Higg, *The Financial System of the United Kingdom*, p. 82.

(g) Royalties and rewards to inventors.

(h) Gifts of public property to public bodies or individuals.

(i) Payment of compensation to a contractor.

(j) Remission of loans.

Durell says: 'The underlying idea in requiring such cases to be submitted to the Treasury is not only to control the Department, but also to secure an impartial tribunal which will examine their merits from an extra-departmental point of view. But, again, while the sanction of the Treasury is obligatory in many classes of expenditure and is not essential in others, cases are likely to arise in which there may be a doubt as to the powers of the accounting department, or in which the circumstances may be so exceptional as to render reference to the Treasury advisable. Even, therefore, when a department may be of opinion that it has the power to take independent action, it may still consider it safer to obtain the concurrence of the Treasury. Having done so, it will be in a stronger position to justify and defend its action before the Public Accounts Committee'.[1]

(iii) *Control over Expenditure*: the annual estimates are made on the basis of anticipated programmes for the year; but it may be that the forecasts of the departments do not come true. There should be some authority, therefore, to make the necessary adjustments when there is excess expenditure or surplus over the amount estimated in the Budget.

It has been already stated that the annual estimates are divided into a number of grants which in their turn are divided into major heads, minor heads and details. It has also been stated (see Chapter XIII) that a grant may contain several major heads while a major head can also be split up and included in more than one grant. The Budget is passed on the basis of the grants, and in the absence of any authority from the legislature, no expenditure can be incurred in excess of the amount of the grant nor can any saving under any grant be diverted into any other grant.

The transfer of money from one major head to another major head within the same grant or from one minor head to another is, however, permissible. But no such transfer, or 'reappropriation' as it is known in India, or 'virement'

----
[1] Durell, p. 335.

as it is known in the United Kingdom, can be made without
the sanction of, or authority delegated by, the Finance Department. In the United Kingdom, however, where there is
virement between votes (as in the Service Departments
Accounts), the sanction of the House is also required (retros-
pectively).

Although the Budget as presented to the legislature shows
the details of the proposed expenditure, the legislature does
not insist that the details should be strictly adhered to in
all cases, and a certain latitude is given to the executive
government to adjust the different items. But certain general
principles have to be observed in sanctioning reappropriation.
The following extract from the *Report of the Public Accounts
Committee of West Bengal* will show how reappropriation can
be made:

'It is true that money is voted by the House and appropriated by the Appropriation Act to the grant as a whole
and not to the sub-heads constituting the grant. Reappropriation from one grant to another is not possible; reappropriation is, however, allowed from one sub-head within a
grant to another.'

But, even so, there are certain general principles which
ordinarily govern such reappropriations. First of all, reappropriation from one sub-head to another can only be
made under the authority and sanction of the Finance Department. And in giving such sanction, the Finance Department
is guided by certain principles. These principles have been
succinctly and correctly laid down by Durell in his book on
Parliamentary Grants as follows:

' "The Public Accounts Committee agrees that there is
nothing unconstitutional in the practice of applying savings
on one sub-head of a vote to meet the deficiency under another
sub-head, as the formal vote of the House of Commons applies
only to the total amount of each estimate; but at the same
time it is of opinion that even here the Treasury should
exercise care that the money is not spent in any way which
seriously differs from the details presented to Parliament.
It is, however, doubtful as to the correctness of sanctioning
transfers between sub-heads if they are not clearly of the
same kind. So far as Civil votes are concerned, this is agreed

to by the Treasury, which never sanctions transfers unless the sub-heads are closely allied." [1]

Another pertinent question may arise, whether it is permissible without the specific sanction of the legislature to restore or increase expenditure on an item the provision for which was specifically omitted or reduced by the vote of the legislature. This involves the question of overriding the wishes of the legislature. There is another question, viz. of providing money by reappropriation for 'new services'.

As regards the practice in the United Kingdom Durell says:

'The Government must adhere to those details as far as is consistent with the interests of the public service, since its good faith is pledged by the details given to Parliament, and the Comptroller and Auditor General would correctly bring divergencies to notice. This being so, it follows that if Parliament wishes to definitely prohibit the use of a vote for a service which would be covered by the terms of the resolution granting the vote, even though no mention is made of it in the details of the estimate, the resolution must obtain a special proviso to that effect. By this means only can Parliament ensure that a particular service is not carried out, for then there would be no funds which could legally be applied to it. In the absence of such a proviso there would be no technical incorrectness in charging the expenditure against the vote, even though the service were for a purpose for which Parliament had not wished to provide. This point is admitted by the Treasury, which points out that, even if the amount of a vote is reduced in supply, there is no guarantee that expenditure will not take place upon the object in respect of which such reduction is made. Unless enforcement is secured by an official record of the specific reduction in the votes and proceedings of the House, the only other method of guarding against expenditure on the service in question is for the Treasury to inform the department concerned and to direct the discontinuance of the expenditure.' [2]

The system of voting grants by means of a resolution of the House does not obtain in legislatures in India. Effective

---

[1] *Report of the Public Accounts Committee for 1949-50*; see also Durell, p. 299.
[2] Durell, p. 296.

parliamentary control, so far as omission of or reduction in amounts of a sub-head under a grant or vote are concerned, can be exercised through the timely caution taken in this regard by the Finance Department which should see that specific wishes of the legislature are not overridden.

It also devolves upon the Finance Department to see that no department continually overestimates an item of expenditure with the deliberate intention of providing funds for transfer to meet deficits wherever they occur on other sub-heads.

If a new but kindred service is introduced, reappropriation for this purpose is permissible, subject to the general principles enunciated above.

In respect of altogether 'new services' not provided for in the estimates, transfer is permissible only for urgent services. 'The Treasury admits that having placed before Parliament a list of new works, it would not hold that it had a free right to apply money to new works of any consequence, except under such urgent circumstances as it would be prepared to justify before Parliament. The Public Accounts Committee recommends that the Treasury shall exhibit the utmost jealousy of any proposal to use savings for the commencement of any new work in the absence of any provision in the estimates. In all such cases Treasury authority can only be given on the understanding that the expenditure on the proposed service can be met from savings on the aggregate'.[1]

As Durell goes on to state 'The sanction of the Treasury is not, and is not to be regarded as, a pure formality, even when the service has been necessarily started and covering sanction is asked for. Its control must not be a shadow, but operative.'[2]

---

[1] Durell, p. 302.
[2] Ibid. p. 304.

CHAPTER XVII

PARLIAMENTARY PRIVILEGE

ARTICLES 105 and 194 of the Constitution of India deal with the powers, privileges and immunities of the legislatures of the Union and the States and of their members and committees. The Articles themselves provide for certain privileges, namely, freedom of speech in the legislatures, immunity of members from any proceedings in any court in respect of anything said or any vote given by them in the legislature or any committee thereof, and also immunity from liability in respect of publication by or under the authority of the legislature of any report, paper, votes or proceedings. The Articles further provide that the legislatures may by law define the powers, privileges and immunities in respect of matters other than those specifically mentioned in the Articles, and that until so defined the privileges, etc. would be those of the British House of Commons and of its members and committees at the date of the commencement of the Constitution.

PRIVILEGES UNDER THE GOVERNMENT OF INDIA ACT, 1935

The Government of India Act, 1935, provided (i) that there should be freedom of speech in the legislature, (ii) that no member should be liable for anything said or any vote given by him in the legislature or in any committee thereof, and (iii) that no person should be liable in respect of the publication, by or under the authority of the legislature, of any report, paper, vote or proceeding. The legislature was empowered to make laws defining the privileges of the members of the legislature in other respects. This power was, however, qualified by the provision that the legislature could not confer upon itself or upon any committee or person, the status of a court, or any punitive or disciplinary powers other than the power to remove or exclude persons infringing any rule or standing order or otherwise behaving in a disorderly manner. The legislature was also empowered by the Government of India

Act, 1935, to provide by legislation for the punishment of any person refusing to give evidence or to produce any document before any committee of the legislature. But the power to punish was to be exercised by the court and not by the legislature, and the Governor had the right to make rules for safeguarding confidential matters from disclosure if government officials were called as witnesses. It was also provided that until legislation regarding privileges was passed, the privileges of the members would be such as were enjoyed by them immediately before the commencement of the Government of India Act, 1935. No Act appears to have been passed by any legislature, excepting Sind and Orissa, either defining the privileges or enforcing the attendance of witnesses. The bill which was passed by the Orissa Assembly was returned by the Governor-General twice, and thereafter the bill was not proceeded with. But it may be noted, however, that in 1956, an Act—the Parliamentary Proceedings (Protection of Publication) Act, 1956—was passed by the Indian Parliament affording protection against publication of proceedings in newspapers. In 1959 a private member sponsored a bill entitled 'The Parliamentary Privilege Bill' in the Lok Sabha with a view to including members' letters to Ministers or to the Presiding Officer of the House and replies thereto within the meaning of the term 'proceedings in Parliament', so that privilege could be claimed in respect of such correspondence. The decision of the British House of Commons in the Strauss's Case[1] where the House disagreeing with the report of its Privileges Committee, decided, though by a slender majority, that such communications between a Member of Parliament and a Minister were not proceedings in Parliament, was the immediate provocation of this Bill. The Bill was, however, rejected by the Lok Sabha.[2]

PRIVILEGES UNDER THE GOVERNMENT OF INDIA ACT, 1919

As we have already seen, the Government of India Act, 1935, preserved all privileges that attached to the legislature or its members or committees at the date of its commencement.

[1] H.C.D. 1957-58, vol. 591, cc. 208-346.
[2] L.S.D. vol. xxv (2nd series), 20 Feb. 1959, cc. 2241-2304.

It is therefore necessary to enquire what, if any, those privileges were. It appears that it was under the Government of India Act, 1919, that (a) freedom of speech in the House, and (b) immunity from liability for publication of any matter in the official proceedings were for the first time ensured by statute. By an amendment in the Civil Procedure Code in 1925, members of legislatures were exempted from arrest or detention under civil process during the continuance of any meeting of the legislature or of any of its committees, and for fourteen days before and after such meeting. By a similar amendment in the Criminal Procedure Code members were exempted from serving as jurors or assessors.

It does not appear that before the Government of India Act, 1919, there was any statutory recognition of any privilege of legislatures, except that of the Bengal Council (Witnesses) Act, 1866. It does not also appear that the question of privilege arose in any legal or other proceedings before the Act of 1919. The question whether the publication of any statement or speech made in the House in any manner other than in the official proceedings was privileged arose in the Central legislature on at least two occasions, and it was decided by the House that no privilege could be claimed in respect of such publication.[1] The point whether the privilege of freedom of speech given by the Government of India Act, 1919, applied to questions put by members, and whether it was absolute or qualified by reason of the use of the words 'subject to the rules and standing orders' in the relevant section, arose in a case in Burma, and it was argued, firstly, that a question was not a speech, freedom of which had been guaranteed and, secondly, that if any speech offended against or was not in conformity with any rule or standing order, such a speech could not be privileged. A Full Bench of the Rangoon High Court repelled both these arguments and held that the privilege was an absolute one.[2]

PRIVILEGES AFTER THE GOVERNMENT OF INDIA ACT, 1935

We therefore find that at the date of the commencement of

---

[1] *Proceedings of the Indian Legislative Assembly*, 27 Feb. 1936, vol. ii, p. 1982.
[2] *Khin Maung* v. *Au Eu Wa*, A.I.R. 1936, Rang. 425.

the Government of India Act, 1935, the privileges enjoyed
by a legislature and its members and committees and recognized by statutes were as follows:

(i) freedom of speech in the House;

(ii) immunity from liability for any publication in the
official proceedings;

(iii) exemption from arrest and detention under civil process
during the continuance of any meeting of the House or of
any committee, and for fourteen days before and after any
such meeting;

(iv) exemption from serving as jurors.

Certain other privileges have been claimed by the legislatures
as matters of convention. For instance, it was considered a
breach of privilege:

(i) to publish or to give for publication any question,
resolution or motion before it is admitted by the Chair;[1]

(ii) to publish reports of Select Committees or minutes of
dissent before they are presented to the House;[2]

(iii) to publish inaccurate reports of proceedings of the
House;[3]

(iv) to molest a member outside the House for his conduct
in the House;[4]

(v) to cast reflection on the House or the Chair.[5]

It appears, however, that there was no power in the legislature to punish any breach of privilege, whether committed
by a member or a stranger except expressing displeasure by
a resolution; in the case of strangers, e.g. newspapers, they
might be excluded from attending the House for the purpose
of reporting the proceedings.[6] It does not appear that the
House had any power to suspend any member who committed a breach of privilege. Under the rules of some legislatures,
a member could be asked by the Speaker to withdraw only
when his conduct was grossly disorderly, and if a member
was asked to withdraw a second time he could be suspended
for the remainder of the session.

---

[1] L.A.D. p. 2655, 27 Mar. 1933.
[2] Ibid. 14 Feb. 1934; ibid. 14 Apr. 1934, vol. iv, p. 3731.
[3] B.L.A.P. vol. lxii, no. 3, p. 42.
[4] Ibid. vol. lii, no. 6, p. 39.
[5] Ibid. vol. lxii, no. 3, p. 42.
[6] Ibid. vol. lxii, no. 3, p. 42.

23

ARREST OR DETENTION OF MEMBER

Another matter which had been exercising the minds of legislators was whether the arrest and detention of a member without trial was a matter of privilege, and what steps, if any, might be taken to secure the attendance of members detained during the session of the legislature. It was ruled by Mr. Speaker Azizul Haque that when a member was arrested or detained, the fact of the arrest or detention should be immediately communicated to the Speaker.[1]

In the British House of Commons the fact of the arrest or conviction of a member has to be communicated to the House. This is ensured by several statutes, and even in cases which are not covered by any statute this practice is followed. The detention of a member without trial came to be considered in several cases before the House of Commons, and it was decided, that no privilege could be claimed against such detention.[2] It appears, however, that Mr. P. Ramamurty, a member of the Rajya Sabha while released on parole, attended the Rajya Sabha and made a speech on 28 March 1966. During the budget session 1966, Mr. Biren Dutta, a member of the Lok Sabha, attended the House also while on parole.

CONSTITUTION OF INDIA, 1950

This was the state of things when the Constitution of India came into force, and whatever might have been their privileges before, the legislatures now enjoy all the powers, privileges and immunities of the British House of Commons as they existed at the date of the commencement of the Constitution. Clause (3) of Article 105 and also of Article 194 are couched in very wide terms and would appear to attract not only the privileges and immunities but also the powers, including, for instance, the power to enforce attendance of persons or to punish for contempt of the House of Commons. It was held in *Keilly* v. *Carson*[3] that the power to commit for contempt, which the House of Commons had, was not in-

---

[1] B.L.A.P. vol. lii, no. 1, p. 148.
[2] *Ramsay's Case*, H.C. 164, 1939-40.
[3] 4 Moore P. C. 63.

herent in the House as a body exercising legislative functions but was derived from the power it had as the High Court of Parliament, and that this power was not necessarily enjoyed by any other body exercising legislative functions as inherent in itself. Where, however, all the powers, privileges and immunities of the House of Commons are vested by a specific enactment, as for instance by the Constitution of India, or by Acts of the British Parliament, in relation to some Dominion Constitutions, the case would be different. It would be interesting to note in this connection that the Government of India Act, 1935, while conferring on the Indian legislatures the powers to legislate regarding privileges, specifically excluded the power to assume to themselves any penal jurisdiction. Whether the intention of the framers of the Constitution was to confer such wide powers on the legislatures we do not know; but under the language of the Articles, it would seem that the legislatures have been vested with very wide and drastic powers.[1]

It will not be out of place here to refer to the decision of the High Court of Australia in the *Queen* v. *Richards; Ex-Parte Fitzpatrick and Browne*,[2] better known as the *Bankstown Observer Case*. The House of Representatives of Australia held the proprietor and the editor of the weekly newspaper *Bankstown Observer* guilty of breach of privilege for publishing an article intended to influence and intimidate a member of the House, and committed them to the custody of the Chief Commissioner of Police of Canberra. The offenders' application for writ of habeas corpus came up before the High Court of Australia. In his judgment, dismissing the application for writ, the Chief Justice referred to Section 49 of the Commonwealth of Australia Constitution Act:

'The powers, privileges and immunities of the Senate and of the House of Representatives, and of the members and the committees of each of the Houses shall be such as are declared by the Parliament, and until declared shall be those of the *Commons House of Parliament* of the United Kingdom, and of its members and Committees, at the establishment of the Commonwealth.'

[1] Con. A. Deb. vol. viii, pp. 143, 582.
[2] 29 Aust. L.J. 1955, pp. 125, 301.

He also pointed out that Parliament had not declared by law their powers, privileges and immunities.

As regards the question whether the law as obtaining in the United Kingdom applied under Section 49 of the Constitution to the House of Representatives, the Chief Justice stated as follows:

'If you take the language of the latter part of Section 49 and read it apart from any other considerations, it is difficult in the extreme to see how any other answer could be given to the question than that that law is applicable in Australia to the House of Representatives.... The language is such as to be apt to transfer to the House the full powers, privileges and immunities of the House of Commons.'

It was also argued that the Australian Constitution was based upon the separation of powers, and the judicial power reposed exclusively in the judicature. It restricted the legislature to the legislative power. It was urged that the House of Representatives in issuing a warrant for the arrest of two persons exercised judicial power which it did not possess.

In reply to the above argument his Lordship observed as follows:

'The consideration we have already mentioned is of necessity an answer to this contention, namely, that in unequivocal terms the powers of the House of Commons have been bestowed upon the House of Representatives. It should be added to that very simple statement that throughout the course of English history there has been a tendency to regard those powers as not strictly judicial but as belonging to the legislature, rather as something essential or, at any rate, proper for its protection.'

The offenders petitioned the Judicial Committee of the Privy Council for special leave to appeal against the decision of the High Court. The Privy Council was of the view that the judgment of the Chief Justice of Australia was unimpeachable and leave to appeal was refused.

The language of Articles 105(3) and 194(3) follows the language used in section 49 of the Commonwealth of Australia Constitution Act word for word. It would therefore be correct to presume that the intention of the constitution-makers of India was to vest very wide powers in the legislatures, so that they could, like the Australian Parliament, take penal action against offenders for breach of privilege or contempt of the legislature.

PRIVILEGES OF THE HOUSE OF COMMONS: GENERAL PRINCIPLES

Be that as it may, we shall now consider what actually are the privileges, etc. of the House of Commons. They are of ancient origin and there are historical reasons for their emergence and growth. It is not necessary for our purpose to probe into past history, but it may perhaps be profitable to enquire what is the fundamental basis on which these privileges are founded. Redlich has defined the privileges of the House of Commons as 'the sum of the fundamental rights of the House and of its individual members as against the prerogatives of the Crown, the authority of the ordinary Courts of Law and the special rights of the House of Lords'.[1] This is not exactly a definition but explains the nature of the privileges by reference to their historical origin. The fundamental fact, however, which emerges on a consideration of the origin and nature of the privileges is that these rights do not attach by reason of any exalted position of the House or its members but are rights which are absolutely necessary for the proper and effective discharge of the functions of a legislative body. As has been said by May: 'The distinctive mark of a privilege is its ancillary character. They are enjoyed by individual members, because the House cannot perform its functions without unimpeded use of the services of its members; and vindication of its own authority and dignity.'[2]

Even as long ago as 1675, the reason for the existence of privileges was given by the House of Commons itself as 'that the members of the House of Commons may freely attend the public affairs in that House without disturbance or interruption.'[3] Certain special rights are therefore enjoyed by the House of Commons and its members which are not enjoyed by other individuals or bodies, and these rights are in their nature in derogation of the ordinary law of the land.

[1] Redlich, vol. 1, p. 46.
[2] May, pp. 42-43.
[3] C.J. 1667-87, vol. ix, p. 342; Hatsell, 3rd ed. vol. i, p. 200.

Another important fact in regard to privileges is that no new privilege can be created by either of the Houses of Parliament. It was agreed as long ago as 1704 'that neither House of Parliament hath any power by any vote, or declaration, to create to themselves any new privilege, that is not warranted by the known laws and customs of Parliament'.[1] This declaration was necessitated by the fact that each House of Parliament claimed to have exclusive right to declare what its privileges were. But this restriction is applicable only to declarations of privileges by resolutions which must be distinguished from the legislative authority which Parliament as a whole undoubtedly has to declare or amend the law relating to privileges. In fact, such legislation has been made in Parliament, and the Parliamentary Papers Act, 1840, may be cited as an example whereby protection was given to the official publication of parliamentary proceedings.

As a necessary corollary to the existence of certain special rights and immunities, the House of Commons claims the exclusive right to punish any person for interfering with the privileges or in vindication of its own authority and dignity. The right is analogous to the right of the superior courts to punish for contempt of court, and in fact was justified in early days by a reference to the mediaevel conception of Parliament as the highest court in the land. The right to declare the lawfulness of its own proceedings, it was said, flowed from the power to punish for contempt. It is natural that this claim of exclusive jurisdiction by Parliament should form the subject-matter of controversy between Parliament and the courts of law. There have been several leading cases[2] which, although the conflict seems to have remained unresolved, appear to have laid down certain general principles. These principles have been summarized by May as follows:

'(1) It seems to be recognized that, for the purpose of adjudicating on questions of privilege, neither House is by itself entitled to claim the supremacy over the ordinary courts of justice which was enjoyed by the undivided High Court of Parliament. The supremacy of Parliament, consisting of the

---

[1] C.J. 1702-4, vol. xiv, p. 555.
[2] *Burdett* v. *Abbot*, 14 East I; *Stockdale* v. *Hansard*, 3 St. Tr. (n.s.), 925; *Bradlaugh* v. *Gosset* (1884), 12 Q.B.D; *Rex* v. *Graham Campbell* (1935), I.K.B. 594.

King and the two Houses, is a legislative supremacy which has nothing to do with the privilege jurisdiction of either House acting singly.

'(2) It is admitted by both Houses that neither House can by its own declaration create a new privilege. This implies that privilege is objective and its extent ascertainable, and reinforces the doctrine that it is known by the Courts....

'(3) That the control of each House over its internal pro- ceedings is absolute and cannot be interfered with by the courts.

'(4) That a committal for contempt by either House is in practice within its exclusive jurisdiction, since the facts consti- tuting the alleged contempt need not be stated on the warrant of committal.'[1]

It is also agreed that the law of Parliament is part of the law of the land, and that the judges are bound to take judicial notice of privilege.

PENAL JURISDICTION OF LEGISLATIVE BODIES

As has already been stated, the penal jurisdiction of the House of Commons was not inherent in it as a legislative body but was derived from the jurisdiction it had as the High Court of Parliament. In the legislatures of the British Domi- nions and Colonies some legislatures have taken power for themselves to punish for contempt by express enactment.[2] But the trend of modern opinion seems to be that the power to punish should be left to the courts of law rather than be assumed by the legislature itself, on the ground that the prosecutors should not also be the judges. In a case in America,[3] which arose out of contempt proceedings and commitment by the House of Representatives, the Supreme Court held that the House had no power by its own action, as distinct

---

[1] May, p. 173.
[2] Western Australia, 54 Vict. no. 4 of 1891; Tasmania Parliamentary Privileges Act, 1853; Victoria Act, 1705, 20 Vict. no. 1; Quebec Act, 53 Vict. C. 5; Queens- land Constitution Act, 1867; South Africa, Powers and Privileges of Parliament Act, 1911; British Columbia, 35 Vict. C. 4, 36 Vict. C. 4, 36 Vict. C. 35, C. 42; Ontario, 1876 C. 9; Manitoba C. 12, 1876; Nova Scotia C. 22, 1876; Ontario, C. 6; New Brunswick and Prince Edward Island; Alberta, 1904, C. 2; Saskat- chewan, 1908, C. 4; Southern Rhodesia, no. 4 of 1924.
[3] *Marshall* v. *Gordon*, (1917) 243 U.S. p. 521.

from such action as might be taken under the criminal laws, to arrest or punish a person for writing and publishing a letter which was held by the House to be defamatory, insulting and as tending to bring that body into public contempt and ridicule. Chief Justice White observed:

'No express power to punish for contempt was granted to the House of Representatives save the power to deal with contempts committed by its own members. The possession by Congress of the commingled legislative and judicial authority to punish for contempts which was exerted by the House of Commons is at variance with the view and tendency existing in this country when the Constitution was adopted, as evidenced by the manner in which the subject was treated in State Constitutions, beginning at or about that time and continuing thereafter. Such commingling of powers would be destructive of the basic constitutional distinction between legislative, executive and judicial power and repugnant to limitations which the Constitution fixes expressly; hence there is no warrant whatever for implying such a dual power in aid of other powers expressly granted to Congress. The House has implied power to deal directly with contempt so far as is necessary to preserve and exercise the legislative authority expressly granted. Being however a power of self-preservation, a means and not an end, the power does not extend to infliction of punishment, as such: it is a power to prevent acts which in and of themselves inherently prevent or obstruct the discharge of legislative duty and to compel the doing of those things which are essential to the performance of the legislative functions.'

It is interesting to note that the Government of India Act, 1935, as already stated, expressly laid down that the legislature could not confer upon itself or upon any committee or person the status of a court or any punitive or disciplinary powers other than the power to remove or exclude persons infringing any rule or standing order or otherwise behaving in a disorderly manner.

POWER OF COMMITTAL OF INDIAN LEGISLATURE

The question whether the Indian legislatures have the power

to commit any person for contempt of the House and how far the Law Courts have the jurisdiction to examine the legality of proceedings taken by the legislature arose in Uttar Pradesh with a conflict between the Judiciary and the Legislature. Keshav Singh was found guilty of contempt of the House and sentenced to seven days' imprisonment. Pursuant to a warrant issued by the Speaker, Keshav Singh was lodged in the District Jail of Lucknow. A petition for habeas corpus was moved before the Allahabad High Court. Two Judges of the Court issued notice on the legislature to show cause why the prisoner should not be set at liberty, and pending hearing of the application Keshav Singh was released on bail. On this fact being brought to the notice of the legislature, the legislature asked the Judges who had issued the notice to explain their conduct, and the Marshal of the House was directed to bring the Judges under arrest before the House. The High Court also issued notice to the legislature to show cause why its order against the Judges should not be set aside and in the meantime stayed operation of the order issued by the legislature. The dispute was heading for a crisis when the President referred the matter to the Supreme Court[1] for its opinion.

Under Article 194 of the Constitution, a State legislature enjoys all the privileges, powers and immunities of the House of Commons as on the date of commencement of the Constitution. It is, therefore, necessary to see whether by virtue of clause (3) of Article 194 the power of committal has devolved on the Indian legislatures. It is now settled by the Bankstown Observer Case[2] that by virtue of the clause 'shall be those of the House of Commons of the Parliament of the United Kingdom' in the Commonwealth of Australia Constitution Act, a dominion legislature has the power to commit a person to jail for contempt of the House. The clause in India is similar; indeed the clause has been copied from the Australia Constitution Act. The Indian legislatures, therefore, have all the power and immunities of the House of Commons, including the power to commit unless there is any provision in the Constitution to the contrary. There is nothing in the

[1] (1965) 1, S.C.A. p. 447
[2] Queen v. Richards. 92 C.L.R. 157.

Constitution which militates against the exercise of the power to commit. Clause (3) of the Article 194 is not subject to the other provisions of the Constitution as is clause (1) of that Article. Consequently the Articles relating to fundamental rights will not apply. Similarly power for committal for contempt has been conferred on the Supreme Court and the High Courts and there can be no question that their powers are not subject to the fundamental rights under Part IV of the Constitution.

In the present case when the Uttar Pradesh legislature sent Keshav Singh to jail it claimed a privilege to do so. Whether the U.P. legislature had that privilege either under Article 194 or otherwise was a question which the Allahabad High Court had the jurisdiction to enquire into. If that privilege was found to exist, then of course the High Court would not go into the question of whether the facts alleged upon which Keshav Singh was found guilty of contempt were sufficient for conviction. What the Allahabad High Court did was just to see whether the legislature had the power to commit. If the privilege existed, then of course the Court would not have gone into the sufficiency or otherwise of the Speaker's warrant. In fact it was just what happened when the matter came to be heard finally by the Allahabad High Court which held that the Speaker's warrant was a valid return to the writ of habeas corpus.

Five questions were referred to the Supreme Court:

(1) Whether, on the facts and circumstances of the case, it was competent for the Lucknow Bench of the High Court of U.P., consisting of the Hon'ble Mr. Justice N. U. Beg and the Hon'ble Mr. Justice G. D. Sahgal, to entertain and deal with the petition of Mr. Keshav Singh challenging the legality of the sentence of imprisonment imposed upon him by the Legislative Assembly of U.P. for its contempt and for infringement of privileges and to pass orders releasing Mr. Keshav Singh on the bail pending disposal of his said petition.

(2) Whether, on the facts and circumstances of the case, Mr. Keshav Singh by causing a petition to be presented on his behalf to the High Court of U.P. as aforesaid, Mr. B. Solomon, Advocate, by presenting the said petition and the

said two Hon'ble Judges by entertaining the dealing with the said petition and ordering the release of Mr. Keshav Singh on bail pending disposal of the said petition committed contempt of the Legislative Assembly of U.P.;

(3) Whether, on the facts and circumstances of the case, it was competent for the Legislative Assembly of U.P. to direct the production of the said two Hon'ble Judges and Mr. B. Solomon, Advocate, before it in custody or to call for their explanation for its contempt;

(4) Whether, on facts and circumstances of the case, it was competent for the Full Bench of the High Court of U.P. to entertain and deal with the petition of the said two Hon'ble judges and Mr. B. Solomon, Advocate, and to pass interim orders restraining the Speaker of the Legislative Assembly of U.P. and other respondents to the said petitions from implementing the aforesaid direction of the said Legislative Assembly; and

(5) Whether a Judge of the High Court who entertains or deals with a petition challenging any order or decision of a legislature imposing any penalty on the petitioner or issuing any process against the petitioner for its contempt or for infringements of its privilege and immunities or who passes any order on such petition commits contempt of the said legislature and whether the said legislature is competent to take proceedings against such a Judge in the exercise and enforcement of its powers, privileges and immunities.

On the facts the Supreme Court held that the Judges while issuing notices upon the application for writ of habeas corpus did not commit contempt of the House and also that they did not commit contempt by staying the order of the Legislative Assembly.

The question was whether clause (3) of Article 194 is subject to other provisions of the Constitution. The Supreme Court has held that even though clause (3) has not been expressed as subject to the provisions of the Constitution in terms yet it would be so subject if for any other valid consideration it appears that the operation of Article 21 may be affected. It seems to be the opinion of the Supreme Court that as Article 21 occurs in the chapter on fundamental rights, all the other particulars of the Constitution should be read as subject to the fundamental rights whether they are made expressly so subject or not. The Supreme Court after discussing English cases on the subject has come to the finding that in England the Court can go into the question whether Parliament has in fact the power to commit for contempt. The learned Judges rely on the observation of Ellenborough C.J. to the effect that even if a valid warrant signed by the Speaker is produced, the Courts will be entitled to enquire into the sufficiency of the ground if on the face of the warrant, it appears that the commitment is an abuse of the power of the Parliament or is a fraudulent use thereof. The substance of the Supreme Court's opinion appears to be that the court, if called upon to decide whether the legislature has validly committed any person to prison, will be entitled to enquire whether the legislature has such power or not. If it is a speaking warrant it seems to be the opinion of the Supreme Court that the Court may enquire into the sufficiency of the reasons. If the warrant is not a speaking one—(the Supreme Court has said that the warrant need not be speaking one) it appears that the aforesaid opinion of the Supreme Court will not be of any avail. If the legislature does not choose to give any reason the Court will have no material before it to judge the sufficiency or otherwise of the reasons for committal. The Supreme Court negatived the assertion of the U.P. legislature that it was the supreme judge of its own powers. In fact Article 194, clause (3), itself points to the conclusion that the court may enquire whether the privileges of the legislature would be the same as those of the House of Commons. There must be somebody to find out what the powers of the House of Commons are and in this respect the legislature will not be in a better position than the Court to find out what are these powers. Therefore, it seems logical that it will be the court which will be entitled to enquire what powers the House of Commons have. Besides it will also be relevant to enquire whether by the language used in clause (3), the Indian legislatures have inherited all the powers including that of committal of the House of Commons. As has been already stated the decision of the Privy Council in the Bankstown Observer Case is conclusive on this point. The Supreme Court limited its decision only to the facts of this case and only to the case of strangers. Whether in the case of members also the position is the same on that point, the Supreme Court has expressed no opinion.

After discussing the case which arose in England the Supreme Court says:

'Having examined the relevant decision on the point, it would, we think, not be inaccurate to observe that the right claimed by the House of Commons not to have its general warrant examined in the habeas corpus proceedings has been based more on the consideration that the House of Commons is in the position of a superior court of record and has the right like other superior courts of record to issue a general warrant for commitment of persons found guilty of contempt. In this connexion we ought to add that even while recognising the validity of such general warrant, Judges have frequently observed that if they were satisfied upon the warrant that such general warrant were issued for frivolous or extravagant reasons, it would be open to them to examine their validity'.

The conclusion of the Supreme Court was that neither the Judge, nor the Advocate, nor the party were guilty of contempt and therefore, it followed that it was competent for the High Court of Allahabad to entertain the petition filed before it by the two Judges and by the Advocate and it was within its jurisdiction to pass the interim orders restraining the operation of the impugned orders passed by the House. Sarkar J. disagreed with the majority on some of the points. He held that the right to commit for contempt by a general warrant was in deprivation of jurisdiction of the courts of law to enquire into the committal and was a privilege of the House of Commons. That privilege was possessed by the U.P. Assembly by reason of Article 194 clause (3) of the Constitution. He also held that Article 194 clause (3) took precedence over the fundamental rights, that is to say, Article 194 clause (3) was not subject to any fundamental right guaranteed under part 3 of the Constitution. The majority of the Supreme Court was of the view that the conflict was not really between the legislature and the Judiciary or whether the legislature or the Judiciary was supreme. The real thing was that the Constitution was supreme and the conflict was

between the U.P. legislature and the citizens whose fundamental rights have been infringed. Although the answers
to the question referred to the Supreme Court could have
been and actually had been framed within short compass,
the Supreme Court has discussed the law on the subject in
detail and the sum total of their conclusion seems to be this:

(1) The legislature has the power to commit a person
who has been found guilty of contempt to the House;

(2) The court is equally competent to enquire whether a
person has been validly committed to prison and for that
purpose to issue notice on the custodian of the prisoner to
make a return;

(3) If there is a valid return showing that the person has
been committed by a warrant duly signed by the Speaker
and the warrant is not a speaking warrant, that is to say, the
warrant does not state on the face of it the reasons for committal, the courts will not further enquire into the matter;

(4) But if there is a speaking warrant, that is to say, if the
warrant states on the face of it the reasons for committal, the
Court will be entitled to examine the reasons stated and to
judge whether the reasons are sufficient for committal or not.

The Supreme Court based its decision on the view that
Article 32 and Article 226 of the Constitution give an over-
riding power to the Courts to examine the validity of any
detention whether the detention is under the order of the
legislature or not.

The rule which was issued by the Lucknow Bench of the
Allahabad High Court came up for hearing, thereafter.
The High Court held that as Keshav Singh had been detained
under an order signed by the Speaker the detention was
valid and the court will not interfere with the order of the
legislature.

PRIVILEGES OF THE HOUSE OF COMMONS

Having discussed the general principles governing the
privileges of the House of Commons, we shall now consider
the privileges in detail. At the outset it will be useful to draw
a distinction between privileges proper and the right to
punish any person or body who interferes with such privileges

or offends the authority and dignity of the House. The latter is more or less in the nature of the jurisdiction of the courts of law in contempt proceedings.

FREEDOM OF SPEECH

Freedom of speech was guaranteed to the House of Commons by the Bill of Rights (section 9) in the following words: 'That the freedom of speech and debates or proceedings in Parliament, ought not to be impeached or questioned in any court or place out of Parliament.' This privilege protects not only members but also strangers in certain circumstances. We shall take up the question of members first.

FREEDOM OF SPEECH OF MEMBERS

It will be noticed that not only 'speeches' and 'debates' but also 'proceedings in Parliament' are mentioned in the Bill of Rights. The Select Committee of the British House of Commons on the Official Secrets Acts (1939)[1] in their Report at paragraph 3 observed:

'While the term "proceedings in Parliament" has never been construed by the courts, it covers both the asking of a question and the giving written notice of such question, and includes everything said or done by a Member in exercise of his functions as a Member in a committee of either House, as well as everything said or done in either House in the transaction of Parliamentary business.'

In a recent case (*Strauss's Case*) the question arose whether a letter from a Member to a Minister about the administration of a nationalized industry could be treated as or included within the scope of 'proceedings in Parliament'. As questions relating to day-to-day administration of nationalized industries could not be asked in the House, a practice had grown up whereby Members of Parliament addressed letters to the Minister if they wanted to elicit information about the working of any nationalized industry. One such letter was written on 8 February 1957 by Mr. G. R. Strauss to the Paymaster-General about the day-to-day maladministration of the

[1] H.C. *Paper* 101 of 1939.

London Electricity Board, and for this he was threatened by the Chairman and Solicitors of the Board with legal action. He thereupon raised a question of privilege, the essence of which was whether his letter to the Minister was covered by the term 'proceedings in Parliament'. As the question and speeches in the House were considered to be within the scope of this term, it was contended that a letter from the Member of Parliament to the Minister should also stand on the same footing. The Privileges Committee came to the conclusion that the letter was well covered by the term 'proceedings in Parliament'.[1] But after a good deal of debate the House disagreed with the conclusion of the Privileges Committee and on 8 July 1958 resolved that Mr. Strauss's letter was not a 'proceeding in Parliament'.[2]

Although this privilege is confined to what is done or said within the House, it has been suggested that it might extend to cases where acts are not done in the immediate presence of the House but are so related to proceedings pending in the House that they might be held to be constructively done in the House. For instance, if a member communicates to a Minister or another member the draft of a question which he intends to put, he may claim privilege for any statement made in it. On the other hand, not all things which are done within the House are protected. A casual conversation between two members on any subject not connected with any matter pending in the House would not be privileged. The relevant clauses of Article 105 and Article 194 of the Constitution lay down that 'there shall be freedom of speech in the Legislature', and amplify the statement by saying that no member 'shall be liable to any proceedings in any court in respect of anything said or any vote given by him in the Legislature'.

It will be noticed that the term 'proceedings in Parliament', which is in the Bill of Rights and on which stress is laid for the extended interpretation of the privilege by the Select Committee of the House of Commons, is absent in this Article. It was held in the case of *Khin Maung* v. *Au Eu Wa*[3] that the expression 'by reason of his speech', occurring

---

[1] *Fifth Report of the Committee of Privileges* 1956-57, p. viii, para 20(a).
[2] H.C.D. 1957-58, vol. 591, cc. 208-346.
[3] A.I.R. 1936, Rang. 425.

in section 72D of the Government of India Act, 1919, protected questions by members; it is interesting to note that in the Government of India Act, 1935, the expression 'by reason of his speech' was changed to 'by reason of anything said', thus covering a wider field, and the latter expression has found a place in the Constitution.

Having regard to the fundamental purpose for which freedom of speech is guaranteed, the correct position seems to have been laid down in the case of *R.* v. *Bunting,*[1] that a member is not liable in ordinary court 'for anything he may say or do within the scope of his duties in the course of parliamentary business for in such matters he is privileged and protected by *lex et consuetudo parliamenti*'. Reference may be made to two other American decisions, *Kilbourn* v. *Thomson*[2] and *Coffin* v. *Coffin,*[3] which also appear to lay down that a member would be protected for anything done in the execution of his duties as a member whether done in the House or out of it.

The privilege of freedom of speech is absolute so far as outsiders are concerned, but the House of Commons has the right to enforce its own discipline upon members, and rules of debate adopted by the House provide for the proper exercise of the right of free speech and against unrestricted licence in the use of unparliamentary language or unparliamentary conduct. This right of the House is derived from the Bill of Rights which lays down that freedom of speech ought not to be questioned in any court or place 'outside Parliament'. Although under the Constitution freedom of speech is absolute, the same restriction seems to have been contemplated by the words 'subject to the rules and standing orders regulating the procedure of the Legislature'. As has already been stated, it was held in the case *Khin Maung* v. *Au Eu Wa*[4] that the privilege of members was absolute, and the words 'subject to rules and standing orders' conferred a right upon the House to control its debates, and did not mean that if any speech offended against any rule or standing order the privilege could not be claimed.

[1] 1884-5, 7 Ontario, 563.
[2] 103 U.S. 168.
[3] 4 Mass. I.
[4] A.I.R. 1936, Rang. 425.

24

MEMBERS AND THE OFFICIAL SECRETS ACT

A question arose in 1939 in the House of Commons as to how far a member disclosing official secrets in the House was protected by the privilege of Parliament. The matter arose in this way. Mr. Duncan Sandys put down for answer by the Home Secretary a question which showed that Mr. Sandys was in possession of certain official secrets. Mr. Sandys was summoned to appear before a court of enquiry so that he might be interrogated as to the source of his information of the secrets. He raised the matter in the House of Commons as a matter of privilege and the matter was referred to a Select Committee. The Select Committee gave it as their opinion that 'disclosures by members in the course of debate or proceedings in Parliament cannot be made the subject of proceedings under the Official Secrets Acts'.[1] As to whether a member can be interrogated for divulging the source of his information, the Select Committee thought that it was a question of some difficulty. The Select Committee, however, observed that as no evidence could be given in relation to any debates or proceedings in Parliament except by the leave of the House, it might well be that the prosecution would be unable to show that the member had information relevant to the investigation of an offence or suspected offence unless they could give evidence of his statement in Parliament.

As regards the solicitation of the disclosure or reception of information affected by the Official Secrets Acts, the Select Committee says:

'Your Committee are of opinion that the soliciting or receipt of information is not a proceeding in Parliament, and that neither the privilege of freedom of speech nor any of the cognate privileges would afford a defence to a member of parliament charged with soliciting, inciting or endeavouring to persuade a person holding office under the Crown to disclose information which such person was not authorized to disclose, or with receiving information knowing, or having reasonable grounds to believe, that the information was communicated to him in contravention of the Official Secrets Acts.'

The Select Committee further observes: 'Although the

[1] H.C. *Paper* 101 of 1939, p. ix, para 10.

legal position with regard to the solicitation of the disclosure by, or the receipt of information from, a person holding office under the Crown is as stated in paragraphs 16 and 17, official information, as the debates of the House show, is frequently obtained by members of Parliament from persons who are not authorized to disclose it. Members' sense of responsibility and discretion have, your Committee believe, prevented them from making use of any information thus obtained in a manner detrimental to the interests or safety of the State. Indeed, the information, though technically confidential, often does not relate to matters affecting the safety of the State. But as the Official Secrets Acts do not distinguish between the solicitation or receipt of information the disclosure of which would be prejudicial to the interests or safety of the State and the solicitation or receipt of information the disclosure of which is merely unauthorized, the Acts, if strictly enforced, would make it difficult for members to obtain the information without which they cannot effectively discharge their duty. Any action which, without actually infringing any privilege enjoyed by members of the House in their capacity as members, yet obstructs or impedes them in the discharge of their duties, or tends to produce such results, even though the act be lawful, may be held to be a contempt of the House.'

PUBLICATION OF SPEECH

So far we have been dealing with the actual utterances of members. Now we shall come to the question of publication of speeches or utterances. As a consequence of the claim of privileges of freedom of speech, the House of Commons has the right to exclude strangers from the House, to prohibit publication of its proceedings or of reports of, or evidence given before, Select Committees before they are presented to the House. The right to prohibit publication of its proceedings is not enforced in practice unless the report published is inaccurate. The privilege asserted in fact is that no inaccurate report of parliamentary proceedings should be published, but when there is a breach of the privilege, the form in which such breach is taken notice of, is, for historical reasons, that the publication infringes the privilege that no publication should take place at all. So far as publication of reports of, or evidence given before, Select Committees is concerned, that right also is not in practice exercised when the public is admitted before such Committees.

In India a question of privilege was raised in the House by Shri Frank Anthony,[1] a member of the Lok Sabha, regarding misrepresentation of his speech delivered in the Lok Sabha on 25 August 1956 in a news item appearing on the front page of the daily newspaper *Hindustan Times*. In view of the regret expressed by the Joint Editor of the newspaper, the House did not take any action. In another case in the Rajya Sabha, Shri Bhupesh Gupta M.P. raised a question of privilege for 'wilfully unfair and mendacious reporting' of the proceedings of the House in the weekly journal *Thought*. The matter was referred to the Privileges Committee, which recommended that in view of the explanations offered and the regrets expressed by the Editor of *Thought* no further time should be occupied by the House in consideration of the matter. The recommendations of the Committee were accepted by the House.[2]

Official publication of debates, etc. is protected under the Parliamentary Papers Act, 1840, passed after the decision in the case of *Stockdale* v. *Hansard*,[3] which had held that there was no protection for the publication of any speech outside the House. Publication of extracts from official reports, if made *bona fide* and without malice, is also protected under this Act. The publication of a fair and faithful report of debates otherwise than in official papers has been held to be a qualified privilege on the analogy of the publication of proceedings in courts of law, and is not actionable. But the publication of a single speech apart from the rest of the debate would not be privileged.[4]

Articles 105 and 194 of the Constitution give protection to the publication of all reports, papers, votes or proceedings under the authority of the House, that is to say, to official publications only.

[1] L.S.D. 1956, vol. 8, part. ii, 28 Aug. 1956, c. 4699.
[2] R.S.D. 9 March 1959, vol. xxiv, cc. 3029-30.
[3] 3 St. Tr. (n.s.), 861.
[4] *Wason* v. *Walter*, 4 Q.B. 94.

Before the passing of the Parliamentary Proceedings (Protection of Publication) Act, 1956, newspapers did not enjoy any privilege, and it was held by the Calcutta High Court in *Suresh Chandra Banerji* v. *Punit Goala*[1] that the case of *Wason* v. *Walter*[2] was not applicable in India. But the position has changed after the passing of the above-mentioned Act. Section 3(1) of this Act, which provides that 'no person shall be liable to any proceedings, civil or criminal, in any court in respect of the publication in a newspaper of a substantially true report of any proceedings of either House of Parliament, unless the publication is proved to have been made with malice', protects substantially true reports of the proceedings of Parliament. Section 4 of the Act extends this privilege to broadcasts from broadcasting stations situated within the territories to which the Act applies. It is interesting to note that this Act protects publication of proceedings of the Indian Parliament and excludes publication of the proceedings of the State legislatures from its scope. Recently the State legislature of Orissa has, however, passed a law on the same lines as the Central Act to give protection to the publication of substantially true reports of the proceedings of the Orissa legislature.

BUDGET DISCLOSURE

Budget proposals are treated as secret until they are placed before the House. But any premature disclosure of such proposals is not deemed to be a breach of privilege of the House although the House has the power to take action otherwise in any manner it chooses. In England two such disclosures have occurred in recent times—one in 1936[3] and the other in 1948.[4] In the first case, a tribunal was appointed under the Tribunal of Enquiry (Evidence) Act, 1921, to enquire into the disclosure alleged to have been made by Mr. J. H. Thomas. In the second case, a Select Committee of the House was appointed to enquire into the circumstances leading to the disclosure of the Budget by Mr. Hugh Dalton. In India a

[1] A.I.R. (38) (1951), Cal. 176.
[2] 1869, 4 Q.B. 73.
[3] H.C.D. 1935-36, vol. 313, cc. 413-16.
[4] Ibid. 1948, vol. 444, cc. 821-823.

Budget disclosure took place in 1860,[1] and Sir Charles Treve-lyan, Governor of Madras, was held responsible for the dis-closure although it appears he was subsequently absolved. Another disclosure took place in 1956, and Mr. Speaker Ayyangar of the House of the people clarified the position by his ruling which was as follows:

'The powers, privileges and immunities of the House are such as were enjoyed by the House of Commons in the United Kingdom at the commencement of our Constitution....

'So far as I can gather only two cases occurred in which the House of Commons took notice of leakage of the Budget proposals. They are known as the Thomas case and the Dalton case. In neither of these cases was the leakage treated as a breach of privileges of the House nor were the cases sent to the Committee of Privileges for inquiry. The prevailing view in the House of Commons is that until the financial proposals are placed before the House of Commons they are an official secret. A reference of the present leakage to the Committee of Privileges does not therefore arise.

'Though the leakage of Budget proposals may not consti-tute a breach of privilege of the House, the Parliament has ample power to inquire into the conduct of a Minister in suitable proceedings in relation to the leakage and the cir-cumstances in which the leakage occurred. In the two English cases aforesaid, matters were brought to the notice of the House of Commons by a resolution or a motion for appoint-ment of Special Committees or tribunal to inquire into the matter and report the facts thereon to the House.

'In the Dalton case, Mr. Dalton, who was the Chancellor of the Exchequer, admitted that he did not think of the consequences at the time of the disclosure and in the Thomas case, it was alleged that he disclosed the Budget secrets, which he got to know as a Cabinet Minister. It is neither alleged nor even suggested in the case before us that the Finance Minister was himself responsible for an unauthorized disclosure of the financial proposals.'[2]

On another occasion in 1959, Mr. Speaker Ayyangar, after quoting his ruling of 1956, observed:

[1] *The Civil Service in Britain* by C.A. Campbell, p. 27.
[2] L.S.D. 19 Mar. 1956, vol. ii, part ii, c. 2913.

'So far as the other matters are concerned—the appointment of a Committee, etc.—there is no proper resolution here as was the case in the House of Commons. It is unnecessary for me to proceed further. Not a word has been alleged that there is any fault on the part of the Hon. Minister. Various persons get into speculation. Possibly this may be or may not be a case of speculation. It is not necessary for me to pronounce one way or the other. So far as the breach of privilege motion is concerned, I withhold my consent to raising the matter as there is no breach of privilege.'[1]

EXTENSION OF PRIVILEGE TO STRANGERS

The qualified privilege of publishers of debates, etc. has already been mentioned. Witnesses who appear before the House or any of its committees to give evidence, persons who present petitions to the House, counsels who appear to argue on behalf of clients, are not liable for any statement made in the evidence, petitions or arguments. This has been made further clear by the (Eng.) Witness (Public Inquiries) Protection Act, 1892, of Great Britain. Although clause (2) of Article 105 and also of Article 194 of the Constitution afford protection to members only, the privilege of witnesses, etc. may be said to be involved in the general provision in clause (1) that there shall be freedom of speech in the legislature.

CRIMINAL ACTS

It has to be remembered that the protection given is in respect of words only and the utterance of words or the publication of such utterances, however criminal or actionable they may be in common law, is privileged. No privilege can, however, be claimed in respect of criminal acts within the House. As Mr. Justice Stephen put it in *Bradlaugh* v. *Gosset*,[2] 'he knew of no authority for the proposition that an ordinary crime committed in the House of Commons would be withdrawn from the ordinary course of criminal justice'. But a

---

[1] L.S.D. 10 Mar. 1959, vol. xxvii, c. 5344.
[2] 12 Q.B.D. 284.

distinction has to be made for cases when the criminal act complained of is in the discharge of parliamentary duties. In the case of *Bradlaugh* v. *Erskine*[1] the Deputy Sergeant-at Arms, who was charged with committing an assault when he tried to exclude Bradlaugh from the House, was held to be justified on the ground that he was taking part in the proceedings of the House.

FREEDOM FROM ARREST AND MOLESTATION

The privilege of freedom from arrest involves two different things, (i) freedom from arrest under process of law and (ii) freedom from illegal detention or molestation. The second one is not actually a privilege but is calculated to prevent a breach of privilege and to punish an infringement thereof. This aspect will be considered in connection with the principles which govern the cases of contempt of the House.

The reason for allowing the privilege has been stated by Hatsell as follows:

'The members, who compose it [i.e. Parliament], should not be prevented by trifling interruptions from their attendance on this important duty but should for a certain time, be excused from obeying any other call, not so immediately necessary for the great services of the nation; it has been therefore, upon these principles, always claimed and allowed, that the Members of both Houses should be, during their attendance in Parliament, exempted from several duties, and not considered as liable to some legal processes, to which other citizens, not entrusted with this most valuable franchise, are by law obliged to pay obedience.'[2]

ARREST UNDER PROCESS OF LAW

Freedom from arrest under process of law extends only to arrest under civil process. A member of the House of Commons is exempt from arrest under civil process during the continuance of a session and for forty days before the commencement of a session and for forty days after prorogation or

---

[1] 12 Q.B.D. 276.
[2] Hatsell, vol. i, p. 1.

dissolution. When a member is under detention at the time privilege accrues, it appears he has to be released.

In India, under section 135A of the Civil Procedure Code, 1908, a member of a legislature is not liable to arrest or detention in prison under civil process during the continuance of any meeting of the legislature or of any committee thereof and during fourteen days before and after such a meeting. Under that section, if a meeting is called when a member is under detention he is to be released, but he is liable to be rearrested and detained after the period of privilege is over.

Keeping in view the provisions of Articles 105 and 194 of the Constitution of India, which place the privileges of members of Parliament and State legislatures on the same footing as those of the British House of Commons where members are exempt from arrest under civil process for forty days before the commencement and for forty days after prorogation or dissolution, it can be argued that the period of fourteen days provided in section 135A of the Civil Procedure Code does no longer hold good.

SUBPOENA AS WITNESS

If a member of the House of Commons is summoned as a witness in any suit or proceeding, he can resist the summons to attend the court by claiming privilege. But this privilege is now normally waived on the ground that non-attendance of a witness would interfere with the administration of justice. On the other hand, it appears, members are granted leave of absence for attending courts as witnesses. Should a *subpoena* be served frivolously, such leave may be refused.[1] In ancient times privilege of exemption from being impleaded as a party in a civil action was also claimed. But this privilege has been taken away by later statutes.

Under section 133 of the Civil Procedure Code, 1908, the Chairman of the Council of States, the Speaker of the House of the People, the Speakers of the State Legislative Assemblies and the Chairmen of the State Legislative Councils are exempted from personal appearance in Civil Courts.

[1] See the incident described in *The Table*, vol. xxii, pp. 129-30.

EVIDENCE AS TO PROCEEDINGS IN HOUSE

No member or officer of the House can give evidence as to the proceedings in the House without the leave of the House. This principle has been established by case law[1] in England.

May says: 'The practice of the Commons regarding evidence sought for outside the walls of Parliament touching proceedings which have occurred therein also conforms to Article 9 of the Bill of Rights. This fact is well recognized by the courts which have held that the evidence of members of proceedings in the House of Commons is not to be received without the permission of the House unless they desire to give it; and the usage of Parliament according to which no member is at liberty to give evidence elsewhere in relation to any debates or proceedings in Parliament except by leave of the House of which he is a member has been held to apply to officers and officials of either House.'[2]

The Indian Parliament has adopted an almost similar procedure for production of documents connected with the proceedings of the House before courts of law. In 1957 the Lok Sabha Secretariat was requested to produce documents relating to the proceedings in the House and also to send an officer to give evidence in the court. The Privileges Committee of the Lok Sabha made the following recommendations:

'...the Committee are of the opinion that no member or officer of the House should give evidence in a Court of Law in respect of any proceedings of the House or any Committee of the House or any other document connected with the proceedings of the House or in the custody of the Secretary of the House without the leave of the House being first obtained.

'When the House is not in session, the Speaker may in emergent cases allow the production of the relevant documents in Courts of Law in order to prevent delays in the administration of justice and inform the House accordingly of the fact when it reassembles. In case, however, the matter involves any question of privilege, especially the privilege of

---

[1] *Chubb* v. *Salomons*, 3 Car. & Kir. 75; ruling of Mr. Justice Hilbery *in re Braddock* v. *Tillotson's Newspaper Ltd.*, 29 Oct. 1948.

[2] May, p. 63.

a witness, or in case the production of the document appears to him to be a subject for the discretion of the House itself, he may decline to grant the required permission and refer the matter to the Committee of Privileges for examination and report.

'Whenever any document relating to the proceedings of the House or any Committees thereof is required to be produced in a Court of Law, the Court or the parties to the legal proceedings should request the House stating precisely the documents required, the purpose for which they are required and the date by which they are required. It should also be specifically stated in each case whether only a certified copy of the document should be sent or an officer of the House should produce it before a Court of Law.

'When a request is received during sessions for producing in a Court of Law a document connected with the proceedings of the House or Committees or which is in the custody of the Secretary of the House, the case may be referred by the speaker to the Committee of Privileges. On a report from the Committee, a motion may be moved in the House by the Chairman or a member of the Committee to the effect that the House agrees with the report and further action should be taken in accordance with the decision of the House.'[1]

When a similar occasion arose in the Rajya Sabha in *Biren Roy's Case*, the Privileges Committee arrived at the same conclusions about the procedure to be adopted for production of documents connected with the proceedings of the House before courts of law, and the House agreed.[2] Privilege can be claimed with regard to proceedings in the House. But it may be argued that the evidence which was called for in *Biren Roy's Case* was not in regard to any proceedings in the House but was in regard to certain contracts of installation of machineries in the Chamber.

EXEMPTION FROM JURY SERVICE

Under the Juries Act, 1870, members of Parliament and

---

[1] *First Report of the Committee of Privileges*, Second Lok Sabha, paras 9 and 10.
[2] *First Report of the Committee of Privileges*, Rajya Sabha, and R.S.D. 2 May 1958, vol. xxi, c. 1295.

officers of the House are exempt from serving as jurors whether during or out of session of the Parliament. Under the Indian Criminal Procedure Code, 1898, members of legislatures are exempt from service as jurors. Officers in the civil employ of the Government above the rank of District Magistrates, and therefore presumably officers of the House, are also exempt.

CRIMINAL OFFENCES

The privilege of freedom from arrest and detention, however, is limited to civil cases and cannot be claimed in respect of criminal cases on the ground that 'Privilege of Parliament is granted in regard to the service of the Commonwealth and is not to be used to the danger of the Commonwealth'. Originally privilege was not claimable in respect of arrest on charges of treason, felony and breach (or surety) of the peace. But the principle has been applied not only to cases of indictable offences but also of criminal cases in general, statutory offences, preventive detention and contempt of court.

Section 10 of the Orissa Legislative Assembly (Powers and Privileges) Act, 1948, provides that if a member is accused of a bailable offence and is arrested or detained in connection therewith, he shall be released on his personal recognition to attend any meeting of the Assembly.

CONTEMPT OF COURT

Immunity from arrest and detention cannot be claimed in respect of contempt of court which is of a criminal nature. What is contempt of a criminal nature cannot be laid down in general terms, and each case will depend upon its particular facts and circumstances. There have been cases both in Parliament and in the courts, and a few instances may be cited as examples:

(i) Privilege cannot be claimed in respect of commitment for contempt of court for publishing certain articles calculated to prejudice the course of justice. *Gray's Case*.[1]

(ii) Similarly in respect of imprisonment for contempt in

[1] C.J. 1882, 487.

appropriating money received by a member as Receiver. *Davis's Case*.[1]

(iii) Privilege was allowed in a case which the alleged contempt was the refusal to comply with an order of the court for payment of certain moneys and documents to the liquidator of a company. *Harrison's Case*.[2]

PREVENTIVE DETENTION

No privilege can be claimed in respect of arrest or detention without trial in cases under Preventive Detention Acts or Ordinances. In *Captain Ramsay's Case* in 1939, the Committee of Privileges of the House of Commons declared the law as follows:

'The precedents lend no support to the view that Members of Parliament are exempted by privilege of Parliament from detention under Regulation 18B of the Defence (General) Regulations, 1939. Preventive arrest under statutory authority by executive order is not within the principle of the cases to which the privilege from arrest has been decided to extend. To claim that the privilege extends to such cases would be either the assertion of a new parliamentary privilege or unjustified extension of an existing one.'[3]

Preventive detention was treated as something of the nature of an arrest on a criminal charge, and the reasons which appeared to have weighed with the Committee seem to have been, firstly, that the purpose of both is the protection of the community as a whole and, secondly, that such a power of arrest can be exercised by the executive only when Parliament has itself conferred the power and required its exercise in accordance with conditions laid down by itself, and that therefore the executive is subject to parliamentary control. Regarding the suggestion that the executive in possession of these powers could in effect avoid parliamentary control by interning all those members who might be likely to challenge its actions, the Privileges Committee pointed out that on a writ of Habeas Corpus in the above-mentioned case, the

[1] C.J. 1888, 488.
[2] 14 Ch. D. 533.
[3] H.C. *Paper* 164 of 1940.

Home Secretary had to swear an affidavit that he had carefully considered the information at his disposal and that in his opinion the detention was justified. The Committee further pointed out that if the real ground of internment was that the member was likely to prove an embarrassment to the executive in Parliament, no such affidavit could be sworn without the commission of gross perjury. It was made clear by the Committee that no arrest or detention under such power could be effected for anything said or done by a member from his place in Parliament; if such be the case, a breach of privilege would be committed.

ARREST AND SERVICE OF PROCESS WITHIN THE PRECINCTS OF THE HOUSE

The general question whether a member is immune from arrest under the Preventive Detention Act or enactments of a similar nature has been answered, as has already been stated, in the negative both in India and in the British Parliament.[1]

The question whether a member can be arrested within the precincts of the House has been asked in certain quarters.

There is one case referred to in May, *Lord Cochrane's Case*, where Lord Cochrane, a Member of Parliament, was taken into custody by the Marshal of the King's Bench while he was sitting on the Privy Councillor's bench in the House of Commons. The House was not sitting at that time. This case, however, is not in point as it was not an instance of serving or executing a process. Lord Cochrane had been convicted of an offence and had escaped from prison and he was retaken into custody. In these circumstances the observation of May seems to be correct, that 'the House will not allow even the sanctuary of its walls to protect a member from the process of criminal law'.

The present question is rather similar to the question whether the service of a criminal process within the precincts of the House is a breach of privilege.

A warrant of arrest under provisions of law similar in nature to the Preventive Detention Act has been held to be in the nature of a criminal process in *Capt. Ramsay's Case*

[1] May, p. 79; Parl. Deb. 1814-15, vol. 30, 309, 336.

referred to above. This view has been taken also by the law courts. Derbyshire C. J. observes in the case of *In re. Niharendu Dutt-Majumdar:*

'If it were necessary for me to decide what it [viz. arrest and detention under Regulation III of 1818 similar to the Preventive Detention Act] was, I should hold that it was something *sui generis* more akin to criminal process than civil process because it is a restraint on the freedom on the subject imposed by the State purporting to be for the safety of the State, which is one of the chief features of arrest on criminal process.'[1]

With regard to the same point, Mitter J. observes: 'I may add that it is not a civil process for the reason that the essence of a civil process is that it is set in motion at the instance of a private person for the enforcement of his rights against another private person.'

Although whether the arrest of a member on a criminal process is a breach of privilege or not has not been specifically raised, the question whether the service of a criminal process within the precincts of the House is a breach of privilege has been raised on several occasions.

It may be said that if the mere service of a criminal process is a breach of privilege, an arrest on a criminal process which stands on a higher footing must certainly be a breach of privilege.

As long ago as 1888, a Select Committee of the British House of Commons expressed the opinion that to attempt to serve a summons upon a member within the precincts of the House, whilst the House was sitting without the leave of the House first obtained, was a breach of privilege.[2]

It also appears that there has been a Police Order in force in England since 1889 which is as follows:

'Criminal process may not be served or executed on any Member of Parliament within the Palace Yard without the leave of the House; and no action whatever will be taken by Police in such cases without the special instruction of the Commissioner.'

This question was thoroughly considered by the Committee

---

[1] 47 C.W.N., 854.
[2] H.C. *Paper* 411 of 1888.

of Privileges of the House of Commons in 1945, and the Committee[1] held that the service of process within the precincts of the House while the House was sitting would be a breach of privilege. The Committee also expressed the opinion that the execution of process, e.g. arrest pursuant to a warrant, would stand on the same footing. The Committee observed:

'While it is not necessary for your Committee to express any opinion with regard to the execution of process within the precincts of the House, it may be convenient if they say that in their view the principles which apply to service of process are equally applicable to execution of process.'

The Privileges Committee approved of the view taken by the Select Committee in 1888 in the following words:

'Although the Report [i.e. of the Select Committee of 1888] was not adopted by the House, your Committee are of the opinion that it may be accepted as a correct, though not necessarily an exhaustive, statement of the law of Parliament. The failure of the House to adopt the Report does not appear to have been due to any disagreement with the finding that a breach of privilege had been committed. Moreover, in Australia, whether the law and custom of Parliament have been applied by Statute, the opinion of the Committee was accepted as a correct statement of the law.'

The reason why the service of process within the precincts of the House is considered to be a breach of privilege is, according to the Committee, not that such a service is an insult to the member but that 'it is deemed disrespectful to the House'. For a stranger admitted within parliamentary precincts with the permission, express or tacit, of the House, to presume to serve the process of an inferior tribunal in the presence, actual or constructive, of the House, is clearly an abuse of the privilege of admission to the House and a violation of the dignity of the High Court of Parliament.

As for what should be the precincts of the House and what should be the time during which the House may be considered to be sitting, the Committee[2] observed as follows:

'As regards service of process within the precincts on sitting days, it would be impracticable to limit the time during

---

[1] H.C. *Paper* 31 of 1945.
[2] See also *Report of the Committee of Privileges*, Mad. L.A. 28 Mar. 1958.

which it would constitute a breach of privilege strictly to the hours during which the House was sitting. It must be extended for at least a reasonable time before the meeting and after the rising of the House. It will clearly include periods when the sitting of the House is suspended, e.g. on the first day of a session after the House returns from attending the King in the House of Peers, when the House is constructively still sitting.

'Indignities offered to Committees of the House are resented as indignities offered to the House itself. It will, therefore, be a breach of privilege to serve process whilst the Committees are sitting, even though the House itself is not sitting at the time. The breach of privilege could not be limited to service of process in the actual view of a Committee, and unless each case is to be decided on its particular facts, it is difficult to see how the area within which protection will be afforded by the dignity of the Committee can be restricted to anything less than the precincts of the House.

'The House has jurisdiction to keep order and maintain decorum within its precincts including the curtilages thereof, and may make rules with respect to the conduct of strangers admitted to those precincts, as well during the intervals between its daily sittings as during the sittings themselves, and your Committee are of opinion that the simplest rule to lay down is that service of process within the precincts of the House on a day on which the House or any Committee thereof is to sit, is sitting or has sat, will constitute a breach of privilege.'

It may be argued that the immunity from service of process, etc. may result in a failure of justice. The Committee furnished the following answer to this argument:

'Your Committee cannot think that the immunity from the service or execution of criminal process which, in their opinion is conferred by the law of Parliament upon all persons within the parliamentary precincts, temporary in its duration and liable to be withheld whenever the House saw fit, could paralyse the arm of the law or obstruct the course of criminal justice. An immunity wider than that claimed by the Committee of 1888, in that it is not limited to the time while the House is sitting, has been enjoyed by Members of Parliament under a Police Order for over fifty years.

25

'If a stranger were to resort to the Palace of Westminster in order to avoid arrest, it would be competent to the Speaker to direct him to be removed from within the precincts. As it would be permissible to serve or execute process within the parliamentary precincts on days on which the House was not sitting, no officer of the House could for long evade arrest or the service of process by living continuously within those precincts. Moreover in such a case application could always be made to the House for leave to serve or execute the process. As regards persons who reside within the Palace of Westminster, the Service of Process (Justices) Act, 1933, enables a summons to be effectively served upon a defendant at his last or usual place of abode by registered post. It is not likely that the service or execution of process would often be a matter of such urgency that to wait until the leave of the House had been obtained to serve or execute it would defeat the ends of justice. If it was feared that such a result would follow, application could be made to the Speaker who would doubtless authorize the process to be served or executed relying on the House to ratify his action.'

There is no immunity when the House is not in session. The Committee observed:

'It is clear that service of process even upon a Member within the precincts of the House during a prorogation or during any periodical recess, or even on a day over which the House had adjourned is not a breach of privilege. To hold that it is would be to confuse what the House is with where the House is.'

The police officer on duty has of course the power to arrest strangers who commit a criminal offence or are about to do so. The Committee said:

'The protection from service or execution of process afforded by the dignity of the House in no way affects the right of police officers on duty within the precincts to arrest strangers who, having been admitted to the Palace of Westminster, commit criminal offences or are thought to be about to do so, subject to this that they must refrain from entering the House itself while it is sitting unless they have previously received its permission.'

Rules of legislatures in India prohibit the arrest of, and

service of summons on, any person within the precincts of
the House.

HOUSE TO BE INFORMED OF ARREST

In England various statutes require that when a member is
arrested or detained in custody the fact of the arrest or detention must be communicated to the House. In cases not covered
by statutes, it is a privilege of the House to be informed of
the arrest or detention. Blackstone has stated the position as
follows:

'The chief, if not the only privilege of Parliament, in such
cases, (i.e. in cases when immunity from arrest cannot be
claimed) seems to be the right of receiving immediate information of the imprisonment or detention of any member
with the reasons for which he is detained.'[1]

Where a member is convicted for a criminal offence, the
court informs the Speaker of the offence and the sentence
passed. When a member is arrested and after conviction
released on bail pending an appeal or otherwise released,
such fact shall also be intimated to the Speaker.[2] It appears
that if a person is already in prison under a sentence of court
when he is elected a member, there is no duty to inform the
Speaker. But it also appears that such communication has,
in fact, been made.[3]

A claim of privilege of being informed of the arrest on
detention of a member was made in Bengal before the Constitution came into force.[4]

In India a question of privilege was raised in the Lok Sabha
by Shri Kansari Halder regarding an attempt to handcuff
a member of the Lok Sabha arrested on a criminal charge.
The Committee of Privileges[5] to which the question was
referred reiterated the stand taken by it in the *Deshpande
Case*, wherein they observed as follows:

'It has to be remembered that the fundamental principle

---

[1] Blackstone, *Commentaries*; *Narasimha Rao's Case*, Hyderabad Assembly Report,
10 Sept. 1952 and *H. K. Vyasa's Case*, Rajasthan Assembly Report, 31 May
1954; C.J. 1924, 17; C. J. 1926, 166.
[2] Rule 230 of the Rules of Procedure and Conduct of Business in the Lok Sabha.
[3] C.J. 1922, 345; H.C.D. 1917-18, 93, c. 1786.
[4] B.L.A.P. 1938, vol. lii, no. 1, p. 148.
[5] *Fourth Report of the Committee of Privileges*, Second Lok Sabha, p. 7, para 11.

is that all citizens including Members of Parliament have to be treated equally in the eyes of law. Unless so specified in the Constitution or in any law a Member of Parliament cannot claim any higher privileges than those enjoyed by any ordinary citizen in the matter of the application of the laws.'

The Committee, on being ordered to do so by the Speaker, reconsidered the whole issue and observed that the Police Rules/Manuals of the various States and the executive instructions issued by the State Governments provided that prisoners, whether undertrials or convicts, should not be handcuffed as a matter of routine, and that 'that use of handcuffs should be restricted to cases where the prisoner is a desperate character or where there are reasonable grounds to believe that he will use violence or attempt to escape or where there are other similar reasons'. The Committee further recommended that the Ministry of Home Affairs be requested to stress upon the State Governments the desirability of strictly complying with the above Rules, especially in the case of Members of Parliament in view of their high status.[1]

PRIVILEGE EXTENDED TO STRANGERS

As in the case of freedom of speech, the privilege of freedom from arrest and molestation has been extended to witnesses summoned to attend before the House or any committee thereof, to persons in personal attendance upon business in Parliament, e.g. petitioners or counsel when coming, staying or returning, and also to officers of the House in immediate attendance upon the service of Parliament. And the same principles as in the case of members apply to them.

CONTEMPT OF HOUSE

We have discussed the specific privileges which the House of Commons in its collective capacity and the individual members of the House enjoy. Now there must be some means for the protection of these privileges or for the prevention of any breach of them. A privilege may be considered in two

[1] *Fifth Report of the Committee of Privileges*, Second Lok Sabha, p. 46.

aspects, a negative and a positive. In its negative aspect, a privilege may be set up as a defence, e.g. in an action for libel for words uttered in Parliament, a defence of privilege may be pleaded; or if a member is arrested under a civil process, he may claim to be released forthwith. In its positive aspect, any person violating or infringing any of the privileges may be met with punishment. In this latter aspect of privileges, the House of Commons is vested with a penal jurisdiction. But this penal jurisdiction is exercised not only in respect of breaches of specific privileges but also in respect of any act which, though not a breach of any specific privilege, is calculated to hamper the due administration of parliamentary business or to offend against the authority or dignity of the House. Such acts, although generally called breaches of privilege, are really in the nature of contempt of the House.

ACTS CONSTITUTING CONTEMPT

Cases of contempt are decided by the House of Commons as and when occasions arise, and it would be difficult to enumerate all the acts which have been construed to be contempt of the House.

The general principle in such cases has been stated by May as follows: '...any act or omission which obstructs or impedes either House of Parliament in the performance of its functions, or which obstructs or impedes any member or officer of such House in the discharge of his duty, or which has a tendency, directly or indirectly, to produce such results may be treated as a contempt....'[1]

A breach of privilege or an act of contempt again may be committed by a member or a stranger. We shall give some examples illustrating the above principle and classify them in two categories, those committed by members and those committed by strangers. These are by no means exhaustive but are given only as illustrations.

MISCONDUCT OF MEMBERS

(1) Acceptance of bribe to influence him in his conduct

[1] May, p. 109.

as a member or of any fee, remuneration or reward for anything done by him in his capacity as a member.

A member was expelled for receiving £500 from the French Merchants for business done in the House;[1] entering into an agreement with a person for money to advocate the claim of such person in the House.[2]

A Committee of Enquiry appointed to investigate into the conduct of Mr. H. G. Mudgal, a member of the Indian Parliament, found that he was to receive certain monetary benefits in exchange for services which included the putting of questions in Parliament, moving amendments to certain bills and arranging interviews with Ministers, etc; it was resolved by the House that the conduct of the member was derogatory to the dignity of the House and inconsistent with the standard which Parliament is entitled to expect from its members, and that he deserved expulsion from the House (the member having previously resigned).[3]

(2) Publication of any report of, or evidence given before, Select Committees before they are presented to the House.[4]

The Committee of Privileges, to which the matter of the disclosure of proceedings of a parliamentary committee was referred in the Lok Sabha, *inter alia* recommended:

'It is in accordance with the law and practice of the Privilege of Parliament that while a Committee of Parliament is holding its sittings from day to day its proceedings should not be published nor any documents or papers which may have been presented to the Committee or the conclusions to which it may have arrived at referred to in the Press.'[5]

(3) Acceptance of payments for the disclosure of information obtained from other members in regard to matters to be brought before Parliament, although not constituting strictly a breach of privilege, has been held to be dishonourable conduct deserving of severe punishment.[6]

---

[1] C.J. 1667-87, p. 24.
[2] Parl. Deb. 1858, vol. 148, c. 1855; H.C. *Paper* 5 of 1941; H.C. *Paper* 63 of 1944-5; *Boothby's Case*, H.C. *Paper* 5 of 1940-41; *Belcher's Case*, (Com. *Paper* 7617 laid on 21 Jan. 1949).
[3] *Mudgal's Case*; proceedings of 24 Sept. 1951.
[4] Resolution of the House of Commons, 21 Apr. 1837 (C.J. 1837, p. 282); H.C.D. 1934-5, vol. 295, c. 389.
[5] *Report of the Sundarryya Case*, 1952, para 11, p. 2, Lok Sabha.
[6] Cases of *Allighan* and *Walkden*, C.J. 1947-8, pp. 22, 23.

(4) Giving evidence before any court or in any other House in regard to debates or proceedings in the House of which he is a member or official without the permission of the House.[1]

In *Biren Roy's Case* the Committee of Privileges recommended that 'no member or officer of the House should give evidence in a Court of Law in respect of any proceedings of the House or any Committee of the House'.[2] On another occasion the Committee held 'that the permission of the House is necessary for giving evidence by a member before the other House or a committee thereof or before a House of the State legislature or a committee thereof'.[3]

MISCONDUCT OR CONTEMPT BY STRANGERS

The following are some instances of misconduct by strangers:

(1) Any disorderly conduct in the House or riotous behaviour to hinder the passing of any bill or other matter pending in the House.[4] Invading the legislature with a large mob, creating noise and disturbance round it, and picketing and preventing the ingress and egress of members is a breach of privilege.[5]

(2) Refusal by witness called to answer questions, to sign statements or to produce any documents.[6]

(3) Disobedience to summons to attend as witness.[7]

(4) Obstructing the execution of any order of the House.[8]

(5) Giving false evidence before the House or any committee.[9]

---

[1] Resolution of the Commons, 26 May 1818, C. J. 1818, p. 389; see also Parl. Deb. 1828, vol. 18, c. 971-2.

[2] *First Report of the Committee of Privileges* Second Lok Sabha, p. 4, para 8.

[3] *Sixth Report of the Committee of Privileges*, Second Lok Sabha, pp. 5-6.

[4] C.J. 1547-1628, p. 258; C.J. (1693-97), 667; C.J. (1699-1702), 230; H.C. Paper 36 of 1946-7.

[5] *Report of the Privileges Committee*, Madhya Pradesh Legislature, 10 Aug. 1951 (*Kumbhare's Case*); Contempt of House Case in Hyderabad P.C. Report, 10 June 1953; (Case of *V. B. Raju and others*), Anti-Communist Demonstration, Punjab L.A. 18 July 1952; Bhooswami Demonstration, Rajasthan Assembly, 10 Apr. 1956.

[6] C.J. 1852-53, p. 320; ibid. 1946-7, p. 377; ibid. p. 378.

[7] Ibid. 1772-4, p. 465; ibid. 1878-9, p. 366.

[8] Ibid. 1851, p. 152; ibid. 1714-18, p. 46.

[9] Ibid. 1842, p. 198; ibid. 1947-8, p. 22. A Government official was admonished for producing a fabricated document, attempting to tamper with a witness and trying to conceal truth from the Committee of Privileges, U.P.L.A.D. 20 Dec. 1954.

(6) Speech or writing casting reflection on the House or its members.[1]

A question of privilege was raised in the Lok Sabha on 10 February 1959 regarding certain remarks[2] made by Shri Mathai in his letter to the Prime Minister. The matter was referred to the Committee of Privileges which found that such remarks which cast aspersions and attribute irresponsibility to Parliament or its members tend to diminish the respect due to Parliament, but recommended that the House would best consult its dignity if it ignored such improprieties.

Certain reflections were made against members of the Mysore legislature by a newspaper *Satya*. It was argued that a person had a fundamental right of freedom of speech under Article 19 (1) of the Constitution, and the right could not be abridged except on the grounds mentioned in Article 19 (2); as the privilege of a legislature was not one of the subjects mentioned in Article 19 (2), a person had a right to criticize a member of the legislature in whatever language he liked and could not be punished for contempt. Article 194, it was said, should be read subject to Article 19 (1). This view, however, did not find favour with the Privileges Committee appointed to hear the case of *Satya*.[3]

In a recent case the Supreme Court held that the provisions of clause (2) of Article 194 indicate that the freedom of speech referred to in clause (1) is different from the freedom of speech and expression guaranteed under Article 19 (1), and cannot be cut down in any way by any law contemplated by clause (2) of Article 19. It was also held that the provisions of Article 19 (1) (a), which are general, must yield to Article

[1] Parl. Deb. 1857-8 vol. 150, c. 1022; ibid. 1836, vol. 35, c. 167; ibid. 1893-4, vol. 20, c. 112; ibid. 1879, vol. 247, c. 1866; *Daily Mail Case*, C. J. 1901, p. 355; *Daily Mail Case*, C.J. 1926, p. 95; *World Press News Case*, C.J. 1947-48, pp. 22, 23; H.C.D. vol. 301, c. 1545. In this case a letter was written to certain members of the House of commons by the Secretary of the League for the Prohibition of Cruel Sports in which the following sentences appeared: 'If we do not hear from you, we shall feel justified in letting your constituency know that you have no objection to cruel sports'; *Times of India Case*, Bombay Legislative Assembly Report, 13 Apr. 1953.

[2] 'But the ever mounting tendency in our Parliament and our Press to attack public servants without caring to verify facts is having devastatingly demoralizing effect. Under such deplorable conditions very few self-respecting persons will care to enter Government service or public life.'

[3] *Satya's Case, Report of the Committee of Privileges*, Mysore Legislative Council, 13 July 1953.

194 (1) and the latter part of its clause (3), which are special.[1]

A letter addressed by an official to the Minister in charge of his department, alleging that certain statements made by a member in the House regarding the official were maliciously false, was read in the House by the Minister concerned. The matter was referred to the Committee of Privileges. The Committee, on being assured that there was no intention to impute malice to the member, found that there had been no breach of privilege but deprecated the reading of such letters in the House.[2] A letter from the Chief Secretary, Vindhya Pradesh, alleged to be intimidating a member and containing reflections upon him, was referred to the Committee of Privileges.[3]

The Chairman of the Stock Exchange of Sydney wrote to Mr. Speaker complaining of a speech made in the House by a member. The member concerned raised a question of privilege in connection with the action of the writer of the letter, and moved a motion that in writing a letter reflecting on the motives and action of a member of the House and in writing a threat, the Chairman of the Stock Exchange was guilty of contempt. A debate ensued on the motion which set out that an individual whose conduct had been criticized in statements made under cover of parliamentary privilege had a right to defend himself, and that the House was of opinion that the remarks of the Chairman of the Stock Exchange were not a breach of privilege but were a defence to charges made against him under cover of privilege. The House, however, considered that in addressing this letter to the Speaker instead of direct to the member the Chairman was in error.[4]

Reflection on the conduct of a member imputing certain motives to him in asking supplementary questions was held to be a breach of privilege.[5]

On 15 April 1961 a despatch from the correspondent of *Blitz* was published in that paper under the heading 'the

[1] *M. S. M. Sharma* v. *Shri Krishna Sinha*, A.I.R. 1959, S.C. 395.
[2] *Report of the Privileges Committee*, W.B.L.A. presented on 10 Mar. 1953 (*S. K. Haldar's Case*).
[3] Vindhya Pradesh L.A.D. 21 Mar. 1956.
[4] *Votes*, 1935, pp. 143, 149 (Australian Federal Parliament).
[5] In the matter of the *Times of India*, *Report of the Committee of Privileges*, Bombay Assembly, 13 Apr. 1953.

Kripaloony impeachment, bad, black, bald lies', in which a strong criticism was made of a speech by Acharya Kripalani in the Lok Sabha. This matter was referred to the Committee of Privileges which reported *inter alia* as follows:

'In the light of what has been stated above the Committee have come to the conclusion that the impugned despatch read as a whole including its heading and the photograph of Shri J. B. Kripalani, M.P. with the caption 'Kripaloony' underneath, in its tenor and content libels Shri Kripalani and casts reflections on him on account of his speech and conduct in the House. The language of the despatch is such that it brings Shri Kripalani into odium, contempt and ridicule by referring to him in a contemptuous and insulting manner by using foul epithets in respect of him.'

The Committee, therefore, found R. K. Karanjia, Editor of *Blitz*, and A. Raghaban, the New Delhi Correspondent of *Blitz*, 'guilty of committing a gross breach of privilege and contempt of the House'.

The House agreed with the report of the Committee on 19 August 1961. The Speaker then summoned R. K. Karanjia to the Bar of the House on 29 August 1961. R. K. Karanjia was brought to the Bar of the House by the Watch and Ward Officer and was formally reprimanded by the Speaker (seated in his Chair).

A criticism of a member for his speech or conduct in the House, however strong, need not necessarily be a breach of privilege. The law of parliamentary privilege should not be administered in a way which will fetter or discourage the free expression of opinion or criticism. It will always be a question of fact in each case whether particular comments come under the category of libel upon a member on account of his speech or conduct in Parliament, or merely constitute *bona fide* criticism though strongly worded. In the *Blitz case* the Committee of Privileges considered this aspect of the matter in their report and came to the conclusion that the comments were libelous.

(7) Reflection upon Presiding Officers.[1]

[1] *Conybeare's Case*, Parl. Deb. 1887, vol. 313, c. 371; ibid. 1888, vol. 329, c. 48; *Atkinson's Case*, ibid. 1890-91, vol. 356, c. 419; *Wedgwood and Ginnell Case*, H.C.D. 1911, vol. 21, c. 1435; *Daily Worker's Case*, C. J. 1937-8, p. 213; H.C.D. 1937-38. vol. 334, c. 1317; in this case certain reflections upon the Speaker were held

(8) Publication of false or inaccurate reports of debates.[1] Putting misleading headlines to reports of proceedings.[2]

(9) Suppressing speeches of particular members.[3]

(10) Publishing a proceeding ordered to be expunged by the House.[4]

On 10 June 1957, a member of the Bihar Legislative Assembly, raising a question of breach of privilege, submitted that in spite of the orders of the Speaker expunging references to the ex-Industries Minister, *Search Light*, a local daily, published all the references which were ordered to be expunged. The motion was moved and the matter was referred to the Committee of Privileges, which resolved that the Editor, the Printer and the Publisher of *Search Light* be called upon to show cause why appropriate action should not be taken against them by reason of the commission of a breach of privilege in respect of the Speaker of the Bihar Legislative Assembly and the Assembly itself, by publishing a perverted and unfaithful report of the proceedings of the Assembly relating to the speech, expunged portions of which were also published.

The Supreme Court, before which the matter came on a petition under Article 32 of the Constitution, held that 'the House of Commons had at the commencement of our Constitution the power or privilege of prohibiting the publication of even a true and faithful report of the debates or proceedings that take place within the House. *A fortiori* the House had at the relevant time the power or privilege of prohibiting the publication of an inaccurate or garbled version of such debates or proceedings. The latter part of Article 194(3) confers all these powers, privileges and immuni-

---

to be gross breach of privilege of the House, but no further action was taken on the ground that there should not be too much made of the matter. A similar course was adopted in the case of the *Jugabani* in West Bengal: *Report of the Privilege Committee*, 9 Nov. 1953; *Case of the Daily Herald*, H.C. Paper 98, 1924; *Case of the Evening News*, C.J. 1928-9, p. 50; Parl. Deb. 1874, vol. 219, c. 752; see also the *Case of Blitz* of Bombay, U.P.L.A.P.; see also *Malayali's Case, Second Report of the Committee of Privileges*, Travancore-Cochin, Oct. 1955.

[1] *Daily News Case*, C.J. 1893-4, p. 324; *Case of The Times* and *The Sun*, Parl. Deb. 1847, vol. 91, c. 1150.

[2] *Sadat Jehan Begum's Case*, Hyderabad Legislative Assembly Report, 10 June 1953; W.B.L.A.P. 25 Mar. 1957, p. 418.

[3] Parl. Deb. 1833, vol. 20, c. 6; ibid. 1849, vol. 104, c. 1054; *Venkataramao's Case* in Hyderabad Legislative Assembly Report, 30 Mar. 1955.

[4] *Case of the Albion and Evening Advertiser*, Lords Journal, 1801-2, p. 104.

ties on the House of the Legislature of the States. Our Constitution clearly provides that until Parliament or the State
Legislature, as the case may be, makes a law defining the
powers, privileges and immunities of the House, its Members
and Committees, they shall have all the powers, privileges
and immunities of the House of Commons as at the date of
the commencement of our Constitution and yet to deny them
those powers, privileges and immunities, after finding that
the House of Commons had them at the relevant time, will
be not to interpret the Constitution but to remake it.'[1]

(11) Premature publication of any report or other paper.[2]

A question of breach of privilege was raised in the Lok
Sabha regarding an article 'Story of the Merchant Shipping
Bill' in the daily newspaper *Hindusthan Standard*, dated 15
August 1958. It was contended that the Joint Committee on
the Merchant Shipping Bill considered the report on 18
August and the report along with the minutes of dissent was
presented to the Lok Sabha on 21 August 1958, and the
article in question referred to the decisions of the Committee
taken on 22 and 24 July 1958. The matter was referred to the
Committee of Privileges, which found that the publication
of the article constituted a breach of privilege as it involved
a premature disclosure of the proceedings of the Joint Committee on the Merchant Shipping Bill, 1958.[3] But having
regard to the unqualified apologies offered by the Editor of
the *Hindusthan Standard* no action was taken by the House.
On another occasion a question of privilege was raised in the
Lok Sabha regarding the publication by the Press Information Bureau of an answer to a question before it was given on
the floor of the House. Keeping in view the assurance given
by the Press Information Bureau that there would be no
repetition of such a lapse in future, the matter was, however,
dropped.[4]

(12) Serving of criminal or civil process within the precincts
of the House while the House is sitting.[5]

[1] *M. S. M. Sharma* v. *Shri Krishna Sinha*, A.I.R. 1959 S.C. 395.
[2] C.J. 1837, p. 282; the *Case of The Times and the Daily News*, Parl. Deb. 1875,
vol. 223, c. 787; *Sheehan's Case*, C.J. 1831-2, p. 360; H.C. *Paper* 87 of 1901; H.C.D.
1934-5, vol. 295, c. 389.
[3] *Seventh Report of the Committee of Privileges*, 1958, p. 9.
[4] L.S.D. 26 July 1957.
[5] *Bell's Case*, Parl. Deb. 1827, vol. 17, c. 34: H.C. *Paper* (report of Select

(13) Causing arrest of member otherwise than in execution of criminal process.[1]

(14) Molestation of members for their conduct in the House or in going to or coming from the House.[2]

(15) Offering bribes or any gratification to a member for influencing his conduct in the House.[3]

(16) Intimidation of members to influence their conduct.[4] But to say that the member could not get support in his election in the future if he pursued certain rules of conduct would not be a breach of privilege.[5]

COMPLAINT OF BREACH OF PRIVILEGE OF ONE HOUSE AGAINST MEMBERS OF THE OTHER HOUSE

There have been occasions in England when one House has complained that a member of the other House has, by words or acts, committed breach of privilege of the other House. Some instances are given below.

The House of Commons sent a message to the Duke of Buckingham asking him to explain his conduct as Lord Admiral in relation to the staying of a ship. There was a conference between the House of Lords and the House of Commons regarding this message, at which the Lords asked whether the message was a summons to Lord Buckingham to make answer. The Commons replied that the Clerk had made a slip in making out the order which had since been corrected.[6]

It was reported to the House of Commons that the Earl of Suffolk had, in conversation with a member of the House of Lords, said that Mr. Selden, a member of the House of Com-

Committee on Privileges re. service of summons) 411 of 1888; H.C. *Paper* 101 of 1938-9 p. 23; *Verney's Case*, H.C. *Paper* 31 of 1945-6.

[1] *Case of Harrod and Pocklington* C.J. 1722-7, p. 504; *Butler's Case*, Parl. Deb. 1809, vol. 14, c. 31.

[2] *Smyth's Case*, Parl. Deb. 1844, vol. 74 c. 286; *O'Donoghue's Case*, C.J. 1862, p. 64; *O'Kelley's Case*, C.J. 1883, p. 232; *Jenning's Case*, Parl. Deb. 1827, vol. 17, c. 282; *Atkinson's Case*, Parl. Deb. 1891, vol. 356, c. 419; *Case of the Guardians of Mullingar*, C.J. 1898, p. 381; H.C.D. 1934-35, vol. 301, c. 1545.

[3] *Cases of Freeman and Dalby Thomas*, C.J. 1697-9, p. 538; H.C. *Paper* 103 of 1942-3.

[4] *Plimsoll's Case*, Parl. Deb. 1873, vol. 214, c. 733; H.C.D. 1934-5, vol. 301, c. 1545; *Mrs. Tennant's Case*, H.C. *Paper* 181 of 1945-6.

[5] H.C.D. 1946-7, vol. 431, c. 1968.

[6] Hatsell III, 48.

mons, deserved to be hanged for erasing a record. The Commons immediately sent a message to the Lords to complain of the conduct of Lord Suffolk.[1]

Sir John Eppealy, a member of the House of Commons, was forbidden by the House to answer a petition filed against him in the House of Lords. The House of Commons sent a message to the House of Lords requesting them to inform the House of Commons whether certain words were spoken by Lord Digby in the House of Lords regarding the House of Commons. The matter was referred to a Committee.[2]

A member of the House of Lords complained of certain words spoken about him by a member of the House of Commons in that House. The House of Lords was of opinion that as the person complained against was a member of the other House and the words were said in that House, the House of Lords could not take any cognizance of what was spoken or done in the House of Commons 'unless it be by themselves in a parliamentary way made known to this House'; neither could the person complained against be called to give reparation without breach of the privilege of Parliament unless the House of Commons consented to it.[3]

From these and other similar cases Hatsell has deduced the following principles:

'The leading principle, which appears to pervade all the proceedings between the two Houses of Parliament is, that there shall subsist a perfect equality with respect to each other; and that they shall be, in every respect, totally independent one of the other. From hence it is, that neither House can claim, much less exercise, any authority over a Member of the other; but, if there is any ground of complaint against an act of the House itself, against any individual Member, or against any of the officers of either House, this complaint ought to be made to that House of Parliament where the offence is charged to be committed; and the nature and mode of redress, or punishment, if punishment is necessary, must be determined upon and inflicted by them.... We see, from the several precedents above cited, that neither House

---

[1] Hatsell III, 49.
[2] Ibid. III, 49, 51.
[3] Ibid III, 51.

of Parliament can take upon themselves to redress any injury, or punish any breach of privilege offered to them by any Member of the other House, but that, in such cases, the usual mode of proceeding is *to examine into the fact, and then to lay a state of that evidence before the House of which the person complained of is a Member.*'[1]

A case[2] arose in which a member of the House of Lords was accused of casting reflections on members of the House of Commons. Lord Mancroft was reported in a newspaper to have said: 'Unlike them [M.Ps] I am not paid a thousand a year for larking about in the Division Lobbies at night with Bessie Braddock and the rest of the girls. I have to earn my living.'

It should be noted that these remarks were made not in the House, as in the cases mentioned above but outside.

The matter was raised in the House of Commons as a matter of privilege, and Lord Mancroft wrote a letter to the Speaker apologizing for and withdrawing the remark.

Mr. Speaker ruled that a *prima facie* case had been made out. The apology was accepted by the House with some reluctance.

In the course of the debate Mr. Ede observed: 'We are in a great difficulty in dealing with a Member of another place because we cannot call him before the Committee of Privileges. What we should have to do if we proceeded further with this matter, according to Erskine May and subject to your Ruling, would be to appoint a Committee to inquire into the matter and, if we thought a *prima facie* case had been established, we should have to send our report to the Lords and ask them to deal with the person we regarded as an offender.'

It may be observed that the procedure laid down by Hatsell was thought to be applicable to the case where remarks had been made not in the House but outside.

The two Houses are, however, agreed that each should respect the privilege of the other. When a message was sent by the House of Commons to the House of Lords 'desiring the Lords to have a regard to the privileges of this House

[1] Hatsell III, 61, 65.
[2] H.C.D. 1952, vol. 499, c. 880-1.

therein', the Lords returned an answer 'that the House of Commons need not doubt but that the Lords would have as due regard to their privileges, as they had to their own'.

A similar question was raised in the House of the People when a Minister who was a member of the Council of States was asked by the House of the People to explain his conduct. There was some controversy between the two Houses but ultimately no decision was reached.[1] Subsequently, the question of the procedure to follow in such cases was referred to a Joint Committee of the two Houses.

The Committee prescribed the following procedure:

'(1) When a question of breach of privilege is raised in any House in which a member, officer or servant of the other House is involved, the Presiding Officer shall refer the case to the Presiding Officer of the other House, unless on hearing the member who raises the question or perusing any document where the complaint is based on a document, he is satisfied that no breach of privilege has been committed or the matter is too trivial to be taken notice of, in which case he may disallow the motion for breach of privilege.

'(2) Upon the case being so referred, the Presiding Officer of the other House shall deal with the matter in the same way as if it were a case of breach of privilege of that House or of a member thereof.

'(3) The Presiding Officer shall thereafter communicate to the Presiding Officer of the House where the question of privilege was originally raised, a report about the enquiry, if any, and the action taken on the reference.

'It is the intention of the Committee that if the offending member, officer or servant tenders an apology to the Presiding Officer of the House in which the question of privilege is raised or the Presiding Officer of the other House to which the reference is made, no further action in the matter may be taken after such apology is tendered.'[2]

CONTEMPT OF ONE LEGISLATURE BY MEMBER OF ANOTHER

If a member of the Central legislature commits contempt

[1] C.S.D. 1 May 1953.
[2] *Report of the Joint Select Committee*, 23 Aug. 1954.

of any State legislature, if a member of a State legislature commits contempt of the Central legislature or of another State legislature, can such a member claim any privilege from being proceeded against by the legislature contemned, and what should be the procedure to be followed in such a case?

Such a contempt may be committed in two different circumstances:

(i) by something said within the House of which the contemner is a member; and

(ii) outside the House.

CONTEMPT COMMITTED INSIDE THE HOUSE

As regards the first point, it will be seen that under Articles 105 and 194 of the Constitution, there is freedom of speech inside the legislature, and no action can be taken in any court for anything said or done within the House. Although legislatures are not expressly mentioned, it may be taken that the immunity extends against action by other legislatures also; for otherwise there would be no meaning in having a freedom which can be set at naught by another legislature. It can, therefore, be said that a member can claim privilege for anything said or done by him within the House, although his speech or action may amount to a contempt of another legislature. But it should not be assumed that the member, if he is guilty of contempt, would get away scot-free. The immunity given by Articles 105 and 194 is subject to the rules of the House. In every legislature there is a rule that no member while speaking shall cast any reflection on any other legislature. If such a reflection is made by a member, the Presiding Officer has the authority to pull him up. If he persists in the act he may be dealt with for disobeying the Presiding Officer, and disciplinary action may be taken against him by admonition, suspension or expulsion according to the circumstances. If any reflection escapes the Presiding Officer a complaint may be made by the legislature contemned, and disciplinary action, if necessary, can certainly be taken against the offending member for having committed an offence. A member is amenable to the jurisdiction of the

26

House for any offence committed within the House. Therefore, so far as a contempt committed within the House is concerned, there should not be any difficulty, and the following propositions may be laid down.

(1) A member of a legislature can claim privilege in regard to anything said or done by him within the House of which he is a member, and no action can be taken against him for his conduct by any other legislature.

(2) The immunity, however, extends only to any action taken by another legislature. The member would be liable to be dealt with under the disciplinary jurisdiction of the House of which he is a member if he is guilty of contempt of another legislature either *suo moto* by the House or on complaint made by the legislature contemned.

CONTEMPT COMMITTED OUTSIDE THE HOUSE

As regards the second point, there would be a great deal of difficulty. This point may be considered in three aspects:

(1) whether any privilege can be claimed;

(2) if it cannot be claimed, what the procedure would be for dealing with the contemner; and

(3) if it can be claimed, what the remedy would be of the legislature contemned.

WHETHER PRIVILEGE CAN BE CLAIMED

The power to punish for contempt of the legislature is 'akin in nature and origin to the power possessed by the Courts of Justice to punish for contempt',[1] and therefore a contempt of a legislature may be taken to be similar in nature to a contempt of court. Where there is a cause of conflict between two legislatures on a question of contempt, a parallel may be found in a case where a member of the legislature is alleged to have committed contempt of court. Let us see, therefore, whether a member can claim privileges of Parliament in such a case.

There have been a number of cases in the House of Commons and, as stated by May, 'it was for some time doubt-

[1] May, p. 89.

ful how far privilege would extend to the protection of a member committed for contempt'. In recent cases members committed for contempt of court have failed to establish any privilege.[1] It seems to be settled now that 'in case of quasi-criminal contempt, members of either House may be committed without an invasion of privilege'.[2] That is to say, no privilege can be claimed by a member committing a quasi-criminal contempt. It may be mentioned here that a reflection on a court of justice is a criminal contempt and not a civil one (e.g. disobedience of a court's order).

If, therefore, the analogy of contempt of court is taken, it would seem that a member cannot or at least should not be allowed to claim privilege if he casts any reflection upon another legislature outside the House.

REMEDY IF PRIVILEGE CANNOT BE CLAIMED

If this position is accepted, the next question is how to deal with such a member. It goes without saying that such a member would be treated just as an ordinary citizen who commits a contempt of the legislature.

It is, however, necessary here to consider the extent of the penal jurisdiction of a legislature. There are two fundamental propositions of International Law laid down by Ulric Hubert:

(1) The laws of a State have force only within the territorial limits of its sovereignty.

(2) All persons who, whether permanently or temporarily, are found within the territory of a sovereign are claimed to be his subjects and as such are bound by his laws.

From these propositions, it may be deduced that the penal jurisdiction of a court extends only within the limits of the territory of the State but not outside, and that within such limits all persons resident within the State, even though subjects of a foreign State, are amenable to such jurisdiction. Although States in India are not sovereign States, the principles of the penal jurisdiction of the courts will be the same. It may be mentioned, however, that section 45 of the Criminal Procedure Code lays down that a warrant of arrest may be

[1] May. p. 82.
[2] Ibid. p. 83.

executed anywhere in India. But for this provision, a warrant of arrest from one State would not have run in another State. The same principle will apply in the case of the penal jurisdiction of legislatures, and it may be taken that the penal jurisdiction of a legislature is coextensive with its legislative jurisdiction, that is to say, it extends only within the territory of the State concerned. In that case, a warrant of arrest issued by the legislature of one State will not have any extraterritorial validity, and such a legislature will not be able to take any action against a contemner unless he voluntarily submits to its jurisdiction.

This question arose in the case of *Blitz* which came up before the Supreme Court, but no decision was given on this aspect of the case. This point might have arisen also in a case before the House of Commons. Mr. D. N. Pritt was committed for contempt of court by a court in Kenya for some statement alleged to have been made by him to certain M.Ps. The matter was raised on a question of privilege. But the specific issue was not decided as the Speaker ruled that the proceedings for contempt had been taken not on the statement made to the M.P. but for the publication of the same in a newspaper in Kenya. With regard to this case, Sir Frederic Metcalfe, the then Clerk of the House of Commons, wrote:

'If such a conflict (between the House of Commons and the Supreme Court of Kenya) had occurred, the question must have arisen whether the House of Commons can exercise jurisdiction outside this country and in the colony of Kenya. What steps the House could take to protect a person who was being penalized by an overseas court has not yet been settled, for in the circumstances the threatened conflict did not arise.'[1]

But there appears to be no doubt that a legislature in India would have the power to commit any person guilty of contempt of the House, if he were within or without the jurisdiction of the State legislature, which would be its legislative jurisdiction, i.e. the territorial limit of the State. For under Articles 105 and 194 the legislatures in India possess all the powers of the House of Commons. Under a section similarly worded in the Commonwealth of Australia Act, it has been held

---

[1] *Table*, vol. xxi, p. 133.

that the Australian Parliament can send a person to jail for contempt.[1]

As regards contempt of the Central legislature, it appears that the Central legislature would have the power to punish for its own contempt a person wherever he may be residing, for its penal jurisdiction would extend to the whole of India, the sphere of its legislative activity.

PROCEDURE IF PRIVILEGE CAN BE CLAIMED

Now we come to the question what would be the procedure if privilege of Parliament is claimed by a member. An analogous case is that in which a member of one House commits a breach of privilege of the other House of the same legislature. It has been stated that a solution has been found by agreement in the Indian Parliament. Such a course can also be adopted in the case of different legislatures by agreement, that in the case of contempt of a legislature by a member of another legislature, the legislature contemned may report to the other legislature, and that legislature can take action against the offending member. But here also there may be some difficulty. The penal jurisdiction which has been conferred by Articles 105 and 194 is with respect to contempt of the legislature which takes action and not of another legislature. Whether by virtue of Article 194 a State legislature would have the power to punish a person guilty of contempt of another legislature is a difficult question. If a member is sent to prison, the action may be challenged by a writ of habeas corpus and the action may be declared *ultra vires*. It appears that in the Kenya Legislative Council certain derogatory reflections were made about a member of the British House of Commons without any question of their admissibility being raised.[2]

REFLECTION AGAINST COMMITTEES OF ANOTHER LEGISLATURE

Reflections against committees of another legislature stand

[1] See article by M. N. Kaul, *Journal of Parliamentary Information*, vol. i, no. 2.
[2] 52 Kenya, *Hansard*, 50.

on the same footing as reflections against the legislature itself, and need not be separately dealt with because such reflections would be treated as contempt of the House itself.

REFLECTION AGAINST MEMBERS OF ANOTHER LEGISLATURE

In the case of reflections against members of another legislature also, any act which obstructs or impedes any member in the discharge of his duty is treated as a contempt of the House itself, and the same considerations will apply. But in the case of a reflection made outside the House, a member may have an additional remedy if no privilege can be claimed by the contemner. He may sue for defamation or libel if the reflection is of such a nature as would be taken cognizance of by a court of law.

PENAL JURISDICTION

The penal jurisdiction of the House of Commons seems to have been derived from the use of the Mace as a symbol of authority. The Sergeant-at-Arms used to carry a Mace from time immemorial and the Mace was used to arrest persons without a warrant. The House of Commons found that they could use the Sergeant-at-Arm's power of arrest without warrant to assist them in their quarrels with other bodies. It enabled them to arrest and commit persons who offended them without having to proceed against them in the ordinary court of law. The Mace in course of time came to represent the authority of the House. There is no Mace in most of the Indian legislatures. The Mace where in existence is merely decorative and does not carry any authority as it does in the House of Commons.[1]

The penal jurisdiction of the House of Commons is exercised in enforcing the attendance of persons by causing them to be arrested and brought before the House, and by punishing, if necessary, any disobedience. The civil power has to aid the officers of the House in enforcing the orders. The punishments which may be inflicted by the House of

[1] House of Commons Library Document no. 1.

Commons are, (a) reprimand and admonition, (b) fine, (c) imprisonment,[1] (d) suspension, and (e) expulsion. The period of imprisonment, however, cannot go beyond the session, and any person imprisoned by an order of the House of Commons, if not released earlier, must be released from custody on prorogation. When the breach of privilege or the alleged contempt is also an offence under the common law, the Attorney-General has in some cases been directed to prosecute the offender in the ordinary court.[2]

CODIFICATION OF PRIVILEGES

The question of codifying the privileges of Parliament has been raised occasionally and particularly by the Press Commission in its report in 1954.[3]

The Constitution has in clear terms conferred the powers, etc. of the House of Commons on the Indian legislatures. The powers and privileges of the House of Commons are well understood and the English people have managed without any legislation. If they have succeeded without any codification, there is no reason why the Indian legislatures should not also succeed without it. The Press Commission has raised two contentions in favour of codification: firstly, that conditions are different in India and the powers, etc. of the House of Commons cannot be engrafted in India without some modification; and secondly, that the privilege, etc. as conferred by Article 194 may conflict with other provisions of the Constitution, and the Press Commission has cited Article 19 and Article 22 with which Article 194 may be in conflict.

As to the first contention, it may be observed that the relevant point of time in which the contention that conditions in India are different and the privileges of the House of Commons cannot be adopted in India *in toto* should have

---

[1] The Rajasthan Assembly punished certain persons (strangers) who were found guilty of riotous behaviour to imprisonment for 15 days and directed the persons to be sent to the Central Jail; Rajasthan Assembly Proceedings, 10 Apr. 1956. See also M. P. Proceedings April 2, 1960; *Ibid*, Aug. 3, 1962.

[2] C.J. 1889, 363; ibid. 1857, 355; ibid. 1860, 258; ibid. 1866, 239.

[3] See also article on codification of the Law of Privilege by M. N. Kaul, Secretary, Lok Sabha, published in *Privilege Digest* vol. i, no. 1, Jan.-Mar. 1957, pp. 35-37.

been raised when the Constitution was framed. If the framers of the Constitution in their wisdom thought fit to confer on the Indian legislatures all the privileges of the House of Commons, they must be presumed to have taken into consideration all the factors and to have decided that the privileges of the House of Commons were the surest guide to go by. The Indian legislatures, of course, have been given the power to pass laws defining this privilege, but that provision is only permissive and does not compel the legislatures to pass any law unless actual necessity arises. The relation between the legislature, a political body and the public or the Press is liable to be adjusted as time goes on, and it would not be in the interests of the growth of a healthy relationship between them to frame rigid laws.

It is true that some legislatures have tended to be oversensitive, as stated by the Press Commission in para 1120. It is also true that the Press Comission has sometimes thought itself to be a privileged body like the courts and the legislatures, and has claimed higher rights than the general public can do. None of these positions is supportable, and it is believed that these would be adjusted in course of time if mutual goodwill and understanding prevail.

As regards the second contention, the passing of any law would not make the position any better. If the provision of the Constitution itself can be challenged, as it was in the *Blitz Case,* any law passed by a legislature would be liable to greater attacks on the ground of *ultra vires* and repugnance to the Constitution. Any legislation by a legislature would surely be of an inferior potency than the Constitutional provisions. If the position is left as it is, any conflict that may arise may be solved by the courts as was done in the case of *Blitz.* If the conferring of all the powers of the House of Commons upon the Indian legislatures by the Constitution has been of any avail, no amount of legislation can help them. No legislation can exhaustively define the circumstances in which a breach of privilege may occur. As regards the specific points raised about publication of reports, etc. the Press Commission seems to be of the opinion that the existing state of things has not in any way inconvenienced the Press. Even under the general law, the Press has to take some risk when they publish material which may be defamatory, seditious or likely to come under the purview of the Penal Code.

APPENDIX I

19.[1] (1) All citizens shall have the right—

(*a*) to freedom of speech and expression;

(*b*) to assemble peaceably and without arms;

(*c*) to form associations or unions;

(*d*) to move freely throughout the territory of India;

(*e*) to reside and settle in any part of the territory of India;

(*f*) to acquire, hold and dispose of property; and

(*g*) to practise any profession, or to carry on any occupation, trade or business.

(2) Nothing in sub-clause (*a*) of clause (1) shall affect the operation of any existing law, or prevent the State from making any law, in so far as such law imposes reasonable restrictions on the exercise of the right conferred by the said sub-clause in the interests of the sovereignty and integrity of India, the security of the State, friendly relations with foreign States, public order, decency or morality, or in relation to contempt of court, defamation or incitement to an offence.

(3) Nothing in sub-clause (*b*) of the said clause shall affect the operation of any existing law in so far as it imposes, or prevent the State from making any law imposing, in the interests of the sovereignty and integrity of India or public order, reasonable restrictions on the exercise of the right conferred by the said sub-clause.

(4) Nothing in sub-clause (*c*) of the said clause shall affect the operation of any existing law in so far as it imposes, or prevent

---

[1] In its application to the State of Jammu and Kashmir, for a period of ten years from the 14 May 1954, Art. 19 shall be subject to the following modifications—

(i) in clauses (3) and (4), after the words 'in the interests of', the words 'the security of the State or' shall be inserted;

(ii) in clause (5), for the words 'or for the protection of the interests of any Scheduled Tribe', the words 'or in the interests of the security of the State' shall be substituted; and

(iii) the following new clause shall be added, namely:—

(7) The words 'reasonable restrictions' occurring in clauses (2), (3), (4) and (5) shall be construed as meaning such restrictions as the appropriate Legislature deems reasonable.

the State from making any law imposing, in the interests of the sovereignty and integrity of India, public order or morality, reasonable restrictions on the exercise of the right conferred by the said sub-clause.

(5) Nothing in sub-clauses (*d*), (*e*) and (*f*) of the said clause shall affect the operation of any existing law in so far as it imposes, or prevent the State from making any law imposing, reasonable restrictions on the exercise of any of the rights conferred by the said sub-clauses either in the interests of the general public or for the protection of the interests of any Scheduled Tribe.

(6) Nothing in sub-clause (*g*) of the said clause shall affect the operation of any existing law in so far as it imposes, or prevent the State from making any law imposing, in the interests of the general public, reasonable restrictions on the exercise of the right conferred by the said sub-clause, and, in particular, nothing in the said sub-clause shall affect the operation of any existing law in so far as it relates to, or prevent the State from making any law relating to,—

(i) the professional or technical qualifications necessary for practising any profession or carrying on any occupation, trade or business; or

(ii) the carrying on by the State or by a corporation owned or controlled by the State, of any trade, business, industry or service, whether to the exclusion, complete or partial, of citizens or otherwise.

31.[1] (1) No person shall be deprived of his property save by authority of law.

(2) No property shall be compulsorily acquired or requisitioned save for a public purpose and save by authority of a law which provides for compensation for the property so acquired or requisitioned and either fixes the amount of the compensation or specifies the principles on which, and the manner in which, the compensation is to be determined and given, and no such

---

[1] In its application to the State of Jammu and Kashmir, in Art. 31, cls. (3), (4) and (6) shall be omitted and for cl. (5) the following clause shall be substituted, namely:—
'(5) Nothing in clause (2) shall affect—
(*a*) the provisions of any existing law; or
(*b*) the provisions of any law which the State may hereafter make—
(i) for the purpose of imposing or levying any tax or penalty; or
(ii) for the promotion of public health or the prevention of danger to life or property; or
(iii) with respect to property declared by law to be evacuee property.'

law shall be called in question in any court on the ground that the compensation provided by that law is not adequate.

(2A) Where a law does not provide for the transfer of the ownership or right to possession of any property to the State or to a corporation owned or controlled by the State, it shall not be deemed to provide for the compulsory acquisition or requisitioning of property, notwithstanding that it deprives any person of his property.

(3) No such law as is referred to in clause (2) made by the Legislature of a State shall have effect unless such law, having been reserved for the consideration of the President, has received his assent.

(4) If any Bill pending at the commencement of this Constitution in the Legislature of a State has, after it has been passed by such Legislature, been reserved for the consideration of the President and has received his assent, then, notwithstanding anything in this Constitution, the law so assented to shall not be called in question in any court on the ground that it contravenes the provisions of clause (2).

(5) Nothing in clause (2) shall affect—

(a) the provisions of any existing law other than a law to which the provisions of clause (6) apply; or

(b) the provisions of any law which the State may hereafter make—

(i) for the purpose of imposing or levying any tax or penalty; or

(ii) for the promotion of public health or the prevention of danger to life or property; or

(iii) in pursuance of any agreement entered into between the Government of the Dominion of India or the Government of India and the Government of any other country, or otherwise, with respect to property declared by law to be evacuee property.

(6) Any law of the State enacted not more than eighteen months before the commencement of this Constitution may within three months from such commencement be submitted to the President for his certification; and thereupon, if the President by public notification so certifies, it shall not be called in question in any court on the ground that it contravenes the provisions of clause (2) of this article or has contravened the provisions of sub-section (2) of section 299 of the Government of India Act, 1935.

75. (1) The Prime Minister shall be appointed by the President

and the other Ministers shall be appointed by the President on the advice of the Prime Minister.

(2) The Ministers shall hold office during the pleasure of the President.

(3) The Council of Ministers shall be collectively responsible to the House of the People.

(4) Before a Minister enters upon his office, the President shall administer to him the oaths of office and of secrecy according to the forms set out for the purpose in the Third Schedule.

(5) A Minister who for any period of six consecutive months is not a member of either House of Parliament shall at the expiration of that period cease to be a Minister.

(6) The salaries and allowances of Ministers shall be such as Parliament may from time to time by law determine and, until Parliament so determines, shall be as specified in the Second Schedule.

79. There shall be a Parliament for the Union which shall consist of the President and two Houses to be known respectively as the Council of States and the House of the People.

80. (1) The Council of States shall consist of—

(a) twelve members to be nominated by the President in accordance with the provisions of clause (3); and

(b) not more than two hundred and thirty-eight representatives of the States and of the Union territories.

(2) The allocation of seats in the Council of States to be filled by representatives of the States and of the Union territories shall be in accordance with the provisions in that behalf contained in the Fourth Schedule.

(3) The members to be nominated by the President under sub-clause (a) of clause (1) shall consist of persons having special knowledge or practical experience in respect of such matters as the following, namely:—

Literature, science, art and social service.

(4) The representatives of each State in the Council of States shall be elected by the elected members of the Legislative Assembly of the State in accordance with the system of proportional representation by means of the single transferable vote.

(5) The representatives of the Union territories in the Council of States shall be chosen in such manner as Parliament may by law prescribe.

81.† (1) Subject to the provisions of Article 331, the House of the People shall consist of—

(*a*) not more than five hundred members chosen by direct election from territorial constituencies in the States; and

(*b*) not more than twenty-five members to represent the Union territories, chosen in such manner as Parliament may by law provide.

(2) For the purposes of sub-clause (*a*) of clause (1),—

(*a*) there shall be allotted to each State a number of seats in the House of the People in such manner that the ratio between that number and the population of the State is, so far as practicable, the same for all States; and

(*b*) each State shall be divided into territorial constituencies in such manner that the ratio between the population of each constituency and the number of seats allotted to it is, so far as practicable, the same throughout the State.

(3) In this article, the expression 'population' means the population as ascertained at the last preceding census of which the relevant figures have been published.

83. (1) The Council of States shall not be subject to dissolution, but as nearly as possible one-third of the members thereof shall retire as soon as may be on the expiration of every second year in accordance with the provisions made in that behalf by Parliament by law.

(2) The House of the People, unless sooner dissolved, shall continue for five years from the date appointed for its first meeting and no longer and the expiration of the said period of five years shall operate as a dissolution of the House:

† NOTE.—Paragraph 2 of the Constitution (Removal of Difficulties) Order No. VIII provides as follows:—

For the period during which the tribal areas specified in Part B of the Table appended to paragraph 20 of the Sixth Schedule to the Constitution or any parts thereof are administered by the President by virtue of sub-paragraph (2) of paragraph 18 of the said Schedule, the Constitution of India shall have effect subject to the following adaptations:—

In Article 81,—

(*a*) in sub-clause (*b*) of cl. (1), after the words 'Union territories', the words, letter and figures 'and the tribal areas specified in Part B of the Table appended to paragraph 20 of the Sixth Schedule' shall be inserted; and

(*b*) to cl. (2), the following proviso shall be added, namely:

'Provided that the constituencies into which the State of Assam is divided shall not comprise the tribal areas specified in Part B of the Table appended to paragraph 20 of the Sixth Schedule.'

Art. 81 shall apply to the State of Jammu and Kashmir subject to the modification that the representatives of the State in the House of the People shall be appointed by the President on the recommendation of the Legislature of the State.

Provided that the said period may, while a Proclamation of Emergency is in operation, be extended by Parliament by law for a period not exceeding one year at a time and not extending in any case beyond a period of six months after the Proclamation has ceased to operate.

84. A person shall not be qualified to be chosen to fill a seat in Parliament unless he—

(a) is a citizen of India, and makes and subscribes before some person authorized in that behalf by the Election Commission an oath or affirmation according to the form set out for the purpose in the Third Schedule;

(b) is, in the case of a seat in the Council of States, not less than thirty years of age and, in the case of a seat in the House of the People, not less than twenty-five years of age; and

(c) possesses such other qualifications as may be prescribed in that behalf by or under any law made by Parliament.

85. (1) The President shall from time to time summon each House of Parliament to meet at such time and place as he thinks fit, but six months shall not intervene between its last sitting in one session and the date appointed for its first sitting in the next session.

(2) The President may from time to time—

(a) prorogue the Houses or either House;

(b) dissolve the House of the People.

87. (1) At the commencement of the first session after each general election to the House of the People and at the commencement of the first session of each year the President shall address both Houses of Parliament assembled together and inform Parliament of the causes of its summons.

(2) Provision shall be made by the rules regulating the procedure of either House for the allotment of time for discussion of the matters referred to in such address.

88. Every Minister and the Attorney-General of India shall have the right to speak in, and otherwise to take part in the proceedings of, either House, any joint sitting of the Houses, and any committee of Parliament of which he may be named a member, but shall not by virtue of this article be entitled to vote.

89. (1) The Vice-President of India shall be *ex-officio* Chairman of the Council of States.

(2) The Council of States shall, as soon as may be, choose a

member of the Council to be Deputy Chairman thereof and, so often as the office of Deputy Chairman becomes vacant, the Council shall choose another member to be Deputy Chairman thereof.

90. A member holding office as Deputy Chairman of the Council of States—

(a) shall vacate his office if he ceases to be a member of the Council;

(b) may at any time, by writing under his hand addressed to the Chairman, resign his office; and

(c) may be removed from his office by a resolution of the Council passed by a majority of all the then members of the Council:

Provided that no resolution for the purpose of clause (c) shall be moved unless at least fourteen days' notice has been given of the intention to move the resolution.

92. (1) At any sitting of the Council of States, while any resolution for the removal of the Vice-President from his office is under consideration, the Chairman, or while any resolution for the removal of the Deputy Chairman from his office is under consideration, the Deputy Chairman, shall not, though he is present, preside, and the provisions of clause (2) of article 91 shall apply in relation to every such sitting as they apply in relation to a sitting from which the Chairman, or, as the case may be, the Deputy Chairman, is absent.

(2) The Chairman shall have the right to speak in, and otherwise to take part in the proceedings of, the Council of States while any resolution for the removal of the Vice-President from his office is under consideration in the Council, but, notwithstanding anything in article 100, shall not be entitled to vote at all on such resolution or on any other matter during such proceedings.

93. The House of the People shall, as soon as may be, choose two members of the House to be respectively Speaker and Deputy Speaker thereof and, so often as the office of Speaker or Deputy Speaker becomes vacant, the House shall choose another member to be Speaker or Deputy Speaker, as the case may be.

94. A member holding office as Speaker or Deputy Speaker of the House of the People—

(a) shall vacate his office if he ceases to be a member of the House of the People;

(b) may at any time, by writing under his hand addressed, if such member is the Speaker, to the Deputy Speaker, and if such member is the Deputy Speaker, to the Speaker, resign his office; and

27

(c) may be removed from his office by a resolution of the House of the People passed by a majority of all the then members of the House:

Provided that no resolution for the purpose of clause (c) shall be moved unless at least fourteen days' notice has been given of the intention to move the resolution:

Provided further that, whenever the House of the People is dissolved, the Speaker shall not vacate his office until immediately before the first meeting of the House of the People after the dissolution.

95. (1) While the office of Speaker is vacant, the duties of the office shall be performed by the Deputy Speaker or, if the office of Deputy Speaker is also vacant, by such member of the House of the People as the President may appoint for the purpose.

(2) During the absence of the Speaker from any sitting of the House of the People the Deputy Speaker or, if he is also absent, such person as may be determined by the rules of procedure of the House, or, if no such person is present, such other person as may be determined by the House, shall act as Speaker.

96. (1) At any sitting of the House of the People, while any resolution for the removal of the Speaker from his office is under consideration, the Speaker, or while any resolution for the removal of the Deputy Speaker from his office is under consideration, the Deputy Speaker, shall not, though he is present, preside, and the provisions of clause (2) of article 95 shall apply in relation to every such sitting as they apply in relation to a sitting from which the Speaker, or, as the case may be, the Deputy Speaker, is absent.

(2) The Speaker shall have the right to speak in, and otherwise to take part in the proceedings of, the House of the People while any resolution for his removal from office is under consideration in the House and shall, notwithstanding anything in article 100, be entitled to vote only in the first instance on such resolution or on any other matter during such proceedings but not in the case of an equality of votes.

98. (1) Each House of Parliament shall have a separate secretarial staff:

Provided that nothing in this clause shall be construed as preventing the creation of posts common to both Houses of Parliament.

(2) Parliament may by law regulate the recruitment, and the conditions of service of persons appointed, to the secretarial staff of either House of Parliament.

(3) Until provision is made by Parliament under clause (2), the President may, after consultation with the Speaker of the House of the People or the Chairman of the Council of States, as the case may be, make rules regulating the recruitment and the conditions of service of persons appointed to the secretarial staff of the House of the People or the Council of States, and any rules so made shall have effect subject to the provisions of any law made under the said clause.

99. Every member of either House of Parliament shall, before taking his seat, make and subscribe before the President, or some person appointed in that behalf by him, an oath or affirmation according to the form set out for the purpose in the Third Schedule.

101. (1) No person shall be a member of both Houses of Parliament and provision shall be made by Parliament by law for the vacation by a person who is chosen a member of both Houses of his seat in one House or the other.

(2) No person shall be a member both of Parliament and of a House of the Legislature of a State, and if a person is chosen a member both of Parliament and of a House of the Legislature of a State, then, at the expiration of such period as may be specified in rules[1] made by the President, that person's seat in Parliament shall become vacant, unless he has previously resigned his seat in the Legislature of the State.

(3) If a member of either House of Parliament—

(a) becomes subject to any of the disqualifications mentioned in clause (1) of Article 102; or

(b) resigns his seat by writing under his hand addressed to the Chairman or the Speaker, as the case may be, his seat shall thereupon become vacant.

(4) If for a period of sixty days a member of either House of Parliament is without permission of the House absent from all meetings thereof, the House may delcare his seat vacant:

Provided that in computing the said period of sixty days no account shall be taken of any period during which the House is prorogued or is adjourned for more than four consecutive days.

102. (1) A person shall be disqualified for being chosen as, and for being, a member of either House of Parliament—

---

[1] See the Prohibition of Simultaneous Membership Rules, 1950, published with the Ministry of Law Notification No. F. 46/50-C, 26 Jan. 1950, *Gazette of India Extraordinary*, p. 678.

(*a*) if he holds any office of profit under the Government of India or the Government of any State, other than an office declared by Parliament by law not to disqualify its holder;

(*b*) if he is of unsound mind and stands so declared by a competent court;

(*c*) if he is an undischarged insolvent;

(*d*) if he is not a citizen of India, or has voluntarily acquired the citizenship of a foreign State, or is under any acknowledgement of allegiance or adherence to a foreign State;

(*e*) if he is so disqualified by or under any law made by Parliament.

(2) For the purposes of this article a person shall not be deemed to hold an office of profit under the Government of India or the government of any State by reason only that he is a Minister either for the Union or for such State.

103. (1) If any question arises as to whether a member of either House of Parliament has become subject to any of the disqualifications mentioned in clause (1) of Article 102, the question shall be referred for the decision of the President and his decision shall be final.

(2) Before giving any decision on any such question, the President shall obtain the opinion of the Election Commission and shall act according to such opinion.

104. If a person sits or votes as a member of either House of Parliament before he has complied with the requirements of Article 99, or when he knows that he is not qualified or that he is disqualified for membership thereof, or that he is prohibited from so doing by the provisions of any law made by Parliament, he shall be liable in respect of each day on which he so sits or votes to a penalty of five hundred rupees to be recovered as a debt due to the Union.

105. (1) Subject to the provisions of this Constitution and to the rules and standing orders regulating the procedure of Parliament, there shall be freedom of speech in Parliament.

(2) No member of Parliament shall be liable to any proceedings in any court in respect of anything said or any vote given by him in Parliament or any committee thereof, and no person shall be so liable in respect of the publication by or under the authority of either House of Parliament of any report, paper, votes or proceedings.

(3) In other respects, the powers, privileges and immunities of each House of Parliament, and of the members and the committees

of each House, shall be such as may from time to time be defined by Parliament by law, and, until so defined, shall be those of the House of Commons of the Parliament of the United Kingdom, and of its members and committees, at the commencement of this Constitution.

(4) The provisions of clauses (1), (2) and (3) shall apply in relation to persons who by virtue of this Constitution have the right to speak in, and otherwise to take part in the proceedings of, a House of Parliament or any committee thereof as they apply in relation to members of Parliament.

107. (1) Subject to the provisions of Articles 109 and 117 with respect to Money Bills and other financial Bills, a Bill may originate in either House of Parliament.

(2) Subject to the provisions of Articles 108 and 109, a Bill shall not be deemed to have been passed by the Houses of Parliament unless it has been agreed to by both Houses, either without amendment or with such amendments only as are agreed to by both Houses.

(3) A Bill pending in Parliament shall not lapse by reason of the prorogation of the Houses.

(4) A Bill pending in the Council of States which has not been passed by the House of the People shall not lapse on a dissolution of the House of the People.

(5) A Bill which is pending in the House of the People, or which having been passed by the House of the People is pending in the Council of States, shall, subject to the provisions of Article 108, lapse on a dissolution of the House of the People.

108. (1) If after a Bill has been passed by one House and transmitted to the other House—

(a) the Bill is rejected by the other House; or

(b) the Houses have finally disagreed as to the amendments to be made in the Bill; or

(c) more than six months elapse from the date of the reception of the Bill by the other House without the Bill being passed by it, the President may, unless the Bill has lapsed by reason of a dissolution of the House of the People, notify to the Houses by message if they are sitting or by public notification if they are not sitting, his intention to summon them to meet in a joint sitting for the purpose of deliberating and voting on the Bill:

Provided that nothing in this clause shall apply to a Money Bill.

(2) In reckoning any such period of six months as is referred to in clause (1), no account shall be taken of any period during which the House referred to in sub-clause (*c*) of that clause is prorogued or adjourned for more than four consecutive days.

(3) Where the President has under clause (1) notified his intention of summoning the Houses to meet in a joint sitting, neither House shall proceed further with the Bill, but the President may at any time after the date of his notification summon the Houses to meet in a joint sitting for the purpose specified in the notification and, if he does so, the Houses shall meet accordingly.

(4) If at the joint sitting of the two Houses the Bill, with such amendments, if any, as are agreed to in joint sitting, is passed by a majority of the total number of members of both Houses present and voting, it shall be deemed for the purposes of this Constitution to have been passed by both Houses:

Provided that at a joint sitting—

(*a*) if the Bill, having been passed by one House, has not been passed by the other House with amendments and returned to the House in which it originated, no amendment shall be proposed to the Bill other than such amendments (if any) as are made necessary by the delay in the passage of the Bill;

(*b*) if the Bill has been so passed and returned, only such amendments as aforesaid shall be proposed to the Bill and such other amendments as are relevant to the matters with respect to which the Houses have not agreed; and the decision of the person presiding as to the amendments which are admissible under this clause shall be final.

(5) A joint sitting may be held under this article and a Bill passed thereat, notwithstanding that a dissolution of the House of the People has intervened since the President notified his intention to summon the Houses to meet therein.

109. (1) A Money Bill shall not be introduced in the Council of States.

(2) After a Money Bill has been passed by the House of the People it shall be transmitted to the Council of States for its recommendations and the Council of States shall within a period of fourteen days from the date of its receipt of the Bill return the Bill to the House of the People with its recommendations and the House of the People may thereupon either accept or reject all or any of the recommendations of the Council of States.

(3) If the House of the People accepts any of the recommendations of the Council of States, the Money Bill shall be deemed to have been passed by both Houses with the amendments recommended by the Council of States and accepted by the House of the People.

(4) If the House of the People does not accept any of the recommendations of the Council of States, the Money Bill shall be deemed to have been passed by both Houses in the form in which it was passed by the House of the People without any of the amendments recommended by the Council of States.

(5) If a Money Bill passed by the House of the People and transmitted to the Council of States for its recommendations is not returned to the House of the People within the said period of fourteen days, it shall be deemed to have been passed by both Houses at the expiration of the said period in the form in which it was passed by the House of the People.

110. (1) For the purposes of this Chapter, a Bill shall be deemed to be a Money Bill if it contains only provisions dealing with all or any of the following matters, namely:

(a) the imposition, abolition, remission, alteration or regulation of any tax;

(b) the regulation of the borrowing of money or the giving of any guarantee by the Government of India, or the amendment of the law with respect to any financial obligations undertaken or to be undertaken by the Government of India;

(c) the custody of the Consolidated Fund or the Contingency Fund of India, the payment of moneys into or the withdrawal of moneys from any such Fund;

(d) the appropriation of moneys out of the Consolidated Fund of India;

(e) the declaring of any expenditure to be expenditure charged on the Consolidated Fund of India or the increasing of the amount of any such expenditure;

(f) the receipt of money on account of the Consolidated Fund of India or the public account of India or the custody or issue of such money or the audit of the accounts of the Union or of a State; or

(g) any matter incidental to any of the matters specified in sub-clauses (a) to (f).

(2) A Bill shall not be deemed to be a Money Bill by reason only that it provides for the imposition of fines or other pecuniary penalties, or for the demand or payment of fees for licences or fees

for services rendered, or by reason that it provides for the imposition, abolition, remission, alteration or regulation of any tax by any local authority or body for local purposes.

(3) If any question arises whether a Bill is a Money Bill or not, the decision of the Speaker of the House of the People thereon shall be final.

(4) There shall be endorsed on every Money Bill when it is transmitted to the Council of States under Article 109, and when it is presented to the President for assent under Article 111, the certificate of the Speaker of the House of People signed by him that it is a Money Bill.

111. When a Bill has been passed by the Houses of Parliament, it shall be presented to the President, and the President shall declare either that he assents to the Bill, or that he withholds assent therefrom:

Provided that the President may, as soon as possible after the presentation to him of a Bill for assent, return the Bill if it is not a Money Bill to the Houses with a message requesting that they will reconsider the Bill or any specified provisions thereof and, in particular, will consider the desirability of introducing any such amendments as he may recommend in his message, and when a Bill is so returned, the Houses shall reconsider the Bill accordingly, and if the Bill is passed again by the Houses with or without amendment and presented to the President for assent, the President shall not withhold assent therefrom.

112. (1) The President shall in respect of every financial year cause to be laid before both the Houses of Parliament a statement of the estimated receipts and expenditure of the Government of India for that year, in this Part referred to as the 'annual financial statement'.

(2) The estimates of expenditure embodied in the annual financial statement shall show separately—

(a) the sums required to meet expenditure described by this Constitution as expenditure charged upon the Consolidated Fund of India; and

(b) the sums required to meet other expenditure proposed to be made from the Consolidated Fund of India,

and shall distinguish expenditure on revenue account from other expenditure.

(3) The following expenditure shall be expenditure charged on the Consolidated Fund of India:

(*a*) the emoluments and allowances of the President and other expenditure relating to his office;

(*b*) the salaries and allowances of the Chairman and the Deputy Chairman of the Council of States and the Speaker and the Deputy Speaker of the House of the People;

(*c*) debt charges for which the Government of India is liable including interest, sinking fund charges and redemption charges, and other expenditure relating to the raising of loans and the service and redemption of debt;

(*d*) (i) the salaries, allowances and pensions payable to or in respect of Judges of the Supreme Court;

(ii) the pensions payable to or in respect of Judges of the Federal Court;

(iii) the pensions payable to or in respect of Judges of any High Court which exercises jurisdiction in relation to any area included in the territory of India or which at any time before the commencement of this Constitution exercised jurisdiction in relation to any area included in a Governor's Province of the Dominion of India;

(*e*) the salary, allowances and pension payable to or in respect of the Comptroller and Auditor-General of India;

(*f*) any sums required to satisfy any judgment, decree or award of any court or arbitration tribunal;

(*g*) any other expenditure declared by this Constitution or by Parliament by law to be so charged.

113. (1) So much of the estimates as relates to expenditure charged upon the Consolidated Fund of India shall not be submitted to the vote of Parliament, but nothing in this clause shall be construed as preventing the discussion in either House of Parliament of any of those estimates.

(2) So much of the said estimates as relates to other expenditure shall be submitted in the form of demands for grants to the House of the People, and the House of the People shall have power to assent, or to refuse to assent, to any demand, or to assent to any demand subject to a reduction of the amount specified therein.

(3) No demand for a grant shall be made except on the recommendation of the President.

114. (1) As soon as may be after the grants under Article 113 have been made by the House of the People, there shall be introduced a Bill to provide for the appropriation out of the Consolidated Fund of India of all moneys required to meet—

(*a*) the grants so made by the House of the People; and

(*b*) the expenditure charged on the Consolidated Fund of India but not exceeding in any case the amount shown in the statement previously laid before Parliament.

(2) No amendment shall be proposed to any such Bill in either House of Parliament which will have the effect of varying the amount or altering the destination of any grant so made or of varying the amount of any expenditure charged on the Consolidated Fund of India, and the decision of the person presiding as to whether an amendment is inadmissible under this clause shall be final.

(3) Subject to the provisions of Articles 115 and 116, no money shall be withdrawn from the Consolidated Fund of India except under appropriation made by law passed in accordance with the provisions of this Article.

115. (1) The President shall—

(*a*) if the amount authorized by any law made in accordance with the provisions of Article 114 to be expended for a particular service for the current financial year is found to be insufficient for the purposes of that year or when a need has arisen during the current financial year for supplementary or additional expenditure upon some new service not contemplated in the annual financial statement for that year; or

(*b*) if any money has been spent on any service during a financial year in excess of the amount granted for that service and for that year;

cause to be laid before both the Houses of Parliament another statement showing the estimated amount of that expenditure or cause to be presented to the House of the People a demand for such excess, as the case may be.

(2) The provisions of Articles 112, 113 and 114 shall have effect in relation to any such statement and expenditure or demand and also to any law to be made authorizing the appropriation of·moneys out of the Consolidated Fund of India to meet such expenditure or the grant in respect of such demand as they have effect in relation to the annual financial statement and the expenditure mentioned therein or to a demand for a grant and the law to be made for the authorization of appropriation of moneys out of the Consolidated Fund of India to meet such expenditure or grant.

116. (1) Notwithstanding anything in the foregoing provisions of this Chapter, the House of the People shall have power—

(*a*) to make any grant in advance in respect of the estimated expenditure for a part of any financial year pending the completion of the procedure prescribed in Article 113 for the voting of such grant and the passing of the law in accordance with the provisions of Article 114 in relation to that expenditure;

(*b*) to make a grant for meeting an unexpected demand upon the resources of India when on account of the magnitude or the indefinite character of the service the demand cannot be stated with the details ordinarily given in an annual financial statement;

(*c*) to make an exceptional grant which forms no part of the current service of any financial year;

and Parliament shall have power to authorize by law the withdrawal of moneys from the Consolidated Fund of India for the purposes for which the said grants are made.

(2) The provisions of Articles 113 and 114 shall have effect in relation to the making of any grant under clause (1) and to any law to be made under that clause as they have effect in relation to the making of a grant with regard to any expenditure mentioned in the annual financial statement and the law to be made for the authorization of appropriation of moneys out of the Consolidated Fund of India to meet such expenditure.

117. (1) A Bill or amendment making provision for any of the matters specified in sub-clauses (*a*) to (*f*) of clause (1) of Article 110 shall not be introduced or moved except on the recommendation of the President and a Bill making such provision shall not be introduced in the Council of States:

Provided that no recommendation shall be required under this clause for the moving of an amendment making provision for the reduction or abolition of any tax.

(2) A Bill or amendment shall not be deemed to make provision for any of the matters aforesaid by reason only that it provides for the imposition of fines or other pecuniary penalties, or for the demand or payment of fees for licences or fees for services rendered, or by reason that it provides for the imposition, abolition, remission, alteration or regulation of any tax by any local authority or body for local purposes.

(3) A Bill which, if enacted and brought into operation, would involve expenditure from the Consolidated Fund of India shall not be passed by either House of Parliament unless the President has recommended to that House the consideration of the Bill.

121. No discussion shall take place in Parliament with respect to the conduct of any Judge of the Supreme Court or of a High Court in the discharge of his duties except upon a motion for presenting an address to the President praying for the removal of the Judge as hereinafter provided.

122. (1) The validity of any proceedings in Parliament shall not be called in question on the ground of any alleged irregularity of procedure.

(2) No officer or member of Parliament in whom powers are vested by or under this Constitution for regulating procedure or the conduct of business, or for maintaining order, in Parliament shall be subject to the jurisdiction of any court in respect of the exercise by him of those powers.

139. Parliament may by law confer on the Supreme Court power to issue directions, orders or writs, including writs in the nature of habeas corpus, mandamus, prohibition, quo warranto and certiorari or any of them, for any purposes other than those mentioned in clause (2) of Article 32.

140. Parliament may by law make provision for conferring upon the Supreme Court such Supplemental powers not inconsistent with any of the provisions of this Constitution as may appear to be necessary or desirable for the purpose of enabling the Court more effectively to exercise the jurisdiction conferred upon it by or under this Constitution.

148. (1) There shall be a Comptroller and Auditor-General of India who shall be appointed by the President by warrant under his hand and seal and shall only be removed from office in like manner and on the like grounds as a Judge of the Supreme Court.

(2) Every person appointed to be the Comptroller and Auditor-General of India shall, before he enters upon his office, make and subscribe before the President, or some person appointed in that behalf by him, an oath or affirmation according to the form set out for the purpose in the Third Schedule.

(3) The salary and other conditions of service of the Comptroller and Auditor-General shall be such as may be determined by Parliament by law and, until they are so determined, shall be as specified in the Second Schedule:

Provided that neither the salary of a Comptroller and Auditor-General nor his rights in respect of leave of absence, pension or age of retirement shall be varied to his disadvantage after his appointment.

(4) The Comptroller and Auditor-General shall not be eligible for further office either under the Government of India or under the Government of any State after he has ceased to hold his office.

(5) Subject to the provisions of this Constitution and of any law made by Parliament, the conditions of service of persons serving in the Indian Audit and Accounts Department and the administrative powers of the Comptroller and Auditor-General shall be such as may be prescribed by rules made by the President after consultation with the Comptroller and Auditor-General.

(6) The administrative expenses of the office of the Comptroller and Auditor-General, including all salaries, allowances and pensions payable to or in respect of persons serving in that office, shall be charged upon the Consolidated Fund of India.

149. The Comptroller and Auditor-General shall perform such duties and exercise such powers in relation to the accounts of the Union and of the States and of any other authority or body as may be prescribed by or under any law made by Parliament and, until provision in that behalf is so made, shall perform such duties and exercise such powers in relation to the accounts of the Union and of the States as were conferred on or exercisable by the Auditor-General of India immediately before the commencement of this Constitution in relation to the accounts of the Dominion of India and the Provinces respectively.

150. The accounts of the Union and of the States shall be kept in such form as the Comptroller and Auditor-General of India may, with the approval of the President, prescribe.

151. (1) The reports of the Comptroller and Auditor-General of India relating to the accounts of the Union shall be submitted to the President, who shall cause them to be laid before each House of Parliament.

(2) The reports of the Comptroller and Auditor-General of India relating to the accounts of a State shall be submitted to the Governor of the State, who shall cause them to be laid before the Legislature of the State.

164.[1] (1) The Chief Minister shall be appointed by the Governor and the other Ministers shall be appointed by the Governor on the advice of the Chief Minister, and the Ministers shall hold

[1] Art. 164 shall not apply to the State of Jammu and Kashmir.

office during the pleasure of the Governor:

Provided that in the States of Bihar, Madhya Pradesh and Orissa, there shall be a Minister in charge of tribal welfare who may in addition be in charge of the welfare of the Scheduled Castes and backward classes or any other work.

(2) The Council of Ministers shall be collectively responsible to the Legislative Assembly of the State.

(3) Before a Minister enters upon his office, the Governor shall administer to him the oaths of office and of secrecy according to the forms set out for the purpose in the Third Schedule.

(4) A Minister who for any period of six consecutive months is not a member of the Legislature of the State shall at the expiration of that period cease to be a Minister.

(5) The salaries and allowances of Ministers shall be such as the Legislature of the State may from time to time by law determine and, until the Legislature of the State so determines, shall be as specified in the Second Schedule.

168.[1] (1) For every State there shall be a Legislature which shall consist of the Governor, and

(a) in the States of Andhra Pradesh, Bihar, Madhya Pradesh, Madras, Maharashtra, Mysore, Punjab, Uttar Pradesh and West Bengal, two Houses;

(b) in other States, one House.

(2) Where there are two Houses of the Legislature of a State, one shall be known as the Legislative Council and the other as the Legislative Assembly, and where there is only one House, it shall be known as the Legislative Assembly.

169.[1] (1) Notwithstanding anything in Article 168, Parliament may by law provide for the abolition of the Legislative Council of a State having such a Council or for the creation of such a Council in a State having no such Council, if the Legislative Assembly of the State passes a resolution to that effect by a majority of the total membership of the Assembly and by a majority of not less than two-thirds of the members of the Assembly present and voting.

(2) Any law referred to in clause (1) shall contain such provisions for the amendment of this Constitution as may be necessary to give effect to the provisions of the law and may also contain such supplemental, incidental and consequential provisions as Parliament may deem necessary.

[1] Arts. 168 and 169 shall not apply to the State of Jammu and Kashmir.

(3) No such law as aforesaid shall be deemed to be an amendment of this Constitution for the purposes of Article 368.

171.[1] (1) The total number of members in the Legislative Council of a State having such a Council shall not exceed one-third of the total number of members in the Legislative Assembly of that State:

Provided that the total number of members in the Legislative Council of a State shall in no case be less than forty.

(2) Until Parliament by law otherwise provides, the composition of the Legislative Council of a State shall be as provided in clause (3).

(3) Of the total number of members of the Legislative Council of a State—

(a) as nearly as may be, one-third shall be elected by electorates consisting of members of municipalities, district boards and such other local authorities in the State as Parliament may by law specify;

(b) as nearly as may be, one-twelfth shall be elected by electorates consisting of persons residing in the State who have been for at least three years graduates of any university in the territory of India or have been for at least three years in possession of qualifications prescribed by or under any law made by Parliament as equivalent to that of a graduate of any such university;

(c) as nearly as may be, one-twelfth shall be elected by electorates consisting of persons who have been for at least three years engaged in teaching in such educational institutions within the State, not lower in standard than that of a secondary school, as may be prescribed by or under any law made by Parliament;

(d) as nearly as may be, one-third shall be elected by the members of the Legislative Assembly of the State from amongst persons who are not members of the Assembly;

(e) the remainder shall be nominated by the Governor in accordance with the provisions of clause (5).

(4) The members to be elected under sub-clauses (a), (b) and (c) of clause (3) shall be chosen in such territorial constituencies as may be prescribed by or under any law made by Parliament, and the elections under the said sub-clauses and under sub-clause (d) of the said clause shall be held in accordance with the system of proportional representation by means of the single transferable vote.

(5) The members to be nominated by the Governor under sub-

[1] Art. 171 shall not apply to the State of Jammu and Kashmir.

clause (*e*) of clause (3) shall consist of persons having special knowledge or practical experience in respect of such matters as the following, namely:—

Literature, science, art, co-operative movement and social service.

172.[1] (1) Every Legislative Assembly of every State, unless sooner dissolved, shall continue for five years from the date appointed for its first meeting and no longer and the expiration of the said period of five years shall operate as a dissolution of the Assembly:

Provided that the said period may, while a Proclamation of Emergency is in operation, be extended by Parliament by law for a period not exceeding one year at a time and not extending in any case beyond a period of six months after the Proclamation has ceased to operate.

(2) The Legislative Council of a State shall not be subject to dissolution, but as nearly as possible one-third of the members thereof shall retire as soon as may be on the expiration of every second year in accordance with the provisions made in that behalf by Parliament by law.

173.[1] A person shall not be qualified to be chosen to fill a seat in the Legislature of a State unless he—

(*a*) is a citizen of India, and makes and subscribes before some person authorized in that behalf by the Election Commission an oath or affirmation according to the form set out for the purpose in the Third Schedule;

(*b*) is, in the case of a seat in the Legislative Assembly, not less than twenty-five years of age and, in the case of a seat in the Legislative Council, not less than thirty years of age; and

(*c*) possesses such other qualifications as may be prescribed in that behalf by or under any law made by Parliament.

174.[1] (1) The Governor shall from time to time summon the House or each House of the Legislature of the State to meet at such time and place as he thinks fit, but six months shall not intervene between its last sitting in one session and the date appointed for its first sitting in the next session.

(2) The Governor may from time to time—

(*a*) prorogue the House or either House;

(*b*) dissolve the Legislative Assembly.

176.[1] (1) At the commencement of the first session after each

[1] Arts. 172, 173, 174 and 176 shall not apply to the State of Jammu and Kashmir.

general election to the Legislative Assembly and at the commencement of the first session of each year, the Governor shall address the Legislative Assembly or, in the case of a State having a Legislative Council, both Houses assembled together and inform the Legislature of the causes of its summons .

(2) Provision shall be made by the rules regulating the procedure of the House or either House for the allotment of time for discussion of the matters referred to in such address.

177.[1] Every Minister and the Advocate-General for a State shall have the right to speak in, and otherwise to take part in the proceedings of, the Legislative Assembly of the State or, in the case of a State having a Legislative Council, both Houses, and to speak in, and otherwise to take part in the proceedings of, any committee of the Legislature of which he may be named a member, but shall not, by virtue of this article, be entitled to vote.

178.[1] Every Legislative Assembly of a State shall, as soon as may be, choose two members of the Assembly to be respectively Speaker and Deputy Speaker thereof and, so often as the office of Speaker or Deputy Speaker becomes vacant, the Assembly shall choose another member to be Speaker or Deputy Speaker, as the case may be.

179.[1] A member holding office as Speaker or Deputy Speaker of an Assembly—

(a) shall vacate his office if he ceases to be a member of the Assembly;

(b) may at any time by writing under his hand addressed, if such member is the Speaker, to the Deputy Speaker, and if such member is the Deputy Speaker, to the Speaker, resign his office; and

(c) may be removed from his office by a resolution of the Assembly passed by a majority of all the then members of the Assembly:

Provided that no resolution for the purpose of clause (c) shall be moved unless at least fourteen days' notice has been given of the intention to move the resolution:

Provided further that, whenever the Assembly is dissolved, the Speaker shall not vacate his office until immediately before the first meeting of the Assembly after the dissolution.

180.[1] (1) While the office of Speaker is vacant, the duties of

[1] Arts. 177, 178, 179 and 180 shall not apply to the State of Jammu and Kashmir.

28

the office shall be performed by the Deputy Speaker or, if the office of Deputy Speaker is also vacant, by such member of the Assembly as the Governor may appoint for the purpose.

(2) During the absence of the Speaker from any sitting of the Assembly the Deputy Speaker or, if he is also absent, such person as may be determined by the rules of procedure of the Assembly, or, if no such person is present, such other person as may be determined by the Assembly, shall act as Speaker.

181.[1] (1) At any sitting of the Legislative Assembly, while any resolution for the removal of the Speaker from his office is under consideration, the Speaker, or while any resolution for the removal of the Deputy Speaker from his office is under consideration, the Deputy Speaker, shall not, though he is present, preside, and the provisions of clause (2) of Article 180 shall apply in relation to every such sitting as they apply in relation to a sitting from which the Speaker or, as the case may be, the Deputy Speaker, is absent.

(2) The Speaker shall have the right to speak in, and otherwise to take part in the proceedings of, the Legislative Assembly while any resolution for his removal from office is under consideration in the Assembly and shall, notwithstanding anything in Article 189, be entitled to vote only in the first instance on such resolution or on any other matter during such proceedings but not in the case of an equality of votes.

182.[1] The Legislative Council of every State having such Council shall, as soon as may be, choose two members of the Council to be respectively Chairman and Deputy Chairman thereof and, so often as the office of Chairman or Deputy Chairman becomes vacant, the Council shall choose another member to be Chairman or Deputy Chairman, as the case may be.

183.[1] A member holding office as Chairman or Deputy Chairman of a Legislative Council—

(a) shall vacate his office if he ceases to be a member of the Council;

(b) may at any time by writing under his hand addressed, if such member is the Chairman, to the Deputy Chairman, and if such member is the Deputy Chairman, to the Chairman, resign his office; and

---

[1] Arts. 181, 182, and 183 shall not apply to the State of Jammu and Kashmir.

(c) may be removed from his office by a resolution of the Council passed by a majority of all the then members of the Council:

Provided that no resolution for the purpose of clause (c) shall be moved unless at least fourteen days' notice has been given of the intention to move the resolution.

185.[1] (1) At any sitting of the Legislative Council, while any resolution for the removal of the Chairman from his office is under consideration, the Chairman, or while any resolution for the removal of the Deputy Chairman from his office is under consideration, the Deputy Chairman, shall not, though he is present, preside, and the provisions of clause (2) of Article 184 shall apply in relation to every such sitting as they apply in relation to a sitting from which the Chairman or, as the case may be, the Deputy Chairman is absent.

(2) The Chairman shall have the right to speak in, and otherwise to take part in the proceedings of, the Legislative Council while any resolution for his removal from office is under consideration in the Council and shall, notwithstanding anything in Article 189, be entitled to vote only in the first instance on such resolution or on any other matter during such proceedings but not in the case of an equality of votes.

187.[1] (1) The House or each House of the Legislature of a State shall have a separate secretarial staff:

Provided that nothing in this clause shall, in the case of the Legislature of a State having a Legislative Council, be construed as preventing the creation of posts common to both Houses of such Legislature.

(2) The Legislature of a State may by law regulate the recruitment, and the conditions of service of persons appointed, to the secretarial staff of the House or Houses of the Legislature of the State.

(3) Until provision is made by the Legislature of the State under clause (2), the Governor may, after consultation with the Speaker of the Legislative Assembly or the Chairman of the Legislative Council, as the case may be, make rules regulating the recruitment, and the conditions of service of persons appointed, to the secretarial staff of the Assembly or the Council, and any rules so made shall have effect subject to the provisions of any law made under the said clause.

188.[1] Every member of the Legislative Assembly or the Legislative

[1] Arts. 185, 187 and 188 shall not apply to be State of Jammu and Kashmir.

Council of a State shall, before taking his seat, make and subscribe before the Governor, or some person appointed in that behalf by him, an oath or affirmation according to the form set out for the purpose in the Third Schedule.

190.[1] (1) No person shall be a member of both Houses of the Legislature of a State and provision shall be made by the Legislature of the State by law for the vacation by a person who is chosen a member of both Houses of his seat in one House or the other.

(2) No person shall be a member of the Legislatures of two or more States specified in the First Schedule and if a person is chosen a member of the Legislatures of two or more such States, then, at the expiration of such period as may be specified in rules made by the President, that person's seat in the Legislatures of all such States shall become vacant, unless he has previously resigned his seat in the Legislatures of all but one of the States.

(3) If a member of a House of the Legislature of a State—

(a) becomes subject to any of the disqualifications mentioned in clause (1) of Article 191; or

(b) resigns his seat by writing under his hand addressed to the Speaker or the Chairman, as the case may be,

his seat shall thereupon become vacant.

(4) If for a period of sixty days a member of a House of the Legislature of a State is without permission of the House absent from all meetings thereof, the House may declare his seat vacant:

Provided that in computing the said period of sixty days no account shall be taken of any period during which the House is prorogued or is adjourned for more than four consecutive days.

191.[1] (1) A person shall be disqualified for being chosen as, and for being, a member of the Legislative Assembly or Legislative Council of a State—

(a) if he holds any office of profit under the Government of India or the Government of any State specified in the First Schedule, other than an office declared by the Legislature of the State by law not to disqualify its holder;

(b) if he is of unsound mind and stands so declared by a competent court;

(c) if he is an undischarged insolvent;

(d) if he is not a citizen of India, or has voluntarily acquired

[1] Arts. 190 and 191 shall not apply to the State of Jammu and Kashmir.

the citizenship of a foreign State, or is under any acknowledgement of allegiance or adherence to a foreign State;

(e) if he is so disqualified by or under any law made by Parliament.

(2) For the purposes of this Article, a person shall not be deemed
to hold an office of profit under the Government of India or the
Government of any State specified in the First Schedule by reason
only that he is a Minister either for the Union or for such State.

192.[1] (1) If any question arises as to whether a member of a
House of the Legislature of a State has become subject to any of
the disqualifications mentioned in clause (1) of Article 191, the
question shall be referred for the decision of the Governor and
his decision shall be final.

(2) Before giving any decision on any such question, the Governor
shall obtain the opinion of the Election Commission and shall act
according to such opinion.

193.[1] If a person sits or votes as a member of the Legislative
Assembly or the Legislative Council of a State before he has
complied with the requirements of Article 188, or when he knows
that he is not qualified or that he is disqualified for membership
thereof, or that he is prohibited from so doing by the provisions
of any law made by Parliament or the Legislature of the State,
he shall be liable in respect of each day on which he so sits or votes
to a penalty of five hundred rupees to be recovered as a debt due
to the State.

194.[1] (1) Subject to the provisions of this Constitution and to
the rules and standing orders regulating the procedure of the
Legislature, there shall be freedom of speech in the Legislature
of every State.

(2) No member of the Legislature of a State shall be liable to
any proceedings in any court in respect of anything said or any
vote given by him in the Legislature or any committee thereof,
and no person shall be so liable in respect of the publication by
or under the authority of a House of such a Legislature of any
report, paper, votes or proceedings.

(3) In other respects, the powers, privileges and immunities
of a House of the Legislature of a State, and of the members
and the committees of a House of such Legislature, shall be such
as may from time to time be defined by the Legislature by law,

---

[1] Arts. 192, 193 and 194 shall not apply to the State of Jammu and
Kashmir.

and, until so defined, shall be those of the House of Commons of the Parliament of the United Kingdom, and of its members and committees, at the commencement of this Constitution.

(4) The provisions of clauses (1), (2) and (3) shall apply in relation to persons who by virtue of this Constitution have the right to speak in, and otherwise to take part in the proceedings of, a House of the Legislature of a State or any committee thereof as they apply in relation to members of that Legislature.

196.[1] (1) Subject to the provisions of Articles 198 and 207 with respect to Money Bills and other financial Bills, a Bill may originate in either House of the Legislature of a State which has a Legislative Council.

(2) Subject to the provisions of Articles 197 and 198, a Bill shall not be deemed to have been passed by the Houses of the Legislature of a State having a Legislative Council unless it has been agreed to by both Houses, either without amendment or with such amendments only as are agreed to by both Houses.

(3) A Bill pending in the Legislature of a State shall not lapse by reason of the prorogation of the House or Houses thereof.

(4) A Bill pending in the Legislative Council of a State which has not been passed by the Legislative Assembly shall not lapse on a dissolution of the Assembly.

(5) A Bill which is pending in the Legislative Assembly of a State, or which having been passed by the Legislative Assembly is pending in the Legislative Council, shall lapse on a dissolution of the Assembly.

197.[1] (1) If after a Bill has been passed by the Legislative Assembly of a State having a Legislative Council and transmitted to the Legislative Council:

(*a*) the Bill is rejected by the Council; or

(*b*) more than three months elapse from the date on which the Bill is laid before the Council without the Bill being passed by it; or

(*c*) the Bill is passed by the Council with amendments to which the Legislative Assembly does not agree;

the Legislative Assembly may, subject to the rules regulating its procedure, pass the Bill again in the same or in any subsequent session with or without such amendments, if any, as have been made, suggested or agreed to by the Legislative Council and then transmit the Bill as so passed to the Legislative Council.

Arts. 196 and 197 shall not apply to the State of Jammu and Kashmir.

(2) If after a Bill has been so passed for the second time by the Legislative Assembly and transmitted to the Legislative Council:

(*a*) the Bill is rejected by the Council; or

(*b*) more than one month elapses from the date on which the Bill is laid before the Council without the Bill being passed by it; or

(*c*) the Bill is passed by the Council with amendments to which the Legislative Assembly does not agree;

the Bill shall be deemed to have been passed by the Houses of the Legislature of the State in the form in which it was passed by the Legislative Assembly for the second time with such amendments, if any, as have been made or suggested by the Legislative Council and agreed to by the Legislative Assembly.

(3) Nothing in this article shall apply to a Money Bill.

198.[1] (1) A Money Bill shall not be introduced in a Legislative Council.

(2) After a Money Bill has been passed by the Legislative Assembly of a State having a Legislative Council, it shall be transmitted to the Legislative Council for its recommendations, and the Legislative Council shall within a period of fourteen days from the date of its receipt of the Bill return the Bill to the Legislative Assembly with its recommendations, and the Legislative Assembly may thereupon either accept or reject all or any of the recommendations of the Legislative Council.

(3) If the Legislative Assembly accepts any of the recommendations of the Legislative Council, the Money Bill shall be deemed to have been passed by both Houses with the amendments recommended by the Legislative Council and accepted by the Legislative Assembly.

(4) If the Legislative Assembly does not accept any of the recommendations of the Legislative Council, the Money Bill shall be deemed to have been passed by both Houses in the form in which it was passed by the Legislative Assembly without any of the amendments recommended by the Legislative Council.

(5) If a Money Bill passed by the Legislative Assembly and transmitted to the Legislative Council for its recommendations is not returned to the Legislative Assembly within the said period of fourteen days, it shall be deemed to have been passed by both Houses at the expiration of the said period in the form in which it was passed by the Legislative Assembly.

[1] Art. 198 shall not apply to the State of Jammu and Kashmir.

199.[1] (1) For the purposes of this Chapter, a Bill shall be deemed to be a Money Bill if it contains only provisions dealing with all or any of the following matters, namely:

(*a*) the imposition, abolition, remission, alteration or regulation of any tax;

(*b*) the regulation of the borrowing of money or the giving of any guarantee by the State, or the amendment of the law with respect to any financial obligations undertaken or to be undertaken by the State;

(*c*) the custody of the Consolidated Fund or the Contingency Fund of the State, the payment of moneys into or the withdrawal of moneys from any such Fund;

(*d*) the appropriation of moneys out of the Consolidated Fund of the State;

(*e*) the declaring of any expenditure to be expenditure charged on the Consolidated Fund of the State, or the increasing of the amount of any such expenditure;

(*f*) the receipt of money on account of the Consolidated Fund of the State or the public account of the State or the custody or issue of such money; or

(*g*) any matter incidental to any of the matters specified in sub-clauses (*a*) to (*f*).

(2) A Bill shall not be deemed to be a Money Bill by reason only that it provides for the imposition of fines or other pecuniary penalties, or for the demand or payment of fees for licences or fees for services rendered, or by reason that it provides for the imposition, abolition, remission, alteration or regulation of any tax by any local authority or body for local purposes.

(3) If any question arises whether a Bill introduced in the Legislature of a State which has a Legislative Council is a Money Bill or not, the decision of the Speaker of the Legislative Assembly of such State thereon shall be final.

(4) There shall be endorsed on every Money Bill when it is transmitted to the Legislative Council under Article 198, and when it is presented to the Governor for assent under Article 200, the certificate of the Speaker of the Legislative Assembly signed by him that it is a Money Bill.

200.[1] When a Bill has been passed by the Legislative Assembly of a State or, in the case of a State having a Legislative Council,

---

[1] Arts. 199 and 200 shall not apply to the State of Jammu and Kashmir.

has been passed by both Houses of the Legislature of the State, it shall be presented to the Governor and the Governor shall declare either that he assents to the Bill or that he withholds assent therefrom or that he reserves the Bill for the consideration of the President:

Provided that the Governor may, as soon as possible after the presentation to him of the Bill for assent, return the Bill if it is not a Money Bill together with a message requesting that the House or Houses will reconsider the Bill or any specified provisions thereof and, in particular, will consider the desirability of introducing any such amendments as he may recommend in his message and, when a Bill is so returned, the House or Houses shall reconsider the Bill accordingly, and if the Bill is passed again by the House or Houses with or without amendment and presented to the Governor for assent, the Governor shall not withhold assent therefrom:

Provided further that the Governor shall not assent to, but shall reserve for the consideration of the President, any Bill which in the opinion of the Governor would, if it became law, so derogate from the powers of the High Court as to endanger the position which that Court is by this Constitution designed to fill.

201.[1] When a Bill is reserved by a Governor for the consideration of the President, the President shall declare either that he assents to the Bill or that he withholds assent therefrom:

Provided that, where the Bill is not a Money Bill, the President may direct the Governor to return the Bill to the House or, as the case may be, the Houses of the Legislature of the State together with such a message as is mentioned in the first proviso to Article 200 and, when a Bill is so returned, the House or Houses shall reconsider it accordingly within a period of six months from the date of receipt of such message and, if it is again passed by the House or Houses with or without amendment, it shall be presented again to the President for his consideration.

202.[1] (1) The Governor shall in respect of every financial year cause to be laid before the House or Houses of the Legislature of the State a statement of the estimated receipts and expenditure of the State for that year, in this Part referred to as the 'annual financial statement'.

(2) The estimates of expenditure embodied in the annual financial statement shall show separately—

[1] Arts. 201 and 202 shall not apply to the State of Jammu and Kashmir.

(*a*) the sums required to meet expenditure described by this Constitution as expenditure charged upon the Consolidated Fund of the State; and

(*b*) the sums required to meet other expenditure proposed to be made from the Consolidated Fund of the State;
and shall distinguish expenditure on revenue account from other expenditure.

(3) The following expenditure shall be expenditure charged on the Consolidated Fund of each State:

(*a*) the emoluments and allowances of the Governor and other expenditure relating to his office;

(*b*) the salaries and allowances of the Speaker and the Deputy Speaker of the Legislative Assembly, and, in the case of a State having a Legislative Council, also of the Chairman and the Deputy Chairman of the Legislative Council;

(*c*) debt charges for which the State is liable including interest, sinking fund charges and redemption charges, and other expenditure relating to the raising of loans and the service and redemption of debt;

(*d*) expenditure in respect of the salaries and allowances of Judges of any High Court;

(*e*) any sums required to satisfy any judgment, decree or award of any court or arbitral tribunal;

(*f*) any other expenditure declared by this Constitution, or by the Legislature of the State by law, to be so charged.

203.¹ (1) So much of the estimates as relates to expenditure charged upon the Consolidated Fund of a State shall not be submitted to the vote of the Legislative Assembly, but nothing in this clause shall be construed as preventing the discussion in the Legislature of any of those estimates.

(2) So much of the said estimates as relates to other expenditure shall be submitted in the form of demands for grants to the Legislative Assembly, and the Legislative Assembly shall have power to assent, or to refuse to assent, to any demand, or to assent to any demand subject to a reduction of the amount specified therein.

(3) No demand for a grant shall be made except on the recommendation of the Governor.

204.¹ (1) As soon as may be after the grants under Article 203 have been made by the Assembly, there shall be introduced a Bill

¹ Arts. 203 and 204 shall not apply to the State of Jammu and Kashmir.

to provide for the appropriation out of the Consolidated Fund of the State of all moneys required to meet:

(*a*) the grants so made by the Assembly; and

(*b*) the expenditure charged on the Consolidated Fund of the State but not exceeding in any case the amount shown in the statement previously laid before the House or Houses.

(2) No amendment shall be proposed to any such Bill in the House or either House of the Legislature of the State which will have the effect of varying the amount or altering the destination of any grant so made or of varying the amount of any expenditure charged on the Consolidated Fund of the State, and the decision of the person presiding as to whether an amendment is inadmissible under this clause shall be final.

(3) Subject to the provisions of Articles 205 and 206, no money shall be withdrawn from the Consolidated Fund of the State except under appropriation made by law passed in accordance with the provisions of this article.

205.[1] (1) The Governor shall—

(*a*) if the amount authorized by any law made in accordance with the provisions of Article 204 to be expended for a particular service for the current financial year is found to be insufficient for the purposes of that year or when a need has arisen during the current financial year for supplementary or additional expenditure upon some new service not contemplated in the annual financial statement for that year; or

(*b*) if any money has been spent on any service during a financial year in excess of the amount granted for that service and for that year;

cause to be laid before the House or the Houses of the Legislature of the State another statement showing the estimated amount of that expenditure or cause to be presented to the Legislative Assembly of the State a demand for such excess, as the case may be.

(2) The provisions of Articles 202, 203 and 204 shall have effect in relation to any such statement and expenditure or demand and also to any law to be made authorizing the appropriation of moneys out of the Consolidated Fund of the State to meet such expenditure or the grant in respect of such demand as they have effect in relation to the annual financial statement and the expenditure mentioned therein or to a demand for a grant and the law to be made for the

[1] Art. 205 shall not apply to the State of Jammu and Kashmir.

authorization of appropriation of moneys out of the Consolidated Fund of the State to meet such expenditure or grant.

206.[1] (1) Notwithstanding anything in the foregoing provisions of this Chapter, the Legislative Assembly of a State shall have power—

(*a*) to make any grant in advance in respect of the estimated expenditure for a part of any financial year pending the completion of the procedure prescribed in Article 203 for the voting of such grant and the passing of the law in accordance with the provisions of Article 204 in relation to that expenditure;

(*b*) to make a grant for meeting an unexpected demand upon the resources of the State when on account of the magnitude or the indefinite character of the service the demand cannot be stated with the details ordinarily given in an annual financial statement;

(*c*) to make an exceptional grant which forms no part of the current service of any financial year;

and the Legislature of the State shall have power to authorize by law the withdrawal of moneys from the Consolidated Fund of the State for the purposes for which the said grants are made.

(2) The provisions of Articles 203 and 204 shall have effect in relation to the making of any grant under clause (1) and to any law to be made under that clause as they have effect in relation to the making of a grant with regard to any expenditure mentioned in the annual financial statement and the law to be made for the authorization of appropriation of moneys out of the Consolidated Fund of the State to meet such expenditure.

207.[1] (1) A Bill or amendment making provision for any of the matters specified in sub-clauses (*a*) to (*f*) of clause (1) of Article 199 shall not be introduced or moved except on the recommendation of the Governor, and a Bill making such provision shall not be introduced in a Legislative Council:

Provided that no recommendation shall be required under this clause for the moving of an amendment making provision for the reduction or abolition of any tax.

(2) A Bill or amendment shall not be deemed to make provision for any of the matters aforesaid by reason only that it provides for the imposition of fines or other pecuniary penalties, or for the demand or payment of fees for licences or fees for services rendered,

[1] Arts. 206 and 207 shall not apply to the State of Jammu and Kashmir.

or by reason that it provides for the imposition, abolition, remission, alteration or regulation of any tax by any local authority or body for local purposes.

(3) A Bill which, if enacted and brought into operation, would involve expenditure from the Consolidated Fund of a State shall not be passed by a House of the Legislature of the State unless the Governor has recommended to that House the consideration of the Bill.

211.[1] No discussion shall take place in the Legislature of a State with respect to the conduct of any Judge of the Supreme Court or of a High Court in the discharge of his duties.

254.[2] (1) If any provision of a law made by the Legislature of a State is repugnant to any provision of a law made by Parliament which Parliament is competent to enact, or to any provision of any existing law with respect to one of the matters enumerated in the Concurrent List, then, subject to the provisions of clause (2), the law made by Parliament, whether passed before or after the law made by the Legislature of such State, or, as the case may be, the existing law, shall prevail and the law made by the Legislature of the State shall, to the extent of the repugnancy, be void.

(2) Where a law made by the Legislature of a State with respect to one of the matters enumerated in the Concurrent List contains any provision repugnant to the provisions of an earlier law made by Parliament or an existing law with respect to that matter, then, the law so made by the Legislature of such State shall, if it has been reserved for the consideration of the President and has received his assent, prevail in that State:

Provided that nothing in this clause shall prevent Parliament from enacting at any time any law with respect to the same matter including a law adding to, amending, varying or repealing the law so made by the Legislature of the State.

265. No tax shall be levied or collected except by authority of law.
266.[3] (1) Subject to the provisions of Article 267 and to the

[1] Art. 211 shall not apply to the State of Jammu and Kashmir.
[2] In its application to the State of Jammu and Kashmir, in Art. 254, the words, brackets and figure 'or to any provision of an existing law with respect to one of the matters enumerated in the Concurrent List, then, subject to the provisions of clause (2)' and the words 'or as the case may be, the existing law' occurring in cl. (1) and the whole of cl. (2) shall be omitted.
[3] In its application to the State of Jammu and Kashmir, in Art. 266, references to the State or States shall be construed as not including references to the State of Jammu and Kashmir.

provisions of this Chapter with respect to the assignment of the whole or part of the net proceeds of certain taxes and duties to States, all revenues received by the Government of India, all loans raised by that Government by the issue of treasury bills, loans or ways and means advances and all moneys received by that Government in repayment of loans shall form one consolidated fund to be entitled 'the Consolidated Fund of India', and all revenues received by the Government of a State, all loans raised by that Government by the issue of treasury bills, loans or ways and means advances and all moneys received by that Government in repayment of loans shall form one consolidated fund to be entitled 'the Consolidated Fund of the State'.

(2) All other public moneys received by or on behalf of the Government of India or the Government of a State shall be credited to the public account of India or the public account of the State, as the case may be.

(3) No moneys out of the Consolidated Fund of India or the Consolidated Fund of a State shall be appropriated except in accordance with law and for the purposes and in the manner provided in this constitution.

267. (1) Parliament may by law establish a Contingency Fund in the nature of an imprest to be entitled 'the Contingency Fund of India' into which shall be paid from time to time such sums as may be determined by such law, and the said Fund shall be placed at the disposal of the President to enable advances to be made by him out of such Fund for the purposes of meeting unforseen expenditure pending authorization of such expenditure by Parliament by law under Article 115 or Article 116.

(2)[1] The Legislature of a State may by law establish a Contingency Fund in the nature of an imprest to be entitled 'the Contingency Fund of the State' into which shall be paid from time to time such sums as may be determined by such law, and the said Fund shall be placed at the disposal of the Governor of the State to enable advances to be made by him out of such Fund for the purposes of meeting unforeseen expenditure pending authorization of such expenditure by the Legislature of the State by law under Article 205 or Article 206.

279. (1) In the foregoing provisions of this Chapter, 'net proceeds' means in relation to any tax or duty the proceeds thereof reduced

---

[1] This clause shall not apply to the State of Jammu and Kashmir.

by the cost of collection, and for the purposes of those provisions the net proceeds of any tax or duty, or of any part of any tax or duty, in or attributable to any area shall be ascertained and certified by the Comptroller and Auditor-General of India, whose certificate shall be final.

(2) Subject as aforesaid, and to any other express provision of this Chapter, a law made by Parliament or an order of the President may, in any case where under this Part the proceeds of any duty or tax are, or may be, assigned to any State, provide for the manner in which the proceeds are to be calculated, for the time from or at which and the manner in which any payments are to be made, for the making of adjustments between one financial year and another, and for any other incidental or ancillary matters.

283. (1) The custody of the Consolidated Fund of India and the Contingency Fund of India, the payment of moneys into such Funds, the withdrawal of moneys therefrom, the custody of public moneys other than those credited to such Funds received by or on behalf of the Government of India, their payment into the public account of India and the withdrawal of moneys from such account and all other matters connected with or ancillary to matters aforesaid shall be regulated by law made by Parliament, and, until provision in that behalf is so made, shall be regulated by rules made by the President.

(2)[1] The custody of the Consolidated Fund of a State and the Contingency Fund of a State, the payment of moneys into such Funds, the withdrawal of moneys therefrom, the custody of public moneys other than those credited to such Funds received by or on behalf of the Government of the State, their payment into the public account of the State and the withdrawal of moneys from such account and all other matters connected with or ancillary to matters aforesaid shall be regulated by law made by the Legislature of the State, and, until provision in that behalf is so made, shall be regulated by rules made by the Governor of the State.

324.[2] (1) The superintendence, direction and control of the preparation of the electoral rolls for, and the conduct of, all elections to Parliament and to the Legislature of every State and of elections

[1] This clause shall not apply to the State of Jammu and Kashmir.
[2] In clause (1) of Art. 324, the reference to the Constitution shall, in relation to elections to either House of the Legislature of Jammu and Kashmir, be construed as a reference to the Constitution of Jammu and Kashmir.

to the offices of President and Vice-President held under this Constitution, including the appointment of election tribunals for the decision of doubts and disputes arising out of or in connection with elections to Parliament and to the Legislatures of States shall be vested in a Commission (referred to in this Constitution as the Election Commission).

(2) The Election Commission shall consist of the Chief Election Commissioner and such number of other Election Commissioners, if any, as the President may from time to time fix and the appointment of the Chief Election Commissioner and other Election Commissioners shall, subject to the provisions of any law made in that behalf by Parliament, be made by the President.

(3) When any other Election Commissioner is so appointed the Chief Election Commissioner shall act as the Chairman of the Election Commission.

(4) Before each general election to the House of the People and to the Legislative Assembly of each State, and before the first general election and thereafter before each biennial election to the Legislative Council of each State having such Council, the President may also appoint after consultation with the Election Commission such Regional Commissioners as he may consider necessary to assist the Election Commission in the performance of the functions conferred on the Commission by clause (1).

(5) Subject to the provisions of any law made by Parliament, the conditions of service and tenure of office of the Election Commissioners and the Regional Commissioners shall be such as the President may by rule determine:

Provided that the Chief Election Commissioner shall not be removed from his office except in like manner and on the like grounds as a Judge of the Supreme Court and the conditions of service of the Chief Election Commissioner shall not be varied to his disadvantage after his appointment:

Provided further that any other Election Commissioner or a Regional Commissioner shall not be removed from office except on the recommendation of the Chief Election Commissioner.

(6) The President, or the Governor of a State, shall, when so requested by the Election Commission, make available to the Election Commission or to a Regional Commissioner such staff as may be necessary for the discharge of the functions conferred on the Election Commission by clause (1).

331.[1] Notwithstanding anything in Article 81, the President may, if he is of opinion that the Anglo-Indian community is not adequately represented in the House of the People, nominate not more than two members of that community to the House of the People.

333.[1] Notwithstanding anything in Article 170, the Governor of a State may, if he is of opinion that the Anglo-Indian community needs representation in the Legislative Assembly of the State and is not adequately represented therein, nominate such number of members of the community to the Assembly as he considers appropriate.

356.[1] (1) If the President on receipt of a report from the Governor of a State or otherwise, is satisfied that a situation has arisen in which the government of the State cannot be carried on in accordance with the provisions of this Constitution, the President may by Proclamation—

(*a*) assume to himself all or any of the functions of the Government of the State and all or any of the powers vested in or exercisable by the Governor, or any body or authority in the State other than the Legislature of the State;

(*b*) declare that the powers of the Legislature of the State shall be exercisable by or under the authority of Parliament;

(*c*) make such incidental and consequential provisions as appear to the President to be necessary or desirable for giving effect to the objects of the Proclamation, including provisions for suspending in whole or in part the operation of any provisions of this Constitution relating to any body or authority in the State:

Provided that nothing in this clause shall authorize the President to assume to himself any of the powers vested in or exercisable by a High Court, or to suspend in whole or in part the operation of any provision of this Constitution relating to High Courts.

(2) Any such Proclamation may be revoked or varied by a subsequent Proclamation.

(3) Every Proclamation under this article shall be laid before each House of Parliament and shall, except where it is a Proclamation revoking a previous Proclamation, cease to operate at the expiration of two months unless before the expiration of that period it has been approved by resolutions of both Houses of Parliament:

Provided that if any such Proclamation (not being a Procla-

[1] Arts. 331, 333 and 356 shall not apply to the State of Jammu and Kashmir.

29

mation revoking a previous Proclamation) is issued at a time when the House of the People is dissolved or the dissolution of the House of the People takes place during the period of two months referred to in this clause, and if a resolution approving the Proclamation has been passed by the Council of States, but no resolution with respect to such Proclamation has been passed by the House of the People before the expiration of that period, the Proclamation shall cease to operate at the expiration of thirty days from the date on which the House of the People first sits after its reconstitution unless before the expiration of the said period of thirty days a resolution approving the Proclamation has been also passed by the House of the People.

(4) A Proclamation so approved shall, unless revoked, cease to operate on the expiration of a period of six months from the date of the passing of the second of the resolutions approving the Proclamation under clause (3):

Provided that if and so often as a resolution approving the continuance in force of such a Proclamation is passed by both Houses of Parliament, the Proclamation shall, unless revoked, continue in force for a further period of six months from the date on which under this clause it would otherwise have ceased to operate, but no such Proclamation shall in any case remain in force for more than three years:

Provided further that if the dissolution of the House of the People takes place during any such period of six months and a resolution approving the continuance in force of such Proclamation has been passed by the Council of States, but no resolution with respect to the continuance in force of such Proclamation has been passed by the House of the People during the said period, the Proclamation shall cease to operate at the expiration of thirty days from the date on which the House of the People first sits after its reconstitution unless before the expiration of the said period of thirty days a resolution approving the continuance in force of the Proclamation has been also passed by the House of the People.

APPENDIX II

List I—Union List

(1) Defence of India and every part thereof including preparation for defence and all such acts as may be conducive in times of war to its prosecution and after its termination to effective demobilization.

(2) Naval, military and air forces; any other armed forces of the Union.

(3)[1] Delimitation of cantonment areas, local self-government in such areas, the constitution and powers within such areas of cantonment authorities and the regulation of house accommodation (including the control of rents) in such areas.

(4) Naval, military and air force works.

(5) Arms, firearms, ammunition and explosives.

(6) Atomic energy and mineral resources necessary for its production.

(7) Industries declared by Parliament by law to be necessary for the purpose of defence or for the prosecution of war.

(8)[2] Central Bureau of Intelligence and Investigation.

(9)[2] Preventive detention for reasons connected with Defence, Foreign Affairs, or the security of India; persons subjected to such detention.

(10) Foreign Affairs: all matters which bring the Union into relation with any foreign country.

(11) Diplomatic, consular and trade representation.

(12) United Nations Organization.

(13) Participation in international conferences, associations and other bodies and implementing of decisions made thereat.

(14) Entering into treaties and agreements with foreign countries and implementing of treaties, agreements and conventions with foreign countries.

---

[1] In its application to the State of Jammu and Kashmir, the following shall be substituted for entry 3:
    '3. Administration of cantonments.'
[2] These entries are not applicable to the State of Jammu and Kashmir.

(15) War and peace.

(16) Foreign jurisdiction.

(17) Citizenship, naturalization and aliens.

(18) Extradition.

(19) Admission into, and emigration and expulsion from, India; passports and visas.

(20) Pilgrimages to places outside India.

(21) Piracies and crimes committed on the high seas or in the air; offences against the law of nations committed on land or the high seas or in the air.

(22) Railways.

(23) Highways declared by or under law made by Parliament to be national highways.

(24) Shipping and navigation on inland waterways, declared by Parliament by law to be national waterways, as regards mechanically propelled vessels; the rule of the road on such waterways.

(25) Maritime shipping and navigation, including shipping and navigation on tidal waters; provision of education and training for the mercantile marine and regulation of such education and training provided by States and other agencies.

(26) Lighthouses, including lightships, beacons and other provisions for the safety of shipping and aircraft.

(27) Ports declared by or under law made by Parliament or existing law to be major ports, including their delimitation, and the constitution and powers of port authorities therein.

(28) Port quarantine, including hospitals connected therewith; seamen's and marine hospitals.

(29) Airways; aircraft and air navigation; provision of aerodromes; regulation and organization of air traffic and of aerodromes; provision for aeronautical education and training and regulation of such education and training provided by States and other agencies.

(30) Carriage of passengers and goods by railway, sea or air, or by national waterways in mechanically propelled vessels.

(31) Posts and telegraphs; telephones, wireless, broadcasting and other like forms of communication.

(32) Property of the Union and the revenue therefrom, but as regards property situated in a State subject to legislation by the State, save in so far as Parliament by law otherwise provides[1]. .

[1] Entry 33 omitted by the Constitution (Seventh Amendment) Act, 1956.

(34)[1] Courts of wards for the estates of Rulers of Indian States.

(35) Public debt of the Union.

(36) Currency, coinage and legal tender; foreign exchange.

(37) Foreign loans.

(38) Reserve Bank of India.

(39) Post Office Savings Bank.

(40) Lotteries organized by the Government of India or the Government of a State.

(41) Trade and commerce with foreign countries; import and export across customs frontiers; definition of customs frontiers.

(42) Inter-State trade and commerce.

(43)[2] Incorporation, regulation and winding up of trading corporations, including banking, insurance and financial corporations but not including co-operative societies.

(44)[3] Incorporation, regulation and winding up of corporations, whether trading or not, with objects not confined to one State, but not including universities.

(45) Banking.

(46) Bills of exchange, cheques, promissory notes and other like instruments.

(47) Insurance.

(48) Stock exchanges and future markets.

(49) Patents, inventions and designs; copyright; trade-marks and merchandise marks.

(50) Establishment of standards of weight and measure.

(51) Establishment of standards of quality for goods to be exported out of India or transported from one State to another.

(52)[3] Industries, the control of which by the Union is declared by Parliament by law to be expedient in the public interest.

(53) Regulation and development of oilfields and mineral oil resources; petroleum and petroleum products; other liquids and substances declared by Parliament by law to be dangerously inflammable.

(54) Regulation of mines and mineral development to the extent to which such regulation and development under the control of the Union is declared by Parliament by law to be expedient in the public interest.

---

[1] Not applicable to the State of Jammu and Kashmir.

[2] In its application to the State of Jammu and Kashmir, the words 'trading corporations, including' in entry 43 shall be omitted.

[3] Not applicable to the State of Jammu and Kashmir.

(55)[1] Regulation of labour and safety in mines and oilfields.

(56) Regulation and development of inter-State rivers and river valleys to the extent to which such regulation and development under the control of the Union is declared by Parliament by law to be expedient in the public interest.

(57) Fishing and fisheries beyond territorial waters.

(58) Manufacture, supply and distribution of salt by Union agencies; regulation and control of manufacture, supply and distribution of salt by other agencies.

(59) Cultivation, manufacture, and sale for export, of opium.

(60)[1] Sanctioning of cinematograph films for exhibition.

(61) Industrial disputes concerning Union employees.

(62) The institutions known at the commencement of this Constitution as the National Library, the Indian Museum, the Imperial War Museum, the Victoria Memorial and the Indian War Memorial, and any other like institution financed by the Government of India wholly or in part and declared by Parliament by law to be an institution of national importance.

(63) The institutions known at the commencement of this Constitution as the Benares Hindu University, the Aligarh Muslim University and the Delhi University, and any other institution declared by Parliament by law to be an institution of national importance.

(64) Institutions for scientific or technical education financed by the Government of India wholly or in part and declared by Parliament by law to be institutions of national importance.

(65) Union agencies and institutions for:

(a) professional, vocational or technical training, including the training of police officers; or

(b) the promotion of special studies or research; or

(c) scientific or technical assistance in the investigation or detection of crime.

(66) Co-ordination and determination of standards in institutions for higher education or research and scientific and technical institutions.

(67)[2] Ancient and historical monuments and records, and archaeological sites and remains, declared by or under law made by Parliament to be of national importance.

[1] Not applicable to the State of Jammu and Kashmir.
[2] In its application to the State of Jammu and Kashmir, the words 'and records' in entry 67 shall be omitted.

(68) The Survey of India, the Geological, Botanical, Zoological and Anthropological Surveys of India; Meteorological organizations.

(69)[1] Census.

(70) Union public services; all-India services; Union Public Service Commission.

(71) Union pensions, that is to say, pensions payable by the Government of India or out of the Consolidated Fund of India.

(72)[2] Elections to Parliament, to the Legislatures of States and to the offices of President and Vice-President; the Election Commission.

(73) Salaries and allowances of members of Parliament, the Chairman and Deputy Chairman of the Council of States and the Speaker and Deputy Speaker of the House of the People.

(74) Powers, privileges and immunities of each House of Parliament and of the members and the committees of each House; enforcement of attendance of persons for giving evidence or producing documents before committees of Parliament or commissions appointed by Parliament.

(75) Emoluments, allowances, privileges, and rights in respect of leave of absence, of the President and Governors; salaries and allowances of the Ministers for the Union; the salaries, allowances, and rights in respect of leave of absence and other conditions of service of the Comptroller and Auditor-General

(76) Audit of the accounts of the Union and of the States.

(77) Constitution, organization, jurisdiction and powers of the Supreme Court (including contempt of such Court), and the fees taken therein; persons entitled to practise before the Supreme Court.

(78)[3] Constitution and organization (including vacation) of the High Courts except provisions as to officers and servants of High Courts; persons entitled to practise before the High Courts.

(79)[3] Extension of the jurisdiction of a High Court to, and exclusion of the jurisdiction of a High Court from, any Union territory.

(80) Extension of the powers and jurisdiction of members of a police force belonging to any State to any area outside that State, but not so as to enable the police of one State to exercise powers and jurisdiction in any area outside that State without the consent of the

---

[1] Made applicable to the State of Jammu and Kashmir. See C.O. 57.

[2] In its application to the State of Jammu and Kashmir, reference to the States shall be construed as not including a reference to the State of Jammu and Kashmir.

[3] Not applicable to the State of Jammu and Kashmir.

Government of the State in which such area is situated; extension of the powers and jurisdiction of members of a police force belonging to any State to railway areas outside that State.

(81)[1] Inter-State migration; inter-State quarantine.

(82) Taxes on income other than agricultural income.

(83) Duties of customs including export duties.

(84) Duties of excise on tobacco and other goods manufactured or produced in India except:

(a) alcoholic liquors for human consumption;

(b) opium, Indian hemp and other narcotic drugs and narcotics, but including medicinal and toilet preparations containing alcohol or any substance included in sub-paragraph (b) of this entry.

(85) Corporation tax.

(86) Taxes on the capital value of the assets, exclusive of agricultural land, of individuals and companies; taxes on the capital of companies.

(87) Estate duty in respect of property other than agricultural land.

(88) Duties in respect of succession to property other than agricultural land.

(89) Terminal taxes on goods or passengers, carried by railway, sea or air; taxes on railway fares and freights.

(90) Taxes other than stamp duties on transactions in stock exchanges and future markets.

(91) Rates of stamp duty in respect of bills of exchange, cheques, promissory notes, bills of lading, letters of credit, policies of insurance, transfer of shares, debentures, proxies and receipts.

(92) Taxes on the sale or purchase of newspapers and on advertisements published therein.

(92A) Taxes on the sale or purchase of goods other than newspapers, where such sale or purchase takes place in the course of inter-State trade or commerce.

(93) Offences against laws with respect to any of the matters in this List.

(94) Inquiries, surveys and statistics for the purpose of any of the matters in this List.

(95) Jurisdiction and powers of all courts, except the Supreme Court, with respect to any of the matters in this List; admiralty jurisdiction.

---

[1] In its application to the State of Jammu and Kashmir, in entry 81, the words 'inter-State migration' shall be omitted.

(96) Fees in respect of any of the matters in this List, but not including fees taken in any court.

(97)[1] Any other matter not enumerated in List II or List III, including any tax not mentioned in either of those Lists.

List II—State List[1]

(1) Public order (but not including the use of naval, military or air forces or any other armed forces of the Union in aid of the civil power).

(2) Police, including railway and village police.

(3) Administration of Justice; constitution and organization of all courts, except the Supreme Court and the High Court; officers and servants of the High Court; procedure in rent and revenue courts; fees taken in all courts except the Supreme Court.

(4) Prisons, reformatories, Borstal institutions and other institutions of a like nature, and persons detained therein; arrangements with other States for the use of prisons and other institutions.

(5) Local government, that is to say, the constitution and powers of municipal corporations, improvement trusts, district boards, mining settlement authorities and other local authorities for the purpose of local self-government or village administration.

(6) Public health and sanitation; hospitals and dispensaries.

(7) Pilgrimages, other than pilgrimages to places outside India.

(8) Intoxicating liquors, that is to say, the production, manufacture, possession, transport, purchase and sale of intoxicating liquors.

(9) Relief of the disabled and unemployable.

(10) Burials and burial grounds; cremations and cremation grounds.

(11) Education including universities, subject to the provisions of entries 63, 64, 65 and 66 of List I and entry 25 of List III.

(12) Libraries, museums and other similar institutions controlled or financed by the State; ancient and historical monuments and records other than those declared by or under law made by Parliament to be of national importance.

(13) Communications, that is to say, roads, bridges, ferries, and other means of communication not specified in List I; municipal

---

[1] Not applicable to the State of Jammu and Kashmir.

tramways; ropeways; inland waterways and traffic thereon subject to the provisions of List I and List III with regard to such waterways; vehicles other than mechanically propelled vehicles.

(14) Agriculture, including agricultural education and research, protection against pests and prevention of plant diseases.

(15) Preservation, protection and improvement of stock and prevention of animal diseases; veterinary training and practice.

(16) Pounds and the prevention of cattle trespass.

(17) Water, that is to say, water supplies, irrigation and canals, drainage and embankments, water storage and water power subject to the provisions of entry 56 of List I.

(18) Land, that is to say, rights in or over land, land tenures including the relation of landlord and tenant, and the collection of rents; transfer and alienation of agricultural land; land improvement and agricultural loans; colonization.

(19) Forests.

(20) Protection of wild animals and birds.

(21) Fisheries.

(22) Courts of wards subject to the provisions of entry 34 of List I; encumbered and attached estates.

(23) Regulation of mines and mineral development subject to the provisions of List I with respect to regulation and development under the control of the Union.

(24) Industries subject to the provisions of entries 7 and 52 of List I.

(25) Gas and gas-works.

(26) Trade and commerce within the State subject to the provisions of entry 33 of List III.

(27) Production, supply and distribution of goods subject to the provisions of entry 33 of List III.

(28) Markets and fairs.

(29) Weights and measures except establishment of standards.

(30) Money-lending and money-lenders; relief of agricultural indebtedness.

(31) Inns and inn-keepers.

(32) Incorporation, regulation and winding up of corporations, other than those specified in List I, and universities; unincorporated trading, literary, scientific, religious and other societies and associations; co-operative societies.

(33) Theatres and dramatic performances; cinemas subject to the

provisions of entry 60 of List I; sports, entertainments and amusements.

(34) Betting and gambling.

(35) Works, lands and buildings vested in or in the possession of the State[1]...

(37) Elections to the Legislature of the State subject to the provisions of any law made by Parliament.

(38) Salaries and allowances of members of the Legislature of the State, of the Speaker and Deputy Speaker of the Legislative Assembly and, if there is a Legislative Council, of the Chairman and Deputy Chairman thereof.

(39) Powers, privileges and immunities of the Legislative Assembly and of the members and the committees thereof, and, if there is a Legislative Council, of that Council and of the members and the committees thereof; enforcement of attendance of persons for giving evidence or producing documents before committees of the Legislature of the State.

(40) Salaries and allowances of Ministers for the State.

(41) State public services; State Public Service Commission.

(42) State pensions, that is to say, pensions payable by the State or out of the Consolidated Fund of the State.

(43) Public debt of the State.

(44) Treasure trove.

(45) Land revenue, including the assessment and collection of revenue, the maintenance of land records, survey for revenue purposes and records of rights, and alienation of revenues.

(46) Taxes on agricultural income.

(47) Duties in respect of succession to agricultural land.

(48) Estate duty in respect of agricultural land.

(49) Taxes on lands and buildings.

(50) Taxes on mineral rights subject to any limitations imposed by Parliament by law relating to mineral development.

(51) Duties of excise on the following goods manufactured or produced in the State and countervailing duties at the same or lower rates on similar goods manufactured or produced elsewhere in India:

(*a*) alcoholic liquors for human consumption;

(*b*) opium, Indian hemp and other narcotic drugs and narcotics; but not including medicinal and toilet preparations containing

[1] Entry 36 omitted by the Constitution (Seventh Amendment) Act, 1956.

alcohol or any substance included in sub-paragraph (b) of this entry.

(52) Taxes on the entry of goods into a local area for consumption, use or sale therein.

(53) Taxes on the consumption or sale of electricity.

(54) Taxes on the sale or purchase of goods other than newspapers, subject to the provisions of entry 92A of List I.

(55) Taxes on advertisements other than advertisements published in the newspapers.

(56) Taxes on goods and passengers carried by road or on inland waterways.

(57) Taxes on vehicles, whether mechanically propelled or not, suitable for use on roads, including tramcars subject to the provisions of entry 35 of List III.

(58) Taxes on animals and boats.

(59) Tolls.

(60) Taxes on professions, trades, callings and employments.

(61) Capitation taxes.

(62) Taxes on luxuries, including taxes on entertainments, amusements, betting and gambling.

(63) Rates of stamp duty in respect of documents other than those specified in the provisions of List I with regard to rates of stamp duty.

(64) Offences against laws with respect to any of the matters in this list.

(65) Jurisdiction and powers of all courts, except the Supreme Court, with respect to any of the matters in this List.

(66) Fees in respect of any of the matters in this List, but not including fees taken in any court.

List III—Concurrent List[1]

(1) Criminal law, including all matters included in the Indian Penal Code at the commencement of this Constitution but excluding offences against laws with respect to any of the matters specified in List I or List II and excluding the use of naval, military or air forces or any other armed forces of the Union in aid of the civil power.

(2) Criminal procedure, including all matters included in the Code of Criminal Procedure at the commencement of this Constitution.

---

[1] Not applicable to the State of Jammu and Kashmir.

(3) Preventive detention for reasons connected with the security of a State, the maintenance of public order, or the maintenance of supplies and services essential to the community; persons subjected to such detention.

(4) Removal from one State to another State of prisoners, accused persons and persons subjected to preventive detention for reasons specified in entry 3 of this List.

(5) Marriage and Divorce; infants and minors; adoption; wills, intestacy and succession; joint family and partition; all matters in respect of which parties in judicial proceedings were immediately before the commencement of this Constitution subject to their personal law.

(6) Transfer of property other than agricultural land; registration of deeds and documents.

(7) Contracts, including partnership, agency, contracts of carriage, and other special forms of contracts, but not including contracts relating to agricultural land.

(8) Actionable wrongs.

(9) Bankruptcy and insolvency.

(10) Trust and Trustees.

(11) Administrators-general and official trustees.

(12) Evidence and oaths; recognition of laws, public acts and records, and judicial proceedings.

(13) Civil procedure, including all matters included in the Code of Civil Procedure at the commencement of this Constitution, limitation and arbitration.

(14) Contempt of court, but not including contempt of the Supreme Court.

(15) Vagrancy; nomadic and migratory tribes.

(16) Lunacy and mental deficiency, including places for the reception or treatment of lunatics and mental deficients.

(17) Prevention of cruelty to animals.

(18) Adulteration of foodstuffs and other goods.

(19) Drugs and poisons, subject to the provisions of entry 59 of List I with respect to opium.

(20) Economic and social planning.

(21) Commercial and industrial monopolies, combines and trusts.

(22) Trade Unions; industrial and labour disputes.

(23) Social security and social insurance; employment and unemployment.

(24) Welfare of labour including conditions of work, provident funds, employers' liability, workmen's compensation, invalidity and old age pensions and maternity benefits.

(25) Vocational and technical training of labour.

(26) Legal, medical and other professions.

(27) Relief and rehabilitation of persons displaced from their original place of residence by reason of the setting up of the Dominions of India and Pakistan.

(28) Charities and charitable institutions, charitable and religious endowments and religious institutions.

(29) Prevention of the extension from one State to another of infectious or contagious diseases or pests affecting men, animals or plants.

(30) Vital statistics including registration of births and deaths.

(31) Ports other than those declared by or under law made by Parliament or existing law to be major ports.

(32) Shipping and navigation on inland waterways as regards mechanically propelled vessels, and the rule of the road on such waterways, and the carriage of passengers and goods on inland waterways subject to the provisions of List I with respect to national waterways.

(33) Trade and commerce in, and the production, supply and distribution of,

(a) the products of any industry where the control of such industry by the Union is declared by Parliament by law to be expedient in the public interest, and imported goods of the same kind as such products;

(b) foodstuffs, including edible oilseeds and oils;

(c) cattle fodder, including oilcakes and other concentrates;

(d) raw cotton, whether ginned or unginned, and cotton seed; and

(e) raw jute.

(34) Price control.

(35) Mechanically propelled vehicles including the principles on which taxes on such vehicles are to be levied.

(36) Factories.

(37) Boilers.

(38) Electricity.

(39) Newspapers, books and printing presses.

(40) Archaeological sites and remains other than those declared by or under law made by Parliament to be of national importance.

(41) Custody, management and disposal of property (including agricultural land) declared by law to be evacuee property.

(42) Acquisition and requisitioning of property.

(43) Recovery in a State of claims in respect of taxes and other public demands, including arrears of land-revenue and sums recoverable as such arrears, arising outside that State.

(44) Stamp duties other than duties or fees collected by means of judicial stamps, but not including rates of stamp duty.

(45) Inquiries and statistics for the purposes of any of the matters specified in List II or List III.

(46) Jurisdiction and powers of all courts, except the Supreme Court, with respect to any of the matters in this List.

(47) Fees in respect of any of the matters in this List, but not including fees taken in any court.

APPENDIX III

(Vide ARTICLES 1 AND 4 OF THE CONSTITUTION)

Name	*Territories*
(1) Andhra Pradesh ..	The territories specified in sub-section (1) of section 3 of the Andhra State Act, 1953, sub-section (1) of section 3 of the States Reorganization Act, 1956, and the First Schedule to the Andhra Pradesh and Madras (alteration of Boundaries) Act, 1959, but excluding the territories specified in the Second Schedule to the last mentioned Act.
(2) Assam ..	The territories which immediately before the commencement of this Constitution were comprised in the Province of Assam, the Khasi States and the Assam Tribal Areas, but excluding the territories specified in the Schedule to the Assam (Alteration of Boundaries) Act, 1951 and the territories specified in sub-section (1) of section 3 of the State of Nagaland Act, 1962.
(3) Bihar ..	The territories which immediately before the commencement of this Constitution were either comprised in the Province of Bihar or were being administered as if they formed part of that Province, but excluding the territories specified in sub-section (1) of section 3 of the

Name	*Territories*
Bihar	Bihar and West Bengal (Transfer of Territories) Act, 1956.
(4) Gujarat ..	The territories referred to in sub-section (1) of section 3 of the Bombay Reorganization Act, 1960.
(5) Kerala ..	The territories specified in sub-section (1) of section 5 of the States Re-organization Act, 1956.
(6) Madhya Pradesh ..	The territories specified in sub-section (1) of section 9 of the States Re-organization Act, 1956 and the First Schedule to the Rajasthan and Madhya Pradesh (Transfer of Terri-tories) Act, 1959.
(7) Madras ..	The territories which immediately be-fore the commencement of this Constitution were either comprised in the Province of Madras or were being administered as if they formed part of that Province and the terri-tories specified in section 4 of the States Reorganization Act, 1956, and the Second Schedule to the Andhra Pradesh and Madras (Alteration of Boundaries) Act, 1959, but ex-cluding the territories specified in sub-section (1) of section 3 and sub-section (1) of section 4 of the Andhra State Act, 1953, and the territories specified in clause (b) of sub-section (1) of section 5, section 6 and clause (d) of sub-section (1) of section 7 of the States Reorganization Act, 1956 and the territories specified in the First Schedule to the Andhra Pradesh and Madras (Alteration of Boun-daries) Act, 1959.
(8) Maharashtra ..	The territories specified in sub-section

30

Name	*Territories*
Maharashtra	(1) of section 8 of the States Re-organization Act, 1956, but excluding the territories referred to in sub-section (1) of section 3 of the Bombay Reorganization Act, 1960.
(9) Mysore ..	The territories specified in sub-section (1) of section 7 of the States Re-organization Act, 1956.
(10) Orissa ..	The territories which immediately before the commencement of this Constitution were either comprised in the Province of Orissa or were being administered as if they formed part of that Province.
(11) Punjab[1] ..	The territories specified in section 11 of the States Reorganization Act, 1956 and the territories referred to in Part II of the First Schedule to the Acquired Territories (Merger) Act, 1960, but excluding the territories referred to in Part II of the First Schedule to the Constitution (Ninth Amendment) Act, 1960.
(12) Rajasthan ..	The territories specified in section 10 of the States Reorganization Act, 1956 but excluding the territories specified in the First Schedule to the Rajasthan and Madhya Pradesh (Transfer of Territories) Act, 1959.
(13) Uttar Pradesh ..	The territories which immediately before the commencement of this Constitution were either comprised in the Province known as the United Provinces or were being administered as if they formed part of that Province.
(14) West Bengal ..	The territories which immediately

[1] Punjab has since been divided into two states Punjabi Suba and Haryana.

Name   *Territories*

before the commencement of this
Constitution were either comprised
in the Province of West Bengal or
were being administered as if they
formed part of that Province and
the territory of Chandernagore as
defined in clause (c) of section 2 of
the Chandernagore (Merger) Act,
1954 and also the territories specified
in sub-section (1) of section 3 of
the Bihar and West Bengal (Transfer
of Territories) Act, 1956.

(15) Jammu and   .. The territory which immediately
    Kashmir   before the commencement of this
                       Constitution was comprised in the
                       Indian State of Jammu and
                       Kashmir.

(16) Nagaland   .. The territories specified in sub-section
                       (1) of section 3 of the State of
                       Nagaland Act, 1962.

THE UNION TERRITORIES

Name   *Extent*

(1) Delhi   .. The territory which immediately
                       before the commencement of this
                       Constitution was comprised in the
                       Chief Commissioner's Province of
                       Delhi.

(2) Himachal Pradesh .. The territories which immediately
                       before the commencement of this
                       Constitution were being adminis-
                       tered as if they were Chief Commis-
                       sioner's Provinces under the names
                       of Himachal Pradesh and Bilaspur.

(3) Manipur   .. The territory which immediately
                       before the commencement of this

Name	*Extent*
Manipur	Constitution was being administered as if it were a Chief Commissioner's Province under the name of Manipur.
(4) Tripura ..	The territory which immediately before the commencement of this Constitution was being administered as if it were a Chief Commissioner's Province under the name of Tripura.
(5) The Andaman and Nicobar Islands ..	The territory which immediately before the commencement of this Constitution was comprised in the Chief Commissioner's Province of the Andaman and Nicobar Islands.
(6) The Laccadive, Minicoy and Amindivi Islands ..	The territory specified in section 6 of the States Reorganization Act, 1956.
(7) Dadra and Nagar Haveli ..	The territory which immediately before the eleventh day of August, 1961 was comprised in Free Dadra and Nagar Haveli.
(8) Goa, Daman and Diu	The territories which immediately before the twentieth day of December, 1961 were comprised in Goa, Daman and Diu.
(9) Pondicherry ..	The territories which immediately before the sixteenth day of August, 1962, were comprised in the French Establishments in India known as Pondicherry, Karikal, Mahe and Yanam.

ALLOCATION OF SEATS IN THE COUNCIL OF STATES
(4th Schedule to the Constitution)

To each State or Union territory specified in the first column of the following table, there shall be allotted the number of seats specified in the second column thereof opposite to that State or that Union territory, as the case may be.

Table

(1) Andhra Pradesh	..	..	18
(2) Assam	..	..	7
(3) Bihar	..	..	22
(4) Gujarat	..	..	11
(5) Kerala	..	..	9
(6) Madhya Pradesh	..	..	16
(7) Madras	..	..	18
(8) Maharashtra ..	..	..	19
(9) Mysore	..	..	12
(10) Orissa	..	..	10
(11) Punjab	..	..	11
(12) Rajasthan	..	..	10
(13) Uttar Pradesh	..	..	34
(14) West Bengal ..	..	..	16
(15) Jammu and Kashmir	..	..	4
(16) Nagaland	..	..	1
(17) Delhi	..	..	3
(18) Himachal Pradesh	..	..	2
(19) Manipur	..	..	1
(20) Tripura	..	..	1
(21) Pondicherry ..	..	..	1
	Total	..	226

APPENDIX IV

PROPORTIONAL REPRESENTATION BY THE METHOD OF THE SINGLE TRANSFERABLE VOTE

The following rules from Part VII of the Conduct of Elections Rules, 1961 framed under the Representation of the People Act, 1951, will show the method of counting votes when an election is held by the system of proportional representation by means of the single transferable vote.

71. *Definitions*—In this Part—

(1) 'continuing candidate' means any candidate not elected and not excluded from the poll at any given time;

(2) 'count' means—

(*a*) all the operations involved in the counting of the first preferences recorded for candidates; or

(*b*) all the operations involved in the transfer of the surplus of an elected candidate; or

(*c*) all the operations involved in the transfer of the total value of votes of an excluded candidate;

(3) 'exhausted paper' means a ballot paper on which no further preference is recorded for a continuing candidate, provided that a paper shall also be deemed to have become exhausted whenever—

(*a*) the names of two or more candidates, whether continuing or not, are marked with the same figure and are next in order of preference; or

(*b*) the name of the candidate next in order of preference, whether continuing or not, is marked by a figure not following consecutively after some other figure on the ballot paper or by two or more figures;

(4) 'first preference' means the figure 1 set opposite the name of a candidate; 'second preference' means the figure 2 set opposite the name of a candidate; 'third preference' means the figure 3 set opposite the name of a candidate, and so on;

(5) 'original vote', in relation to any candidate, means a vote derived from a ballot paper on which a first preference is recorded for such candidate;

(6) 'surplus' means the number by which the value of the votes, original and transferred, of any candidate exceeds the quota;

(7) 'transferred vote', in relation to any candidate, means a vote the value or the part of the value of which is credited to such candidate and which is derived from a ballot paper on which a second or a subsequent preference is recorded for such candidate; and

(8) 'unexhaustee paper' means a ballot paper on which a further preference is recorded for a continuing candidate.

72. *Application of certain rules*—The provisions of rules 51 to 54 shall apply to the counting of votes at any election by assembly members or in a council constituency as they apply to the counting of votes at an election in a parliamentary or assembly constituency.

73. *Scrutiny and opening of ballot boxes and packets of postal ballot papers*—(1) The returning officer shall—

(*a*) first open the ballot boxes, take out from each box and count the ballot papers contained therein, and record their number in a statement;

(*b*) then deal with the covers containing the postal ballot papers, if any, in the manner provided in sub-rules (2) to (7) of rule 62;

(*c*) scrutinize the ballot papers taken out of the ballot boxes as well as the postal ballot papers taken out from the covers; and

(*d*) separate the ballot papers which he deems valid from those which he rejects endorsing on each of the latter the word 'Rejected' and the ground of rejection.

(2) A ballot paper shall be invalid on which—

(*a*) the figure 1 is not marked; or

(*b*) the figure 1 is set opposite the name of more than one candidate or is so placed as to render it doubtful to which candidate it is intended to apply; or

(*c*) the figure 1 and some other figures are set opposite the name of the same candidate; or

(*d*) there is any mark or writing by which the elector can be identified.

74. *Arrangement of valid ballot papers in parcels*—After rejecting the ballot papers which are invalid, the returning officer shall—

(*a*) arrange the remaining ballot papers in parcels according to the first preference recorded for each candidate;

(*b*) count and record the number of papers in each parcel and the total number; and

(*c*) credit to each candidate the value of the papers in his parcel.

75. *Counting of votes where only one seat is to be filled*—(1) At any

election where only one seat is to be filled, every valid ballot paper shall be deemed to be of the value of 1 at each count, and the quota sufficient to secure the return of a candidate at the election shall be determined as follows:—

(a) add the values credited to all the candidates under clause (c) of rule 74;

(b) divide the total by 2; and

(c) add 1 to the quotient ignoring the remainder, if any and the resulting number is the quota.

(2) If, at the end of the first or any subsequent count, the total value of the ballot papers credited to any candidate is equal to, or greater than the quota or there is only one continuing candidate, that candidate shall be declared elected.

(3) If, at the end of any count, no candidate can be declared elected the returning officer shall—

(a) exclude from the poll the candidate who up to that stage has been credited with the lowest value;

(b) examine all the ballot papers in his parcel and sub-parcels, arrange the unexhausted papers in sub-parcels according to the next available preferences recorded thereon for the continuing candidates, count the number of papers in each sub-parcel and credit it to the candidate for whom such preference is recorded, transfer the sub-parcel to that candidate, and make a separate sub-parcel of all the exhausted papers; and

(c) see whether any of the continuing candidates has, after such transfer and credit, secured the quota.

(4) If, when a candidate has to be excluded under clause (a) of sub-rule (3), two or more candidates have been credited with the same value and stand lowest on the poll, the candidate for whom the lowest number of original votes are recorded shall be excluded, and if this number also is the same in the case of two or more candidates, the returning officer shall decide by lot which of them shall be excluded.

COUNTING OF VOTES WHEN MORE THAN ONE SEAT IS TO BE FILLED

76. *Ascertainment of quota*—At any election where more than one seat is to be filled, every valid ballot paper shall be deemed to be of the value of 100, and the quota sufficient to secure the return of a candidate at the election shall be determined as follows:—

(*a*) add the values credited to all the candidates under clause (*c*) of rule 74;

(*b*) divide the total by a number which exceeds by 1 the number of vacancies to be filled; and

(*c*) add 1 to the quotient ignoring the remainder, if any, and the resulting number is the quota.

77. *General instruction*—In carrying out the provisions of rules 78 to 82, the returning officer shall disregard all fractions and ignore all preferences recorded for candidates already elected or excluded from the poll.

78. *Candidates with quota elected*—If at the end of any count or at the end of the transfer of any parcel or sub-parcel of an excluded candidate the value of ballot papers credited to a candidate is equal to, or greater than the quota, that candidate shall be declared elected.

79. *Transfer of surplus*—(1) If at the end of any count the value of the ballot papers credited to a candidate is greater than the quota, the surplus shall be transferred, in accordance with the provisions of this rule, to the continuing candidates indicated on the ballot papers of that candidate as being next in order of the elector's preference.

(2) If more than one candidate have a surplus, the largest surplus shall be dealt with first and the others in order of magnitude;

Provided that every surplus arising on the first count shall be dealt with before those arising on the second count and so on.

(3) Where there are more surpluses than one to distribute and two or more surpluses are equal, regard shall be had to the original votes of each candidate and the candidate for whom most original votes are recorded shall have his surplus first distributed; and if the values of their original votes are equal, the returning officer shall decide by lot which candidate shall have his surplus first distributed.

(4) (*a*) If the surplus of any candidate to be transferred arises from original votes only, the returning officer shall examine all the papers in the parcel belonging to that candidate, divide the unexhausted papers into sub-parcels according to the next preferences recorded thereon and make a separate sub-parcel of the exhausted papers;

(*b*) He asshall certain the value of the papers in each sub-parcel and of all the unexhausted papers;

(c) If the value of the unexhausted papers is equal to or less than the surplus, he shall transfer all the unexhausted papers at the value at which they were received by the candidate whose surplus is being transferred.

(d) If the value of the unexhausted papers is greater than the surplus, he shall transfer the sub-parcels of unexhausted papers, and the value at which each paper shall be transferred shall be ascertained by dividing the surplus by the total number of unexhausted papers.

(5) If the surplus of any candidate to be transferred arises from transferred as well as original votes, the returning officer shall re-examine all the papers in the sub-parcel last transferred to the candidate, divide the unexhausted papers into sub-parcels according to the next preference recorded thereon, and then deal with the sub-parcels in the same manner as is provided in the case of sub-parcels referred to in sub-rule (4).

(6) The papers transferred to each candidate shall be added in the form of a sub-parcel to the papers already belonging to such candidate.

(7) All papers in the parcel or sub-parcel of an elected candidate not transferred under this rule shall be set apart as finally dealt with

80. *Exclusion of candidates lowest on the poll*—(1) If after all surpluses have been transferred as hereinbefore provided, the number of candidates elected is less than the required number, the returning officer shall exclude from the poll the candidate lowest on the poll and shall distribute his unexhausted papers among the continuing candidates according to the next preferences recorded thereon; and any exhausted papers shall be set apart as finally dealt with.

(2) The papers containing original votes of an excluded candidate shall first be transferred, the transfer value of each paper being one hundred.

(3) The papers containing transferred votes of an excluded candidate shall then be transferred in the order of the transfers in which, and as the value at which he obtained them.

(4) Each of such transfers shall be deemed to be a separate transfer but not a separate count.

(5) If, as a result of the transfer of papers, the value of votes obtained by a candidate is equal to or greater than the quota, the count then proceeding shall be completed but no further papers shall be transferred to him.

(6) The process directed by this rule shall be repeated on the successive exclusions one after another of the candidates lowest on the poll until such vacancy is filled either by the election of a candidate with the quota or as hereinafter provided.

(7) If at any time it becomes necessary to exclude a candidate and two or more candidates have the same value of votes and are the lowest on the poll, regard shall be had to the original votes of each candidate and the candidate for whom fewest original votes are recorded shall be excluded; and if the values of their original votes are equal the candidate with the smallest value at the earliest count at which these candidates had unequal values shall be excluded.

(8) If two or more candidates are lowest on the poll and each has the same value of votes at all counts the returning officer shall decide by lot which candidate shall be excluded.

81. *Filling the last vacancies*—(1) When at the end of any count the number of continuing candidates is reduced to the number of vacancies remaining unfilled, the continuing candidates shall be declared elected.

(2) When at the end of any count only one vacancy remains unfilled and the value of the papers of some one candidate exceeds the total value of the papers of all the other continuing candidates together with any surplus not transferred, that candidate shall be declared elected.

(3) When at the end of any count only one vacancy remains unfilled and there are only two continuing candidates and each of them has the same value of votes and no surplus remains capable of transfer, the returning officer shall decide by lot which of them shall be excluded; and after excluding him in the manner aforesaid, declare the other candidate to be elected.

82. *Provision for re-counts*—(1) Any candidate or, in his absence, his election agent or counting agent may, at any time during the counting of the votes, either before the commencement or after the completion of any transfer of votes (whether surplus or otherwise), request the returning officer to re-examine and re-count the papers of all or any candidates (not being papers set aside at any previous transfer as finally dealt with), and the returning officer shall forthwith re-examine and re-count the same accordingly.

(2) The returning officer may in his discretion re-count the votes either once or more than once in any case in which he is not satisfied as to the accuracy of any previous count:

Provided that nothing in this sub-rule shall make it obligatory on the returning officer to re-count the same votes more than once.

The following illustration is given of the procedure as to the counting of votes at, and the declaration of the result of, an election conducted on the system of the single transferable vote.

Assume that there are seven members to be elected, sixteen candidates, and one hundred and forty electors.

The valid ballot papers are arranged in separate parcels according to the first preference recorded for each candidate, and the papers in each parcel counted.

Let it be assumed that the result is as follows:

A	12
B	8
C	6
D	9
E	10
F	7
G	4
H	19
I	13
J	5
K	14
L	8
M	10
N	6
O	4
P	5
Total	140

Each valid ballot paper is deemed to be of the value of one hundred and the values of the votes obtained by the respective candidates are as shown in the first column of the result sheet.

The values of all the papers are added together and the total 14,000 is divided by eight (i.e. the number which exceeds by one the number of vacancies to be filled) and 1,751 (i.e. the quotient 1,750 increased by one) is the number sufficient to secure the return of a member and is called the quota.

The operation may be shown thus:

$$\text{Quota} = \frac{14,000}{8} + 1 = 1,750 + 1 = 1,751$$

The candidate H, the value of whose votes exceeds the quota, is declared elected.

As the value of the papers in H's parcel exceeds the quota, his surplus must be transferred. His surplus is 149 (i.e. 1,900 less 1,175).

The surplus arises from original votes, and therefore the whole of H's papers are divided into sub-parcels according to the next preferences recorded thereon, a separate parcel of the exhausted papers being also made. Let it be assumed that the result is as follows:

	Papers
B is marked as next available preference on ..	7
D is marked as next available preference on ..	4
E is marked as next available preference on ..	4
F is marked as next available preference on ..	3
Total of unexhausted papers ..	18
No. of exhausted papers ..	1
Total of papers ..	19

The values of the papers in the sub-parcels are as follows:

B	..	..	..	..	700
D	..	..	..	..	400
E	..	..	..	..	400
F	..	..	..	..	300
Total value of unexhausted papers ..					1,800
Value of exhausted papers ..					100
Total value ..					1,900

The value of the unexhausted papers is 1,800 and is greater than the surplus. This surplus is, therefore, transferred as follows:

All the unexhausted papers are transferred, but at a reduced value, which is ascertained by dividing the surplus by the number of unexhausted papers.

The reduced value of all the papers, when added together, with the addition of any value lost as the result of the neglect of fractions, equals the surplus. In this case the new value of each paper

$$\text{transferred is} \quad \frac{149 \text{ (the surplus)}}{18 \text{ (the number of unexhausted papers)}} = 8, \text{ the}$$

residue of the value of each paper $(100-8 = 92)$, being required by H for the purpose of constituting his quota, i.e. one exhausted paper (value 100) plus the value (1,656) of 18 unexhausted papers.

These values of the sub-parcels transferred are:

B $= 56$ (i.e. seven papers at the value of 8);
D $= 32$ (i.e. four papers at the value of 8);
E $= 32$ (i.e. four papers at the value of 8);
F $= 24$ (i.e. three papers at the value of 8).

These operations can be shown on a transfer sheet as follows:

Transfer Sheet

Value of surplus (H's) to be transferred	149
Number of papers in H's parcel	19
Value of each paper in parcel	100
Number of unexhausted papers	18
Value of unexhausted papers	1,800

New value of each paper transferred $=$

$$\frac{\text{Surplus}}{\text{Number of unexhausted papers}} = \frac{149}{18} = \quad 8$$

Names of Candidates marked as the next available preference	Number of papers to be transferred	Value of sub-parcel to be transferred
B	7	56
D	4	32
E	4	32
F	3	24
Total	18	144

Number of exhausted papers	1	..
Loss of value owing to neglect of fractions		5
Total ..	19	149

The values of the sub-parcels are added to the values of the votes already credited to the candidates B, D, E and F. This operation is shown on the result sheet.

There being no further surplus, the candidate lowest on the poll has now to be excluded. G and O both have 400.

The Returning Officer casts lots and G is chosen to be excluded.

Being original votes, G's papers are transferred at the value of 100 each. A who was marked as next preference on two papers receives 200, while D and E were each next preference on one paper and receiving 100 each. O now being lowest is next excluded and his 400 is similarly transferred to I, B and K. I receiving 200 and B and K 100 each.

This leaves J and P lowest with 500 each and J is chosen by lot for exclusion first. His papers are transferred at the value of 100 each to A, B, D and I, the three first named receiving 100 each, and I who had the next preference on two papers receiving 200. P is then excluded and his papers are transferred to E, L and K, the two first named receiving 100 each, and K, who had the next preference on three papers, receiving 300.

K now exceeds the quota and is declared elected.

Prior to further exclusion, K's surplus of 49 has to be distributed.

The sub-parcel last transferred to K consisted of 3 votes transferred at the value of 100 each. This sub-parcel is examined; there are no exhausted papers and B, F and I are each next preference on one paper, and one paper is transferred to each of them at a reduced value determined by dividing the surplus (49) by the number of unexhausted papers (3). B, F and I accordingly receive 16 each.

The process of exclusion is now proceeded with.

C and N have 600 each, and C is chosen by lot for exclusion first. He has 6 original votes; B, D and E are each next preference on two papers, and each receives 200. N is then excluded; A is next preference on 3 of his papers, and receives 300; F, I and L are each next preference on one paper and receive 100 each.

This brings A and I above the quota and they are declared elected. Their surplus have now to be distributed and I's surplus which is the larger, 65, is dealt with first.

The last sub-parcel transferred to I consisted of one paper transferred at the value of 100. D is next preference on this paper, and receives the whole surplus of 65.

A's surplus of 49 is then dealt with. The last sub-parcel transferred to him consisted of 3 papers transferred at the value of 100 each. B was next preference on two of these papers and E on one, and the papers are transferred accordingly. The value to be transferred is 16 per paper, i.e. the surplus (49), divided by the number of the unexhausted papers (3). B accordingly receives 32 and E 16.

No other candidate having reached the quota, the process of exclusion is proceeded with, and F, who is now lowest with 840, is excluded.

His seven original votes are next transferred first. B, D and E are next preference on three, two and two papers, respectively, and receive respectively 300, 200 and 200.

The transferred votes are next transferred in the order of their transfers to F. The 3 votes received at the value of eight each at the distribution of H's surplus are transferred at the same value to L who was next preference on all 3 papers. The vote valued at sixteen received by F at the distribution of K's surplus, goes at the same value to M, who was next preference on that paper. The vote transferred at the value of 100 on the exclusion of N is then transferred at the same value to D, who thus receives a total of 300.

No continuing candidate having yet reached the surplus, M, who is now lowest with 1,016, is excluded.

His ten original votes are transferred first. B and D are first preference on three papers each, and E and L on two each. B and D accordingly receive 300 each, and E and L 200 each. This brings B, D and E above the quota, and they are declared elected. The requisite number of candidates having now been elected, the election is at an end, and it is unnecessary to proceed to the transfer of M's transferred votes.

Full details are shown in the result sheet.

Value of votes 14,000

RESULT SHEET

$$\text{Quota} = \frac{14,000}{8} + 1 = 1,751$$

Name of candidates	Value of votes at first count	Distribution of H's surplus	Result	Distribution of votes of G and O	Result	Distribution of votes of J and P	Result	Distribution of K's surplus	Result
1	2	3	4	5	6	7	8	9	10
A	1,200		1,200	+200	1,400	+100	1,500	+16	1,500
B	800	+56	856	+100	956	+100	1,056	+16	1,072
C	600		600		600		600		600
D	900	+32	932	+100	1,032	+100	1,132		1,132
E	1,000	+32	1,032	+100	1,132	+100	1,232		1,232
F	700	+24	724		724		724	+16	740
G	400		400	−400					
H	1,900	−149	1,751		1,751		1,751		1,751
I	1,300		1,300	+200	1,500	+200	1,700	+16	1,716
J	500		500		500	−500			
K	1,400		1,400	+100	1,500	+300	1,800	−49	1,751
L	800		800		800	+100	900		900
M	1,000		1,000		1,000		1,000		1,000
N	600		600		600		600		600
O	400		400	−400					
P	500		500		500	−500			
Loss of value by neglect of fractions		+5	5		5		5	+1	6
Total	14,000		14,000		14,000		14,000		14,000

RESULT SHEET—contd.

Value of votes 14,000

$$\text{Quota} = \frac{14,000}{8} + 1 = 1,751$$

Name of candidates	Distribution of votes of C and N	Result	Distribution of surplus of I and A	Result	Distribution of F's votes	Result	Distribution of M's votes	Result	Result of Election
	11	12	13	14	15	16	17	18	19
A	+300	1,800	−49	1,751		1,751		1,751	Elected
B	+200	1,272	+32	1,304	+300	1,604	+300	1,904	Elected
C	−600								Not Elected
D	+200	1,332	+65	1,397	+300	1,697	+300	1,997	Elected
E	+200	1,432	+16	1,448	+200	1,648	+200	1,848	Elected
F	+100	840		840	−840				Not Elected
G									Not Elected
H		1,751		1,751		1,751		1,751	Elected
I	+100	1,816	−65	1,751		1,751		1,751	Elected
J									Not Elected
K		1,751		1,751		1,751		1,751	Elected
L	+100	1,000		1,000	+24	1,024	+200	1,224	Not Elected
M		1,000		1,000	+16	1,016	−1,006	+16	Not Elected
N	−600								Not Elected
O									Not Elected
P									Not Elected
Loss of value by neglect of fractions		6	+1	7		7		7	
TOTAL		14,000		14,000		14,000		14,000	

INDEX

31A

complaint of one House against member of other, 400

disposal of adjournment motion by Speaker, Lok Sabha, 129-30

election of Presiding Officer, 41-4

Estimates Committee, 311-12

supplementary estimate, same as for main estimates, 292

Upper House for Appropriation Bill, 304

Proceedings:
no member or officer to give evidence as to, 378

Public Accounts Committee, usually devoid of party feelings, 314

reference to, as reported in newspapers, not allowed, 161

Select Committee, confidential, 234

written statements included in, 153

Proceedings in Parliament, meaning of, 367

Prorogation: 63
effect of, on committee, 64, 65

effect of, on pending business, 63, 64

effect on notices of questions, 96

Public Accounts, 282

Public Accounts Committee:
assistance by Comptroller and Auditor General and/or Accountant General, 314-15

association of members of Upper House with, 321

chairmanship of, 315-16

discussion of report of, 321

examination of excess expenditure, 317

functions of, 265-6; 316-17

mode of investigation by, 314

not concerned with questions of policy, 317-18

origin (in India) of, 312-13

proceedings of, usually devoid of party feelings, 314

report of, 318-19

role of, 313-14

Publication:
bills directed by Presiding Officer, 217

speech, 371

Public documents:
minister not bound to produce if summary of contents given, 162-3

quoted by minister to be laid, if not confidential, 162-3

Public finance:
classification of general control of Finance Department, 344-9

Finance Department vested with control over, 339

importance of Finance Department as to, 342-4

Public funds, amendments to bill imposing charge upon, inadmissible unless recommended by Head of State, 240

Public interest, minister may not answer question in, 96

Punishments, inflicted by House of Commons, 407

Q

QUALIFICATIONS FOR MEMBERSHIP, see Member

Questions:
absent members, 94

admissibility decided by Presiding Officer, 82

admissibility rules, 82-6

answers not available beforehand, 93

Autonomous Bodies, 86-8

edited if not properly framed, 89

half-an-hour discussion on, 73

history of right of putting, 78-80

manner of putting and answering, 94

matter within jurisdiction of Speaker, 89

member granted leave of absence, 92

member under legal detention, 90, 91

ministers not bound to answer, 96

not put or withdrawn, answered in public interest, 94

notices lapse after prorogation, 96

number of, by a member on a day 92

period of notice of, 92

President's or Governor's household, 89, 90

Presiding Officer's decision cannot be challenged, 82

putting and answering of manner of, 94

putting of, 176

remaining unanswered for want of time, 94

starred and unstarred, 80

supplementary, 95, 96

suspended member's, 92

utility of, 97, 98

whom to be put, 80-2

withdrawal of, 96

Question House, Select Committee cannot sit during, 230

494

INDEX